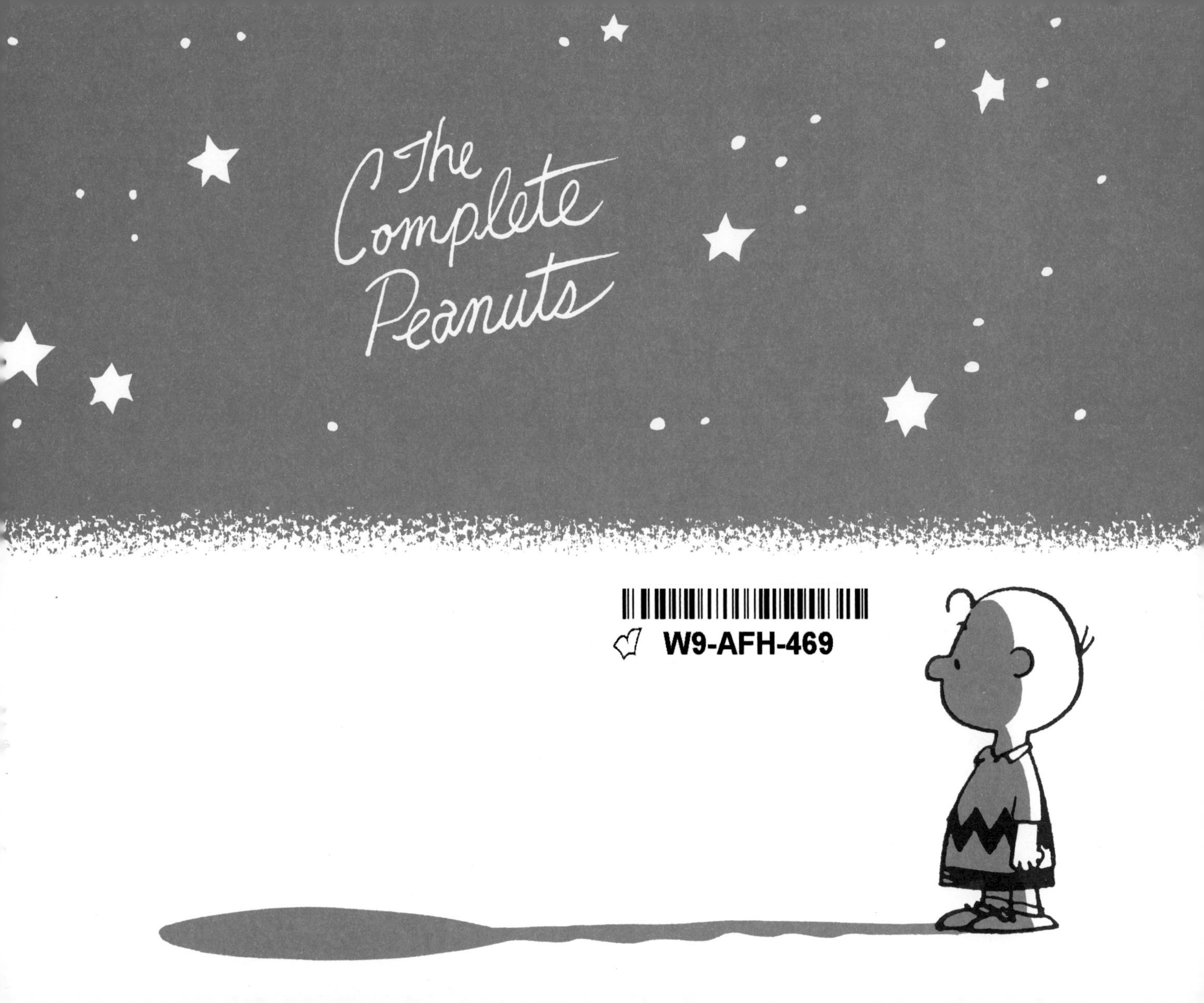
The Complete Peanuts

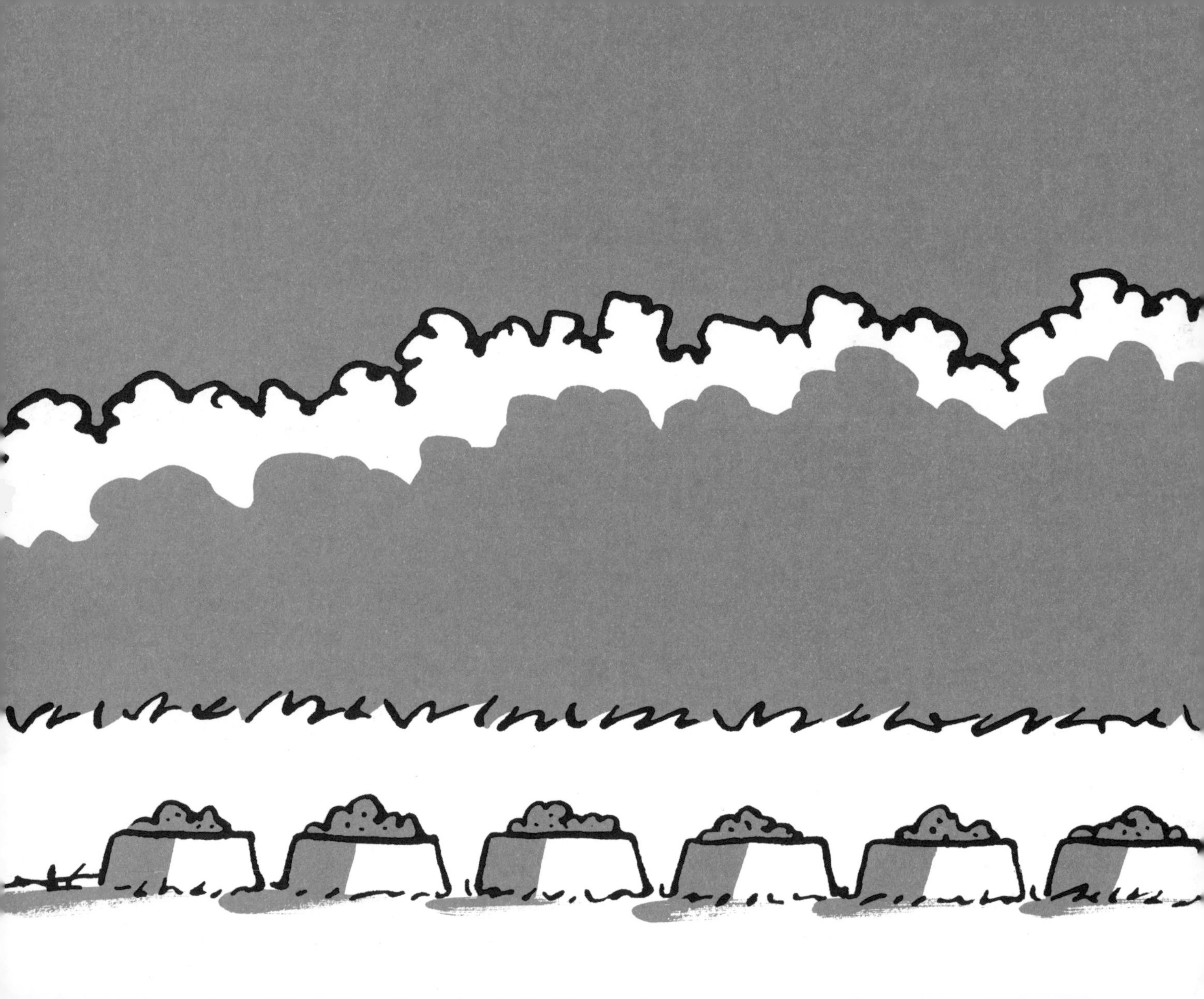

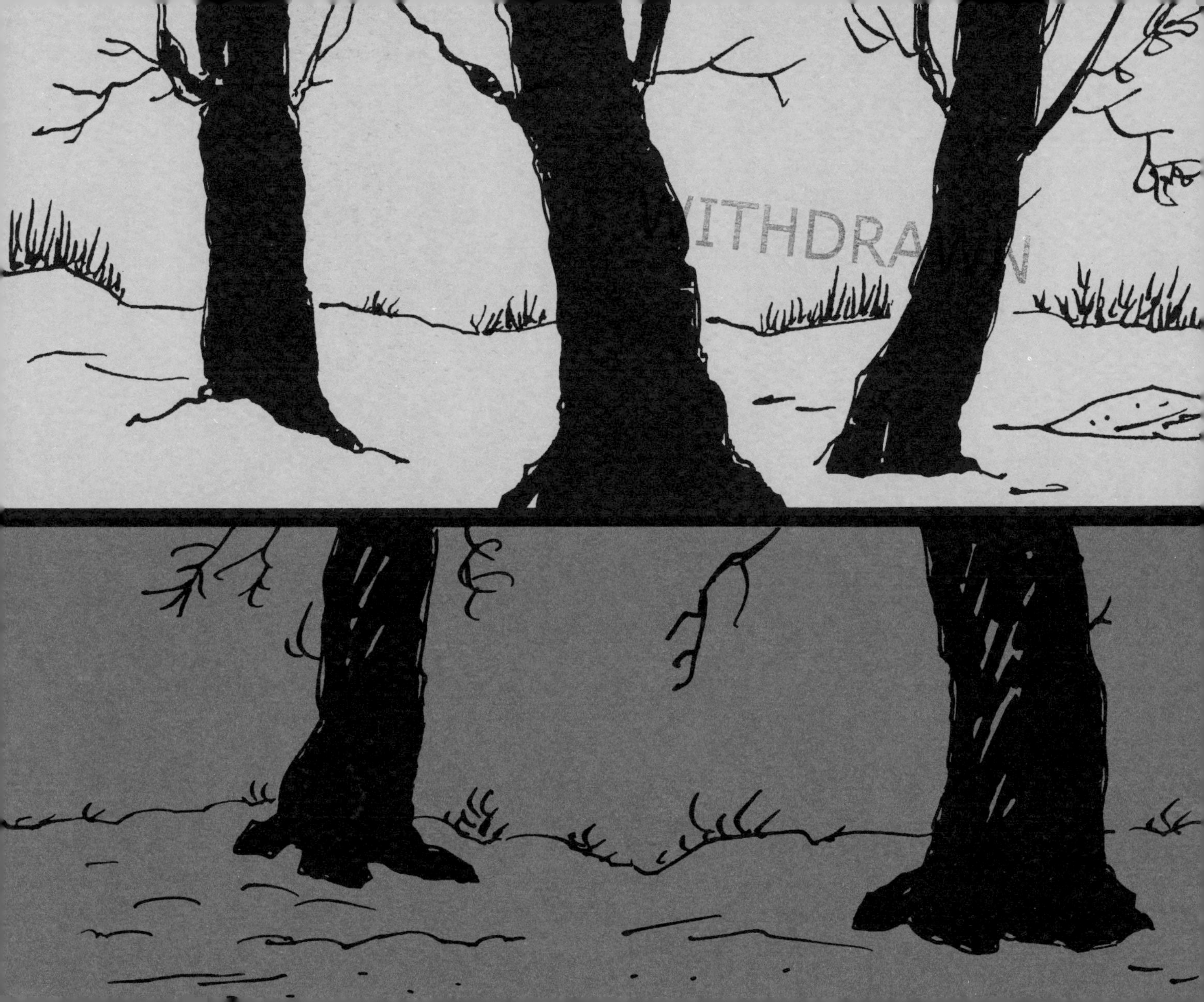

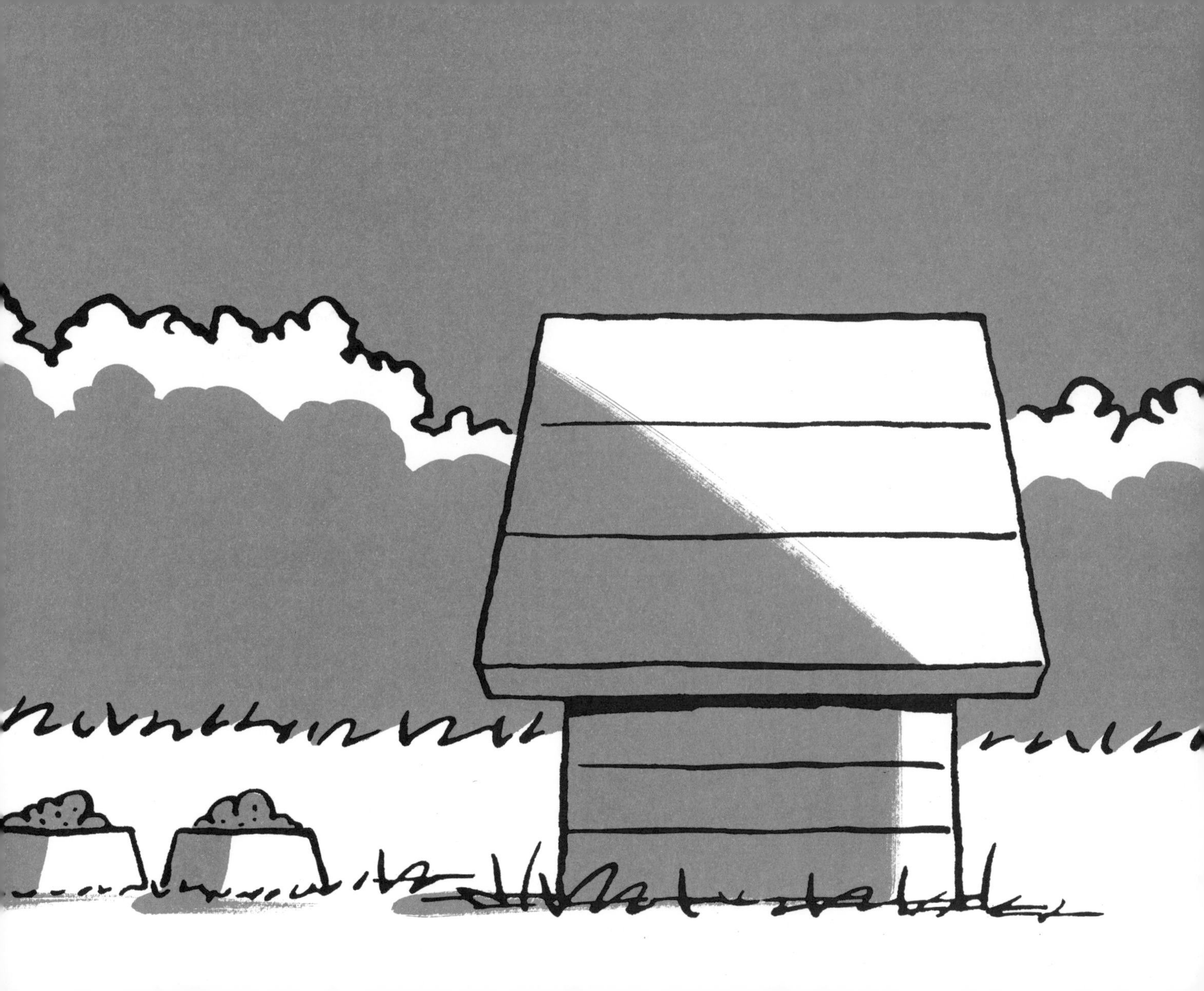

THE COMPLETE PEANUTS
by Charles M. Schulz
published by
Fantagraphics Books

Editor: Gary Groth
Designer: Seth
Production, assembly, and restoration: Paul Baresh
Archival assistance: Marcie Lee
Associate Publisher: Eric Reynolds
Publisher: Gary Groth

Special thanks to Jean Schulz, without whom this project would not have come to fruition.

Fantagraphics Books, 7563 Lake City Way NE, Seattle, WA 98115, USA.
Call 1-800-657-1100 or visit Fantagraphics.com, Facebook.com/Fantagraphics, or Twitter @fantagraphics.

ISBN: 978-1-60699-957-8
Library of Congress Control Number: 2016936900
First printing: October 2016   Printed in China

CHARLES M. SCHULZ

THE COMPLETE PEANUTS

COMICS AND STORIES

" THE FUTURE FRIGHTENS ME ! "

◾ FANTAGRAPHICS BOOKS ◾

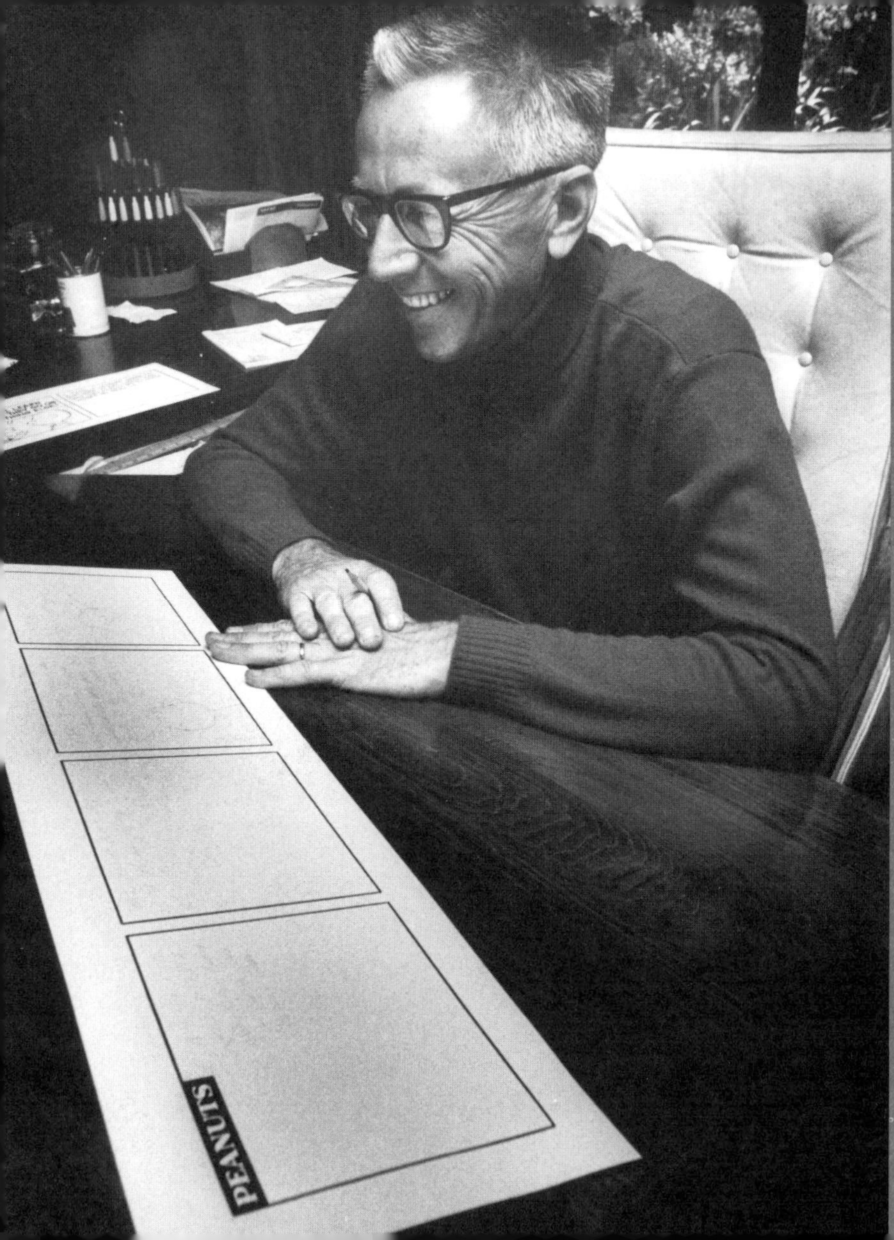
PEANUTS

Charles M. Schulz in his home studio at the drawing board, Santa Rosa, California, 1969. Photo © Jean F. Schulz, courtesy of the Charles M. Schulz Museum and Research Center

INTRODUCTION

The newspaper strip is obviously the heart and soul of *Peanuts*, but Charles Schulz created a large amount of material that was not part of his daily creative focus. Getting a complete picture of Schulz's *Peanuts* requires looking at some of that extracurricular work.

This volume is not a complete collection of *Peanuts* beyond the strip. There is so much out there that we had to make judgment calls. The absolute requirement was that it had to be *Peanuts*; this is not the home for Schulz's non-*Peanuts* work. For a piece to be included, Schulz had to have drawn it himself, rather than any of the various artists who worked on beyond-the-strip projects (even those that might bear the Schulz signature). When possible, we have relied on sources such as Schulz's widow Jean, who verified that certain books were indeed illustrated by him, and Schulz's former studiomate and *Peanuts* comic book artist Jim Sasseville, who identified which comic book stories Schulz drew. In other instances, we made our best guess as to whether a given piece looks like the real deal or whether it was a project in which Schulz was likely to have invested his time.

Material that never had been in a book before, or which had not seen print in the twenty-first century, was given preferential treatment; for example, you will not find the contents of the best-selling book *Happiness is a Warm Puppy* here, as that title has been reprinted frequently. Also, the more a given item resembled a comic strip, the more we wanted to include it. Indeed, some of the following content is flat-out strips, but beyond that, we weighed whether each had multiple-image continuity, dialogue, and humor.

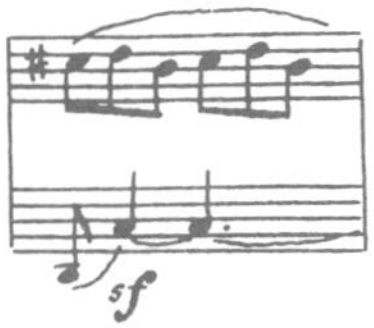

sf

Illustrations that were merely cute drawings, lovely as they were, generally did not make the final cut.

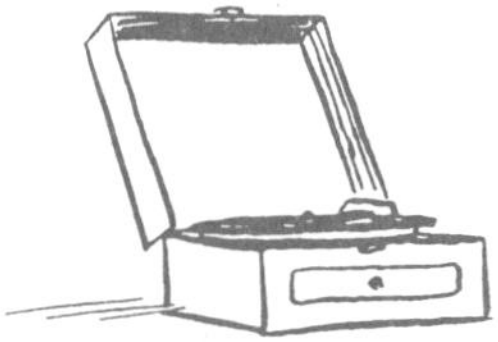

So what did pass our rigorous (if occasionally arbitrary) filtering system? In these pages you'll find dozens of strips never seen in any book, as well as ones that have not been printed in more than half a century. Six complete books are here — four storybooks, two volumes on life's lessons — plus new cartoon stories done for two other books, which had been mixed in with strip reprints. You'll also find seven comic book stories, dozens of single-panel gags, one recipe, and assorted odd bits. The material covers a wide swath of *Peanuts* history, with every decade of the strip's run from the 1950s to the 1990s represented.

This compilation would not be nearly so full and satisfying without the support and cooperation of Jean Schulz, Alexis Fajardo, and Paige Braddock of Charles M. Schulz Creative Associates; without information supplied by Cesar Gallegos and his staff at the Charles M. Schulz Museum's Research Center; and without such kindly folks as Caren Pilgrim of CollectPeanuts.com, John Pilgrim, Dr. Michael J. Vassallo, and Jeff Trexler providing access to (and scanning of) obscure materials that otherwise were beyond the reach and budget of this effort.

—Nat Gertler, Derrick Bang, and Timothy Chow, July 2016

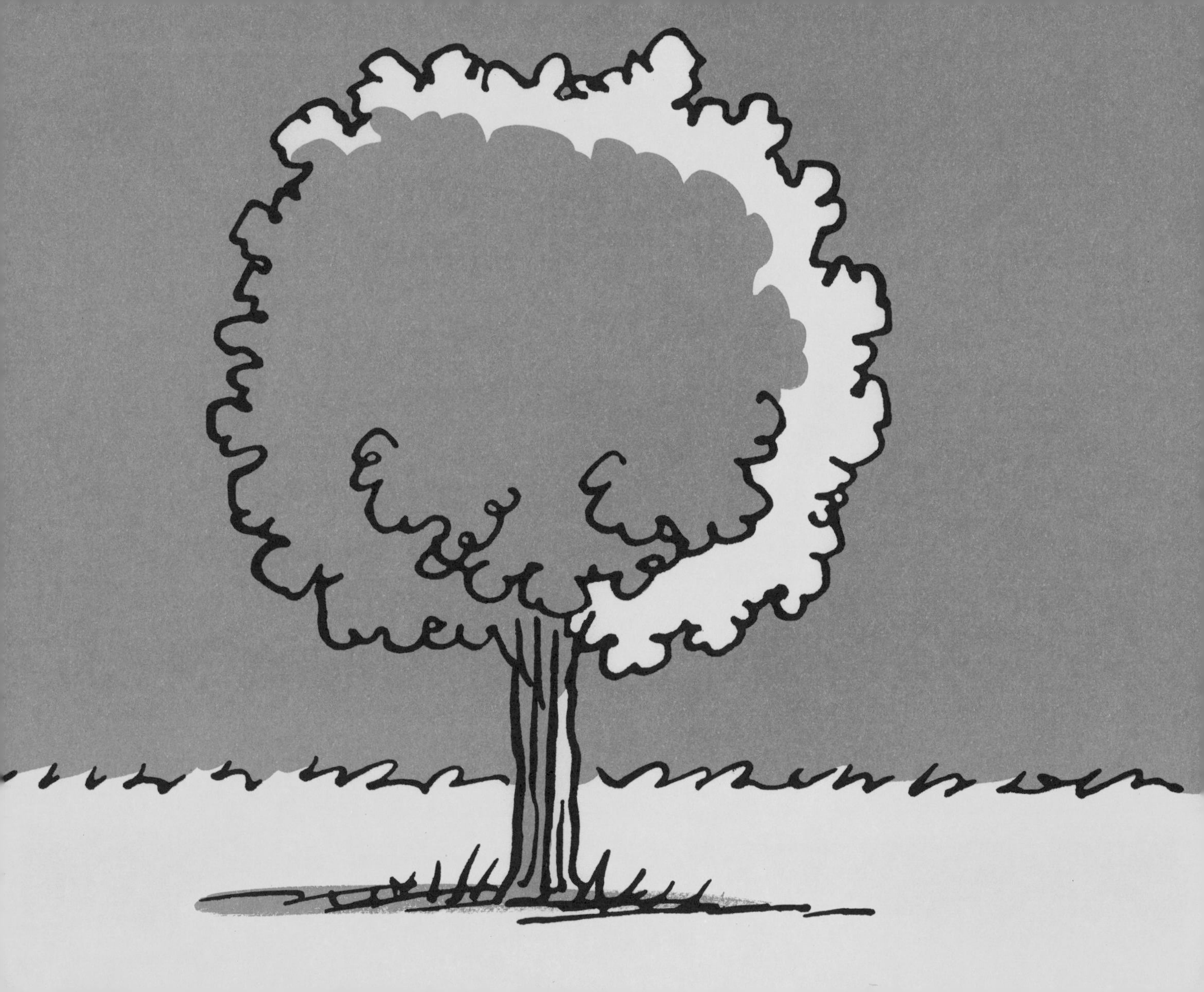

DESIGNER'S NOTE

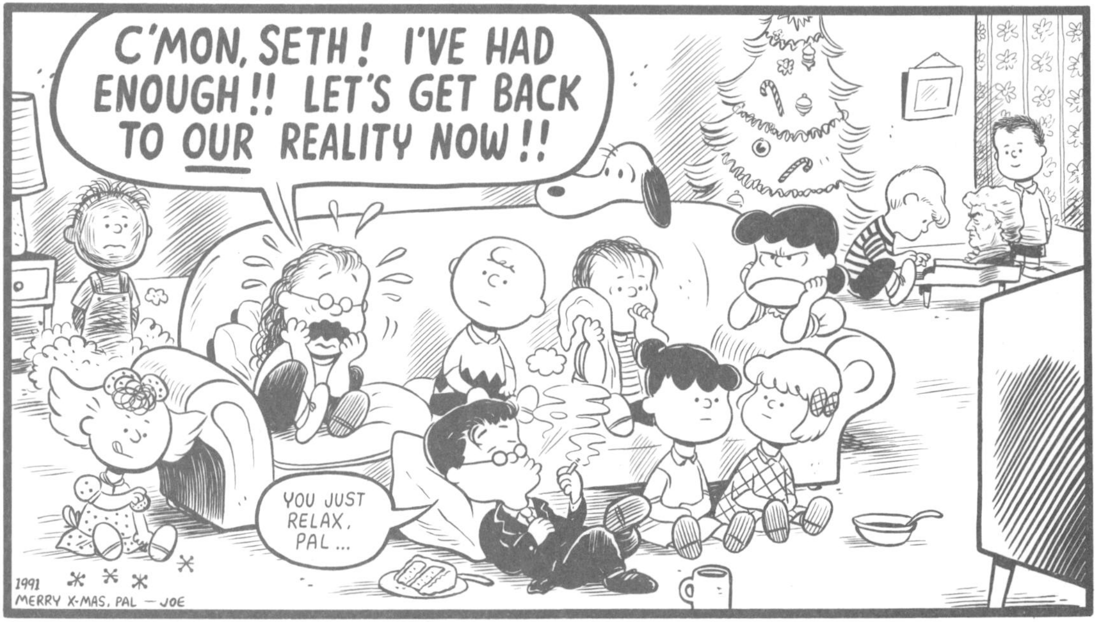
C'MON, SETH! I'VE HAD ENOUGH!! LET'S GET BACK TO OUR REALITY NOW!!
YOU JUST RELAX, PAL...
1991
MERRY X-MAS, PAL — JOE

Moments ago, I completed the last design elements for this volume, placed them in a FedEx box, and set them on the porch for the courier. With that, *The Complete Peanuts* is done. Thirteen years, two volumes a year, twenty-six volumes in all — I can't believe it's over. I recall, in perfect detail, the trip publisher Gary Groth, my wife Tania, and I made to Santa Rosa when we first proposed the series to Jean Schulz. That seems like it was just the other day. I was somewhat nervous going into that meeting. I very much wanted to design these books, but I was also grimly determined to try and sell my low-key vision for the series. I worried it would be a hard sell, but when I met Jean Schulz, many of those worries evaporated. It was clear she genuinely understood Sparky's work and regarded her husband as a genius. That didn't guarantee anything, of course, but it hinted I was halfway there in my argument. As it turned out, there was very little argument. All went smoothly. Since then, I've plodded along, volume by volume, and did what I thought best. Miraculously, nobody seemed to mind.

What did I want from these books, though?

Well, obviously I wished them to look and feel respectful and dignified, and maybe even a bit sad. I wanted the beauty of the strip to shine. And, I admit, I wanted something else, too — something more an act of sympathetic magic than design. I wished to pay *personal* tribute to Charles Schulz. To thank the man. To offer something of a spiritual quality and — let's be honest — to somehow connect myself to him, one cartoonist to another.

Like so many of my generation, it was his brilliant work (first seen, practically, in infancy) that set me on the cartoonist path. He was, literally, the first artist I ever noticed. Grade school or not, I could tell that there was something "bigger" about *Peanuts* than everything else I was looking at, then. I noticed his signature and thought, "Who is this magical person who signs his name in the last box of *Peanuts*?" I have continued to think about the man ever since — as an inspiration, as an object lesson, as a mentor … as a goalpost, even. I'm not sorry to have never met him in the flesh. I think I met him in the best way, through the work.

The drawing that sits at the beginning of this note might be perplexing on first glance. It was a gift to me, many Christmases ago, from my dear friend, cartoonist Joe Matt. Back then, in the early 1990s, Joe and I talked about Charles Schulz compulsively. Long telephone conversations, in which we would yak *Peanuts, Peanuts, Peanuts* … We knew the first thirty years of the strip practically by heart, and would quiz each other on them. Joe might ask, "In panel one, Lucy is saying: 'Charlie Brown, do you care if I hit you with this paper?'" Then, I'd need to produce the dialogue from the final panel*. We were both surprisingly good at this game. Perhaps we loved *Peanuts* a bit too much! I certainly did — embarrassing as this sounds today, I once confessed to Joe that, when falling asleep at night, I often entertained the fantasy of visiting Charlie Brown's world and interacting there as "one of the gang." And so, Mr. Matt's drawing explained.

I suppose I've included it here as just another spiritual offering to Sparky. To show him that *Peanuts* hasn't just been something I've been entertained by. It has always been personal. Held close. Work that changed my life.

When we began *The Complete Peanuts*, I envisioned the series as as an austere setting for the beautiful, multifaceted jewel that was *Peanuts* … but as the years rolled by and the end approached, I recognized that I was probably constructing a monument instead. I don't wish this to sound morbid, but I'd rather these books be seen as headstones than as jewel cases. A marker that spells out the man's name, reminds us that he was here, and of what he left behind.

Seth
Palookaville, 2016
*"I never know what's good for me."

THE SATURDAY EVENING POST

From 1948 to 1950 Charles Schulz sold seventeen gag-cartoons to the *Saturday Evening Post*. Quite a coup for a cartoonist who was just starting out. These cartoons, like the *Li'l Folks* strips he was drawing concurrently (reprinted in the previous volume) are, of course, not the Peanuts characters, but it is impossible to look at them and not see their prototypes here. This is the first time all seventeen of these cartoons have been reprinted together.

"Sure . . . you've seen me before . . . That night on the screen porch
. . . remember?"

"Good grief, woman, get out of the way!
Do you want to be trampled to death?"

"We must be approaching civilization . . . I can see my mother!"

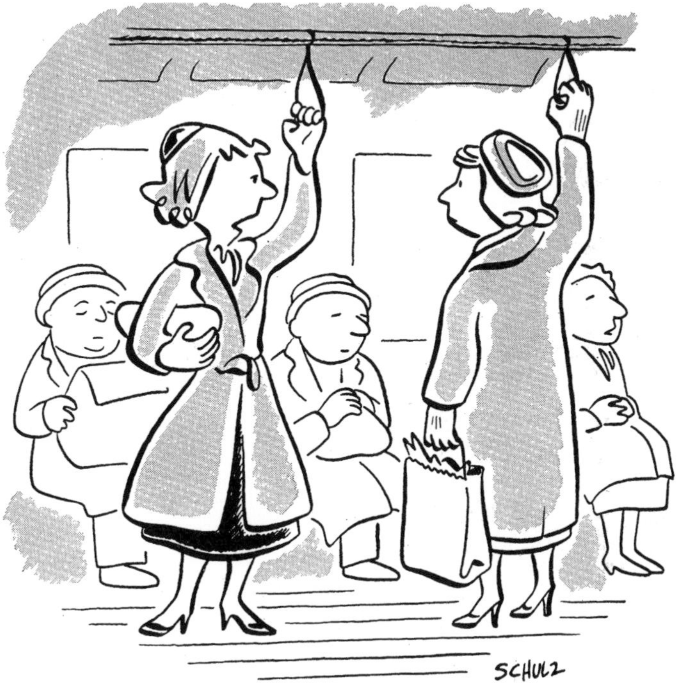
SCHULZ

"I sleep well enough at night . . . it's living during the day that I find so hard!"

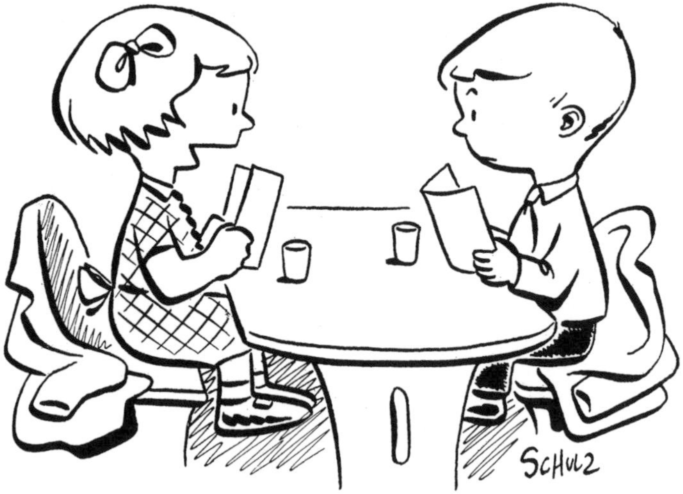
SCHULZ

"I'm taking it for granted that you're very anxious to impress me!"

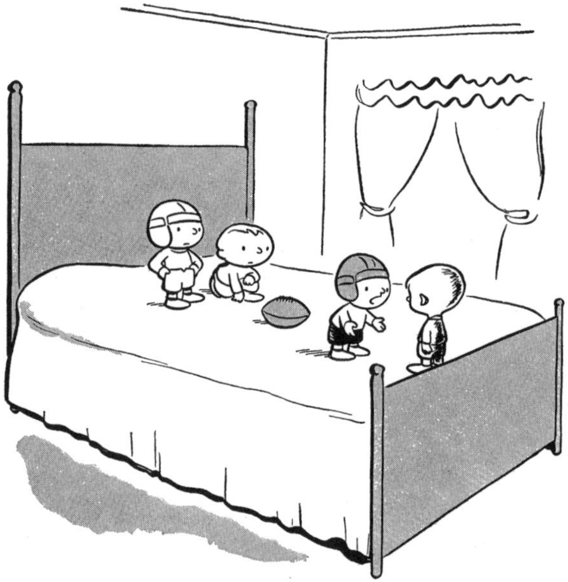

"We're close enough . . . Let's try for a field goal!"

"Everybody hang on real tight in case he starts with a sudden jerk!"

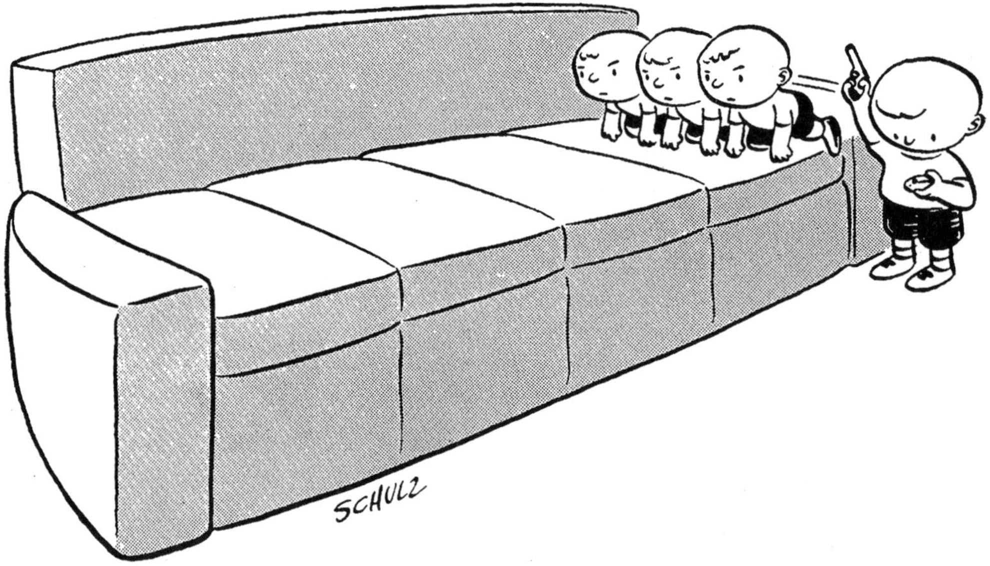
SCHULZ

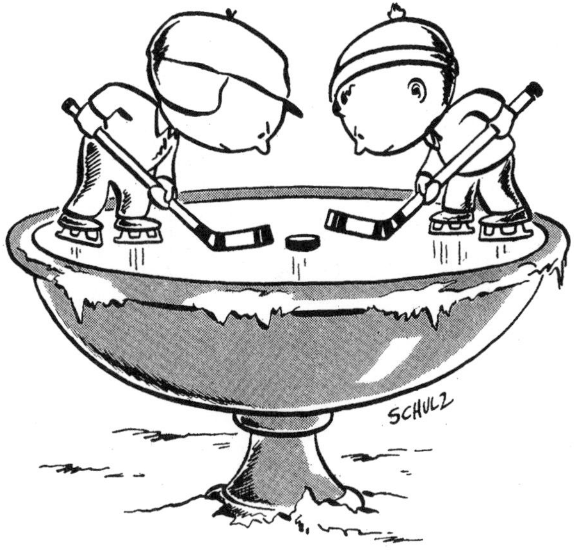
SCHULZ

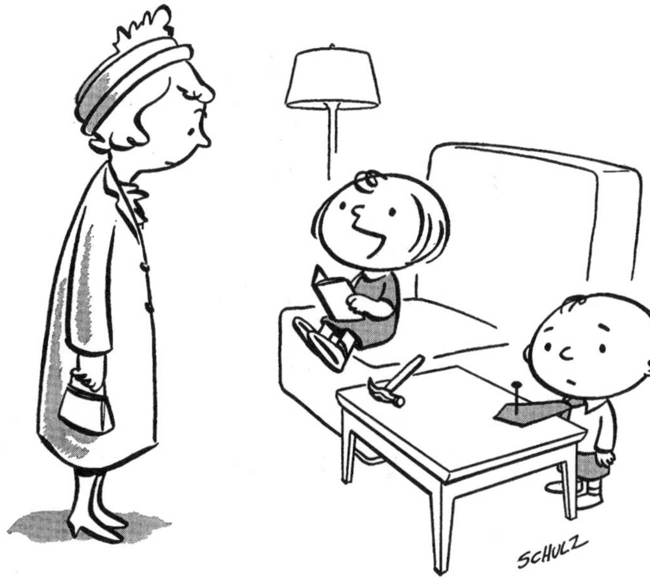
SCHULZ

"Oh, we get along swell . . . he hasn't moved from my side all afternoon!"

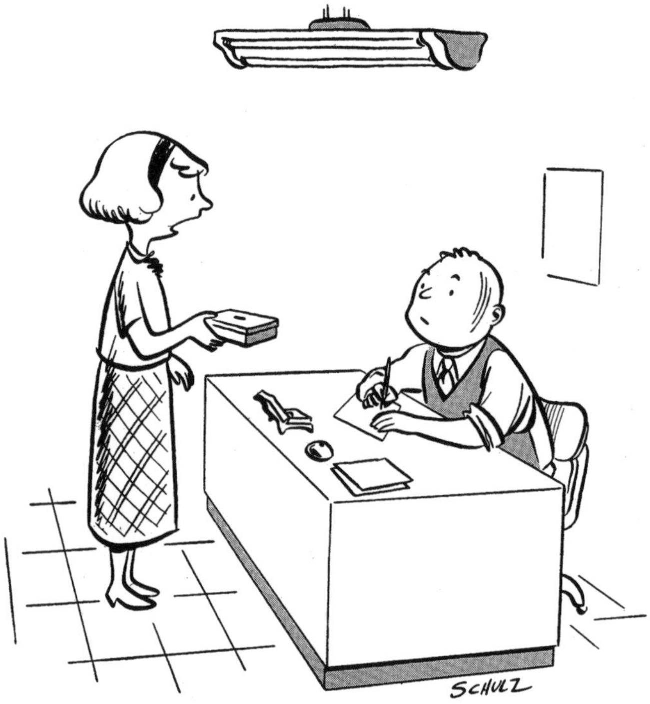
SCHULZ

"We're taking up a collection for one of the girls in the office who is not going to get married or leave, but feels that she is stuck here for the rest of her life."

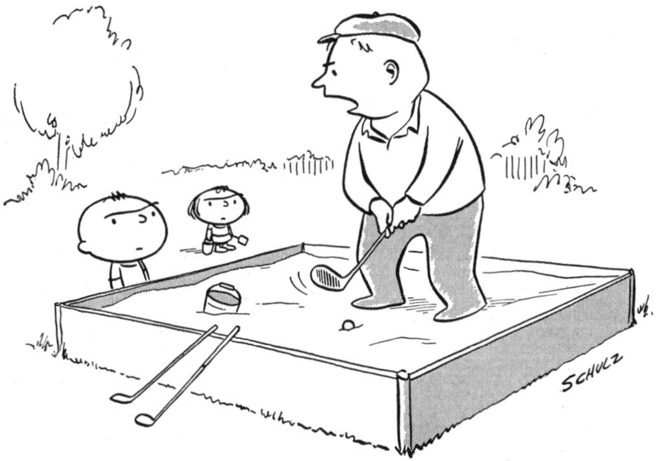
SCHULZ

"I need practice, I tell you . . . surely you don't begrudge your father a little practice!"

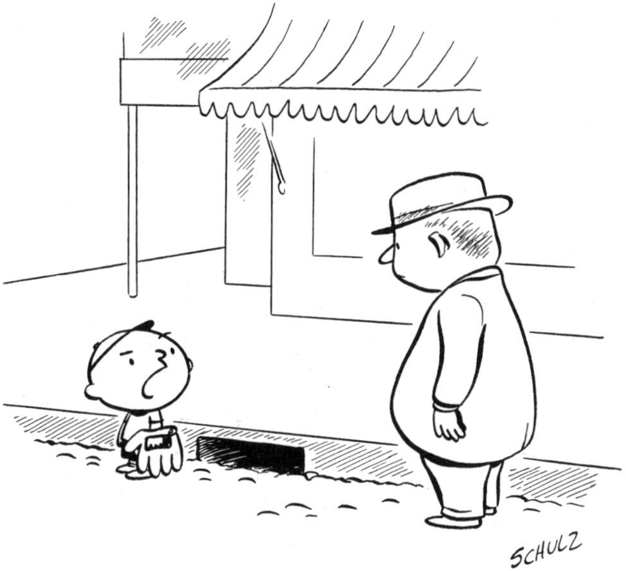
SCHULZ

"This is the most important position on the team . . . I'm here to see that the ball doesn't go down the sewer!"

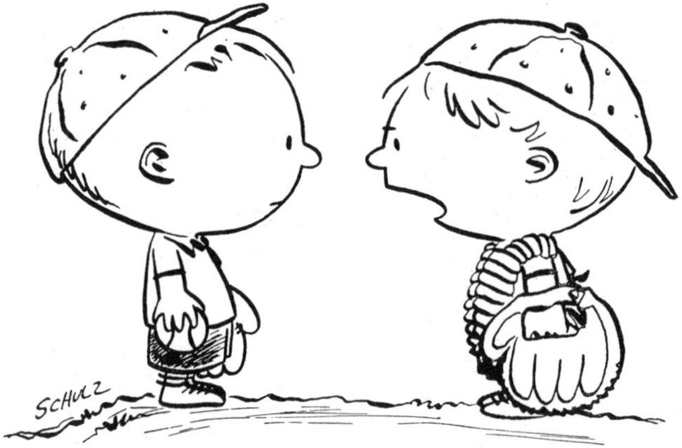
SCHULZ

"I think we'd better change our signals . . . One finger will mean the high straight ball, and two fingers will mean the low straight ball!"

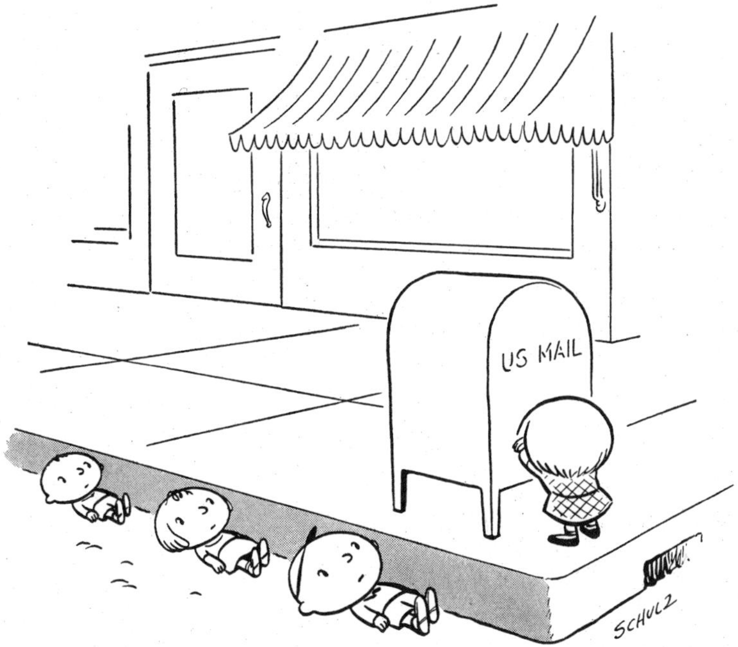
US MAIL
SCHULZ

“Forty-eight, forty-nine, fifty . . . here I come . . . ready or not!”

COMIC BOOKS

While the majority of the original Peanuts comic book stories of the 1950s and 1960s were drawn by other hands, Schulz collaborator Jim Sasseville has identified seven stories from 1957 and 1959 as being Schulz's own work.

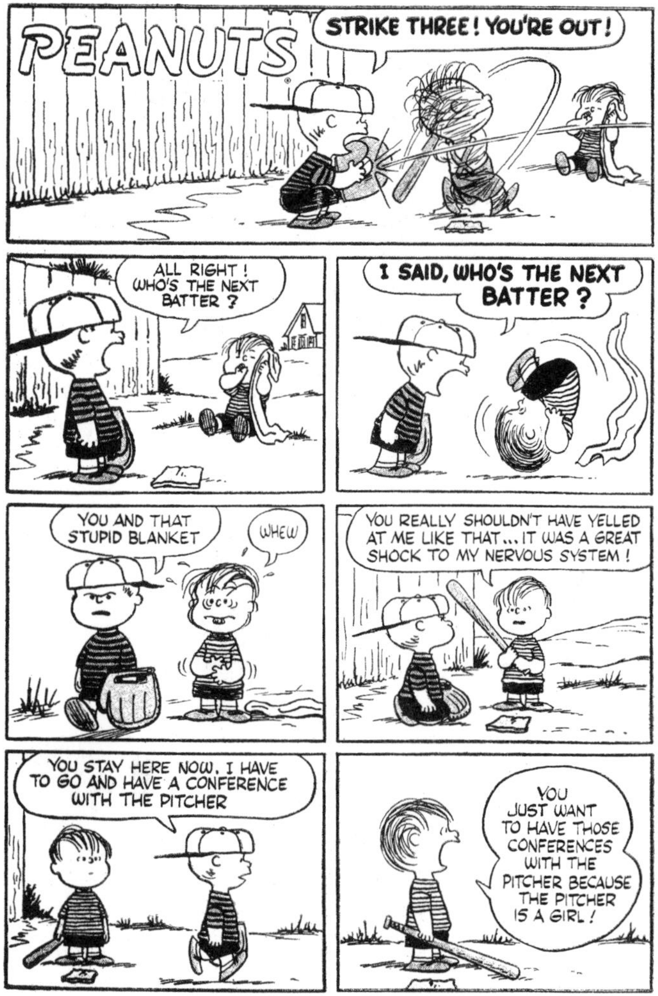
PEANUTS
STRIKE THREE! YOU'RE OUT!
ALL RIGHT! WHO'S THE NEXT BATTER ?
I SAID, WHO'S THE NEXT BATTER ?
YOU AND THAT STUPID BLANKET
WHEW
YOU REALLY SHOULDN'T HAVE YELLED AT ME LIKE THAT... IT WAS A GREAT SHOCK TO MY NERVOUS SYSTEM!
YOU STAY HERE NOW. I HAVE TO GO AND HAVE A CONFERENCE WITH THE PITCHER
YOU JUST WANT TO HAVE THOSE CONFERENCES WITH THE PITCHER BECAUSE THE PITCHER IS A GIRL!

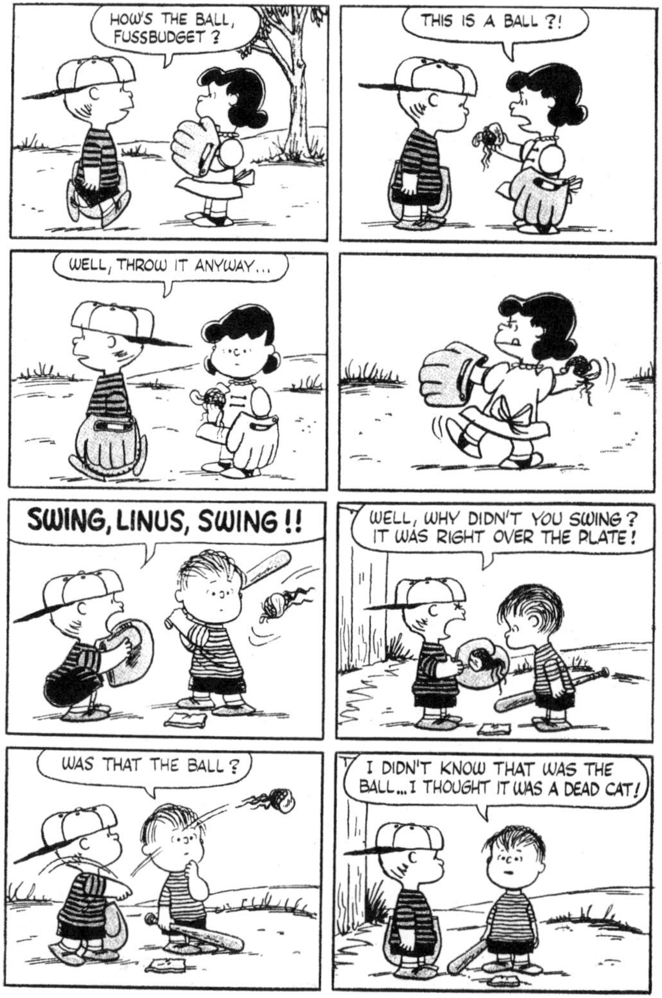
HOW'S THE BALL, FUSSBUDGET ?
THIS IS A BALL ?!
WELL, THROW IT ANYWAY...
SWING, LINUS, SWING!!
WELL, WHY DIDN'T YOU SWING? IT WAS RIGHT OVER THE PLATE!
WAS THAT THE BALL ?
I DIDN'T KNOW THAT WAS THE BALL... I THOUGHT IT WAS A DEAD CAT!

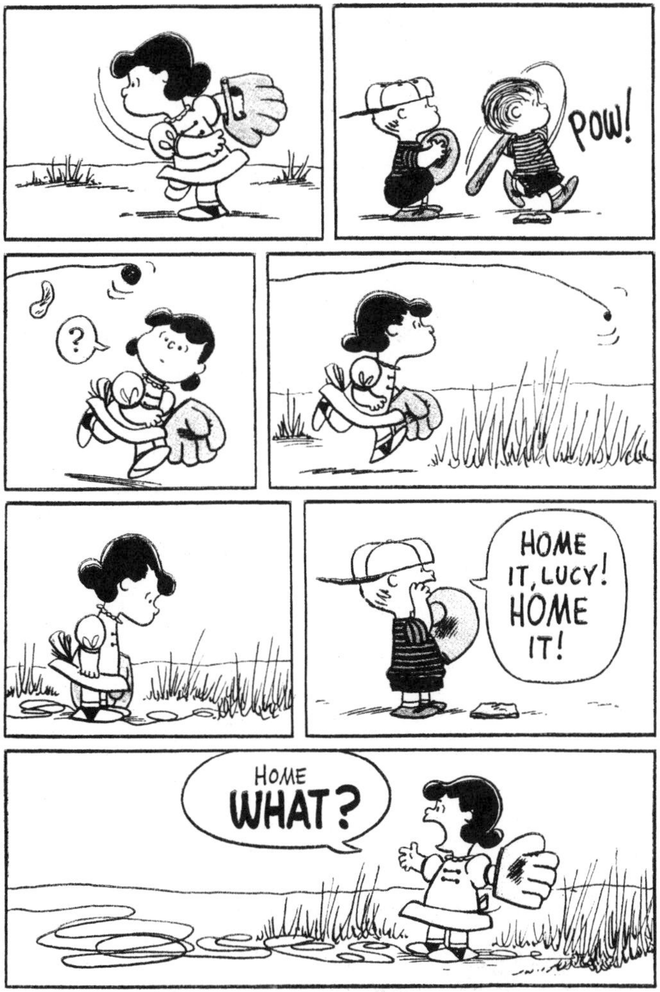
POW!
?
HOME IT, LUCY! HOME IT!
HOME WHAT?

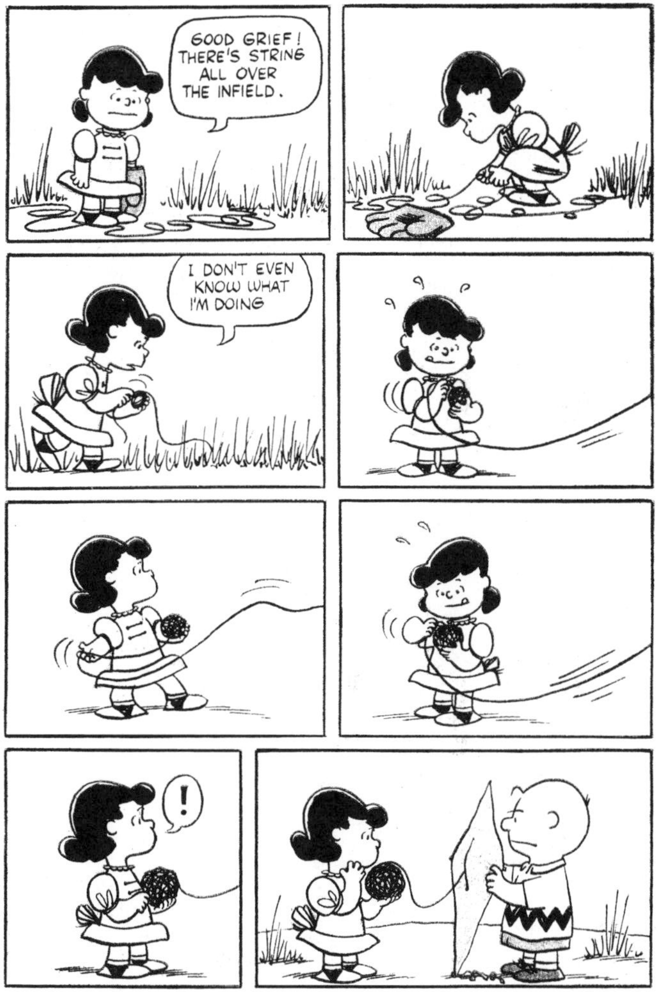
GOOD GRIEF! THERE'S STRING ALL OVER THE INFIELD.
I DON'T EVEN KNOW WHAT I'M DOING
!

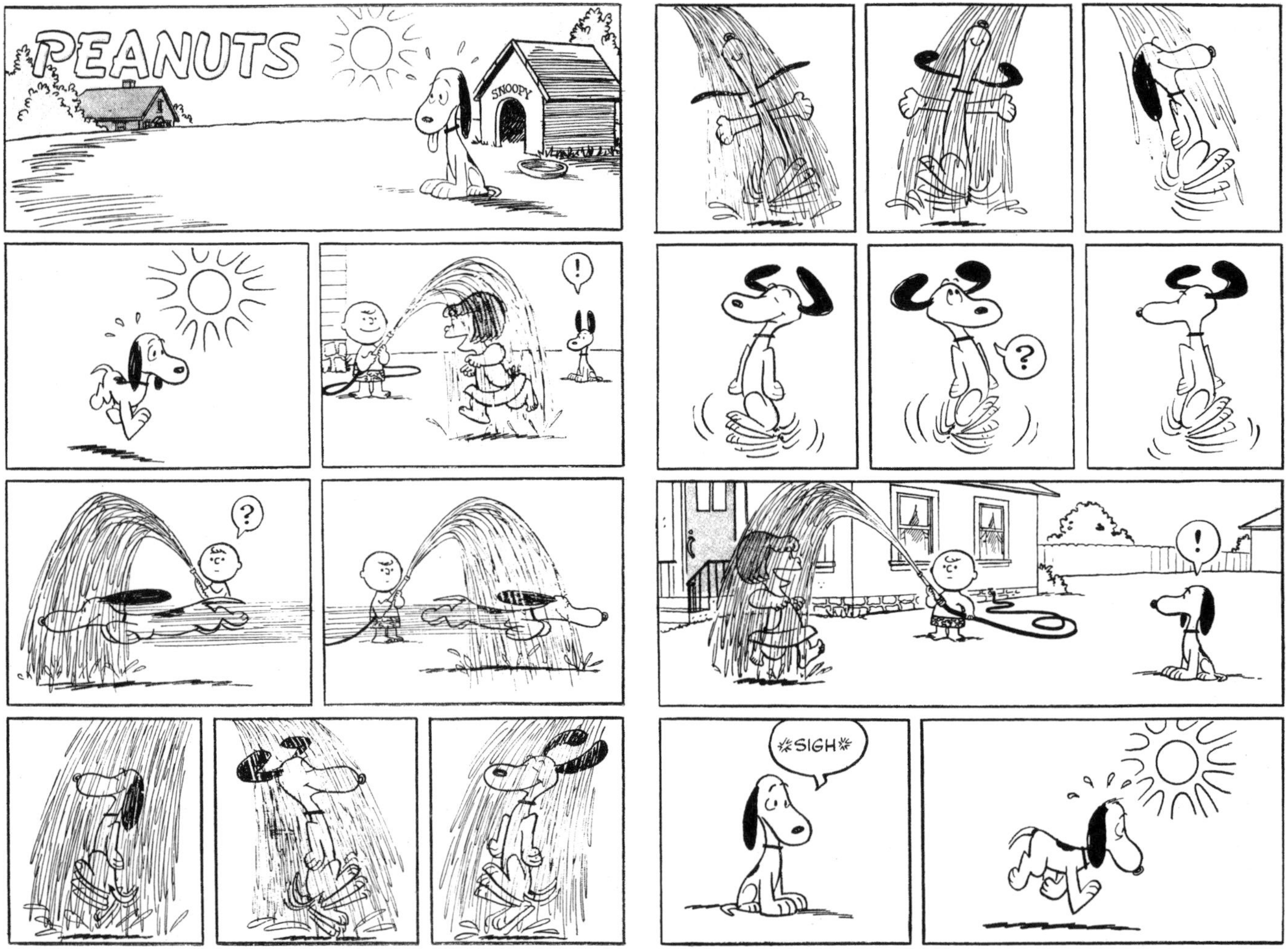
PEANUTS
SNOOPY
!
?
?
!
SIGH

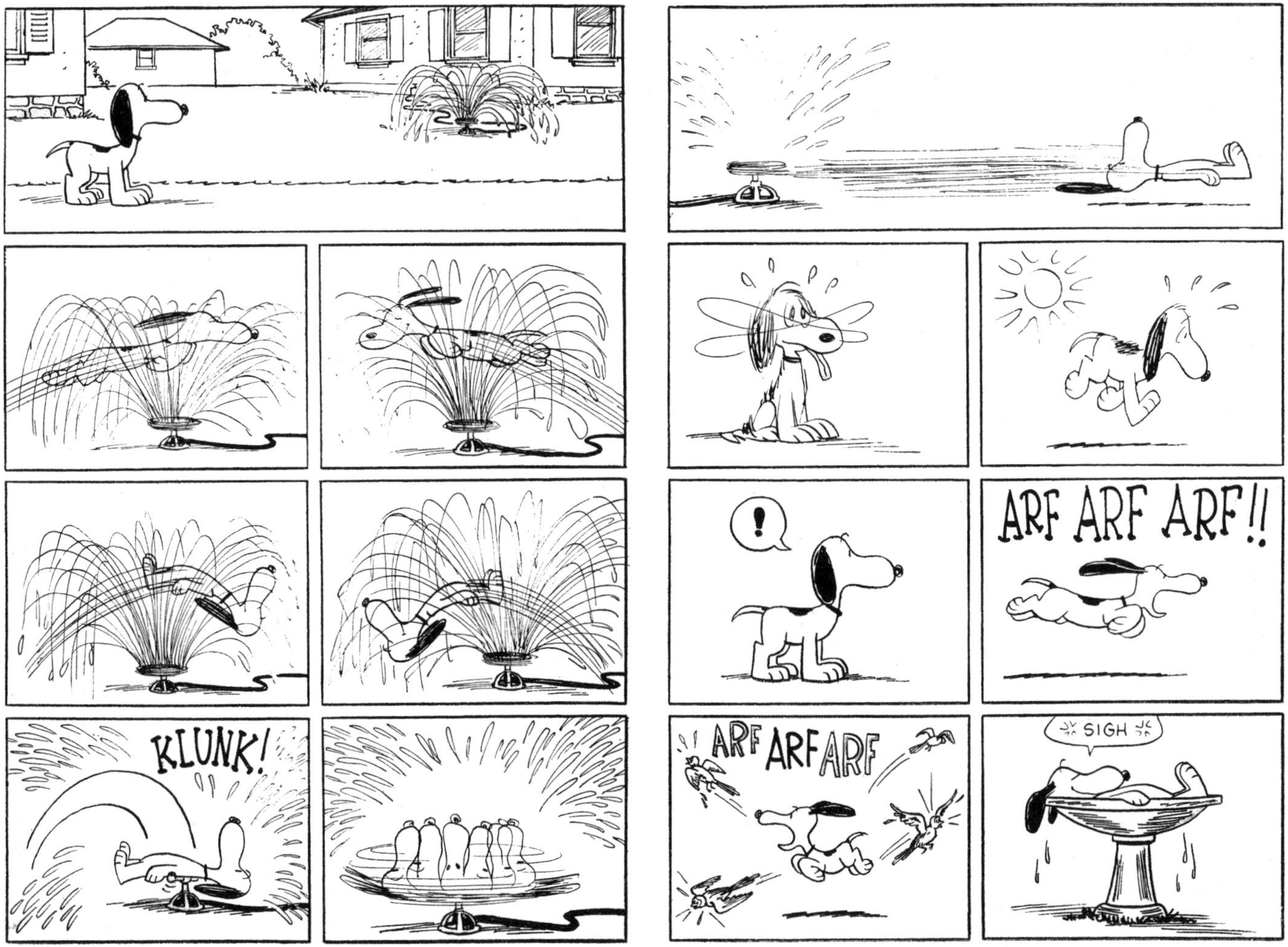
KLUNK!
!
ARF ARF ARF!!
ARF ARF ARF
SIGH

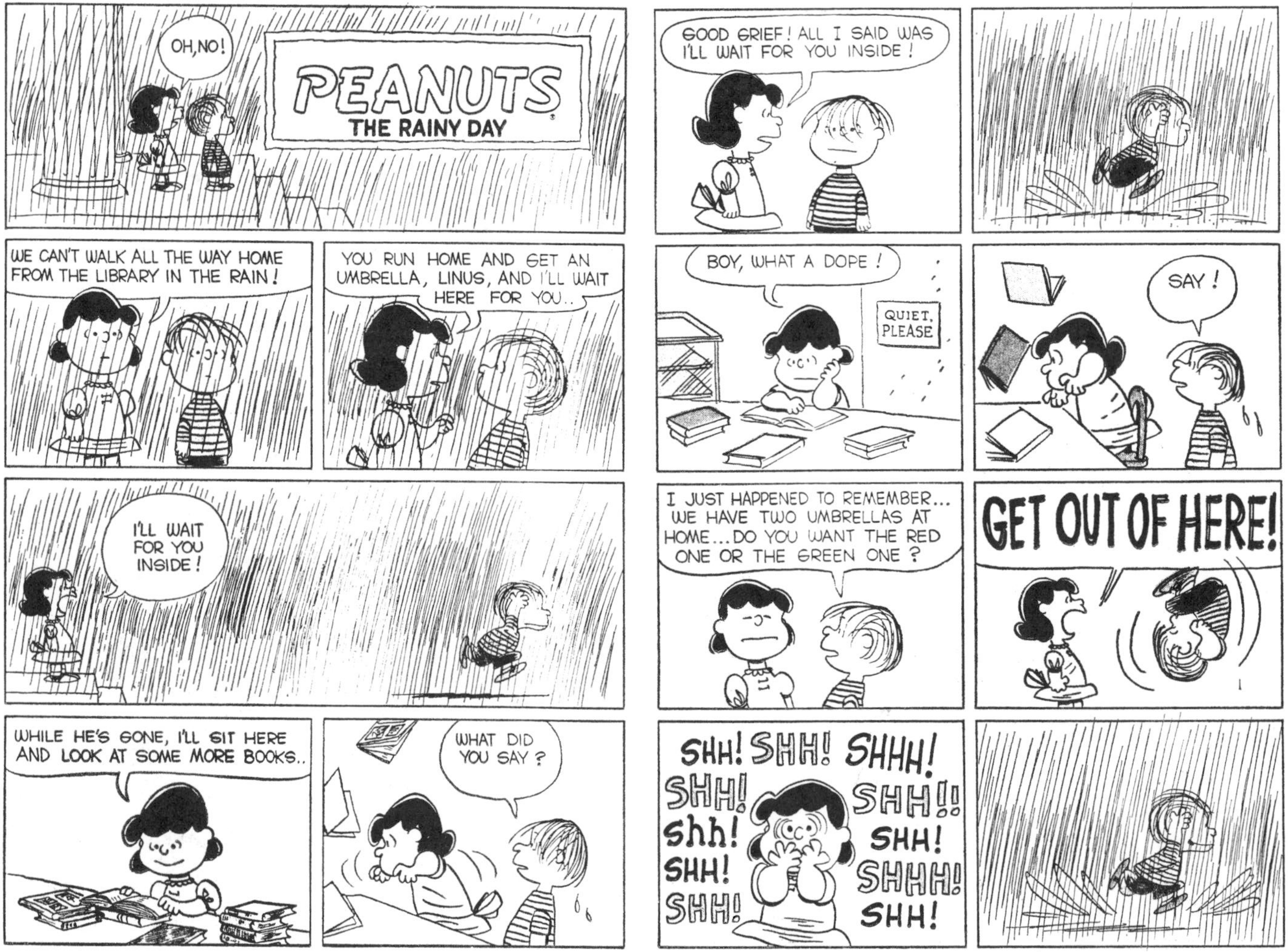
OH, NO!
PEANUTS
THE RAINY DAY
WE CAN'T WALK ALL THE WAY HOME FROM THE LIBRARY IN THE RAIN!
YOU RUN HOME AND GET AN UMBRELLA, LINUS, AND I'LL WAIT HERE FOR YOU..
I'LL WAIT FOR YOU INSIDE!
WHILE HE'S GONE, I'LL SIT HERE AND LOOK AT SOME MORE BOOKS..
WHAT DID YOU SAY?
GOOD GRIEF! ALL I SAID WAS I'LL WAIT FOR YOU INSIDE!
BOY, WHAT A DOPE!
QUIET, PLEASE
SAY!
I JUST HAPPENED TO REMEMBER... WE HAVE TWO UMBRELLAS AT HOME... DO YOU WANT THE RED ONE OR THE GREEN ONE?
GET OUT OF HERE!
SHH! SHH! SHHH!
SHH! SHH!!
shh! SHH!
SHH! SHHH!
SHH! SHH!

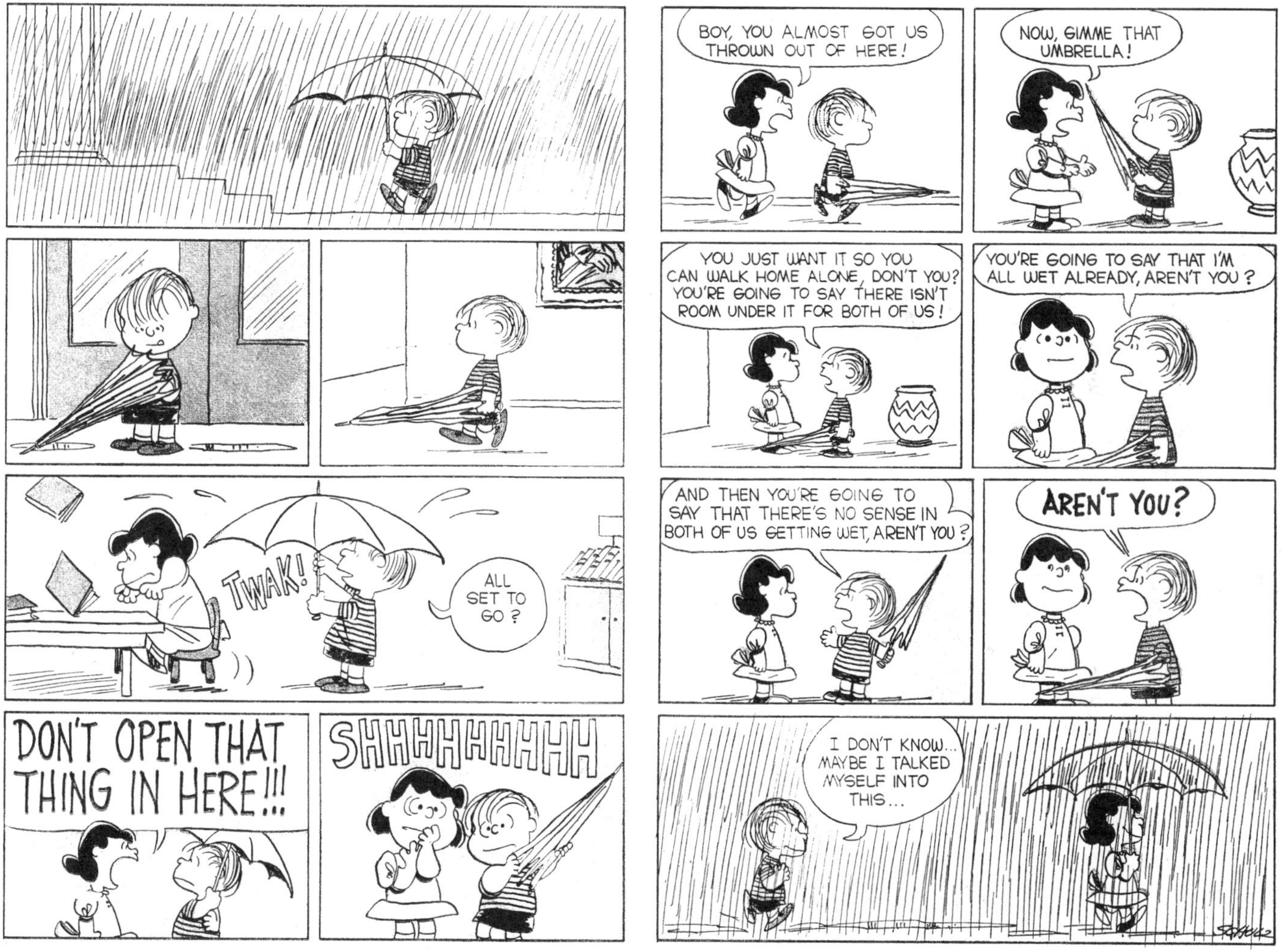
TWAK!
ALL SET TO GO?
DON'T OPEN THAT THING IN HERE!!!
SHHHHHHHHH
BOY, YOU ALMOST GOT US THROWN OUT OF HERE!
NOW, GIMME THAT UMBRELLA!
YOU JUST WANT IT SO YOU CAN WALK HOME ALONE, DON'T YOU? YOU'RE GOING TO SAY THERE ISN'T ROOM UNDER IT FOR BOTH OF US!
YOU'RE GOING TO SAY THAT I'M ALL WET ALREADY, AREN'T YOU?
AND THEN YOU'RE GOING TO SAY THAT THERE'S NO SENSE IN BOTH OF US GETTING WET, AREN'T YOU?
AREN'T YOU?
I DON'T KNOW... MAYBE I TALKED MYSELF INTO THIS...

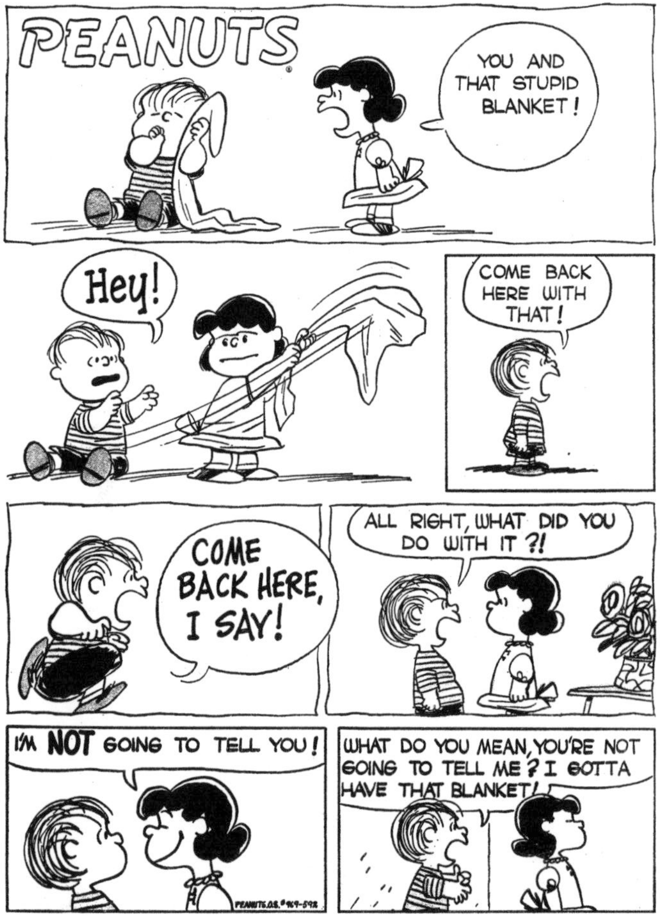
PEANUTS
YOU AND THAT STUPID BLANKET!
Hey!
COME BACK HERE WITH THAT!
COME BACK HERE, I SAY!
ALL RIGHT, WHAT DID YOU DO WITH IT ?!
I'M **NOT** GOING TO TELL YOU!
WHAT DO YOU MEAN, YOU'RE NOT GOING TO TELL ME? I GOTTA HAVE THAT BLANKET!

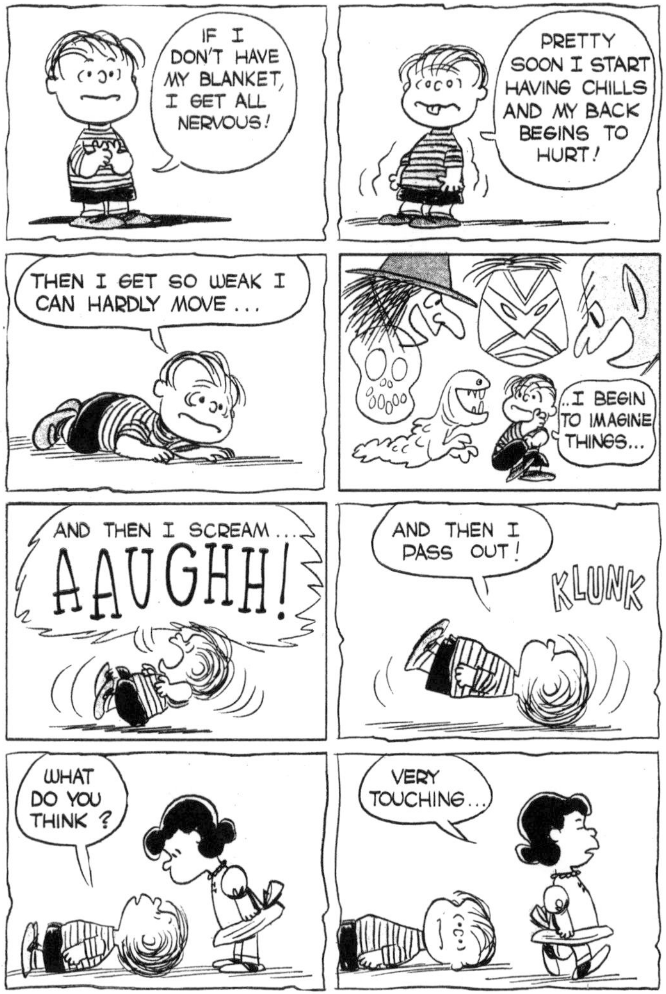
IF I DON'T HAVE MY BLANKET, I GET ALL NERVOUS!
PRETTY SOON I START HAVING CHILLS AND MY BACK BEGINS TO HURT!
THEN I GET SO WEAK I CAN HARDLY MOVE...
..I BEGIN TO IMAGINE THINGS...
AND THEN I SCREAM...
AAUGHH!
AND THEN I PASS OUT!
KLUNK
WHAT DO YOU THINK ?
VERY TOUCHING...

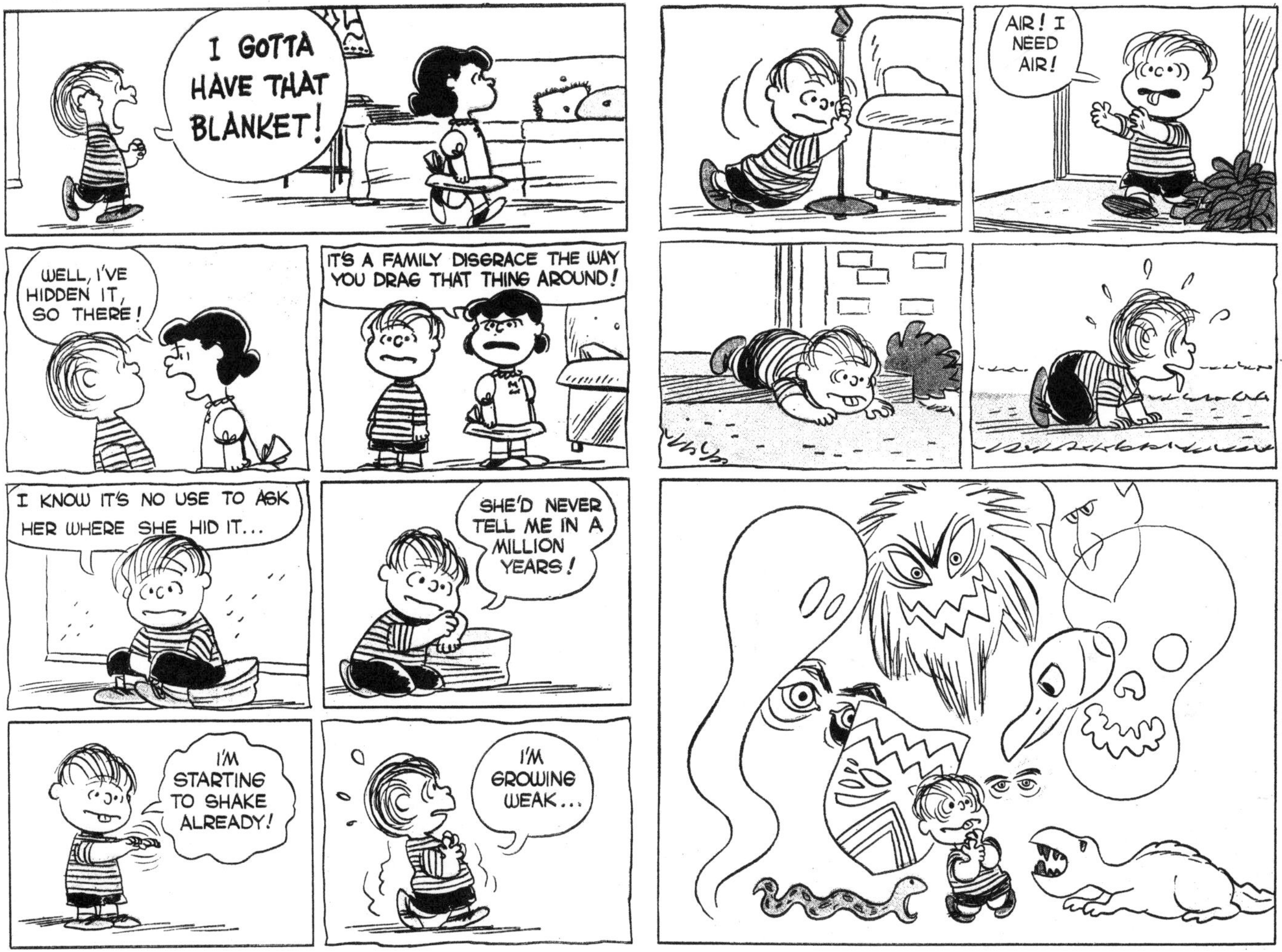
I GOTTA HAVE THAT BLANKET!
AIR! I NEED AIR!
WELL, I'VE HIDDEN IT, SO THERE!
IT'S A FAMILY DISGRACE THE WAY YOU DRAG THAT THING AROUND!
I KNOW IT'S NO USE TO ASK HER WHERE SHE HID IT...
SHE'D NEVER TELL ME IN A MILLION YEARS!
I'M STARTING TO SHAKE ALREADY!
I'M GROWING WEAK...

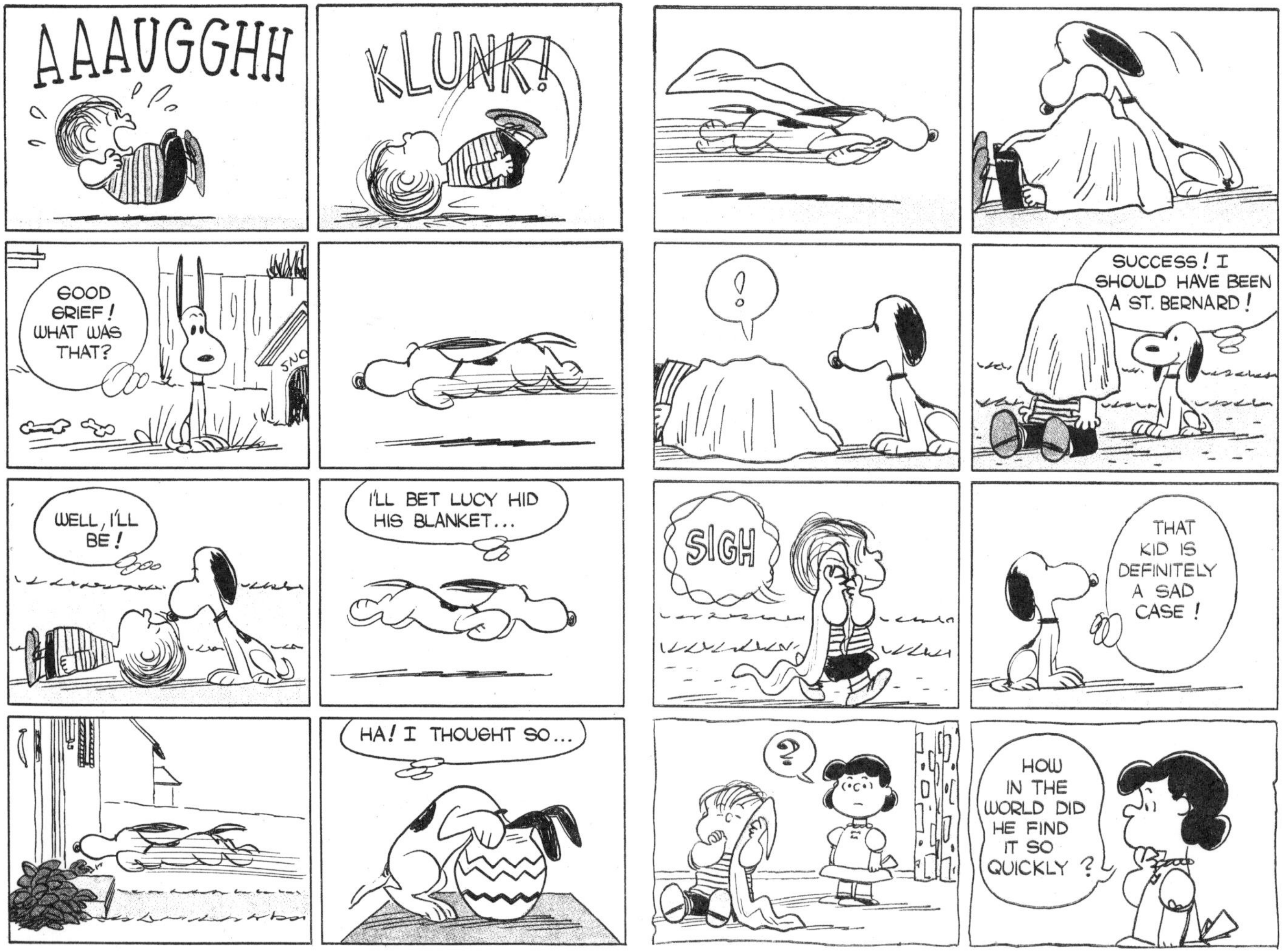
AAAUGGHH
KLUNK!
GOOD GRIEF! WHAT WAS THAT?
WELL, I'LL BE!
I'LL BET LUCY HID HIS BLANKET...
HA! I THOUGHT SO...
!
SUCCESS! I SHOULD HAVE BEEN A ST. BERNARD!
SIGH
THAT KID IS DEFINITELY A SAD CASE!
?
HOW IN THE WORLD DID HE FIND IT SO QUICKLY ?

RATS!

I JUST CAN'T STAND TO SEE HIM SIT THERE WITH THAT BLANKET!

HE LOOKS LIKE A FOOL, AND WHEN ONE MEMBER OF A FAMILY IS A FOOL, IT MAKES THE OTHER MEMBERS OF THE FAMILY LOOK LIKE FOOLS!

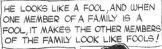

WELL, I'M NOT GOING TO BE MADE TO LOOK LIKE A FOOL!

I'LL TAKE IT AWAY FROM HIM AGAIN!

THIS TIME I'LL HIDE IT WHERE HE'LL **NEVER** FIND IT!

BZZZZZ

A BEE!

TWACK!!

GOT HIM!

WHAT WERE YOU DOING DOWN THERE ON THE FLOOR?

OH, NOTHING..NOTHING..JUST FORGET YOU EVER SAW ME...

AND DON'T EVER LET ANYTHING HAPPEN TO THAT BLANKET!

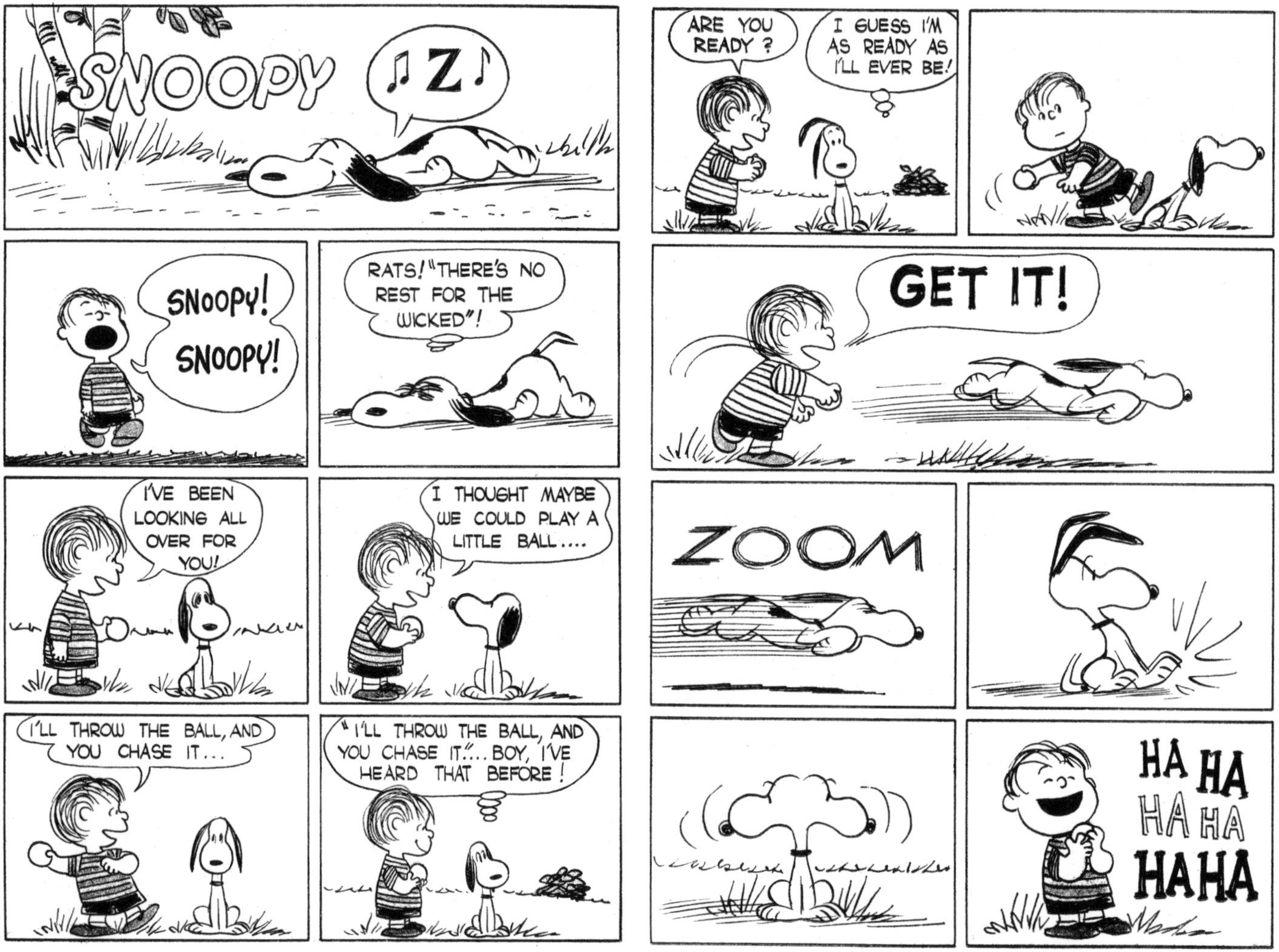
SNOOPY
♪Z♪
SNOOPY! SNOOPY!
RATS! "THERE'S NO REST FOR THE WICKED"!
I'VE BEEN LOOKING ALL OVER FOR YOU!
I THOUGHT MAYBE WE COULD PLAY A LITTLE BALL....
I'LL THROW THE BALL, AND YOU CHASE IT...
"I'LL THROW THE BALL, AND YOU CHASE IT!"... BOY, I'VE HEARD THAT BEFORE!
ARE YOU READY ?
I GUESS I'M AS READY AS I'LL EVER BE!
GET IT!
ZOOM
HA HA HA HA HAHA

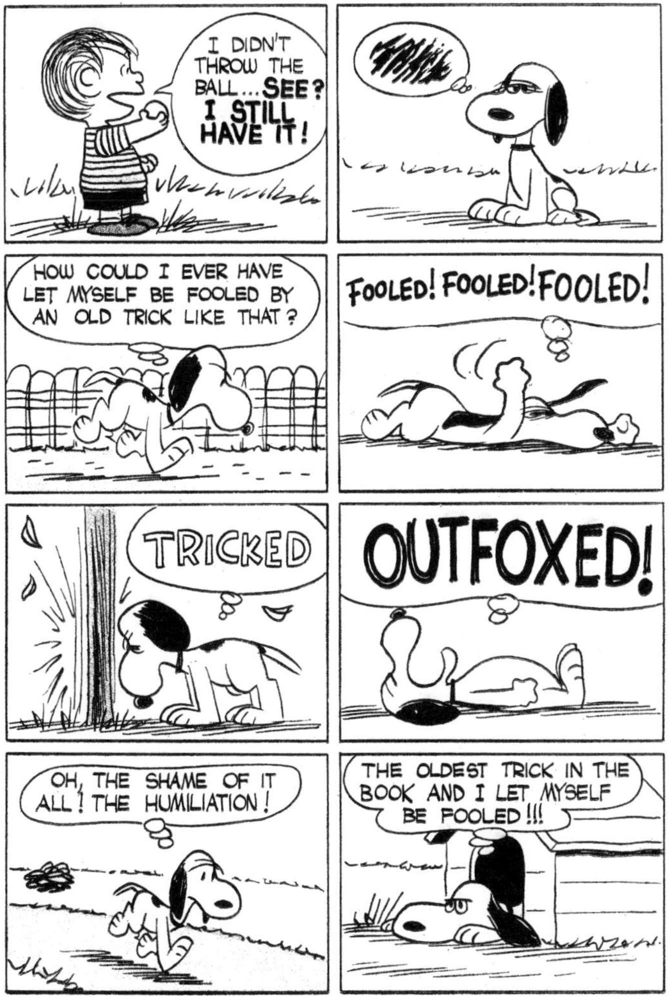
I DIDN'T THROW THE BALL... SEE? I STILL HAVE IT!
HOW COULD I EVER HAVE LET MYSELF BE FOOLED BY AN OLD TRICK LIKE THAT?
FOOLED! FOOLED! FOOLED!
TRICKED
OUTFOXED!
OH, THE SHAME OF IT ALL! THE HUMILIATION!
THE OLDEST TRICK IN THE BOOK AND I LET MYSELF BE FOOLED!!!

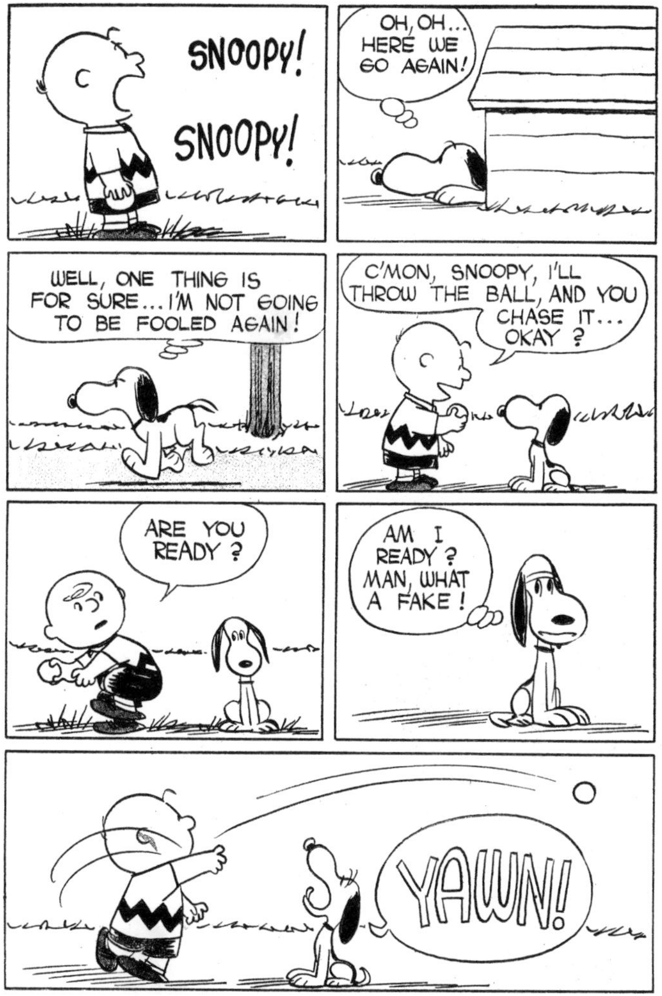
SNOOPY!
SNOOPY!
OH, OH... HERE WE GO AGAIN!
WELL, ONE THING IS FOR SURE... I'M NOT GOING TO BE FOOLED AGAIN!
C'MON, SNOOPY, I'LL THROW THE BALL, AND YOU CHASE IT... OKAY?
ARE YOU READY?
AM I READY? MAN, WHAT A FAKE!
YAWN!

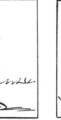

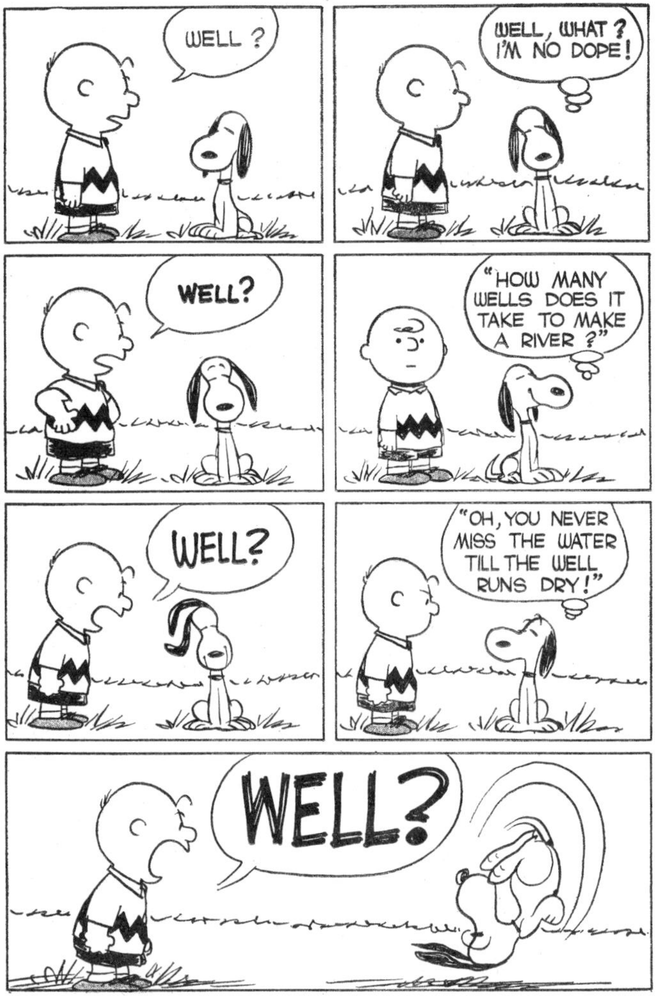
WELL ?
WELL, WHAT ? I'M NO DOPE !
WELL?
"HOW MANY WELLS DOES IT TAKE TO MAKE A RIVER ?"
WELL?
"OH, YOU NEVER MISS THE WATER TILL THE WELL RUNS DRY !"
WELL?

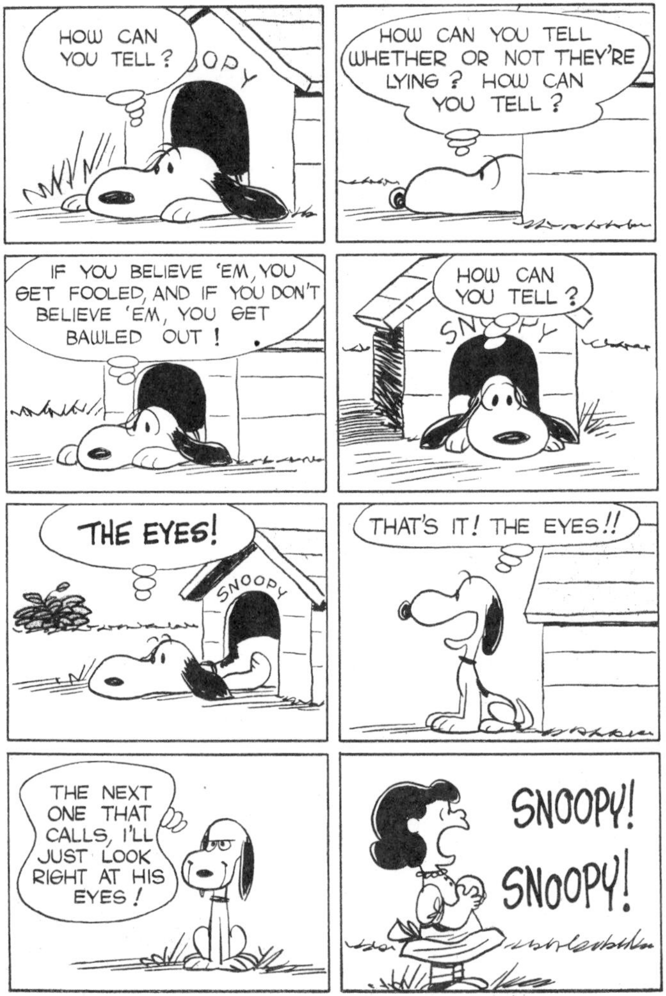
HOW CAN YOU TELL ?
HOW CAN YOU TELL WHETHER OR NOT THEY'RE LYING ? HOW CAN YOU TELL ?
IF YOU BELIEVE 'EM, YOU GET FOOLED, AND IF YOU DON'T BELIEVE 'EM, YOU GET BAWLED OUT !
HOW CAN YOU TELL ?
THE EYES!
THAT'S IT! THE EYES!!
THE NEXT ONE THAT CALLS, I'LL JUST LOOK RIGHT AT HIS EYES !
SNOOPY!
SNOOPY!

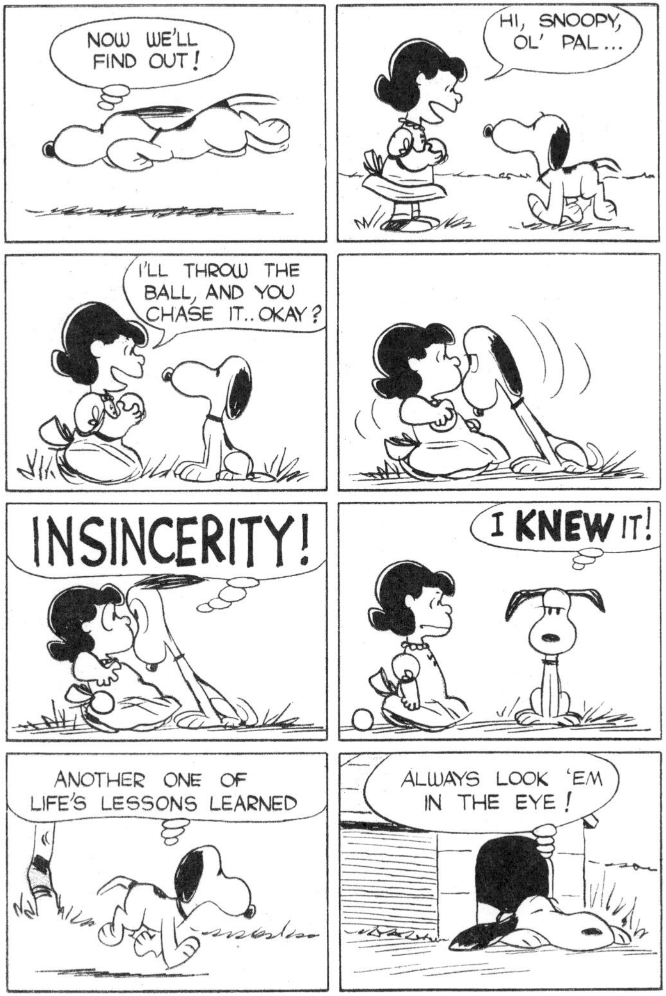
NOW WE'LL FIND OUT!
HI, SNOOPY, OL' PAL...
I'LL THROW THE BALL, AND YOU CHASE IT.. OKAY?
INSINCERITY!
I KNEW IT!
ANOTHER ONE OF LIFE'S LESSONS LEARNED
ALWAYS LOOK 'EM IN THE EYE!

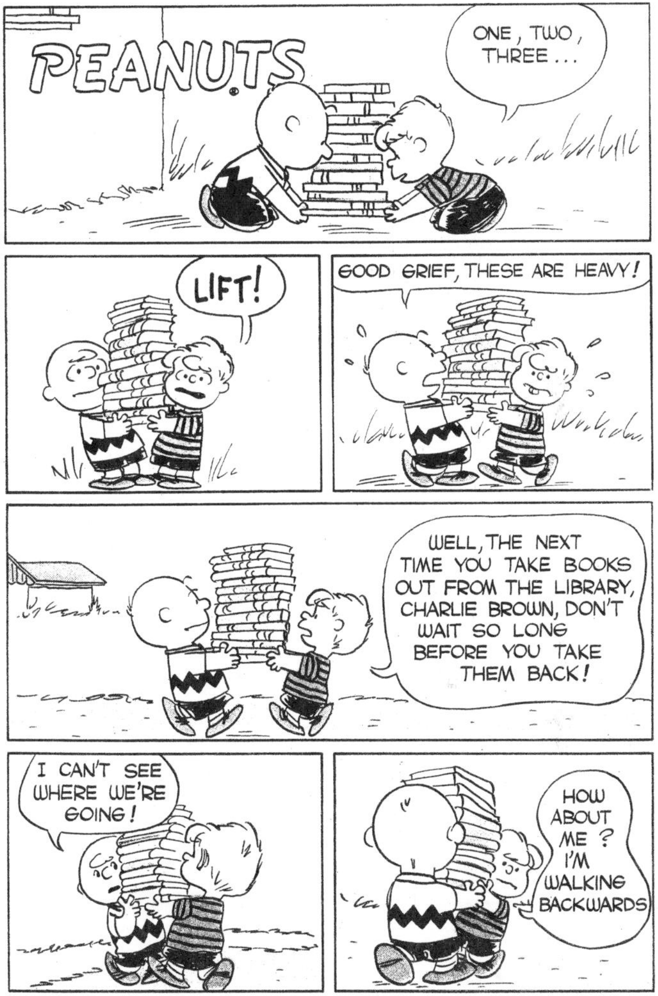
PEANUTS
ONE, TWO, THREE...
LIFT!
GOOD GRIEF, THESE ARE HEAVY!
WELL, THE NEXT TIME YOU TAKE BOOKS OUT FROM THE LIBRARY, CHARLIE BROWN, DON'T WAIT SO LONG BEFORE YOU TAKE THEM BACK!
I CAN'T SEE WHERE WE'RE GOING!
HOW ABOUT ME? I'M WALKING BACKWARDS

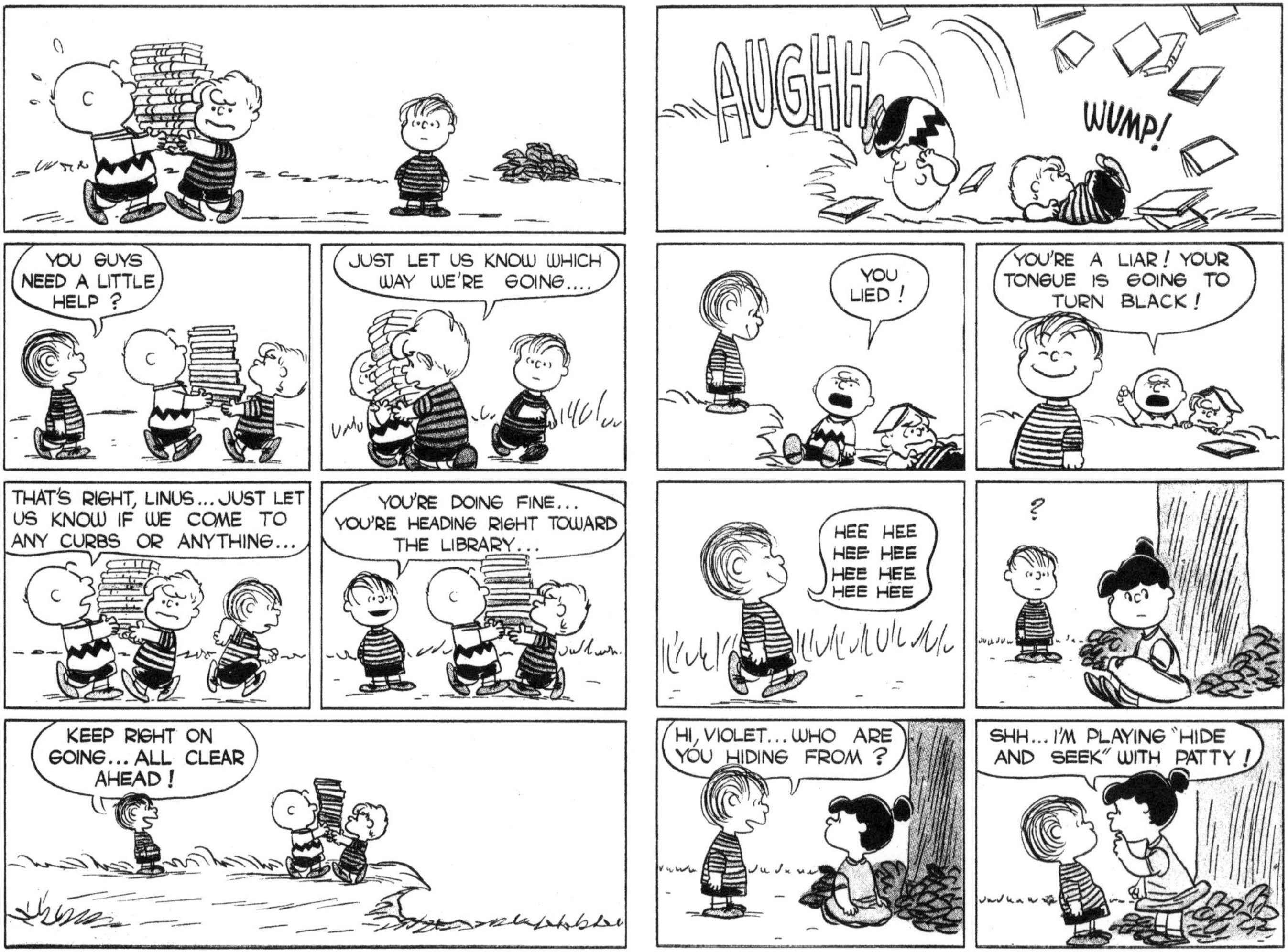
YOU GUYS NEED A LITTLE HELP ?
JUST LET US KNOW WHICH WAY WE'RE GOING....
THAT'S RIGHT, LINUS... JUST LET US KNOW IF WE COME TO ANY CURBS OR ANYTHING...
YOU'RE DOING FINE... YOU'RE HEADING RIGHT TOWARD THE LIBRARY...
KEEP RIGHT ON GOING... ALL CLEAR AHEAD !
AUGHH
WUMP!
YOU LIED !
YOU'RE A LIAR ! YOUR TONGUE IS GOING TO TURN BLACK !
HEE HEE HEE HEE HEE HEE HEE HEE
?
HI, VIOLET... WHO ARE YOU HIDING FROM ?
SHH... I'M PLAYING "HIDE AND SEEK" WITH PATTY !

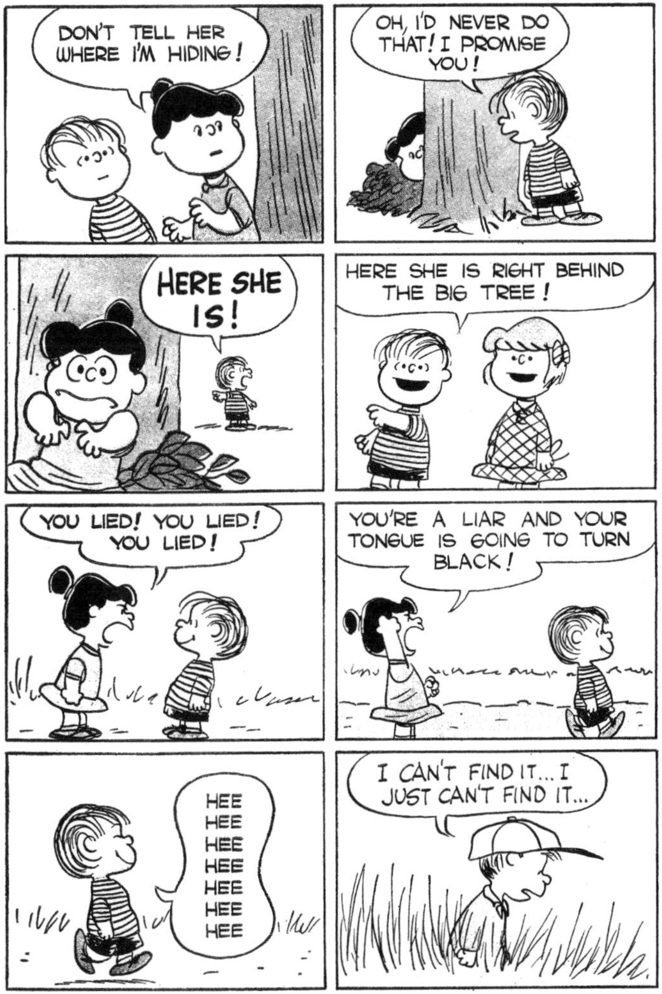
DON'T TELL HER WHERE I'M HIDING!
OH, I'D NEVER DO THAT! I PROMISE YOU!
HERE SHE IS!
HERE SHE IS RIGHT BEHIND THE BIG TREE!
YOU LIED! YOU LIED! YOU LIED!
YOU'RE A LIAR AND YOUR TONGUE IS GOING TO TURN BLACK!
HEE HEE HEE HEE HEE HEE HEE

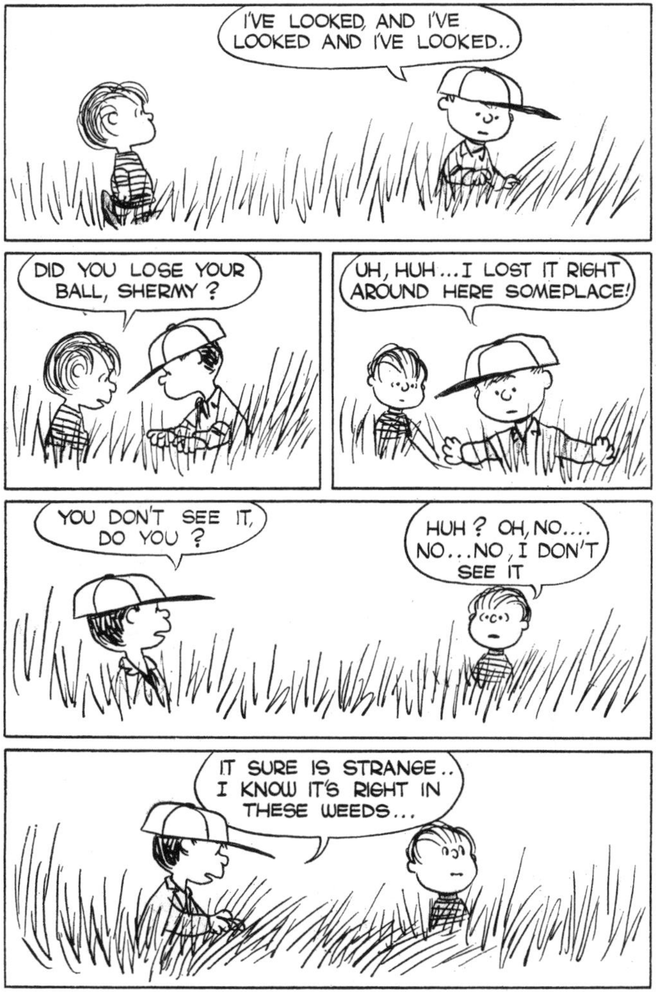
I CAN'T FIND IT... I JUST CAN'T FIND IT...
I'VE LOOKED, AND I'VE LOOKED AND I'VE LOOKED..
DID YOU LOSE YOUR BALL, SHERMY ?
UH, HUH... I LOST IT RIGHT AROUND HERE SOMEPLACE!
YOU DON'T SEE IT, DO YOU ?
HUH ? OH, NO.... NO...NO, I DON'T SEE IT
IT SURE IS STRANGE.. I KNOW IT'S RIGHT IN THESE WEEDS...

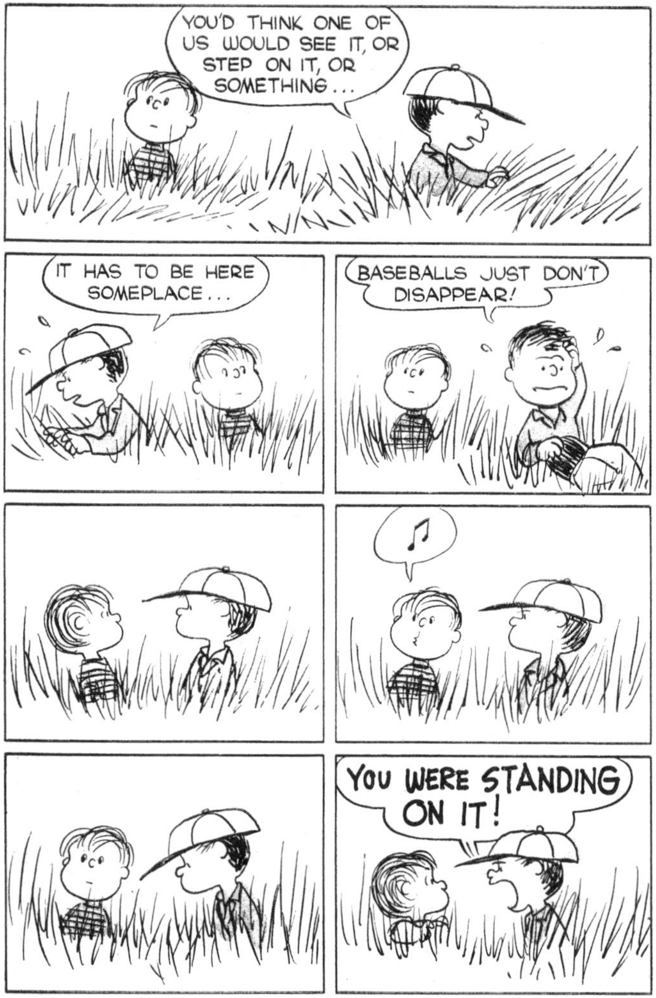
YOU'D THINK ONE OF US WOULD SEE IT, OR STEP ON IT, OR SOMETHING...
IT HAS TO BE HERE SOMEPLACE...
BASEBALLS JUST DON'T DISAPPEAR!
♪
YOU WERE STANDING ON IT!
YOU SAID YOU DIDN'T KNOW WHERE IT WAS AND YOU WERE STANDING ON IT!
LINUS, YOU'RE A LIAR, AND YOUR TONGUE IS GOING TO TURN BLACK!
HEE HEE HEE HEE HEE HEE

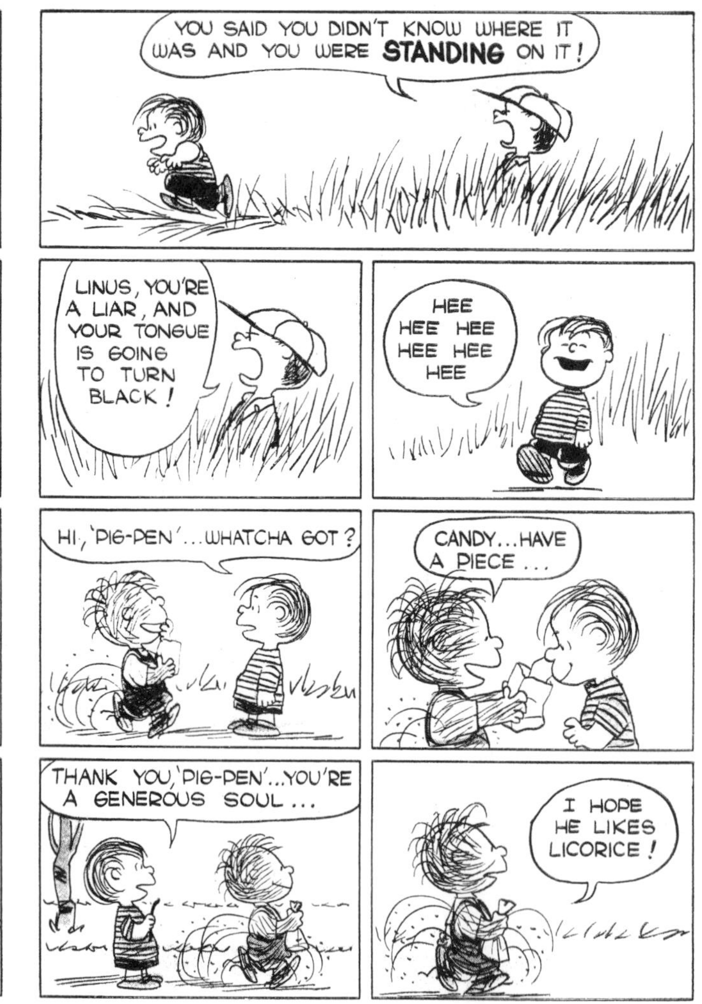
HI, 'PIG-PEN'...WHATCHA GOT?
CANDY...HAVE A PIECE...
THANK YOU, 'PIG-PEN'...YOU'RE A GENEROUS SOUL...
I HOPE HE LIKES LICORICE!

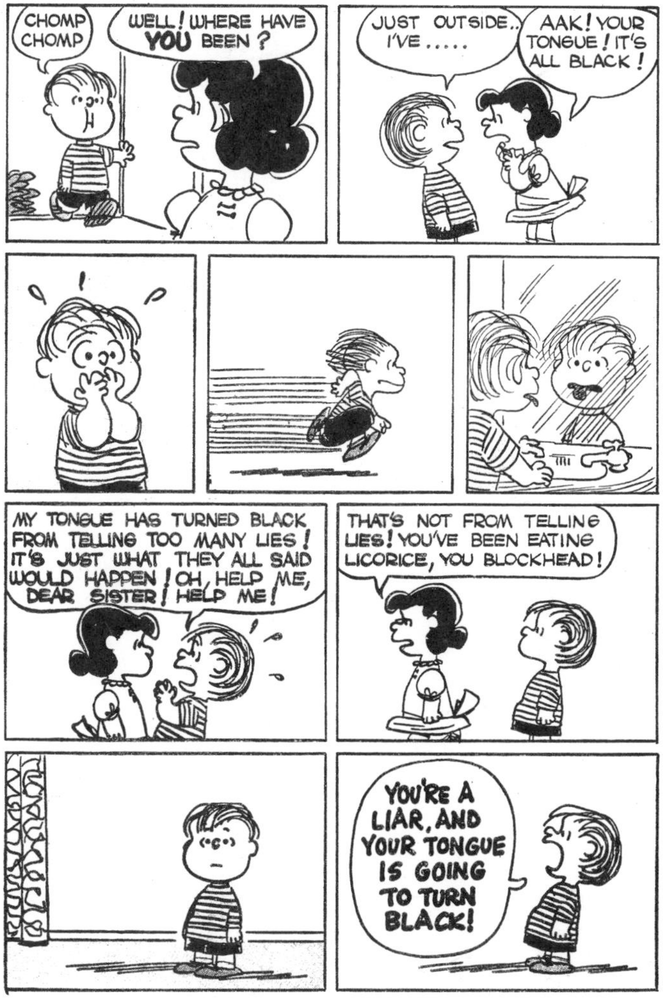
CHOMP CHOMP
WELL! WHERE HAVE YOU BEEN ?
JUST OUTSIDE... I'VE .....
AAK! YOUR TONGUE! IT'S ALL BLACK!
MY TONGUE HAS TURNED BLACK FROM TELLING TOO MANY LIES! IT'S JUST WHAT THEY ALL SAID WOULD HAPPEN! OH, HELP ME, DEAR SISTER! HELP ME!
THAT'S NOT FROM TELLING LIES! YOU'VE BEEN EATING LICORICE, YOU BLOCKHEAD!
YOU'RE A LIAR, AND YOUR TONGUE IS GOING TO TURN BLACK!

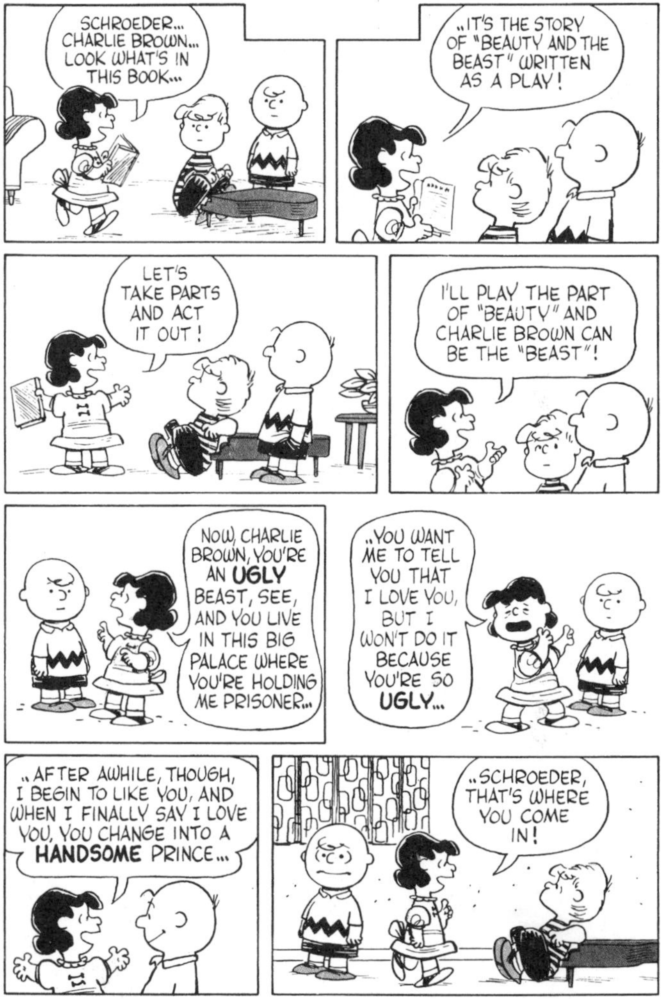
SCHROEDER... CHARLIE BROWN... LOOK WHAT'S IN THIS BOOK...
..IT'S THE STORY OF "BEAUTY AND THE BEAST" WRITTEN AS A PLAY!
LET'S TAKE PARTS AND ACT IT OUT!
I'LL PLAY THE PART OF "BEAUTY" AND CHARLIE BROWN CAN BE THE "BEAST"!
NOW, CHARLIE BROWN, YOU'RE AN UGLY BEAST, SEE, AND YOU LIVE IN THIS BIG PALACE WHERE YOU'RE HOLDING ME PRISONER...
..YOU WANT ME TO TELL YOU THAT I LOVE YOU, BUT I WON'T DO IT BECAUSE YOU'RE SO UGLY...
..AFTER AWHILE, THOUGH, I BEGIN TO LIKE YOU, AND WHEN I FINALLY SAY I LOVE YOU, YOU CHANGE INTO A HANDSOME PRINCE...
..SCHROEDER, THAT'S WHERE YOU COME IN!

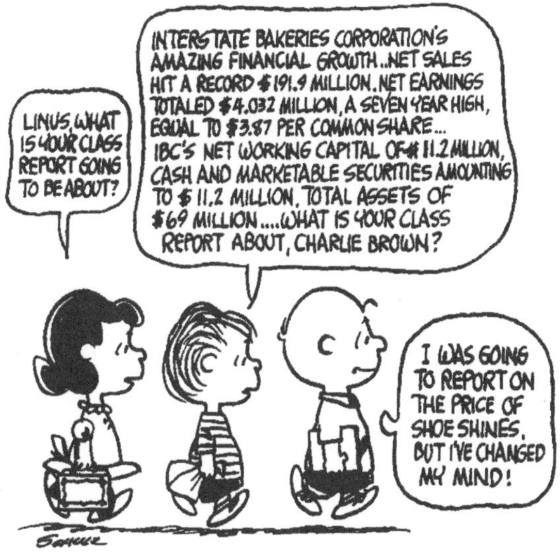
LINUS, WHAT IS YOUR CLASS REPORT GOING TO BE ABOUT?
INTERSTATE BAKERIES CORPORATION'S AMAZING FINANCIAL GROWTH..NET SALES HIT A RECORD $191.9 MILLION. NET EARNINGS TOTALED $4.032 MILLION, A SEVEN YEAR HIGH, EQUAL TO $3.87 PER COMMON SHARE... IBC'S NET WORKING CAPITAL OF $11.2 MILLION, CASH AND MARKETABLE SECURITIES AMOUNTING TO $11.2 MILLION, TOTAL ASSETS OF $69 MILLION....WHAT IS YOUR CLASS REPORT ABOUT, CHARLIE BROWN?
I WAS GOING TO REPORT ON THE PRICE OF SHOE SHINES, BUT I'VE CHANGED MY MIND!

ADVERTISING

The Peanuts characters have been used to advertise many products over the years. This section is not meant to be an encyclopedic collection of this material. Rather it showcases some of the more interesting work Schulz drew with his own hand in his early years as a professional cartoonist.

On pages 36 to 41 are strips and illustrations from 1955's *The Brownie Book of Picture-Taking*, a Kodak instructional booklet on using your Brownie camera.

Pages 42 to 58 present a sampling of the very many strips and drawings Schulz did for the Ford Motor Company's new compact car, the Ford Falcon. This advertising campaign ran from January 1960 through mid- '64, and included animated TV spots, brochures, and a series of ads in major magazine with original multi-panel strips.

On pages 59 to 63 are some charming drawings licensed to promote Interstate Bakeries Corporation's Dolly Madison Cakes and Butternut Bread.

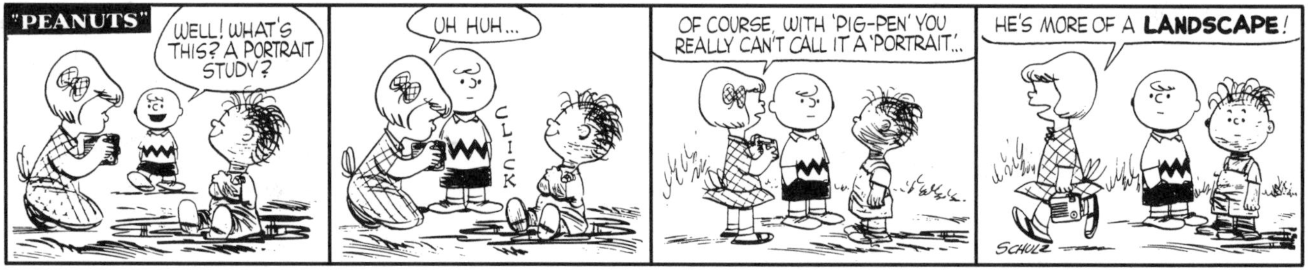
"PEANUTS"
WELL! WHAT'S THIS? A PORTRAIT STUDY?
UH HUH...
CLICK
OF COURSE, WITH 'PIG-PEN' YOU REALLY CAN'T CALL IT A 'PORTRAIT'..
HE'S MORE OF A **LANDSCAPE**!
SCHULZ

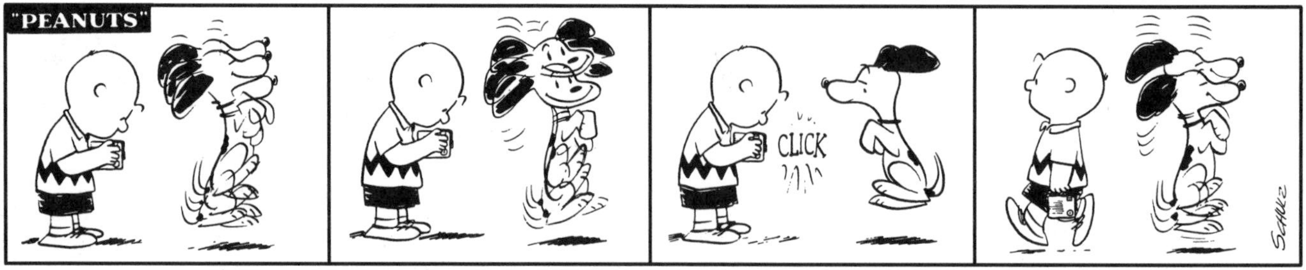
"PEANUTS"
CLICK
SCHULZ

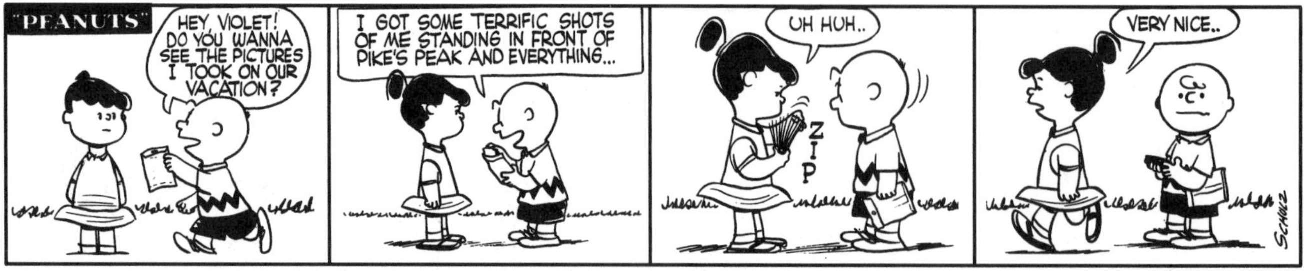
"PEANUTS"
HEY, VIOLET! DO YOU WANNA SEE THE PICTURES I TOOK ON OUR VACATION?
I GOT SOME TERRIFIC SHOTS OF ME STANDING IN FRONT OF PIKE'S PEAK AND EVERYTHING...
UH HUH..
ZIP
VERY NICE..
SCHULZ

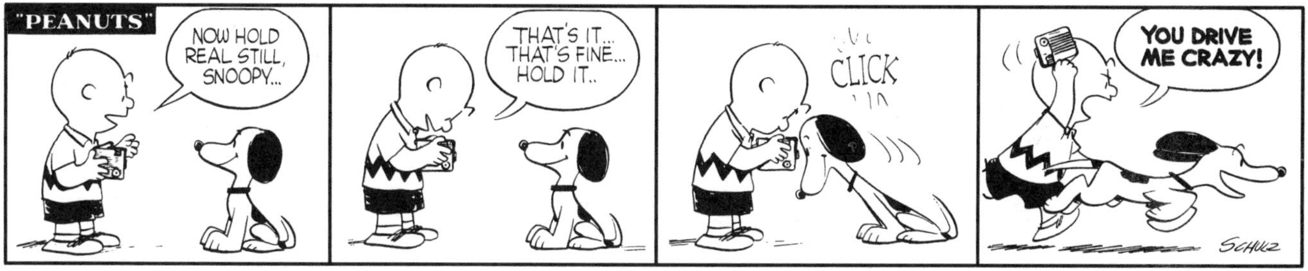
"PEANUTS"
NOW HOLD REAL STILL, SNOOPY...
THAT'S IT... THAT'S FINE... HOLD IT..
CLICK
YOU DRIVE ME CRAZY!
SCHULZ

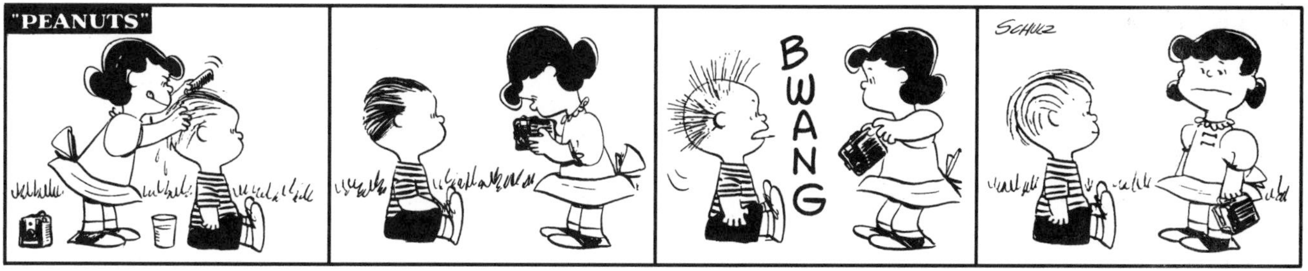
"PEANUTS"
BWANG
SCHULZ

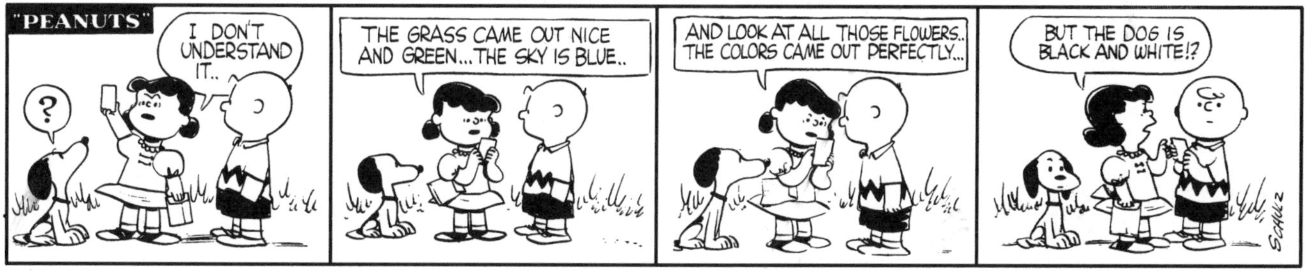
"PEANUTS"
I DON'T UNDERSTAND IT..
?
THE GRASS CAME OUT NICE AND GREEN... THE SKY IS BLUE..
AND LOOK AT ALL THOSE FLOWERS.. THE COLORS CAME OUT PERFECTLY...
BUT THE DOG IS BLACK AND WHITE!?
SCHULZ

"PEANUTS"
I'M GOING TO TRY AN INDOOR SHOT TODAY, CHARLIE BROWN..
CAN YOU REMEMBER EVERYTHING I TOLD YOU ABOUT TAKING INDOOR PICTURES?
I SURE CAN
OH ONE OTHER THING, LUCY...DON'T FORGET TO STAY FIVE FEET AWAY FROM YOUR SUBJECT..
THAT'S EASIER SAID THAN DONE!
SNOOPY
SCHULZ

"PEANUTS"
CLICK!
!
?
HOT!
SCHULZ

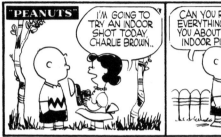

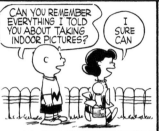

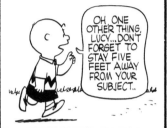

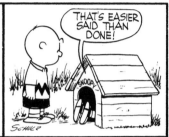

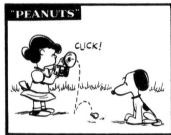

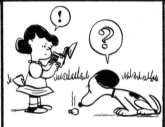

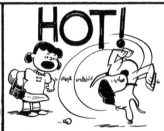

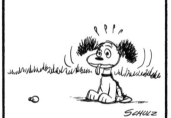

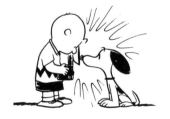

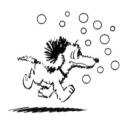

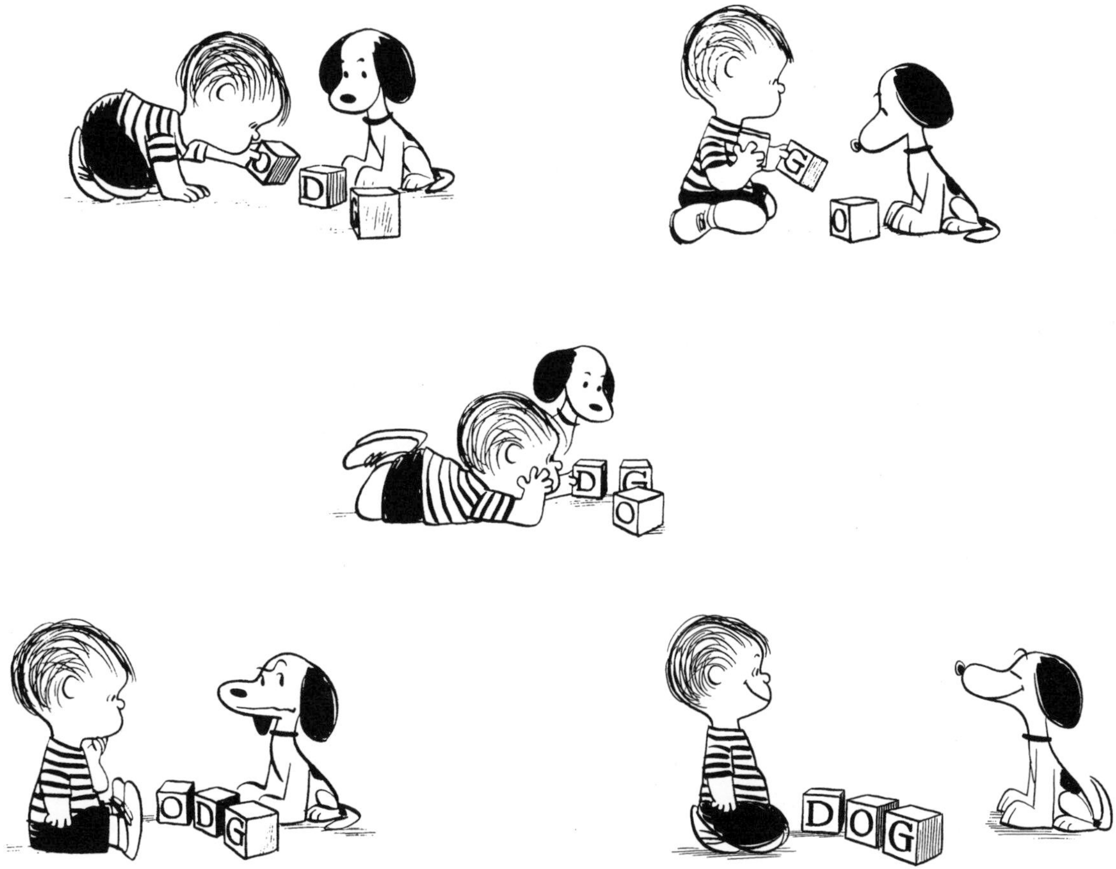
D
G
O
D G
O
O D G
D O G

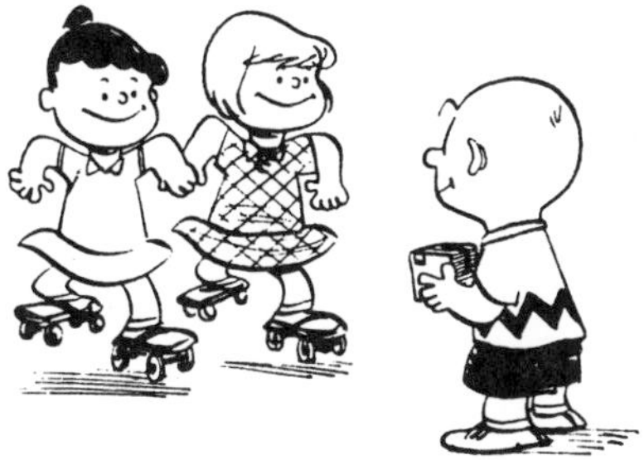

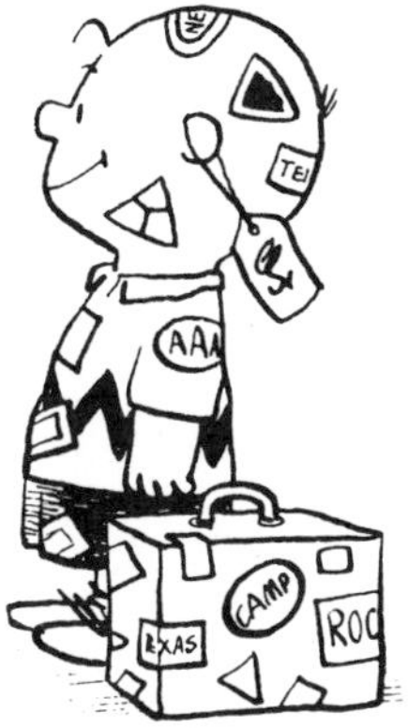
CAMP

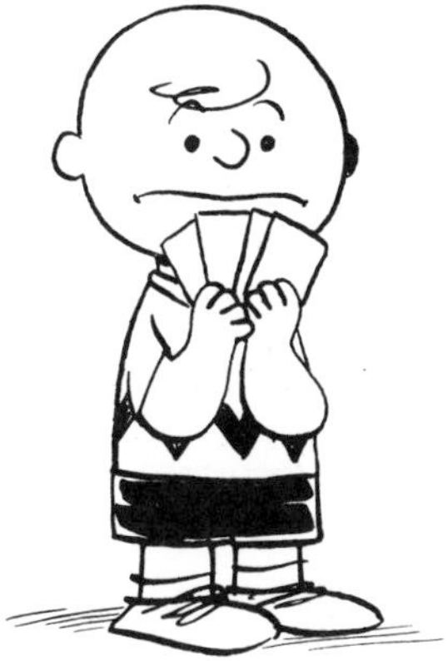

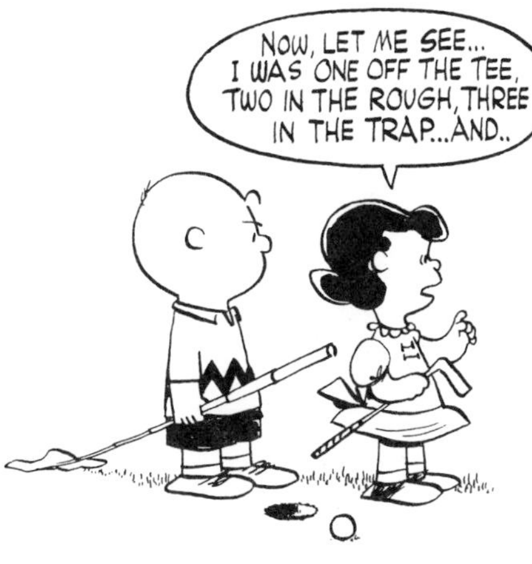
NOW, LET ME SEE... I WAS ONE OFF THE TEE, TWO IN THE ROUGH, THREE IN THE TRAP...AND..

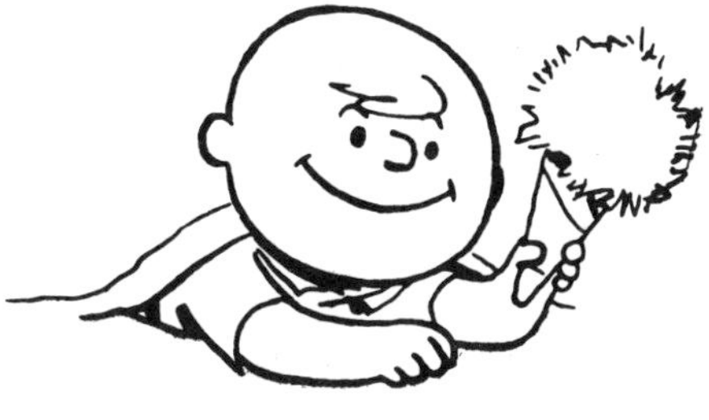

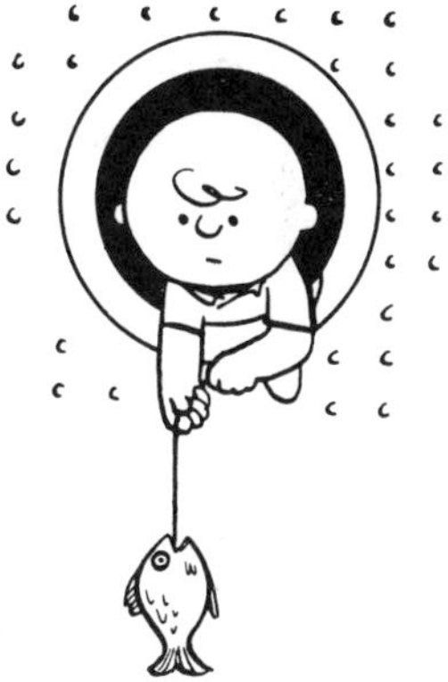

IF EACH FORD ECONOMY TWIN HOLDS SIX BIG PEOPLE, HOW MANY IS THAT ALTOGETHER?

DEFINE "BIG"... IN FACT, DEFINE "PEOPLE"!

THESE FORD ECONOMY TWINS SURE ARE THRIFTY WITH YOUR MONEY!

WHAT GOOD IS MONEY WITHOUT EMOTIONAL SECURITY?

I THINK IT WAS VERY SMART OF FORD TO FASHION THE FALCON AFTER THE FAIRLANE 500...

YOU ALWAYS SOUND SO SMUG, CHARLIE BROWN... FOR ALL YOU KNOW, THEY FASHIONED THE FAIRLANE 500 AFTER THE FALCON!

SCHROEDER, DO YOU KNOW, "YOU'RE AHEAD IN A FORD ALL THE WAY"?

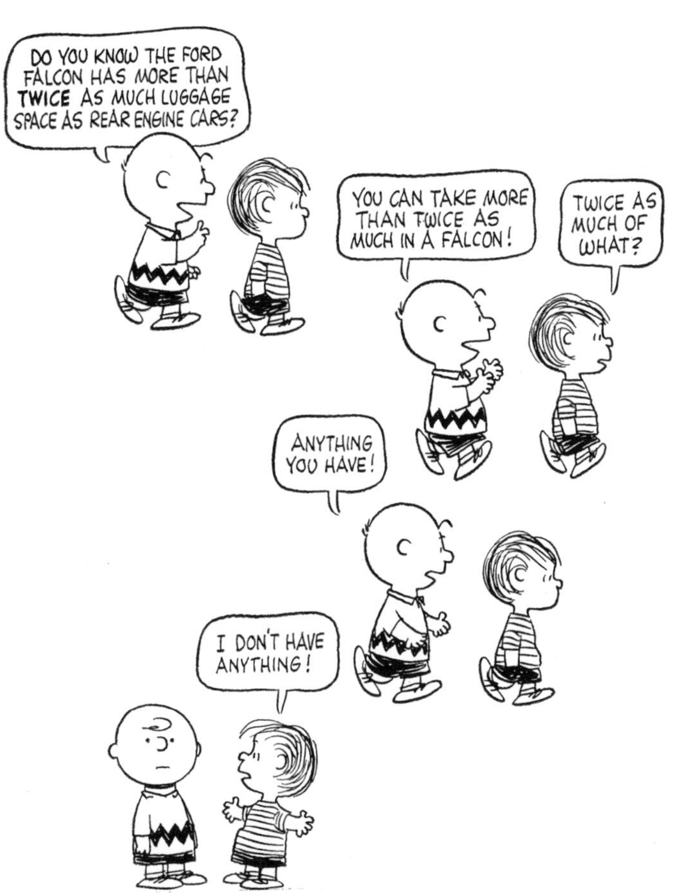
DO YOU KNOW THE FORD FALCON HAS MORE THAN TWICE AS MUCH LUGGAGE SPACE AS REAR ENGINE CARS?
YOU CAN TAKE MORE THAN TWICE AS MUCH IN A FALCON!
TWICE AS MUCH OF WHAT?
ANYTHING YOU HAVE!
I DON'T HAVE ANYTHING!

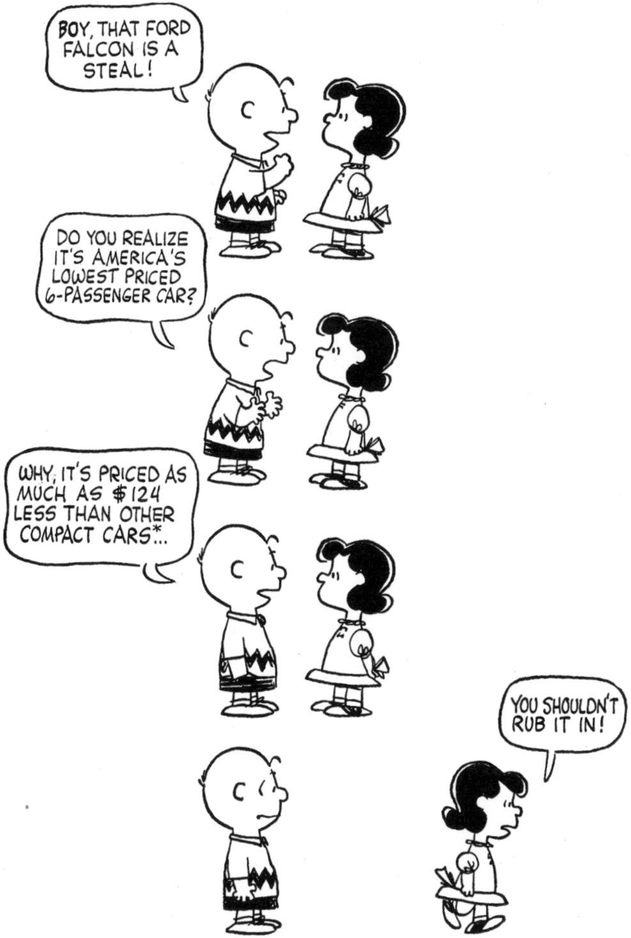
BOY, THAT FORD FALCON IS A STEAL!
DO YOU REALIZE IT'S AMERICA'S LOWEST PRICED 6-PASSENGER CAR?
WHY, IT'S PRICED AS MUCH AS $124 LESS THAN OTHER COMPACT CARS*...
YOU SHOULDN'T RUB IT IN!

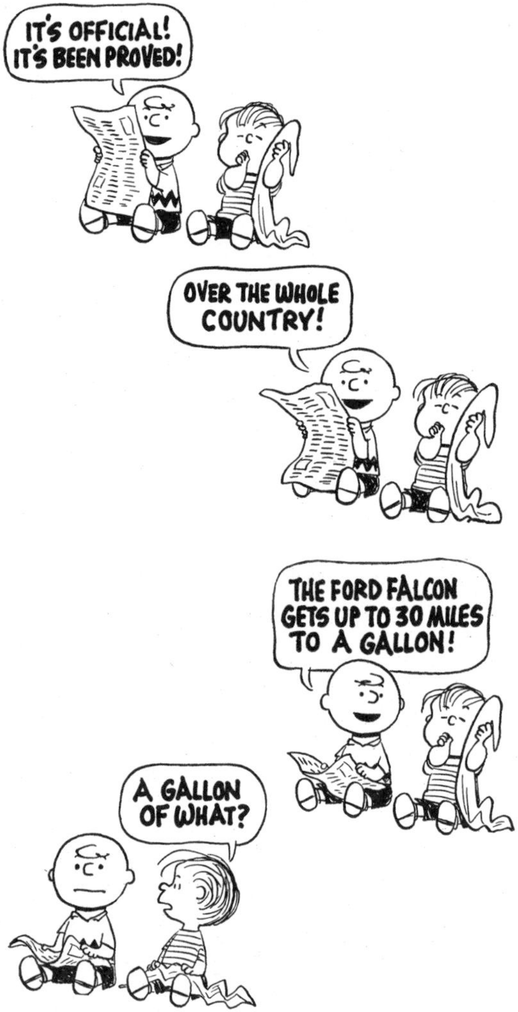
IT'S OFFICIAL! IT'S BEEN PROVED!
OVER THE WHOLE COUNTRY!
THE FORD FALCON GETS UP TO 30 MILES TO A GALLON!
A GALLON OF WHAT?

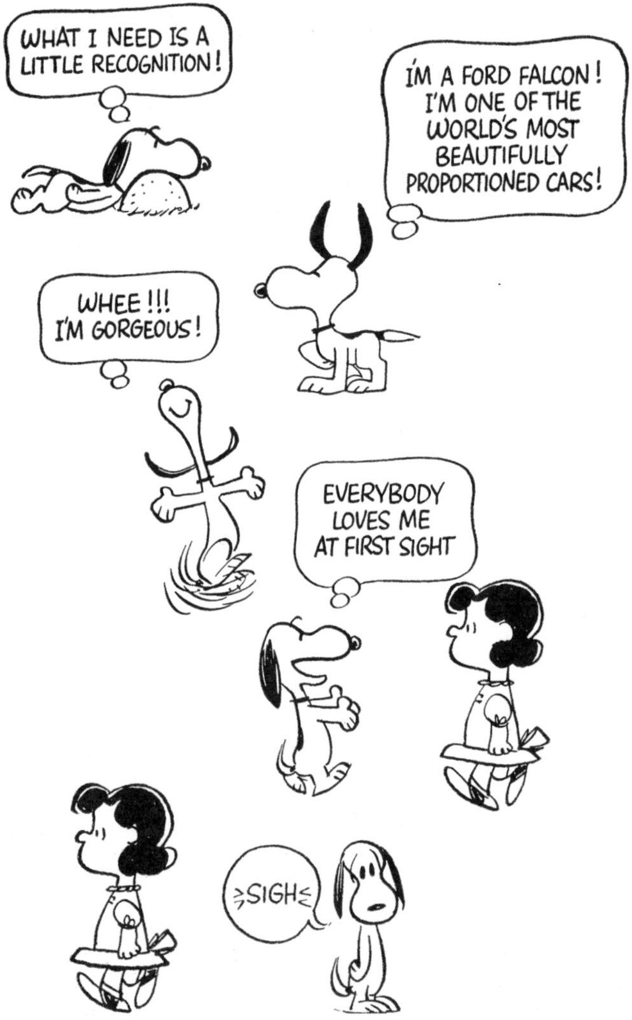
WHAT I NEED IS A LITTLE RECOGNITION!
I'M A FORD FALCON! I'M ONE OF THE WORLD'S MOST BEAUTIFULLY PROPORTIONED CARS!
WHEE!!! I'M GORGEOUS!
EVERYBODY LOVES ME AT FIRST SIGHT
SIGH

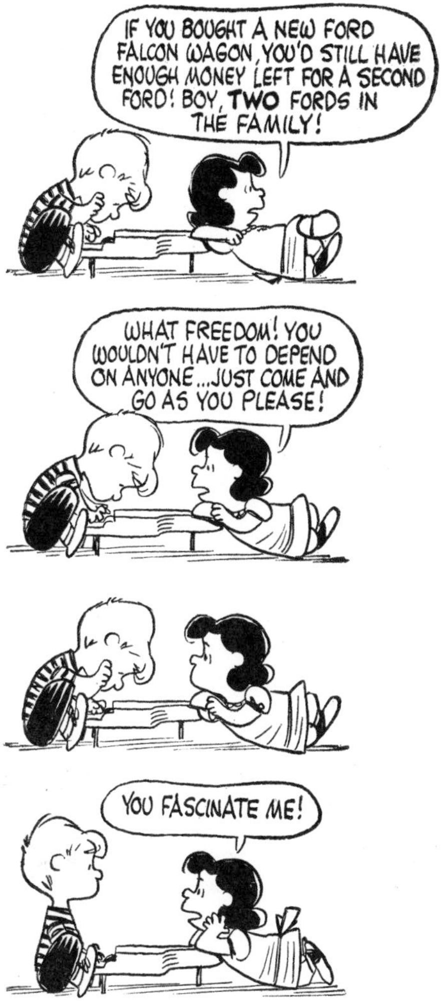
IF YOU BOUGHT A NEW FORD FALCON WAGON, YOU'D STILL HAVE ENOUGH MONEY LEFT FOR A SECOND FORD! BOY, TWO FORDS IN THE FAMILY!
WHAT FREEDOM! YOU WOULDN'T HAVE TO DEPEND ON ANYONE...JUST COME AND GO AS YOU PLEASE!
YOU FASCINATE ME!

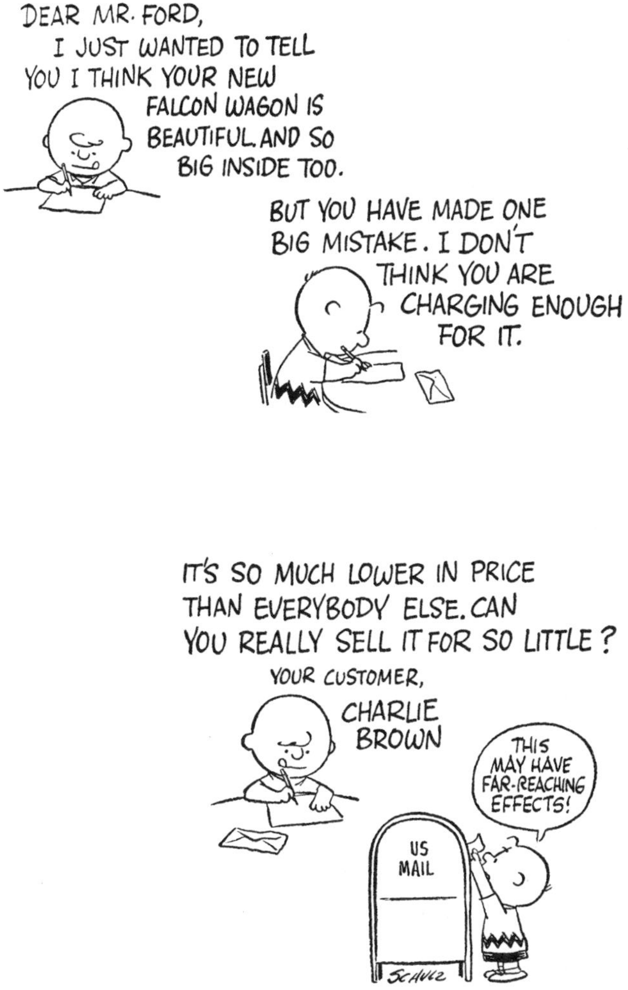
DEAR MR. FORD,
I JUST WANTED TO TELL YOU I THINK YOUR NEW FALCON WAGON IS BEAUTIFUL. AND SO BIG INSIDE TOO.
BUT YOU HAVE MADE ONE BIG MISTAKE. I DON'T THINK YOU ARE CHARGING ENOUGH FOR IT.
IT'S SO MUCH LOWER IN PRICE THAN EVERYBODY ELSE. CAN YOU REALLY SELL IT FOR SO LITTLE?
YOUR CUSTOMER,
CHARLIE BROWN
THIS MAY HAVE FAR-REACHING EFFECTS!
US MAIL
SCHULZ

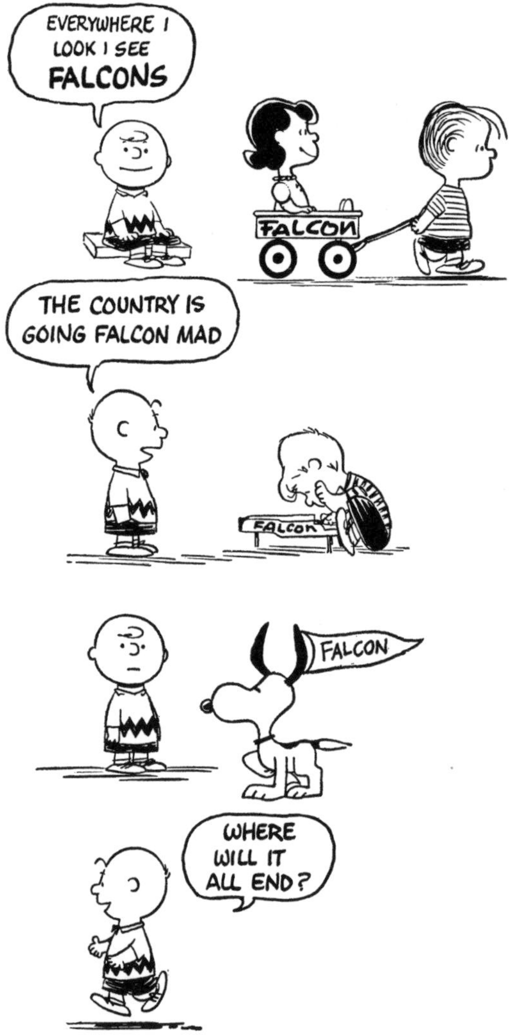
EVERYWHERE I LOOK I SEE FALCONS
FALCON
THE COUNTRY IS GOING FALCON MAD
FALCON
FALCON
WHERE WILL IT ALL END?

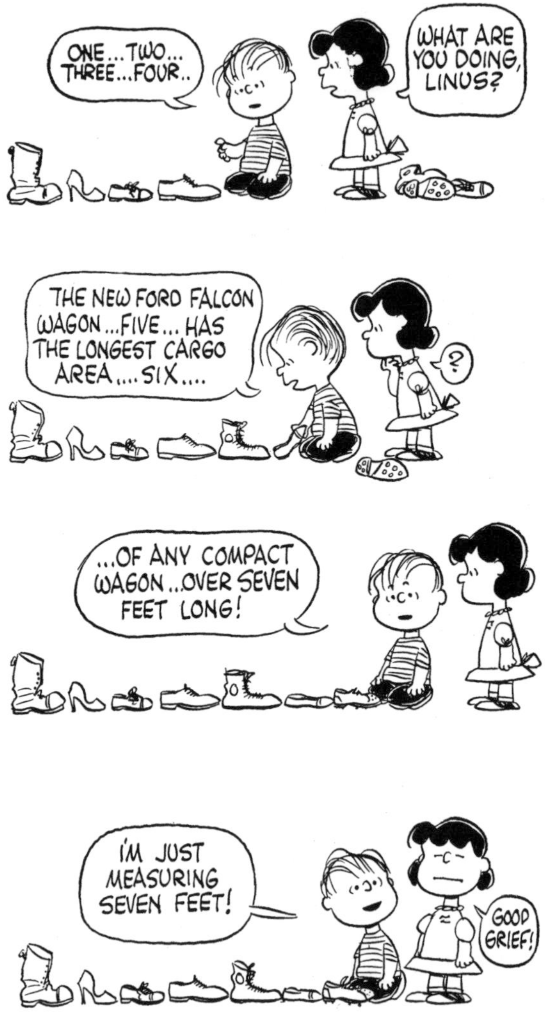
ONE...TWO... THREE...FOUR..
WHAT ARE YOU DOING, LINUS?
THE NEW FORD FALCON WAGON...FIVE... HAS THE LONGEST CARGO AREA.... SIX....
?
...OF ANY COMPACT WAGON...OVER SEVEN FEET LONG!
I'M JUST MEASURING SEVEN FEET!
GOOD GRIEF!

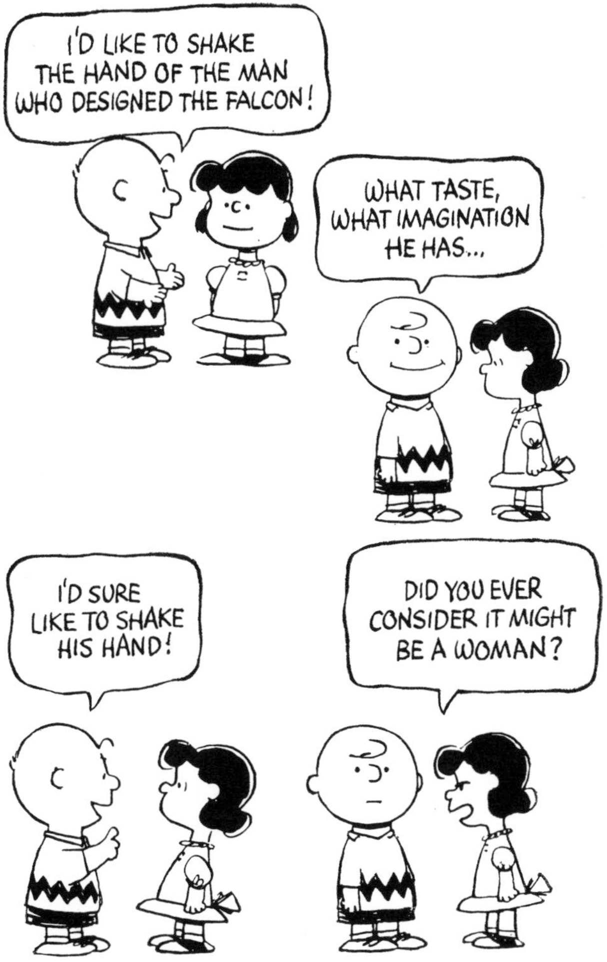
I'D LIKE TO SHAKE THE HAND OF THE MAN WHO DESIGNED THE FALCON!
WHAT TASTE, WHAT IMAGINATION HE HAS...
I'D SURE LIKE TO SHAKE HIS HAND!
DID YOU EVER CONSIDER IT MIGHT BE A WOMAN?

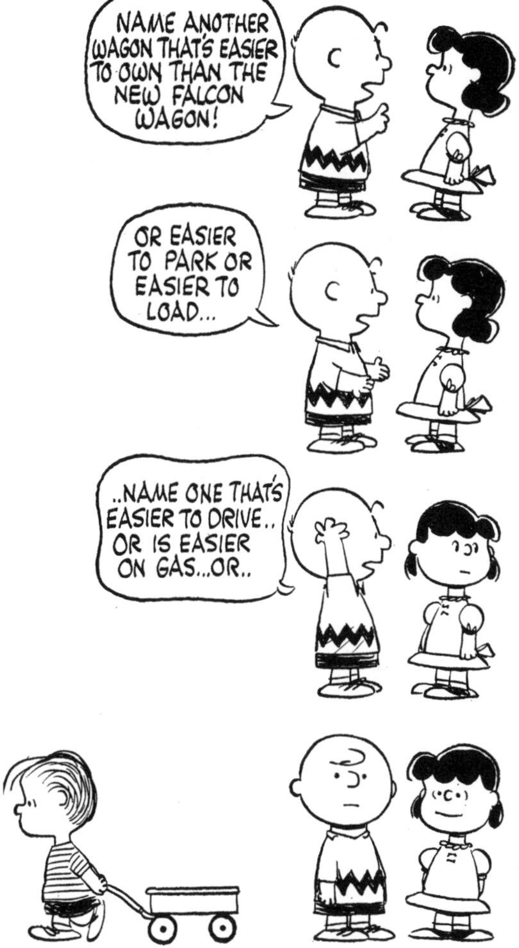
NAME ANOTHER WAGON THAT'S EASIER TO OWN THAN THE NEW FALCON WAGON!
OR EASIER TO PARK OR EASIER TO LOAD...
..NAME ONE THAT'S EASIER TO DRIVE.. OR IS EASIER ON GAS...OR..

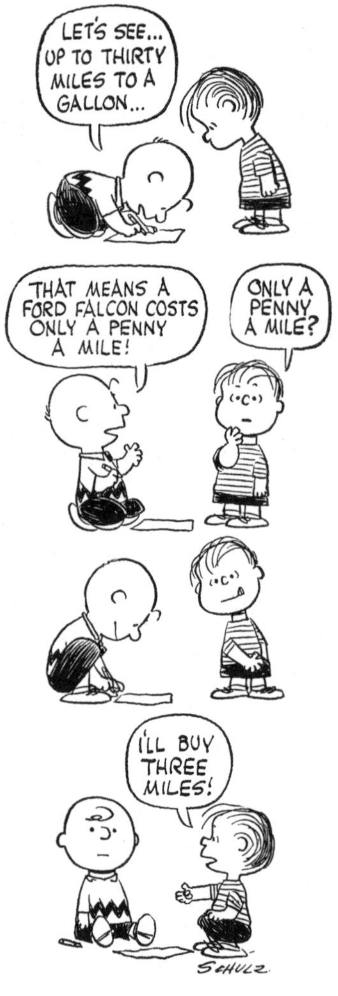
LET'S SEE... UP TO THIRTY MILES TO A GALLON...
THAT MEANS A FORD FALCON COSTS ONLY A PENNY A MILE!
ONLY A PENNY A MILE?
I'LL BUY THREE MILES!
SCHULZ

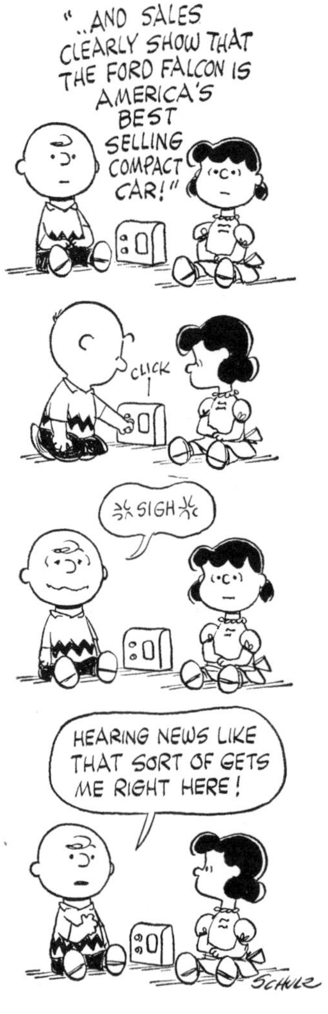
"...AND SALES CLEARLY SHOW THAT THE FORD FALCON IS AMERICA'S BEST SELLING COMPACT CAR!"
CLICK
SIGH
HEARING NEWS LIKE THAT SORT OF GETS ME RIGHT HERE!
SCHULZ

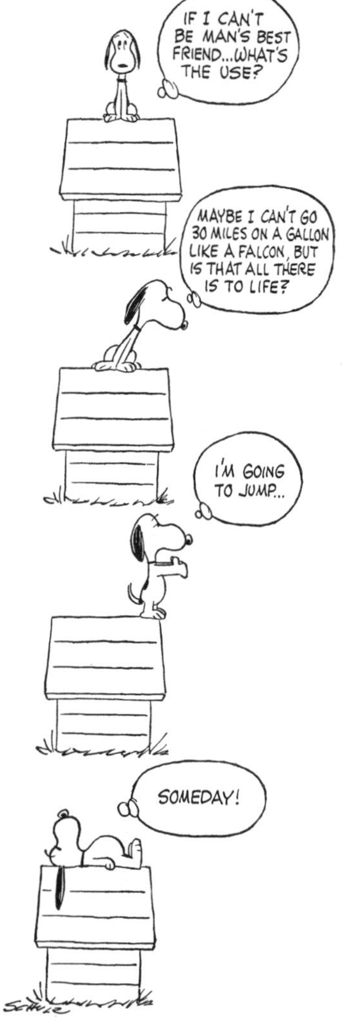
IF I CAN'T BE MAN'S BEST FRIEND...WHAT'S THE USE?
MAYBE I CAN'T GO 30 MILES ON A GALLON LIKE A FALCON, BUT IS THAT ALL THERE IS TO LIFE?
I'M GOING TO JUMP...
SOMEDAY!
SCHULZ

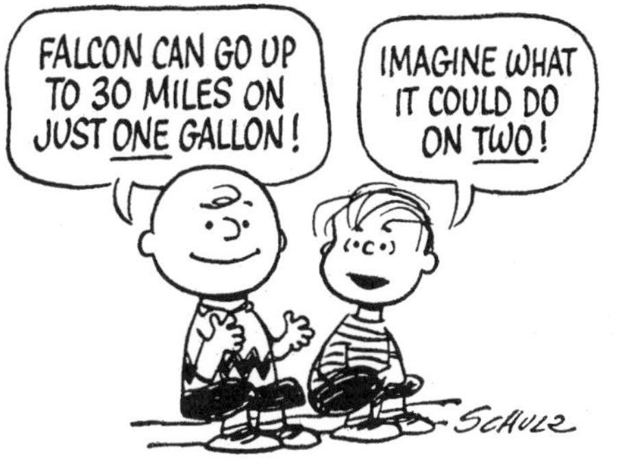
FALCON CAN GO UP TO 30 MILES ON JUST ONE GALLON!
IMAGINE WHAT IT COULD DO ON TWO!

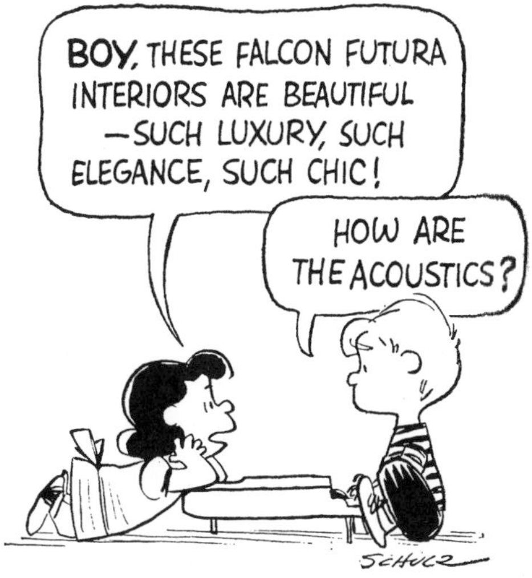
BOY, THESE FALCON FUTURA INTERIORS ARE BEAUTIFUL —SUCH LUXURY, SUCH ELEGANCE, SUCH CHIC!
HOW ARE THE ACOUSTICS?

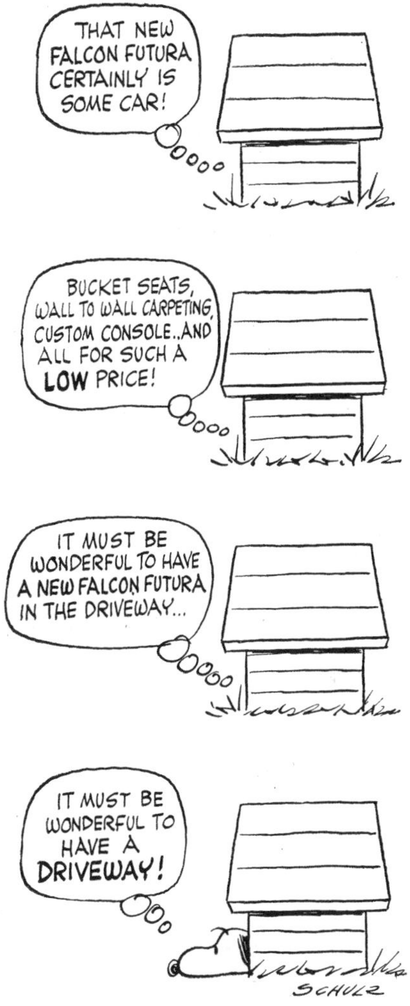
THAT NEW FALCON FUTURA CERTAINLY IS SOME CAR!
BUCKET SEATS, WALL TO WALL CARPETING, CUSTOM CONSOLE..AND ALL FOR SUCH A LOW PRICE!
IT MUST BE WONDERFUL TO HAVE A NEW FALCON FUTURA IN THE DRIVEWAY...
IT MUST BE WONDERFUL TO HAVE A DRIVEWAY!

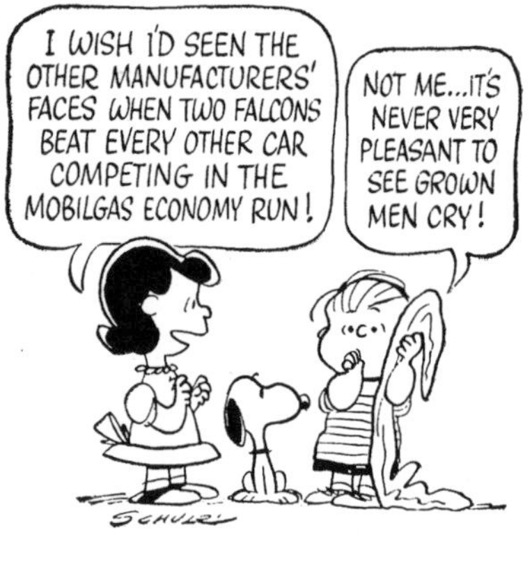

I WISH I'D SEEN THE OTHER MANUFACTURERS' FACES WHEN TWO FALCONS BEAT EVERY OTHER CAR COMPETING IN THE MOBILGAS ECONOMY RUN!
NOT ME...IT'S NEVER VERY PLEASANT TO SEE GROWN MEN CRY!
SCHULZ

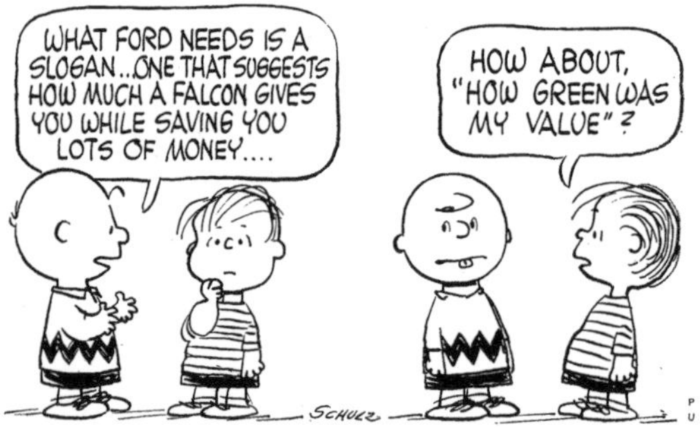

WHAT FORD NEEDS IS A SLOGAN...ONE THAT SUGGESTS HOW MUCH A FALCON GIVES YOU WHILE SAVING YOU LOTS OF MONEY....
HOW ABOUT, "HOW GREEN WAS MY VALUE"?
SCHULZ

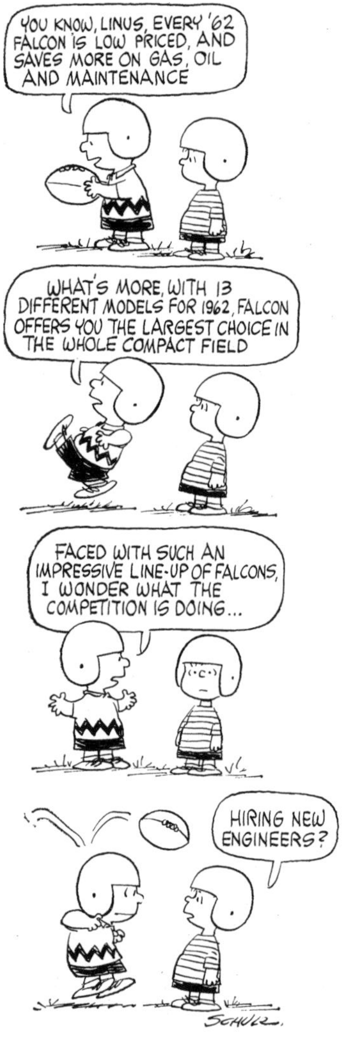

YOU KNOW, LINUS, EVERY '62 FALCON IS LOW PRICED, AND SAVES MORE ON GAS, OIL AND MAINTENANCE
WHAT'S MORE, WITH 13 DIFFERENT MODELS FOR 1962, FALCON OFFERS YOU THE LARGEST CHOICE IN THE WHOLE COMPACT FIELD
FACED WITH SUCH AN IMPRESSIVE LINE-UP OF FALCONS, I WONDER WHAT THE COMPETITION IS DOING...
HIRING NEW ENGINEERS?
SCHULZ

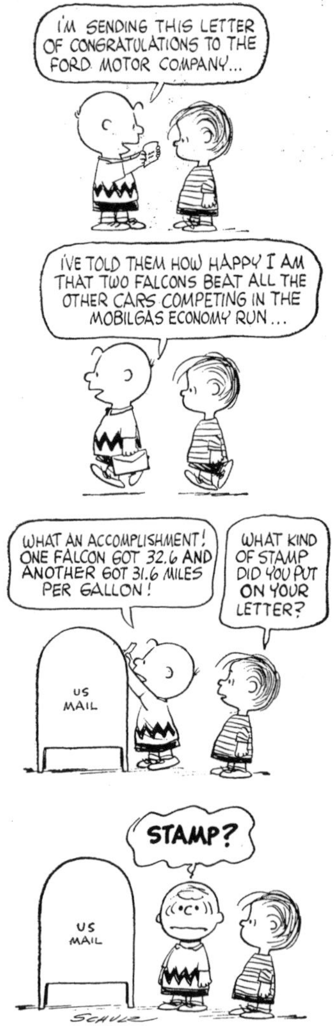

I'M SENDING THIS LETTER OF CONGRATULATIONS TO THE FORD MOTOR COMPANY...
I'VE TOLD THEM HOW HAPPY I AM THAT TWO FALCONS BEAT ALL THE OTHER CARS COMPETING IN THE MOBILGAS ECONOMY RUN...
WHAT AN ACCOMPLISHMENT! ONE FALCON GOT 32.6 AND ANOTHER GOT 31.6 MILES PER GALLON!
WHAT KIND OF STAMP DID YOU PUT ON YOUR LETTER?
US MAIL
STAMP?
US MAIL
SCHULZ

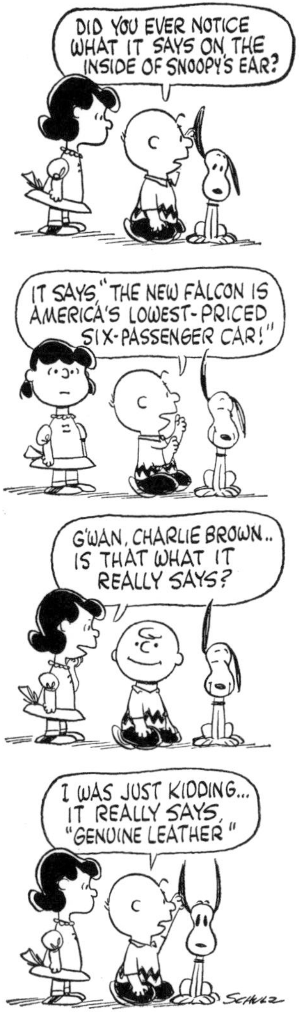
DID YOU EVER NOTICE WHAT IT SAYS ON THE INSIDE OF SNOOPY'S EAR?
IT SAYS, "THE NEW FALCON IS AMERICA'S LOWEST-PRICED SIX-PASSENGER CAR!"
G'WAN, CHARLIE BROWN.. IS THAT WHAT IT REALLY SAYS?
I WAS JUST KIDDING... IT REALLY SAYS, "GENUINE LEATHER"
SCHULZ

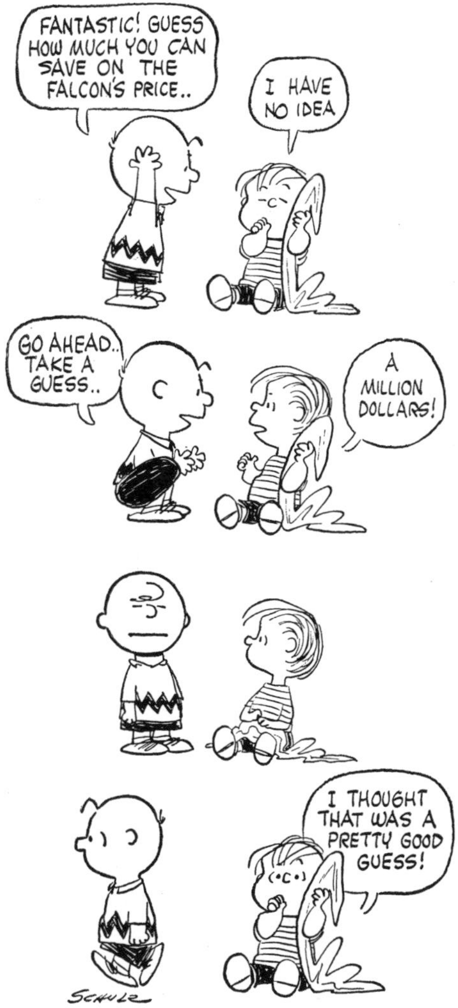
FANTASTIC! GUESS HOW MUCH YOU CAN SAVE ON THE FALCON'S PRICE..
I HAVE NO IDEA
GO AHEAD.. TAKE A GUESS..
A MILLION DOLLARS!
I THOUGHT THAT WAS A PRETTY GOOD GUESS!
SCHULZ

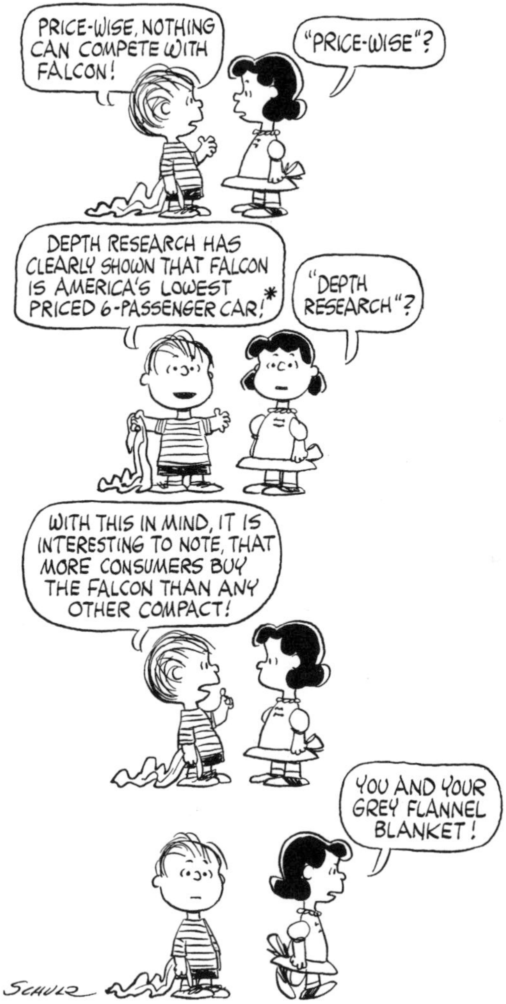
PRICE-WISE, NOTHING CAN COMPETE WITH FALCON!
"PRICE-WISE"?
DEPTH RESEARCH HAS CLEARLY SHOWN THAT FALCON IS AMERICA'S LOWEST PRICED 6-PASSENGER CAR!*
"DEPTH RESEARCH"?
WITH THIS IN MIND, IT IS INTERESTING TO NOTE, THAT MORE CONSUMERS BUY THE FALCON THAN ANY OTHER COMPACT!
YOU AND YOUR GREY FLANNEL BLANKET!
SCHULZ

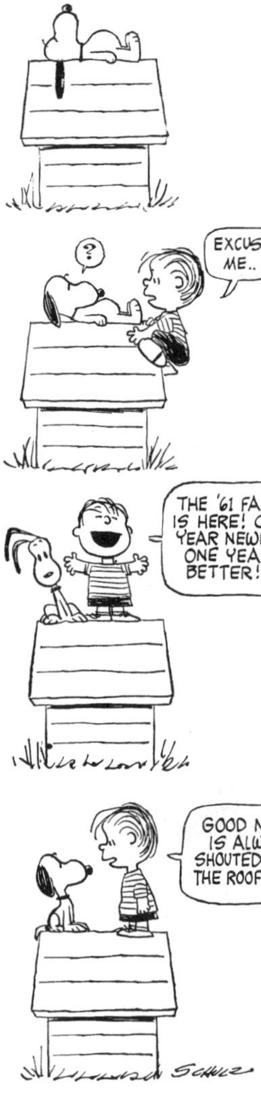
EXCUSE ME..
THE '61 FALCON IS HERE! ONE YEAR NEWER... ONE YEAR BETTER!
GOOD NEWS IS ALWAYS SHOUTED FROM THE ROOF TOPS!
SCHULZ

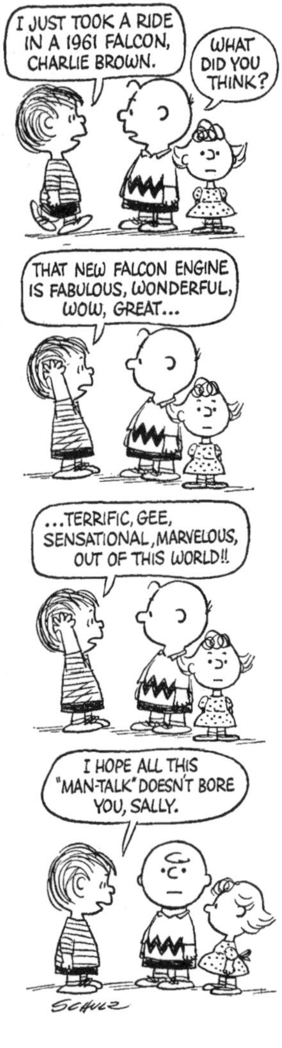
I JUST TOOK A RIDE IN A 1961 FALCON, CHARLIE BROWN.
WHAT DID YOU THINK?
THAT NEW FALCON ENGINE IS FABULOUS, WONDERFUL, WOW, GREAT...
...TERRIFIC, GEE, SENSATIONAL, MARVELOUS, OUT OF THIS WORLD!!
I HOPE ALL THIS "MAN-TALK" DOESN'T BORE YOU, SALLY.
SCHULZ

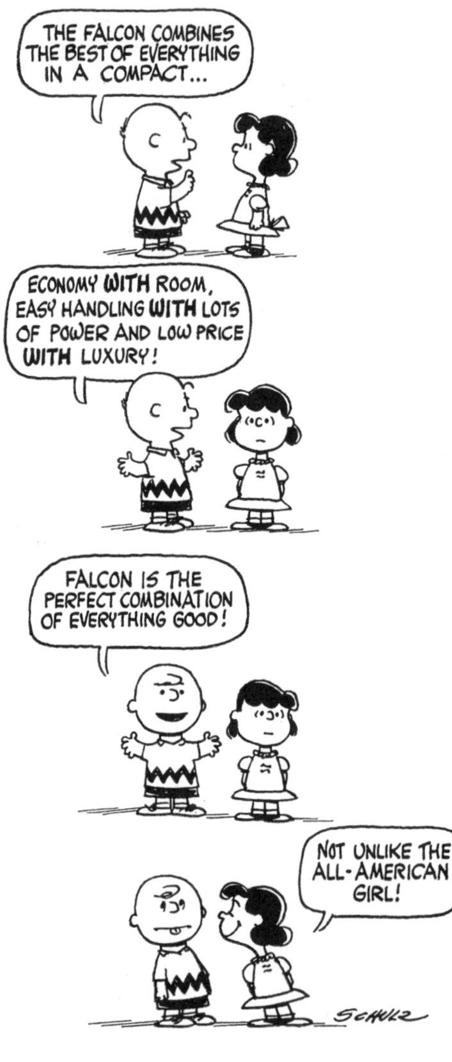
THE FALCON COMBINES THE BEST OF EVERYTHING IN A COMPACT...
ECONOMY WITH ROOM, EASY HANDLING WITH LOTS OF POWER AND LOW PRICE WITH LUXURY!
FALCON IS THE PERFECT COMBINATION OF EVERYTHING GOOD!
NOT UNLIKE THE ALL-AMERICAN GIRL!
SCHULZ

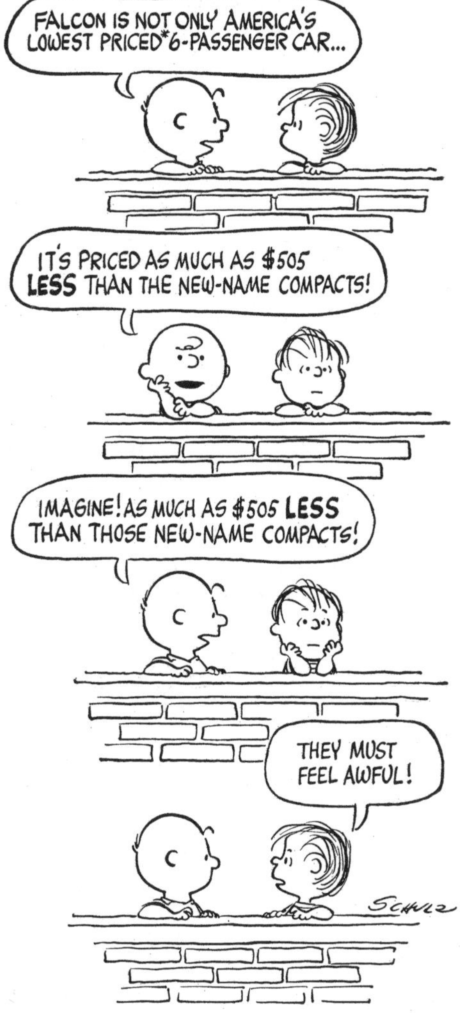
FALCON IS NOT ONLY AMERICA'S LOWEST PRICED*6-PASSENGER CAR...
IT'S PRICED AS MUCH AS $505 LESS THAN THE NEW-NAME COMPACTS!
IMAGINE! AS MUCH AS $505 LESS THAN THOSE NEW-NAME COMPACTS!
THEY MUST FEEL AWFUL!
SCHULZ

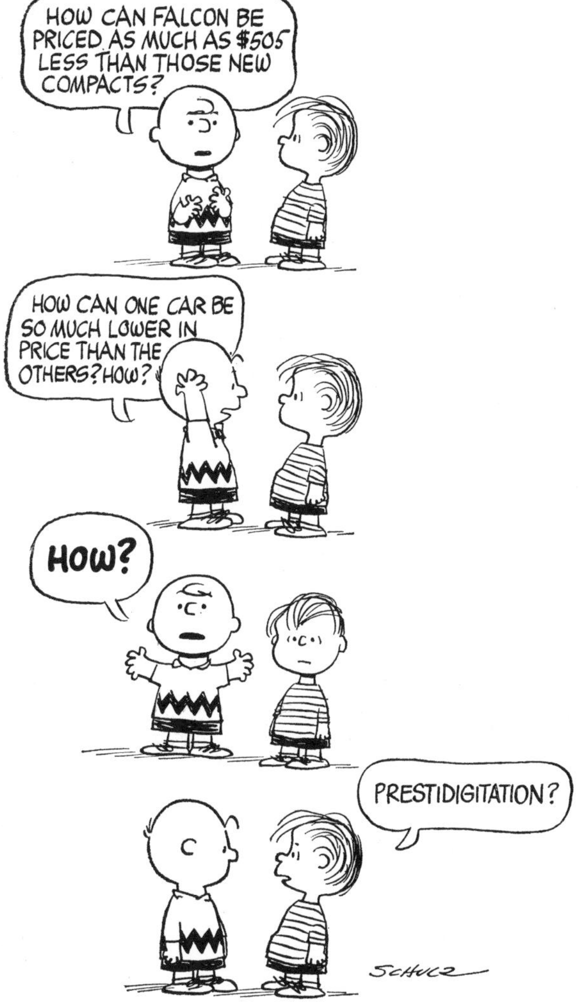
HOW CAN FALCON BE PRICED AS MUCH AS $505 LESS THAN THOSE NEW COMPACTS?
HOW CAN ONE CAR BE SO MUCH LOWER IN PRICE THAN THE OTHERS? HOW?
HOW?
PRESTIDIGITATION?
SCHULZ

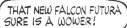

WHEN IT COMES TO GREAT GAS MILEAGE, YOU JUST CAN'T BEAT FALCON..

THAT NEW FALCON FUTURA SURE IS A WOWER!

NOW, YOU TAKE A LOT OF THOSE **NEW** COMPACTS... THEY'RE JUST TOO **HEAVY** TO GO UP TO 30 MILES ON A GALLON LIKE FALCON...

BUCKET SEATS, CONSOLE.. BOY, THAT'S SNAZZ!!

YOU'VE GOT TO BE **COMPACT** LIKE FALCON TO GO UP TO 30 MILES ON A GALLON!

AND ON THE TURNPIKE... *VAROOOM!!*

ENGLISH IS A BEAUTIFUL LANGUAGE!

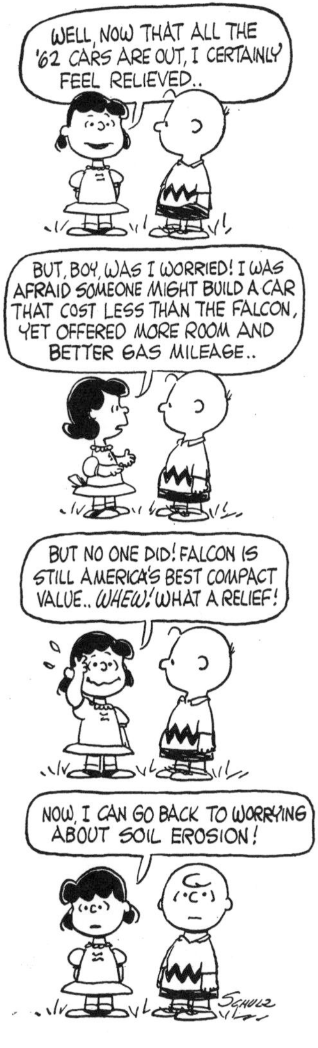
WELL, NOW THAT ALL THE '62 CARS ARE OUT, I CERTAINLY FEEL RELIEVED..
BUT, BOY, WAS I WORRIED! I WAS AFRAID SOMEONE MIGHT BUILD A CAR THAT COST LESS THAN THE FALCON, YET OFFERED MORE ROOM AND BETTER GAS MILEAGE..
BUT NO ONE DID! FALCON IS STILL AMERICA'S BEST COMPACT VALUE.. WHEW! WHAT A RELIEF!
NOW, I CAN GO BACK TO WORRYING ABOUT SOIL EROSION!
SCHULZ

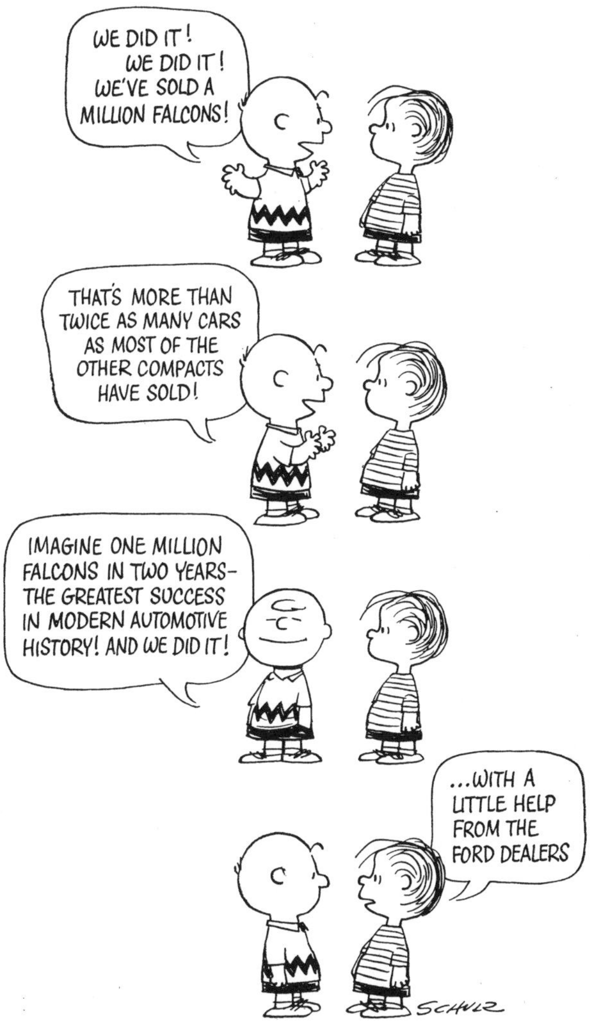
WE DID IT! WE DID IT! WE'VE SOLD A MILLION FALCONS!
THAT'S MORE THAN TWICE AS MANY CARS AS MOST OF THE OTHER COMPACTS HAVE SOLD!
IMAGINE ONE MILLION FALCONS IN TWO YEARS- THE GREATEST SUCCESS IN MODERN AUTOMOTIVE HISTORY! AND WE DID IT!
...WITH A LITTLE HELP FROM THE FORD DEALERS
SCHULZ

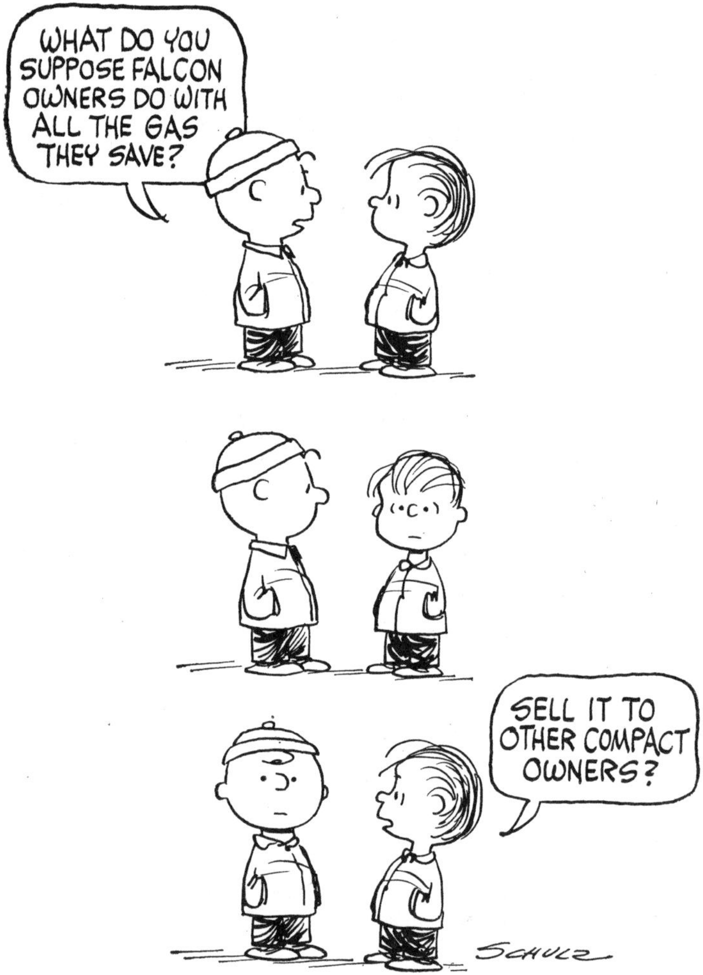
WHAT DO YOU SUPPOSE FALCON OWNERS DO WITH ALL THE GAS THEY SAVE?
SELL IT TO OTHER COMPACT OWNERS?
SCHULZ

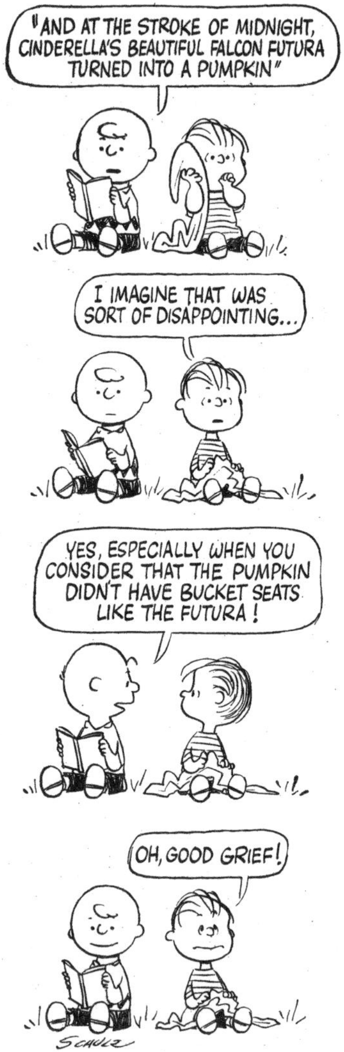
"AND AT THE STROKE OF MIDNIGHT, CINDERELLA'S BEAUTIFUL FALCON FUTURA TURNED INTO A PUMPKIN"
I IMAGINE THAT WAS SORT OF DISAPPOINTING...
YES, ESPECIALLY WHEN YOU CONSIDER THAT THE PUMPKIN DIDN'T HAVE BUCKET SEATS LIKE THE FUTURA!
OH, GOOD GRIEF!
SCHULZ

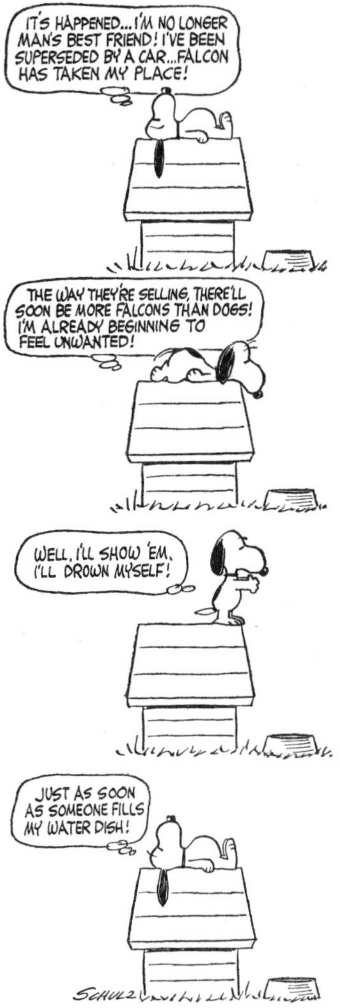
IT'S HAPPENED... I'M NO LONGER MAN'S BEST FRIEND! I'VE BEEN SUPERSEDED BY A CAR...FALCON HAS TAKEN MY PLACE!
THE WAY THEY'RE SELLING, THERE'LL SOON BE MORE FALCONS THAN DOGS! I'M ALREADY BEGINNING TO FEEL UNWANTED!
WELL, I'LL SHOW 'EM, I'LL DROWN MYSELF!
JUST AS SOON AS SOMEONE FILLS MY WATER DISH!
SCHULZ

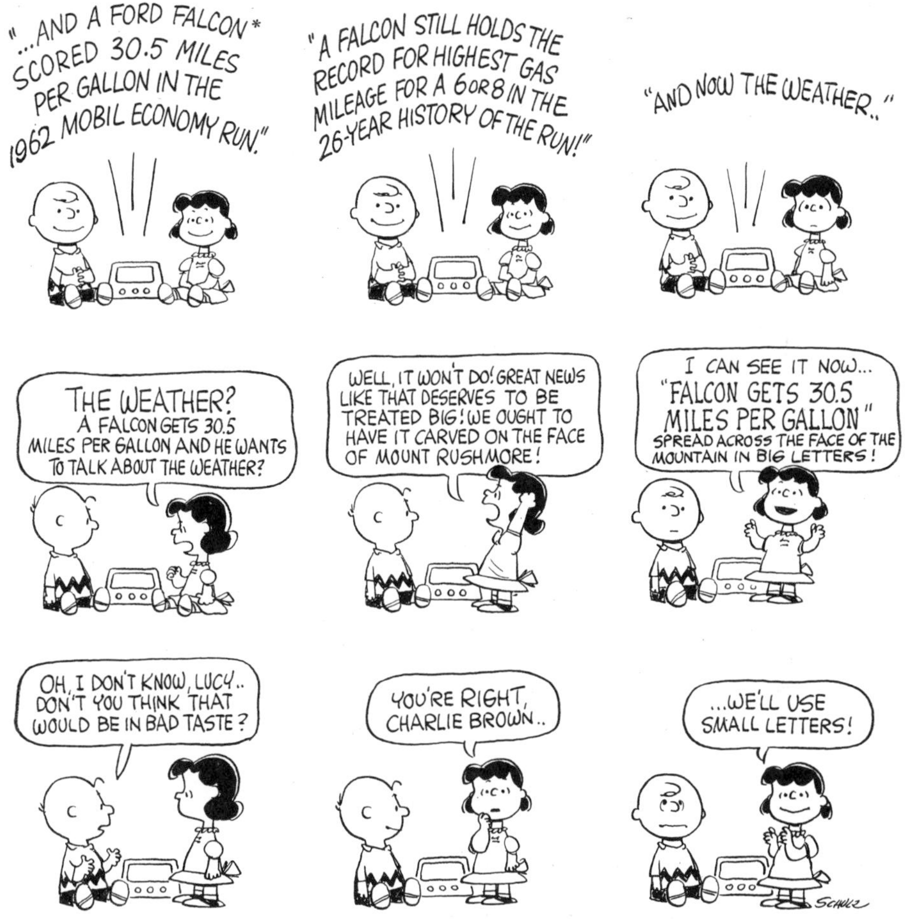
"...AND A FORD FALCON* SCORED 30.5 MILES PER GALLON IN THE 1962 MOBIL ECONOMY RUN."
"A FALCON STILL HOLDS THE RECORD FOR HIGHEST GAS MILEAGE FOR A 6 OR 8 IN THE 26-YEAR HISTORY OF THE RUN!"
"AND NOW THE WEATHER.."
THE WEATHER? A FALCON GETS 30.5 MILES PER GALLON AND HE WANTS TO TALK ABOUT THE WEATHER?
WELL, IT WON'T DO! GREAT NEWS LIKE THAT DESERVES TO BE TREATED BIG! WE OUGHT TO HAVE IT CARVED ON THE FACE OF MOUNT RUSHMORE!
I CAN SEE IT NOW... "FALCON GETS 30.5 MILES PER GALLON" SPREAD ACROSS THE FACE OF THE MOUNTAIN IN BIG LETTERS!
OH, I DON'T KNOW, LUCY.. DON'T YOU THINK THAT WOULD BE IN BAD TASTE?
YOU'RE RIGHT, CHARLIE BROWN..
...WE'LL USE SMALL LETTERS!
SCHULZ

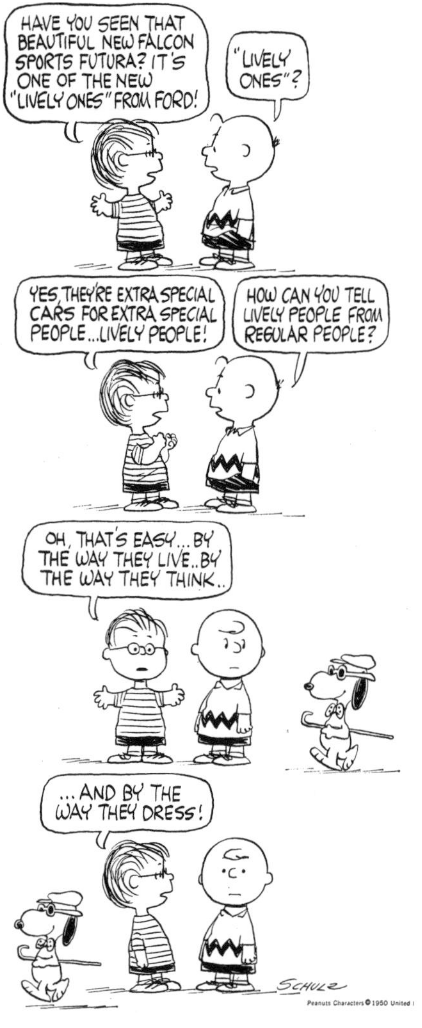
HAVE YOU SEEN THAT BEAUTIFUL NEW FALCON SPORTS FUTURA? IT'S ONE OF THE NEW "LIVELY ONES" FROM FORD!
"LIVELY ONES"?
YES, THEY'RE EXTRA SPECIAL CARS FOR EXTRA SPECIAL PEOPLE...LIVELY PEOPLE!
HOW CAN YOU TELL LIVELY PEOPLE FROM REGULAR PEOPLE?
OH, THAT'S EASY...BY THE WAY THEY LIVE..BY THE WAY THEY THINK..
...AND BY THE WAY THEY DRESS!
SCHULZ
Peanuts Characters © 1950 United

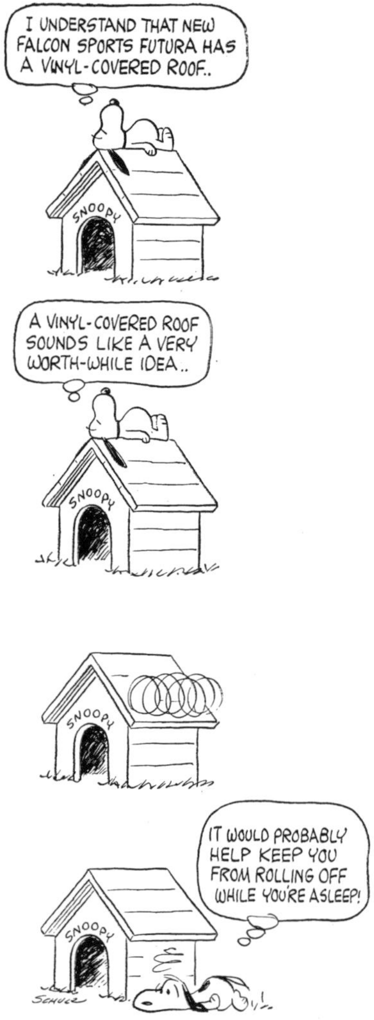
I UNDERSTAND THAT NEW FALCON SPORTS FUTURA HAS A VINYL-COVERED ROOF..
SNOOPY
A VINYL-COVERED ROOF SOUNDS LIKE A VERY WORTH-WHILE IDEA..
SNOOPY
SNOOPY
IT WOULD PROBABLY HELP KEEP YOU FROM ROLLING OFF WHILE YOU'RE ASLEEP!
SNOOPY
SCHULZ

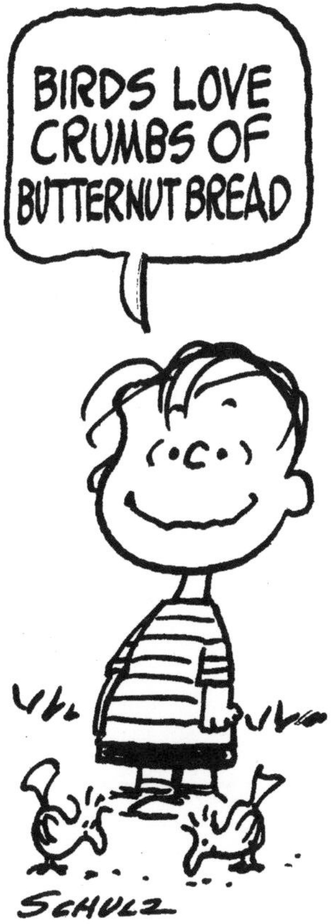
BIRDS LOVE CRUMBS OF BUTTERNUT BREAD
SCHULZ

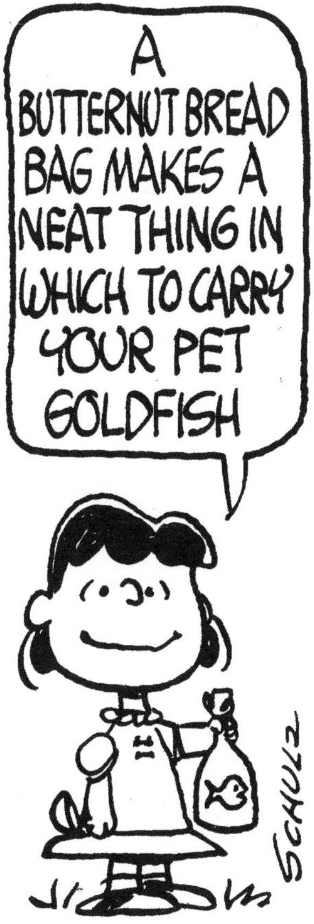
A BUTTERNUT BREAD BAG MAKES A NEAT THING IN WHICH TO CARRY YOUR PET GOLDFISH
SCHULZ

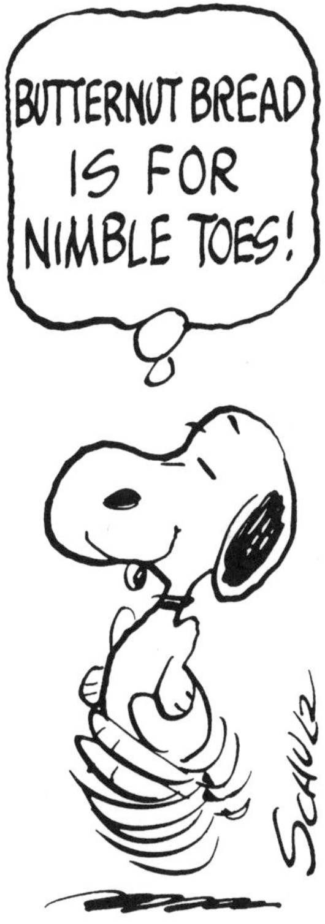
BUTTERNUT BREAD IS FOR NIMBLE TOES!
SCHULZ

BUTTERNUT BREAD WILL MAKE YOU FLIP!
SCHULZ

DEAR BUTTERNUT BREAD PEOPLE... WILL YOU PLEASE MAKE GREEN AND YELLOW STRIPED BREAD?
SCHULZ

EATING BUTTERNUT BREAD WILL HELP YOU TO GET BETTER MARKS IN LUNCH!
SCHULZ

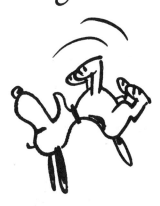

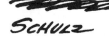

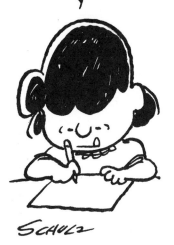

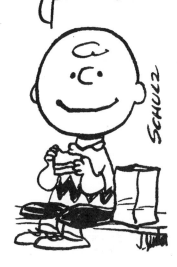

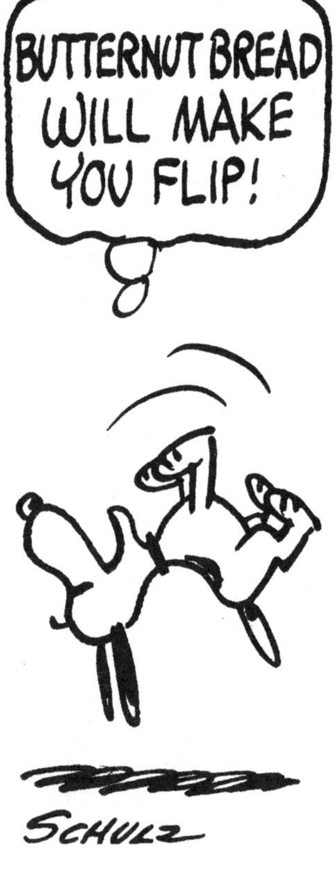

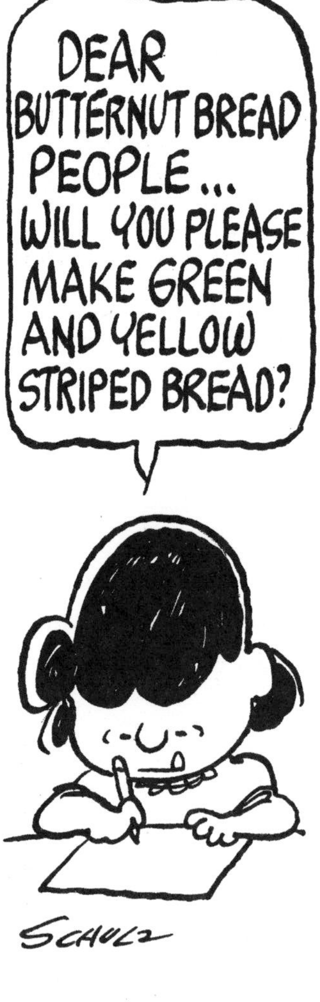

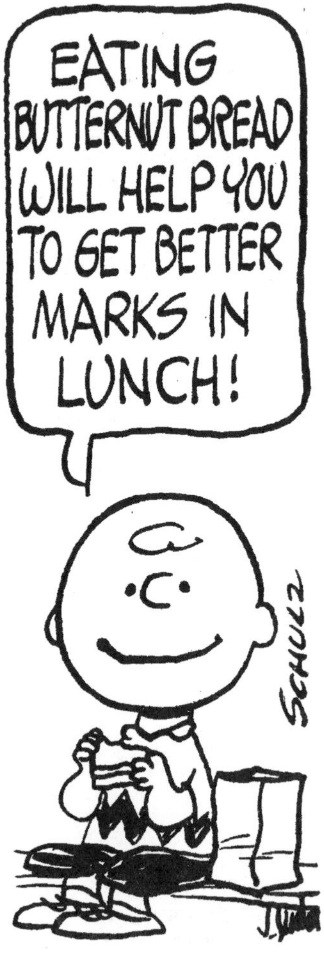

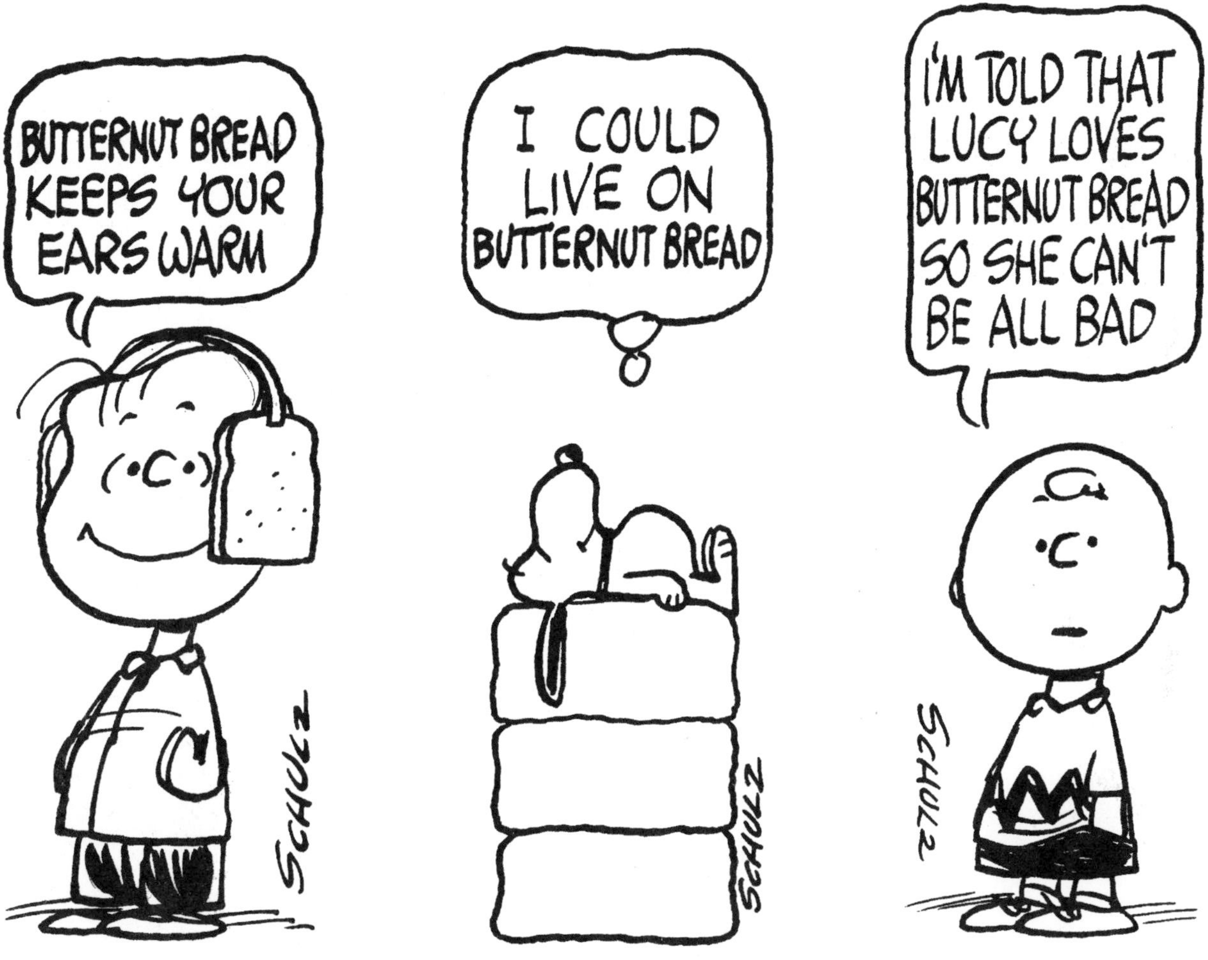
BUTTERNUT BREAD KEEPS YOUR EARS WARM
I COULD LIVE ON BUTTERNUT BREAD
I'M TOLD THAT LUCY LOVES BUTTERNUT BREAD SO SHE CAN'T BE ALL BAD

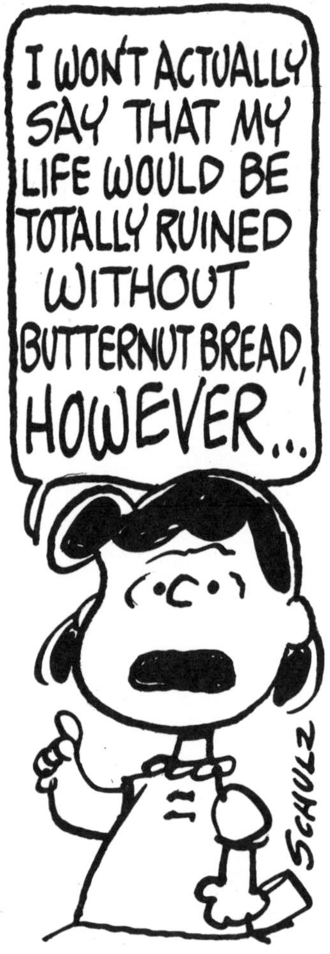
I WON'T ACTUALLY SAY THAT MY LIFE WOULD BE TOTALLY RUINED WITHOUT BUTTERNUT BREAD, HOWEVER...
SCHULZ

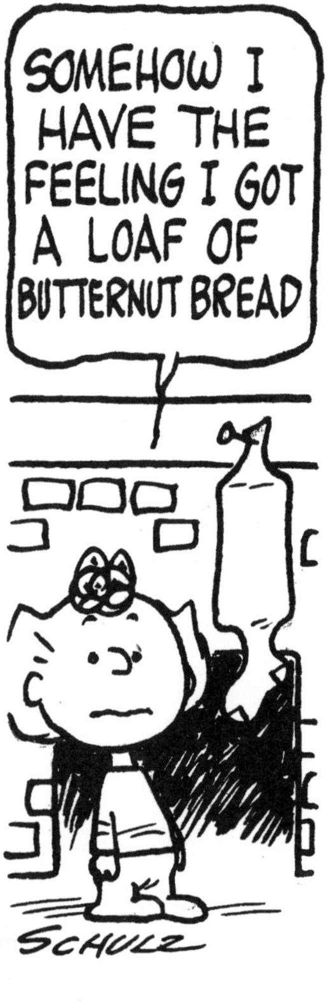
SOMEHOW I HAVE THE FEELING I GOT A LOAF OF BUTTERNUT BREAD
SCHULZ

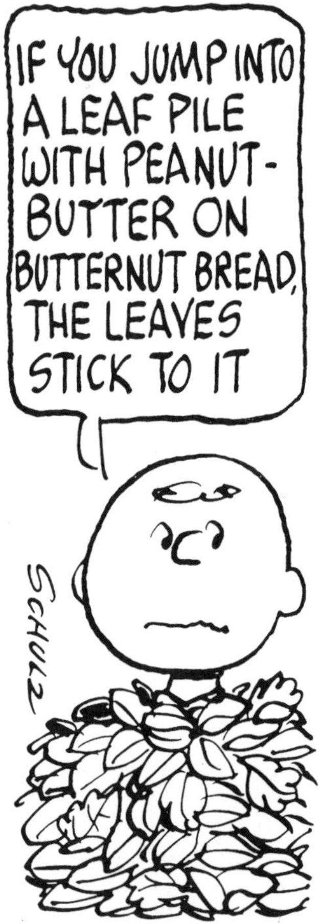
IF YOU JUMP INTO A LEAF PILE WITH PEANUT-BUTTER ON BUTTERNUT BREAD, THE LEAVES STICK TO IT
SCHULZ

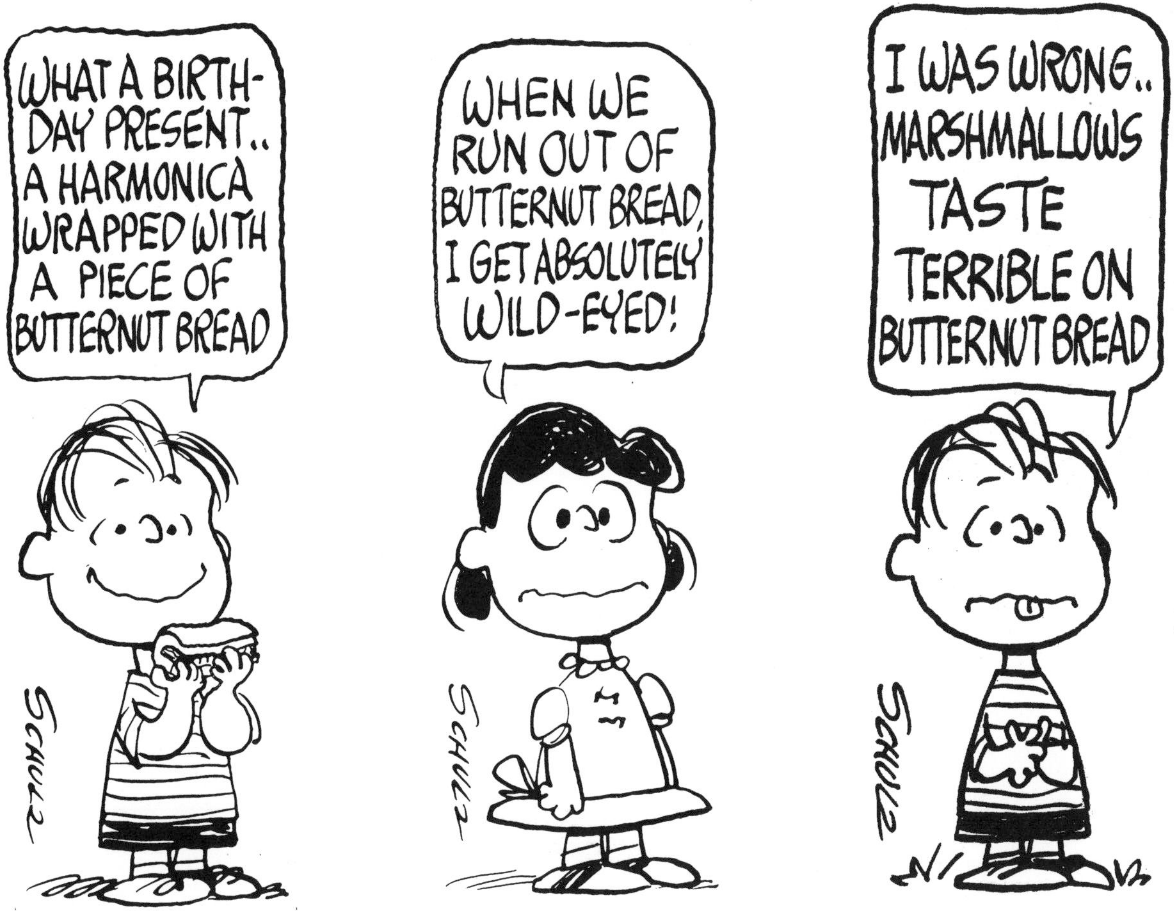
WHAT A BIRTH-DAY PRESENT.. A HARMONICA WRAPPED WITH A PIECE OF BUTTERNUT BREAD
WHEN WE RUN OUT OF BUTTERNUT BREAD, I GET ABSOLUTELY WILD-EYED!
I WAS WRONG.. MARSHMALLOWS TASTE TERRIBLE ON BUTTERNUT BREAD
SCHULZ
SCHULZ
SCHULZ

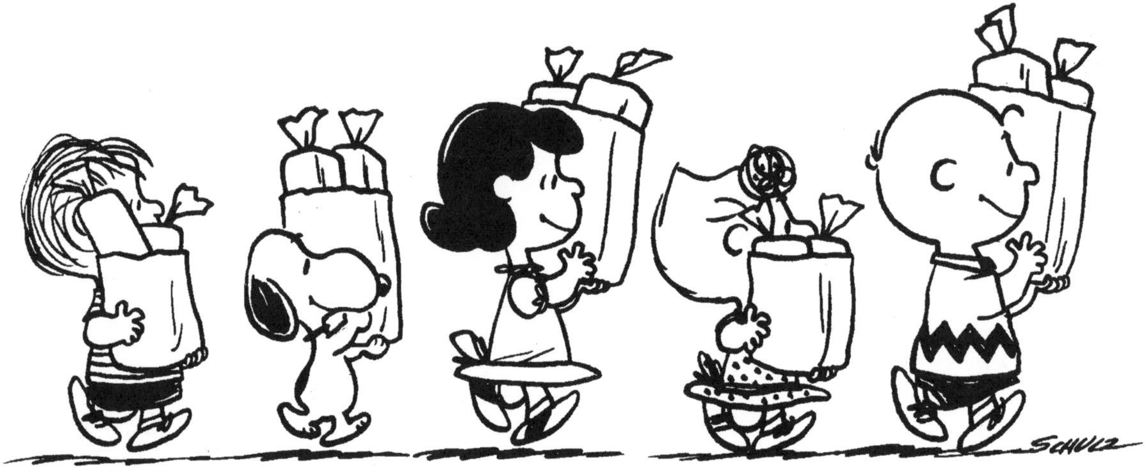
SCHULZ

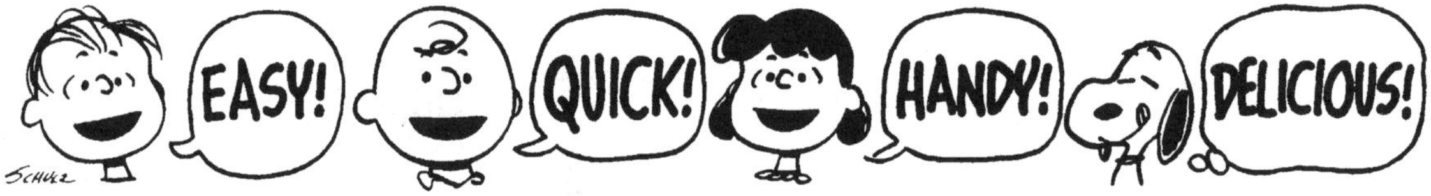
EASY!
QUICK!
HANDY!
DELICIOUS!
SCHULZ

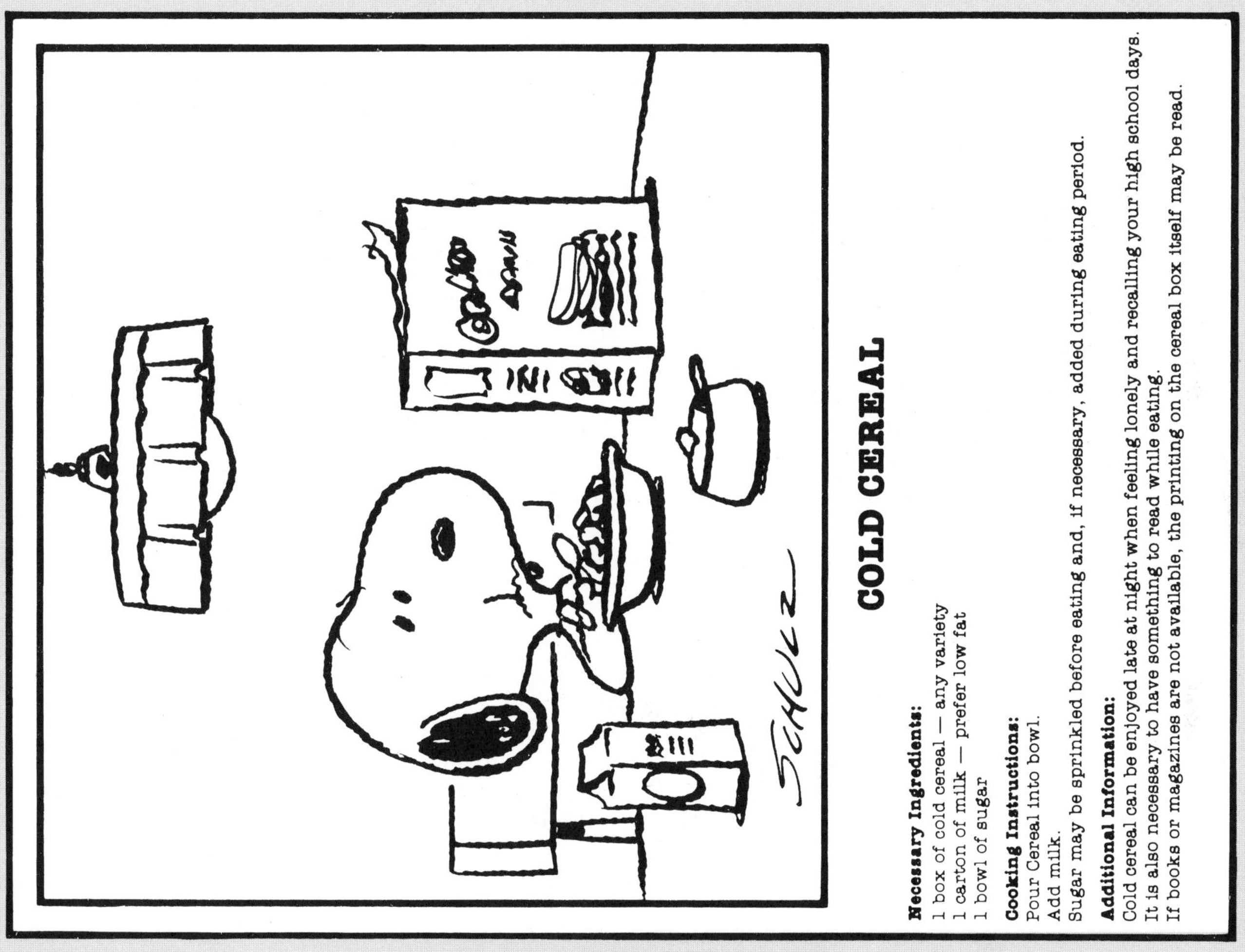
COLD CEREAL
Necessary Ingredients:
1 box of cold cereal — any variety
1 carton of milk — prefer low fat
1 bowl of sugar
Cooking Instructions:
Pour Cereal into bowl.
Add milk.
Sugar may be sprinkled before eating and, if necessary, added during eating period.
Additional Information:
Cold cereal can be enjoyed late at night when feeling lonely and recalling your high school days.
It is also necessary to have something to read while eating.
If books or magazines are not available, the printing on the cereal box itself may be read.
SCHULZ

Schulz was on the Board of Trustees of the Women's Sports Foundation, and provided this cover to a cookbook they issued in 1983.

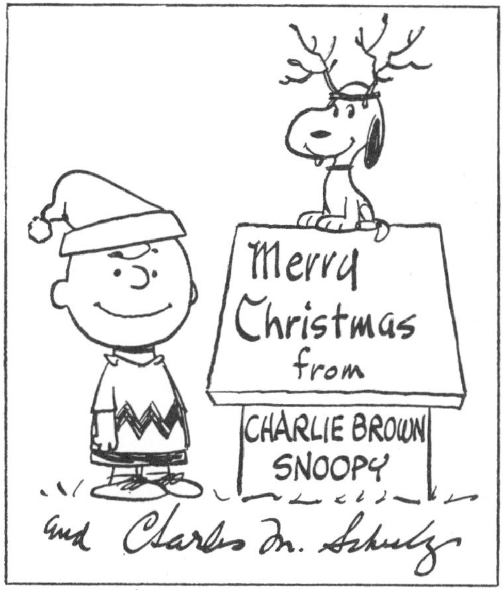
Merry
Christmas
from
CHARLIE BROWN
SNOOPY
and Charles M. Schulz

CHRISTMAS

Peanuts and Christmas have become inseparable in many people's eyes. Here are some little-seen works involving the *Peanuts* characters at the most joyous time of year.

While the Christmas strip seen on page 68 has been reprinted many times, the first half of the story has not been seen since its original appearance in the December, 1958 issue of *Better Homes and Gardens*.

"Charlie Brown's Christmas Stocking" appeared as a booklet bound into the December, 1963 issue of *Good Housekeeping*. It was reprinted in 2012 by Fantagraphics as a small hardcover stand-alone book.

The original tale "A Christmas Story" was the cover feature for the December, 1968 issue of *Women's Day*.

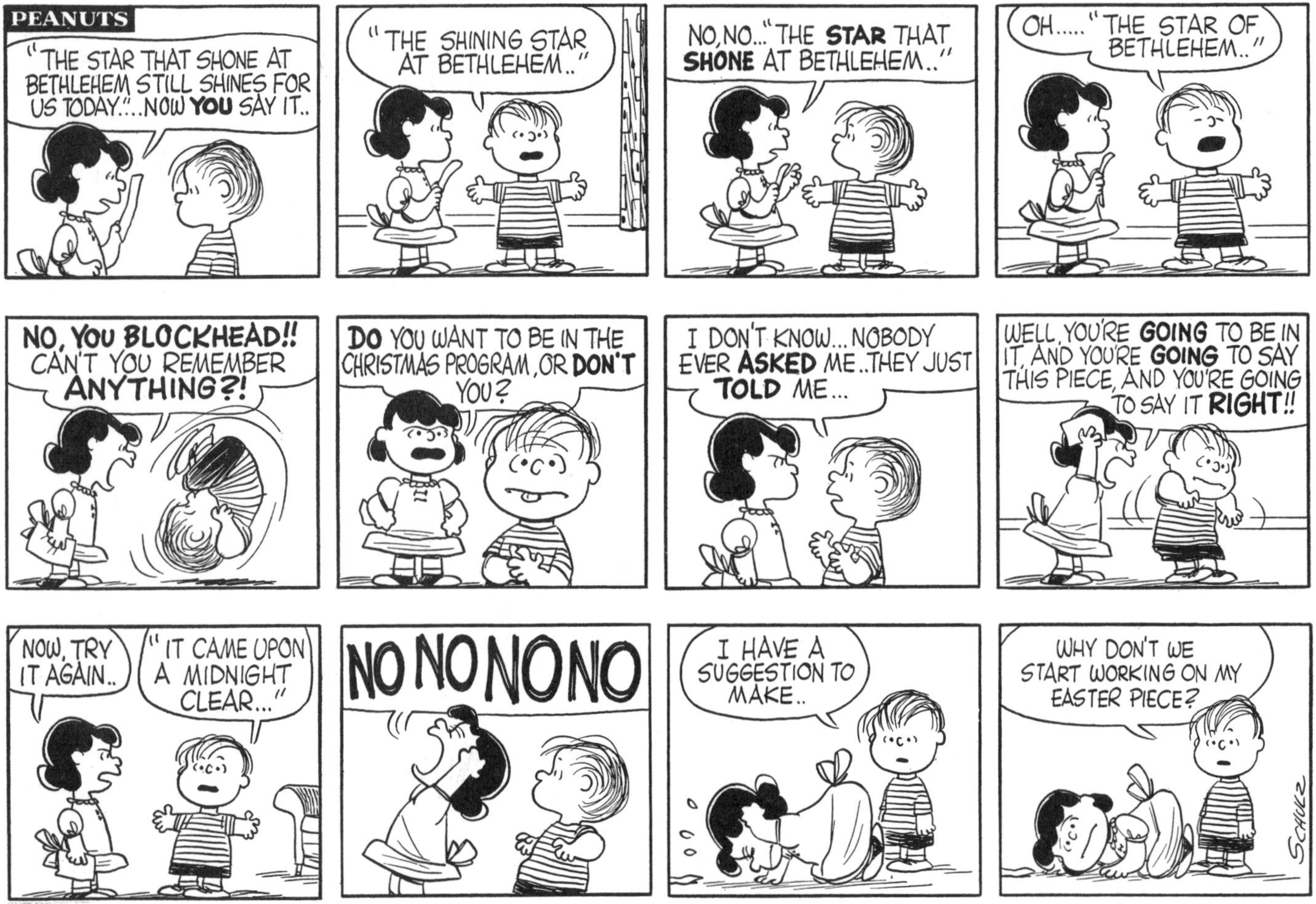
PEANUTS
"THE STAR THAT SHONE AT BETHLEHEM STILL SHINES FOR US TODAY."...NOW YOU SAY IT..
"THE SHINING STAR AT BETHLEHEM.."
NO, NO..."THE STAR THAT SHONE AT BETHLEHEM.."
OH....."THE STAR OF BETHLEHEM.."
NO, YOU BLOCKHEAD!! CAN'T YOU REMEMBER ANYTHING?!
DO YOU WANT TO BE IN THE CHRISTMAS PROGRAM, OR DON'T YOU?
I DON'T KNOW...NOBODY EVER ASKED ME..THEY JUST TOLD ME...
WELL, YOU'RE GOING TO BE IN IT, AND YOU'RE GOING TO SAY THIS PIECE, AND YOU'RE GOING TO SAY IT RIGHT!!
NOW, TRY IT AGAIN..
"IT CAME UPON A MIDNIGHT CLEAR..."
NO NO NO NO
I HAVE A SUGGESTION TO MAKE..
WHY DON'T WE START WORKING ON MY EASTER PIECE?
SCHULZ

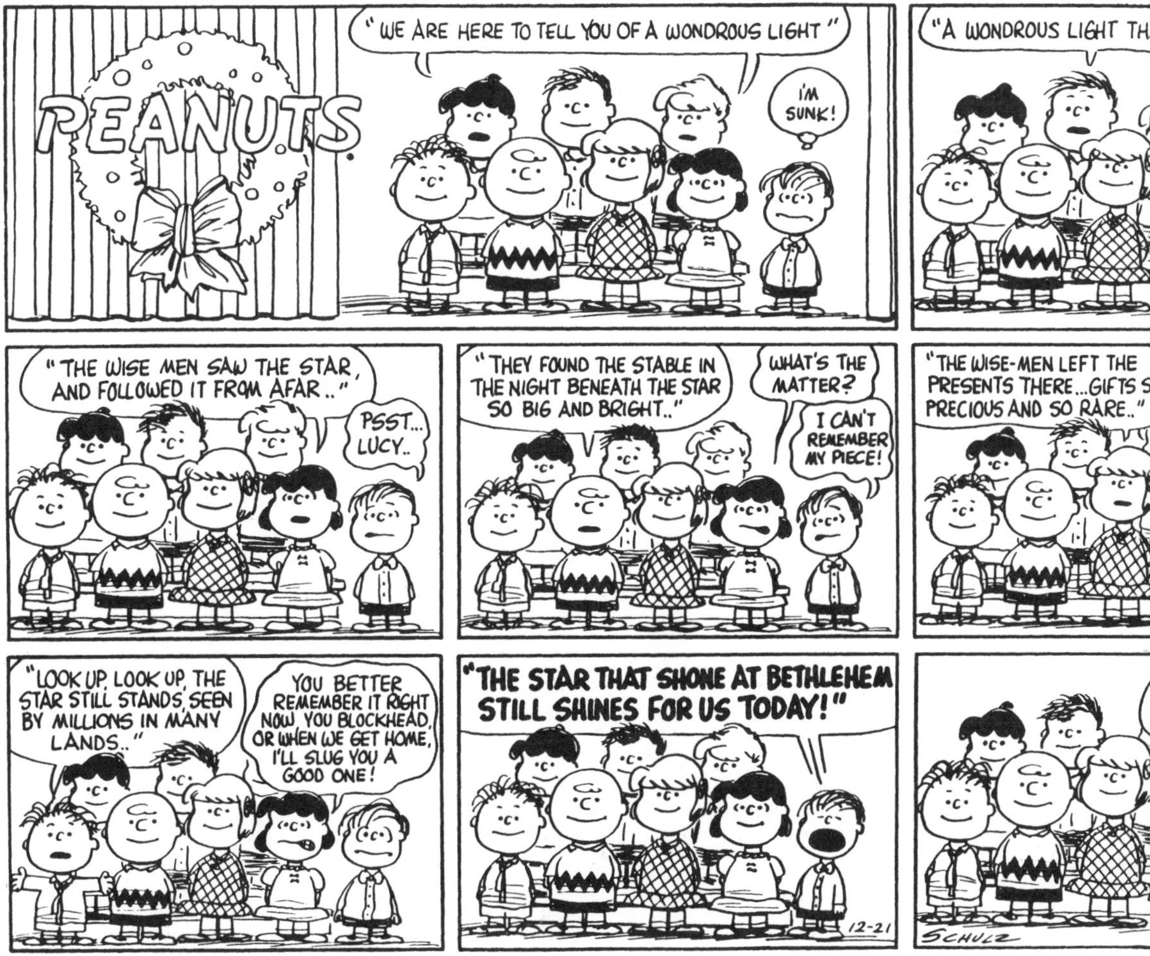
PEANUTS
"WE ARE HERE TO TELL YOU OF A WONDROUS LIGHT"
I'M SUNK!
"A WONDROUS LIGHT THAT WAS A STAR"
I WONDER IF THERE'S ANY WAY I COULD GET OUT OF HERE...
"THE WISE MEN SAW THE STAR, AND FOLLOWED IT FROM AFAR.."
PSST... LUCY..
"THEY FOUND THE STABLE IN THE NIGHT BENEATH THE STAR SO BIG AND BRIGHT.."
WHAT'S THE MATTER?
I CAN'T REMEMBER MY PIECE!
"THE WISE-MEN LEFT THE PRESENTS THERE...GIFTS SO PRECIOUS AND SO RARE.."
WADDYA MEAN, YOU CAN'T REMEMBER IT?
I CAN'T REMEMBER IT!
"LOOK UP, LOOK UP, THE STAR STILL STANDS, SEEN BY MILLIONS IN MANY LANDS.."
YOU BETTER REMEMBER IT RIGHT NOW, YOU BLOCKHEAD, OR WHEN WE GET HOME, I'LL SLUG YOU A GOOD ONE!
"THE STAR THAT SHONE AT BETHLEHEM STILL SHINES FOR US TODAY!"
12-21
SCHULZ
MERRY CHRISTMAS
THANK YOU..

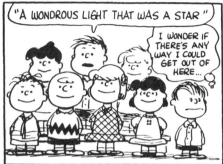

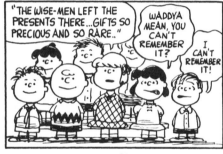

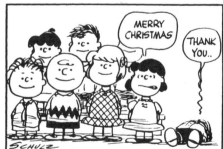

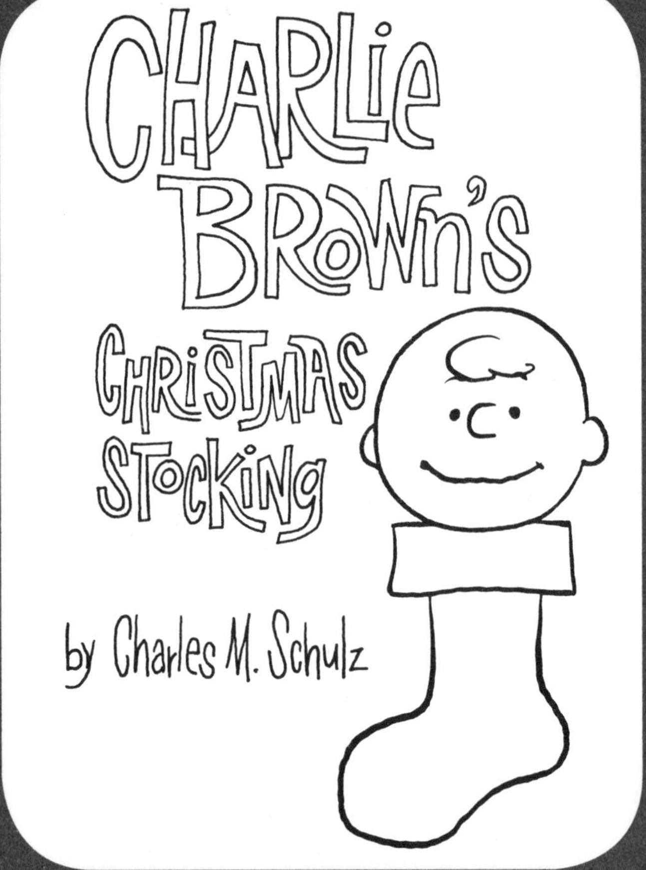
CHARLIE BROWN'S
CHRISTMAS STOCKING
by Charles M. Schulz

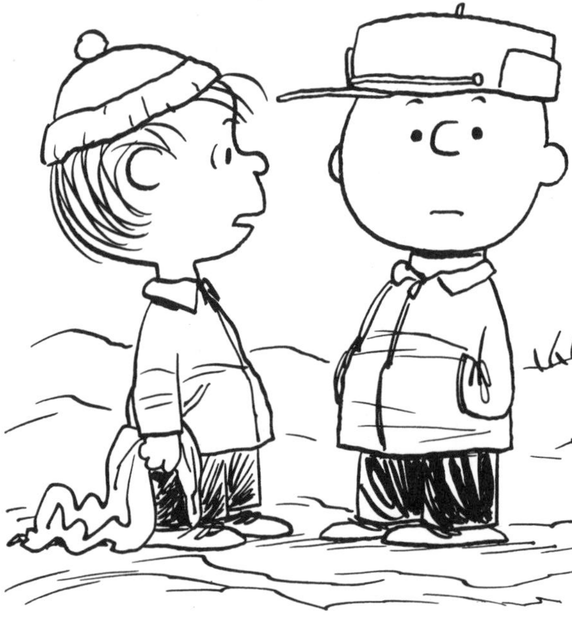

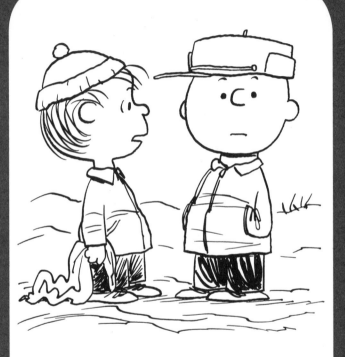

"I'm not going to hang up a Christmas stocking this year . . . I've decided it's not scriptural!"

"Two stockings? Why not two stockings?
I have two feet, don't I?"

"A Christmas stocking? I don't know if I will or not...
Did Beethoven hang up a Christmas stocking?"

"I'm not a bit worried... The way I see it,
how can Santa help but bring a lot of presents to a
little girl who has naturally curly hair?"

"Grownups are the ones who puzzle me at Christmastime...
Who, but a grownup, would ruin a beautiful holiday
season for himself by suddenly attempting to correspond
with four hundred people he doesn't see all year?"

"What worries me the most is how Santa Claus
is going to find where I live...On our block, all
the houses look alike!"

"Do you realize there's no place
in this house to hang a Christmas stocking?
I say let's sue the architect!"

"She's right... How can you hang a Christmas
stocking on a thermostat?"

"A house with no fireplace! Oh, the trials
of being part of the wrong generation!"

"Somehow this doesn't seem to be the solution…"

"It's almost midnight... Good grief! I feel like
the Chairman of the Board during an industrial crisis!"

"Think of something! Think of something!
Santa Claus will be here any minute, and all you
can do is say your stomach hurts!"

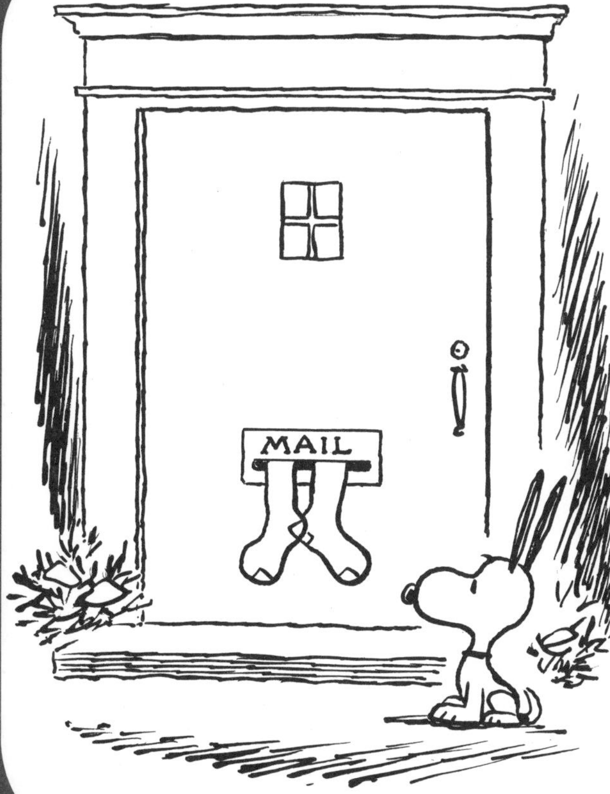
MAIL

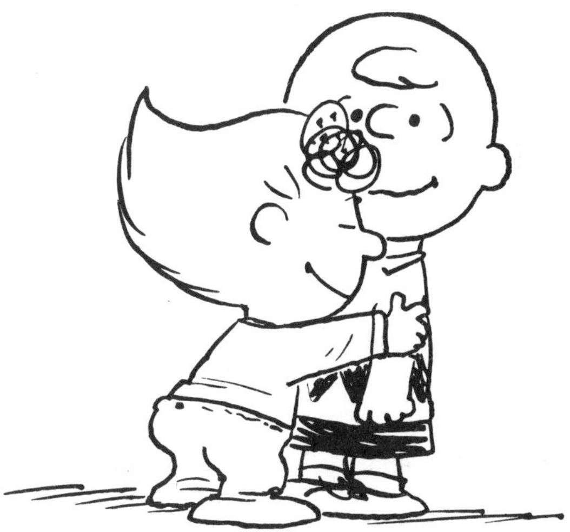

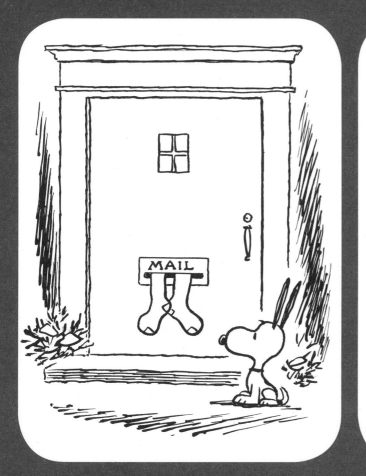

"Big brothers know everything...
Merry Christmas, Charlie Brown!"

A CHRISTMAS STORY

BY CHARLES M. SCHULZ

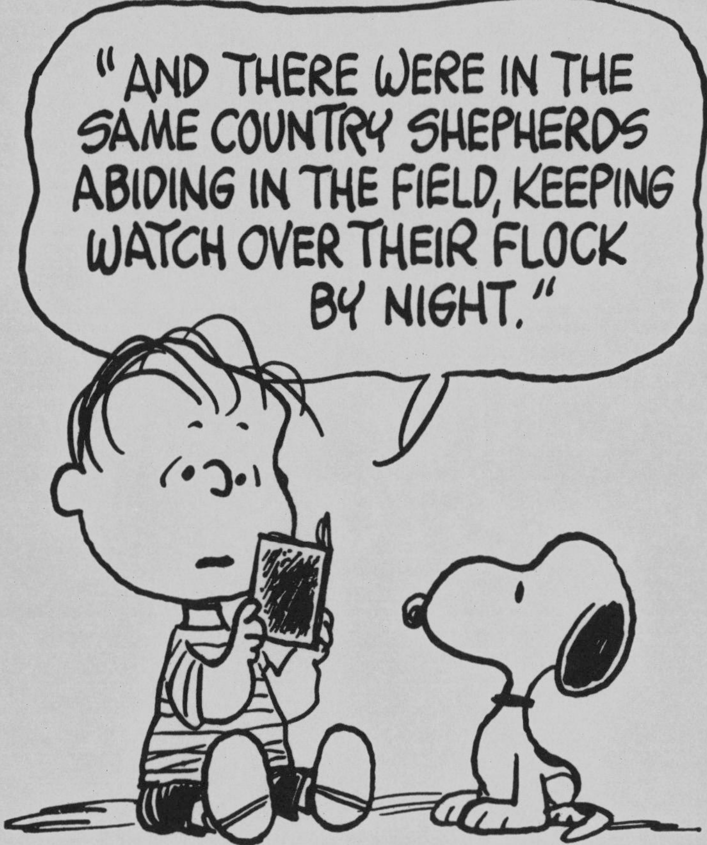
"AND THERE WERE IN THE SAME COUNTRY SHEPHERDS ABIDING IN THE FIELD, KEEPING WATCH OVER THEIR FLOCK BY NIGHT."

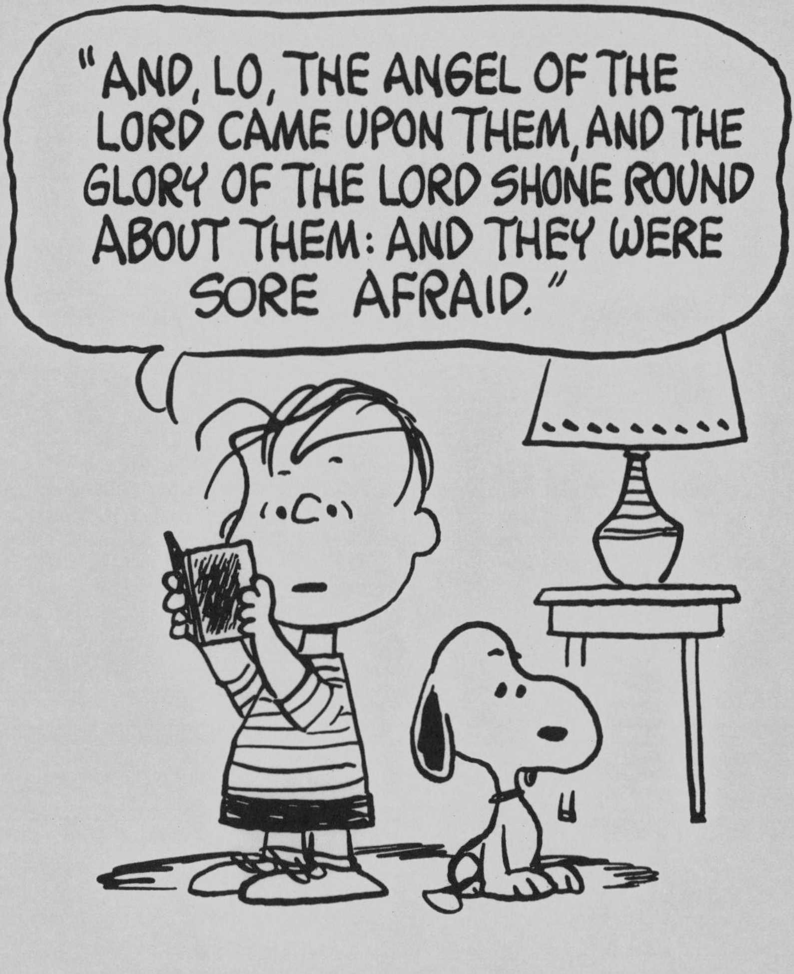
"AND, LO, THE ANGEL OF THE LORD CAME UPON THEM, AND THE GLORY OF THE LORD SHONE ROUND ABOUT THEM: AND THEY WERE SORE AFRAID."

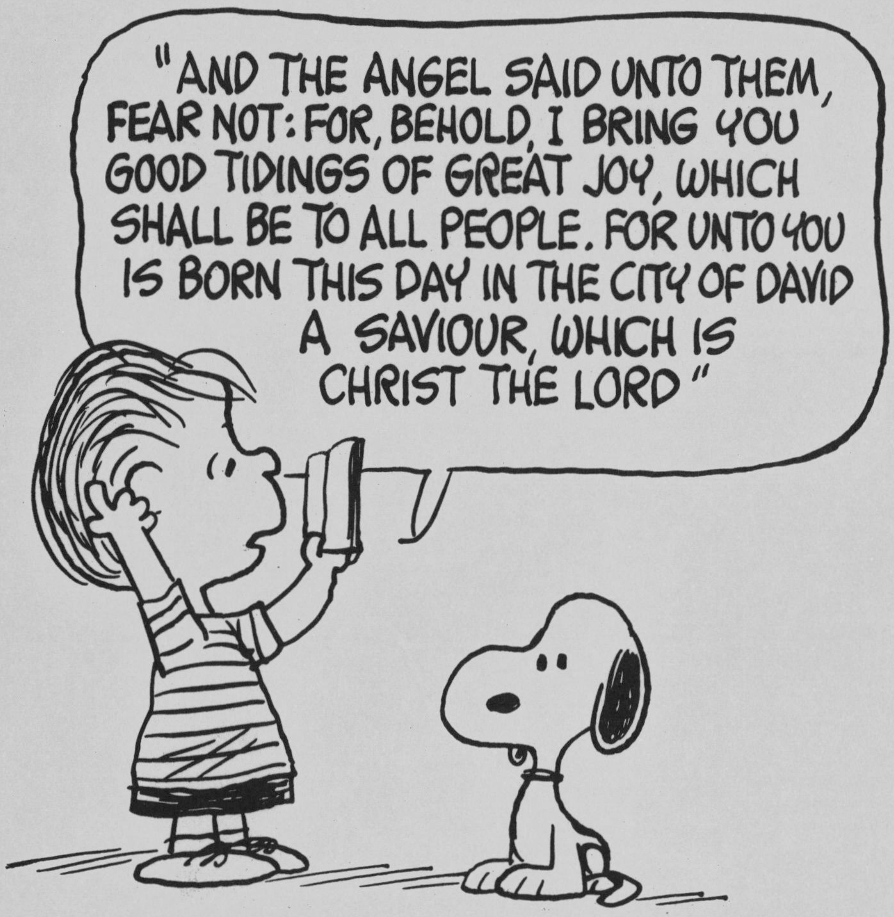
"AND THE ANGEL SAID UNTO THEM, FEAR NOT: FOR, BEHOLD, I BRING YOU GOOD TIDINGS OF GREAT JOY, WHICH SHALL BE TO ALL PEOPLE. FOR UNTO YOU IS BORN THIS DAY IN THE CITY OF DAVID A SAVIOUR, WHICH IS CHRIST THE LORD"

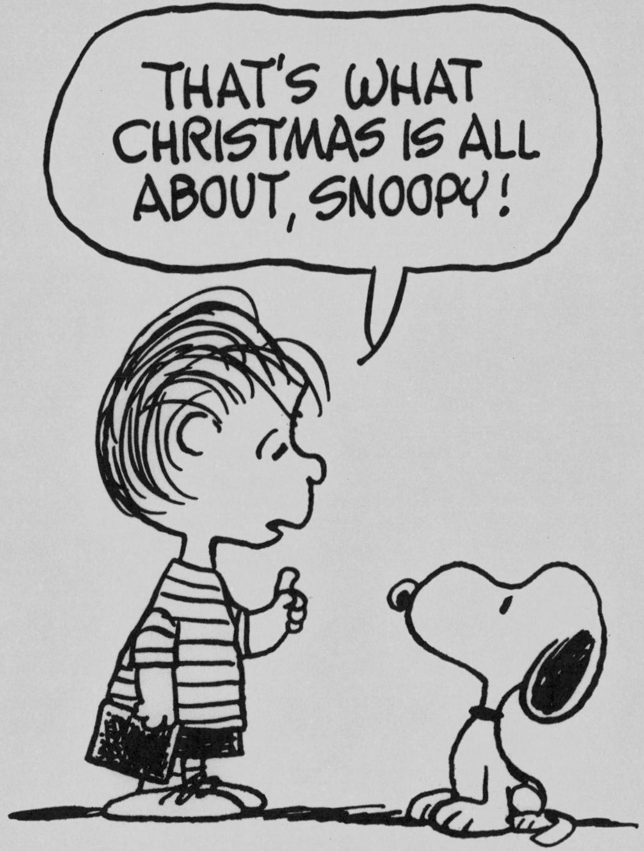
THAT'S WHAT CHRISTMAS IS ALL ABOUT, SNOOPY!

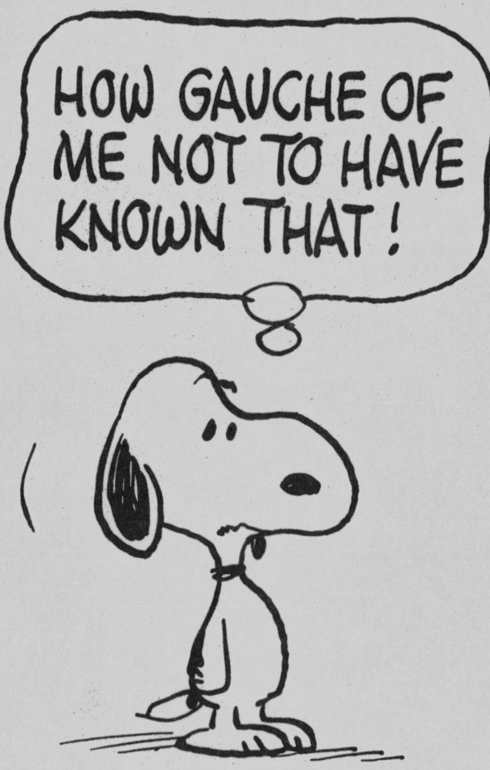
HOW GAUCHE OF ME NOT TO HAVE KNOWN THAT!

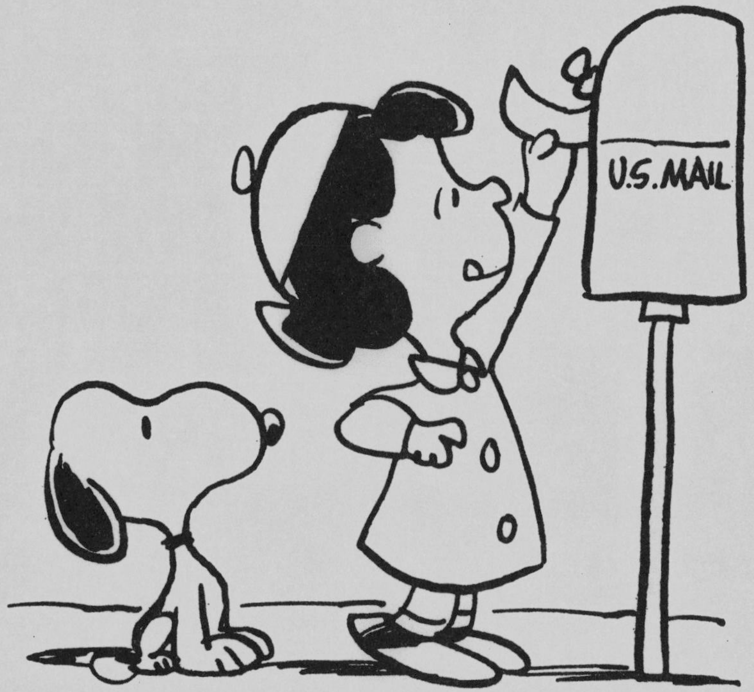
U.S. MAIL

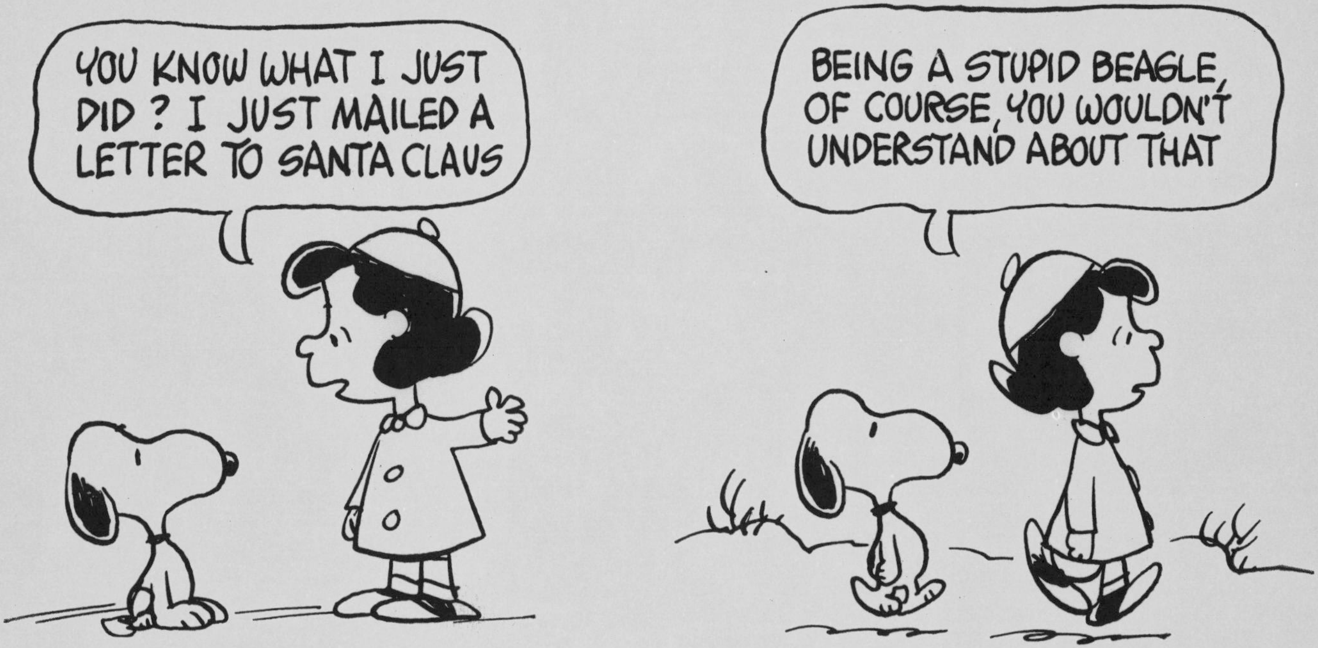
YOU KNOW WHAT I JUST DID ? I JUST MAILED A LETTER TO SANTA CLAUS
BEING A STUPID BEAGLE, OF COURSE, YOU WOULDN'T UNDERSTAND ABOUT THAT

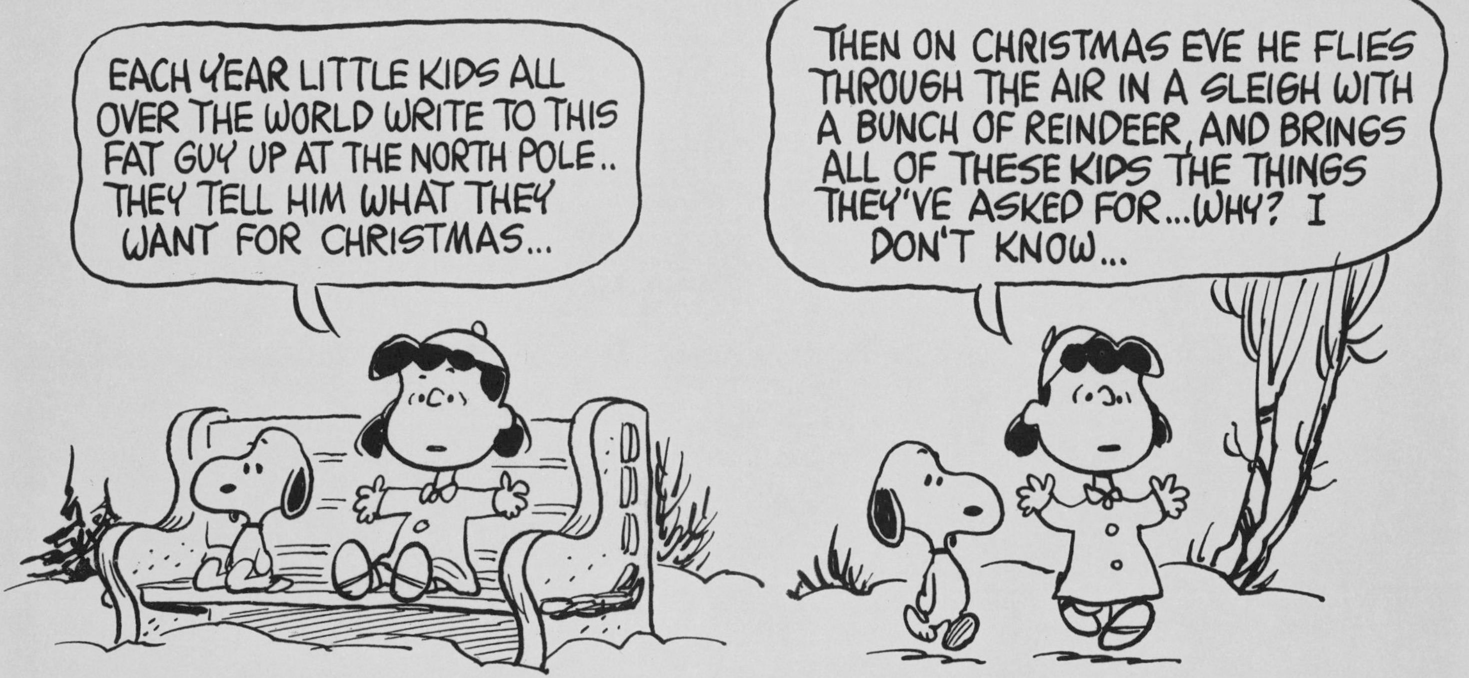
EACH YEAR LITTLE KIDS ALL OVER THE WORLD WRITE TO THIS FAT GUY UP AT THE NORTH POLE.. THEY TELL HIM WHAT THEY WANT FOR CHRISTMAS...
THEN ON CHRISTMAS EVE HE FLIES THROUGH THE AIR IN A SLEIGH WITH A BUNCH OF REINDEER, AND BRINGS ALL OF THESE KIDS THE THINGS THEY'VE ASKED FOR...WHY? I DON'T KNOW...

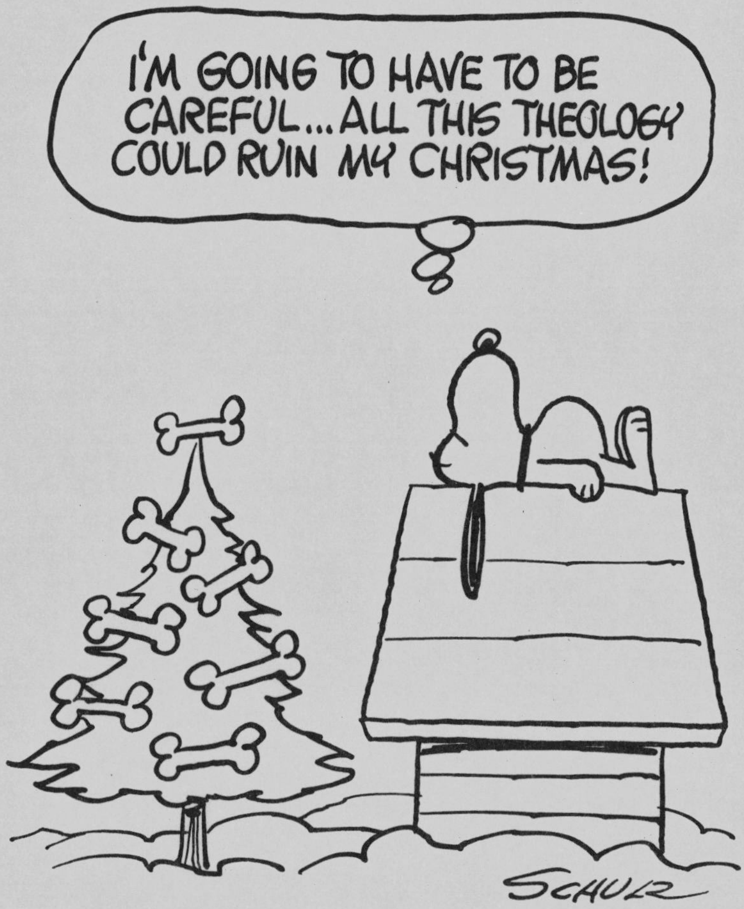
I'M GOING TO HAVE TO BE CAREFUL... ALL THIS THEOLOGY COULD RUIN MY CHRISTMAS!
SCHULZ

PEANUTS STORYBOOKS

These four storybooks published by Holt, Rinehart and Winston from 1966 through 1976 were made mainly from gags reworked from the strip, but Schulz drew entirely new artwork for them.

SNOOPY and the Red Baron

BY CHARLES M. SCHULZ

Here's the World War I flying ace posing beside his Sopwith "Camel."

The Red Baron has been reported
in the vicinity of Saint-Mihiel.
I must bring him down.
"Switch off!" cries my mechanic.
"Coupez!" I reply. "Contact?"
"Contact it is!"

"I think my dog has finally
flipped!"

Here I am flying high over France
in my Sopwith "Camel" searching
for the infamous Red Baron!

Suddenly antiaircraft fire begins to burst below my plane. "Archie" we call it.

"Nyahh, nyahh, nyahh! You can't hit me!"

Actually, tough flying aces never said, "Nyahh, nyahh, nyahh!"

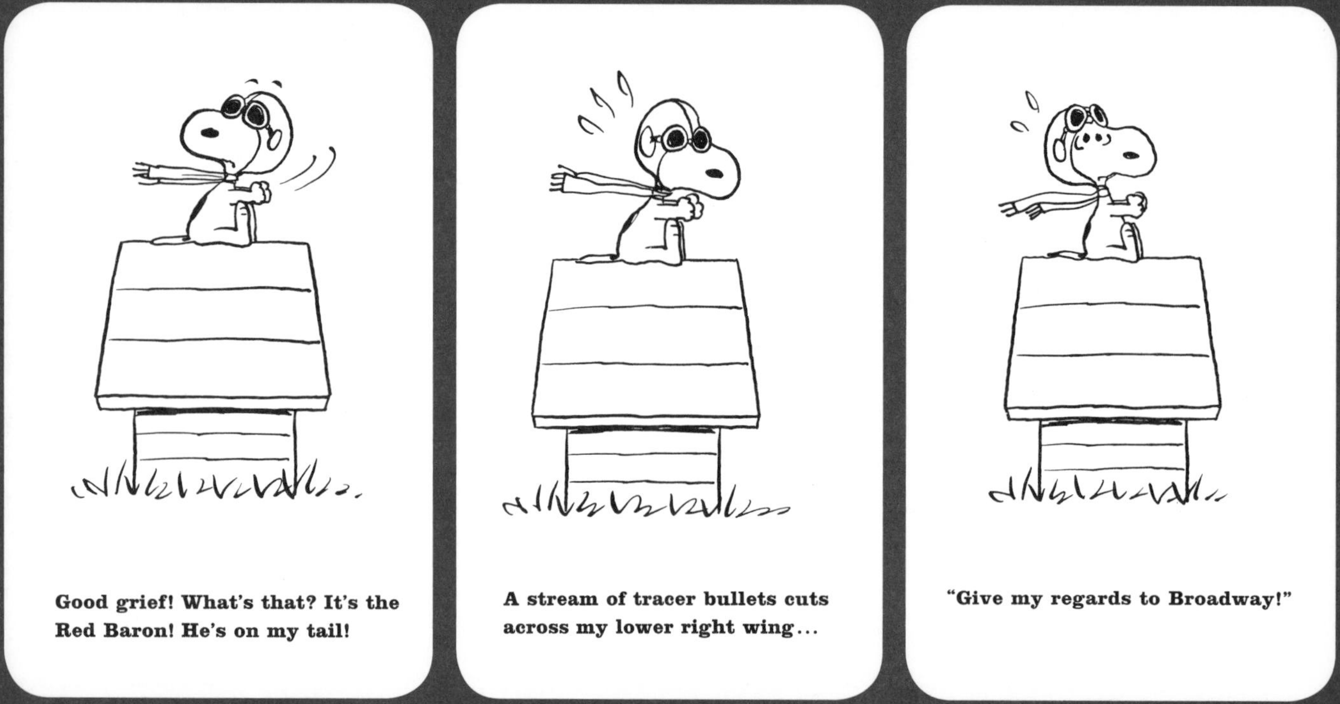
Good grief! What's that? It's the Red Baron! He's on my tail!
A stream of tracer bullets cuts across my lower right wing...
"Give my regards to Broadway!"

As my plane strikes the ground, I leap from the cockpit!

Right in my supper dish....How embarassing!

"Curse you, Red Baron!"

Here's the World War I pilot asleep in his bunk being awakened to fly another dawn patrol.

"Good morning, chaps! Another important mission today, eh what? But, I dare say they all are important, eh what?"

Drat this fog! It's bad enough having to fight the Red Baron without having to fly in weather like this. When I get back I'm going to write a letter to President Wilson!

Ah, the sun has broken through...
I can see the woods of Montsec
below...And what's that? It's a
Fokker Triplane!

"Ha! This time I've got you, Red
Baron! This time you've met
your match!"

"I hate that Red Baron!"

The scene: An aerodrome somewhere in France. The World War I
flying ace is asleep on his bunk.
Little does he realize that he is
about to face the most terrible
experience of his life!

"Good morning, ground crew!"

Here's the pilot standing next to his Sopwith "Camel" chatting with his faithful mechanics. Even at this early hour, they admire his calm courage.

"Switch off!" "Coupez!" "Contact?" "Contact!"

Soon I am flying high over France. I can see the little city of Pont-a-Mousson below...

My strategy today is to cross
the enemy lines near Verdun...I
must find the Red Baron, and
bring him down!

"All right, Red Baron! Where are
you? You can't hide forever!"

"Aaugh! There he is! He's diving
down out of the sun! He's tricked
me again!"

"I've got to run! Come on, Sopwith Camel, let's go! Go, Camel, go!!!"

"I can't shake him! He's riddling my plane with bullets! It bursts into flames!"

"Curse you, Red Baron!"

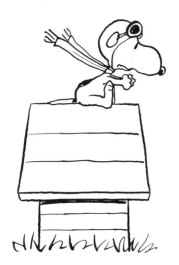

"I'm coming in right over the trees!"

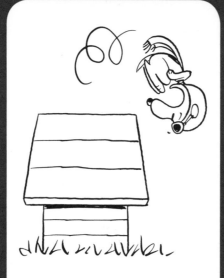

"AAUGH!"

Here's the World War I pilot trapped behind enemy lines.

"I'll never make it back! I'll be captured, and shot at dawn! I never should have left the Daisy Hill Puppy Farm!"

"I miss my buddies!"

That night I sneak through abandoned trenches.

By day I sleep on haystacks.

Dusk approaches...I must be on my way!

"Good grief! A sentry!"

I'll sneak up on him, grab him by the arm, and fling him over my back....Easy now...Mustn't let him see me....Easy...

Okay, here he goes! One big flip, and over he goes! This is it...One big flip! Over he goes! One big flip! Okay, here he goes!

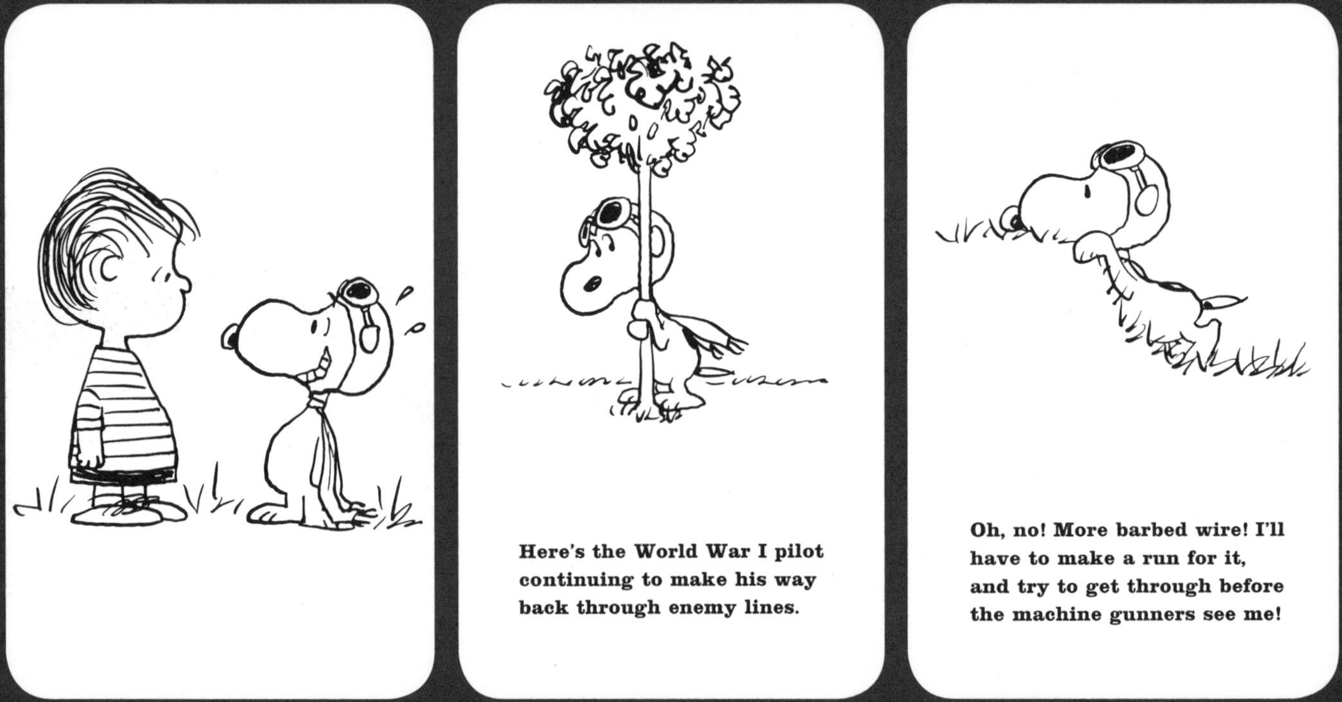
Here's the World War I pilot continuing to make his way back through enemy lines.
Oh, no! More barbed wire! I'll have to make a run for it, and try to get through before the machine gunners see me!

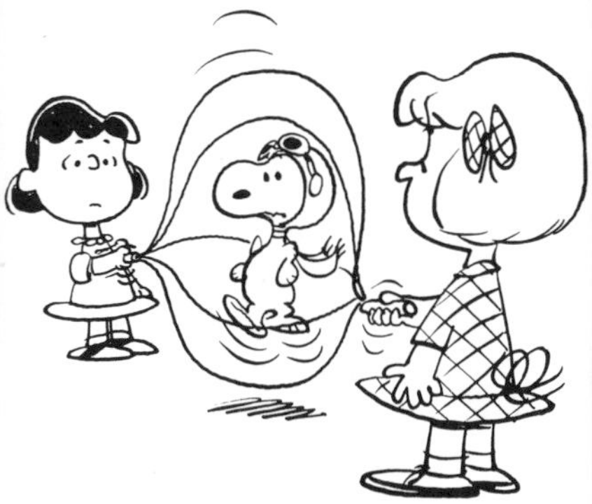

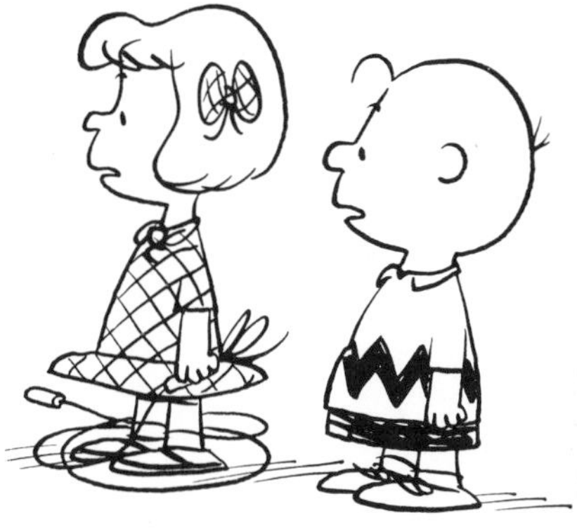

“What was that?” “I’m not sure, but I think it was a World War I pilot going through some barbed wire…”

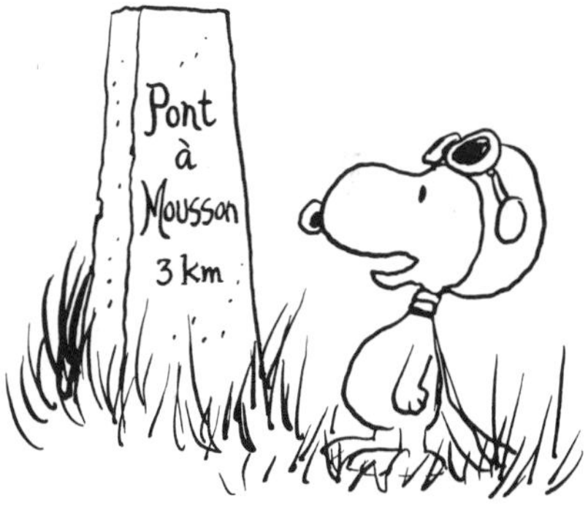
Pont à Mousson 3 km

“Ah! My journey is almost over….”

What's this? A small French farm house!

"Ah, mademoiselle...Do not be afraid....I am a pilot with the Allies....My plane was shot down by the Red Baron..."

She does not understand ze English....Ah, but she will understand that I am a handsome young pilot...And she? She is a beautiful French girl...

"Soup? Ah, yes, mademoiselle...
That would be wonderful! A little
potato soup, and I will be on
my way..."

But how can I bear to leave her?
Perhaps someday I can return...
"Au revoir, mademoiselle...Au
revoir!" Ah, what a pity....Her
heart is breaking."Do not cry, my
little one....Do not cry..."

"Farewell! Farewell!"

"Curse the Red Baron and his kind! Curse the wickedness in this world! Curse the evil that causes all this unhappiness!"

Here's the World War I flying ace back at the aerodrome in France....He is exhausted and yet he does not sleep, for one thought runs continuously through his mind...

"Someday I'll get you, Red Baron!"

SNOOPY and His Sopwith Camel

BY CHARLES M. SCHULZ

Part One

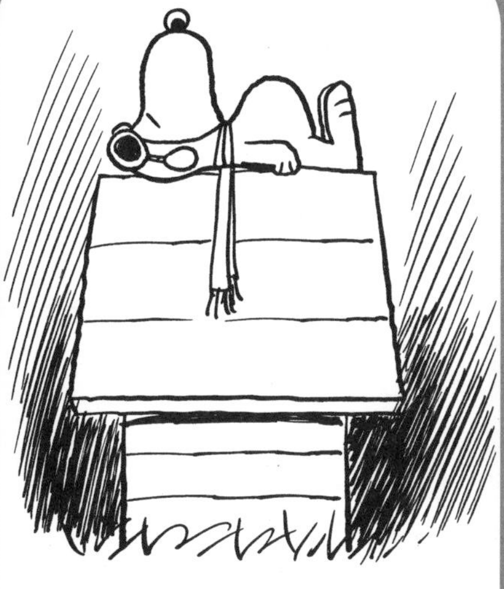

Here's the World War I flying ace being awakened to fly another dawn patrol.

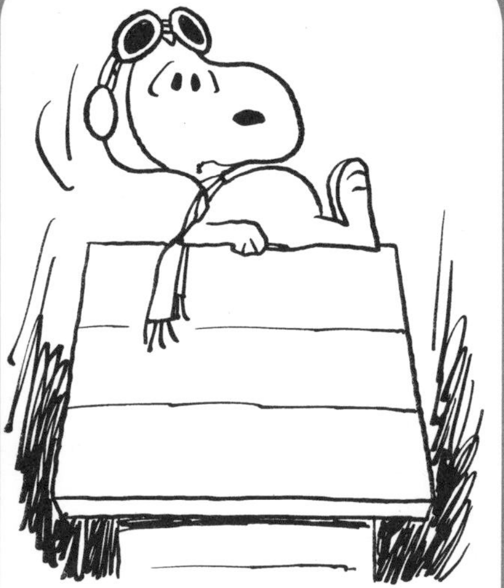

"AT THREE O'CLOCK IN THE MORNING?!"

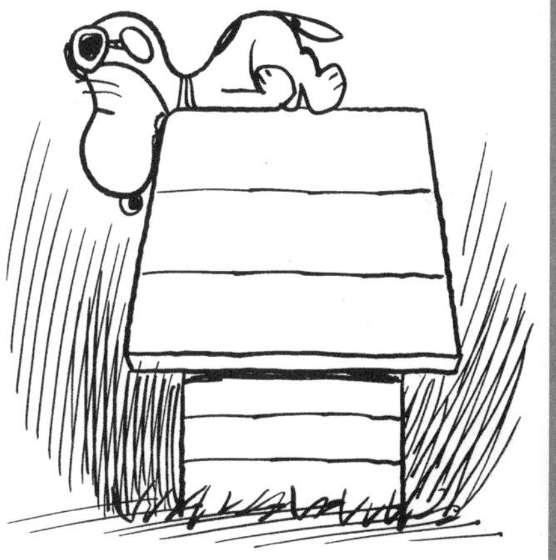

"Tell President Wilson to call me at ten."

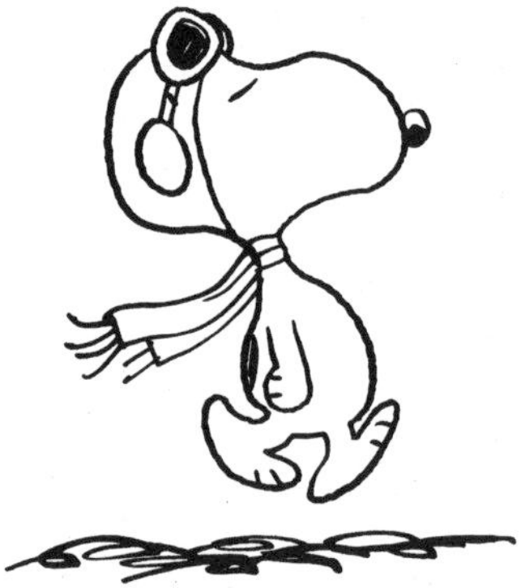

Here's the World War I flying ace walking out onto the aerodrome somewhere in France.

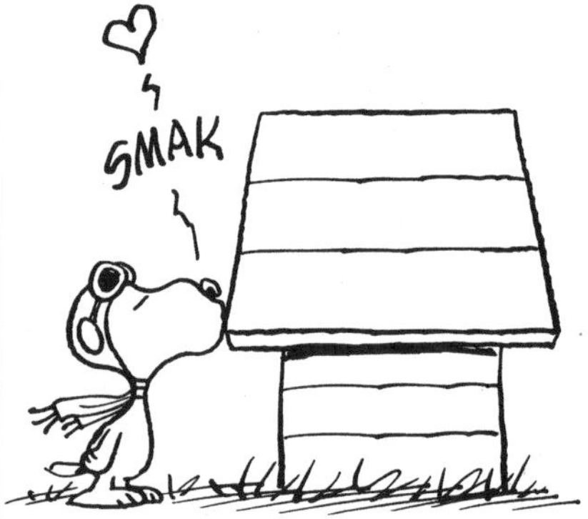
SMAK

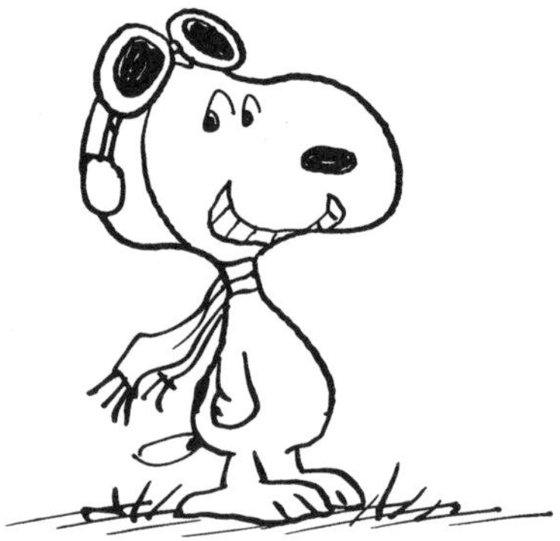

I love my Sopwith Camel.

"Where's my stupid mechanic?"

"I hate it when he's late with my toasted English muffin."

Here's the World War I flying ace taking off on a dangerous mission ...our supply sergeant has told me to take good care of my Sopwith Camel.

Our supply sergeant hates me!

"Some people have dogs who chase cars, some people have dogs who bite the mailman, some people have dogs who dig up gardens...."

Here's the World War I flying ace back at the base...he is very depressed...he is sitting alone in a small French café drinking root beer...

Actually, World War I flying aces very seldom drank root beer...

Ah! A shy country lass
approaches...

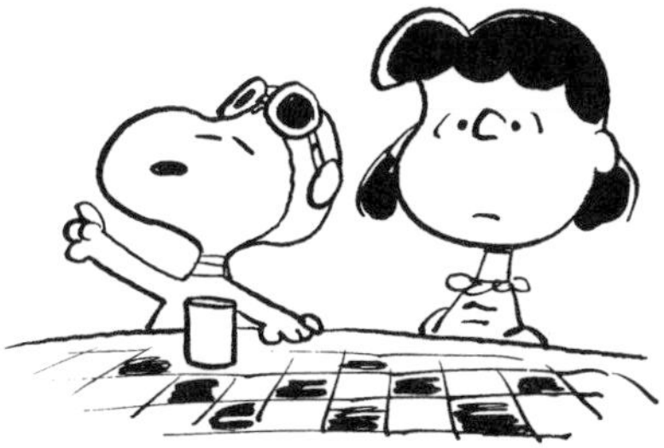

I shall buy her a root beer and impress her with my tales of heroic deeds.

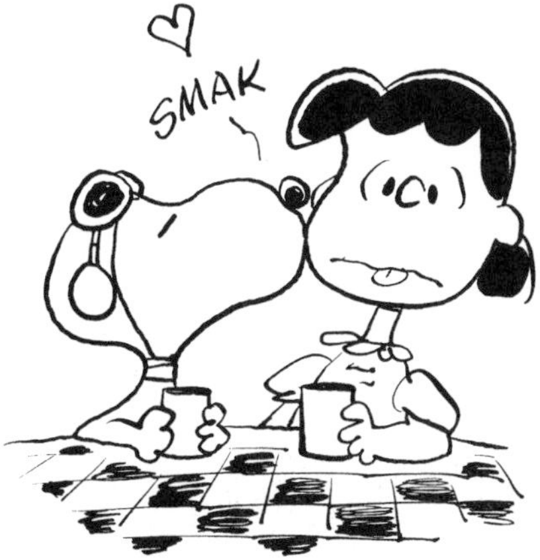
SMAK

As the night goes on, we become very friendly...

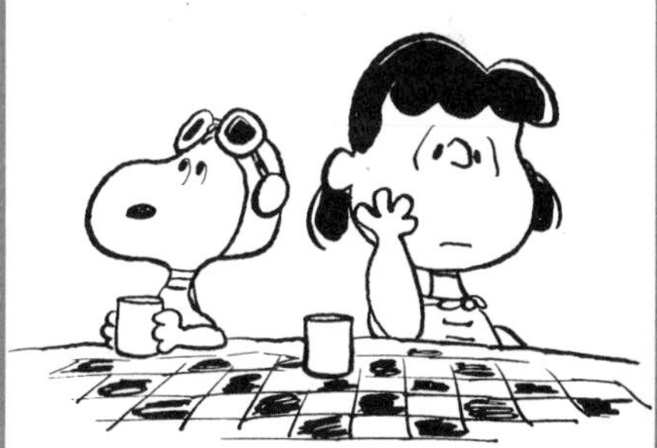

I think this simple country lass has fallen for me...I could probably become fond of her, too, if she weren't so ugly!

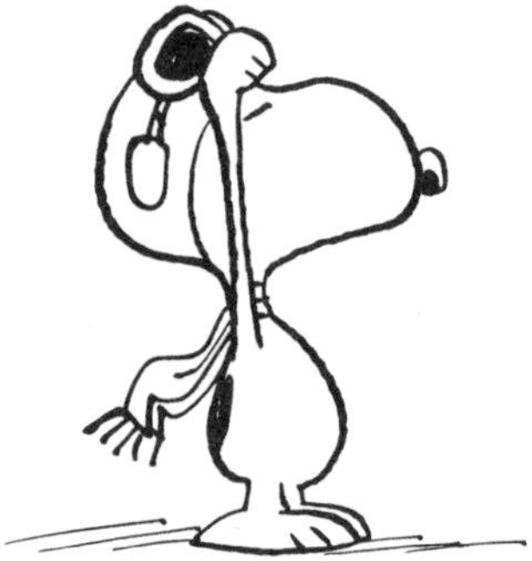

The next morning I report to my commanding officer for orders... he is always impressed by my snappy salute!

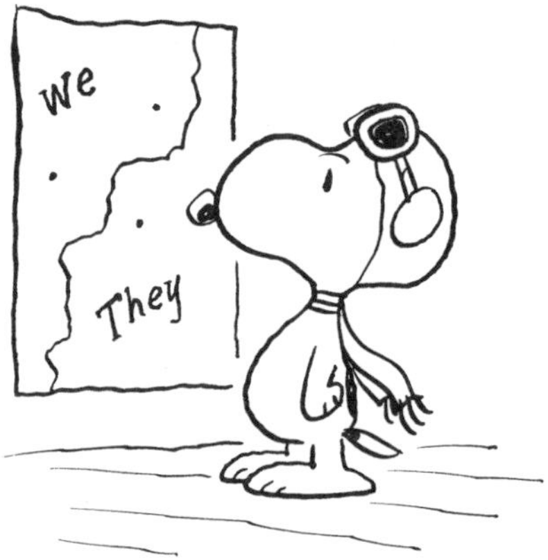
We
They

Word has it that the Red Baron has been sighted near Toul... my mission is to search him out, and shoot him down.... I study the map on the wall...

Here's the World War I flying ace taking off again in his Sopwith Camel.

As I fly south following the Moselle River, I scan the skies for that familiar red Fokker Triplane.[1]

[1] As I recall, it was a shade between International Orange and Stearman Vermilion.

Too late! He has seen me first! A burst of tracers cuts across my wing!

This is what I get for sitting up all night drinking root beer.

Only my great skill as a pilot enables me to return safely...my ground crew is overjoyed to see me.

The next day I am put on KP for losing too many Sopwith Camels! How humiliating!

Part Two

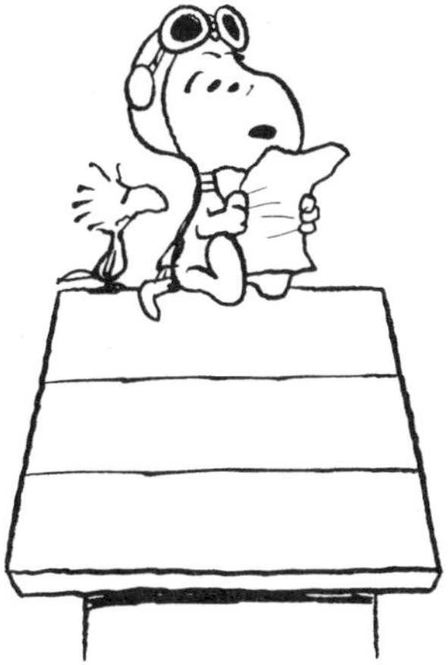

The war drags on.... News from the front is all bad. A big enemy push is expected at any moment.

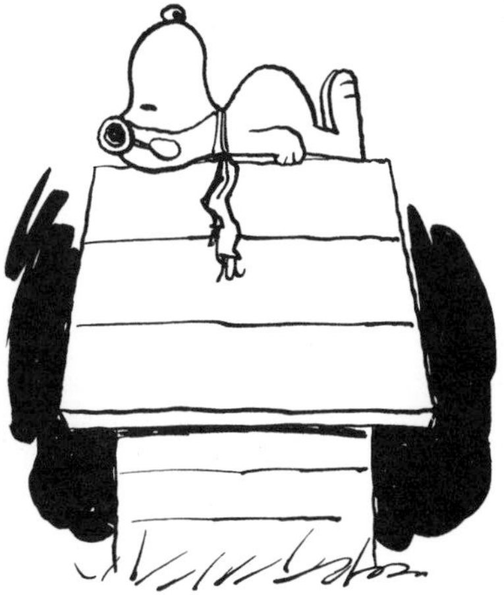

It is difficult to sleep... one longs for the comfortable beds of home.

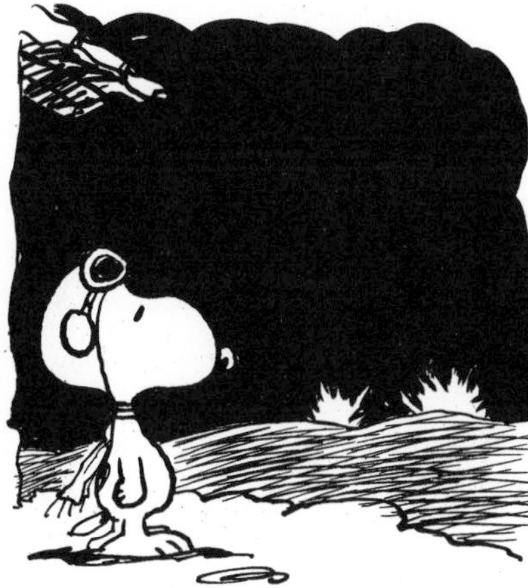

Outside, flashes of artillery fire can be seen in the distance... a siren wails in the night... the sky is dark...[2]

[2]For more on dark skies, see my novel, IT WAS A DARK AND STORMY NIGHT.

"What are we all doing here? This war is madness."

What's this? All pilots are instructed to report to headquarters immediately.

My first reaction is to realize that something is up.

We crowd into the briefing room. The other pilots are inspired by my quiet confidence.

This is the news we have been waiting for. An ammunition train is leaving Fère-en-Tardenois in the morning. It will be well guarded, but one lone plane flying very low just might be able to get through to it.

I, of course, immediately volunteer!

A few hours' rest before my important mission...I wonder if that shy country lass is thinking of me....

When I awaken, the first faint rays of dawn are beginning to lighten the sky...it is cold...curse this stupid war!

"Good morning, chaps...another important mission, eh what? But I daresay they are all important, eh what?"

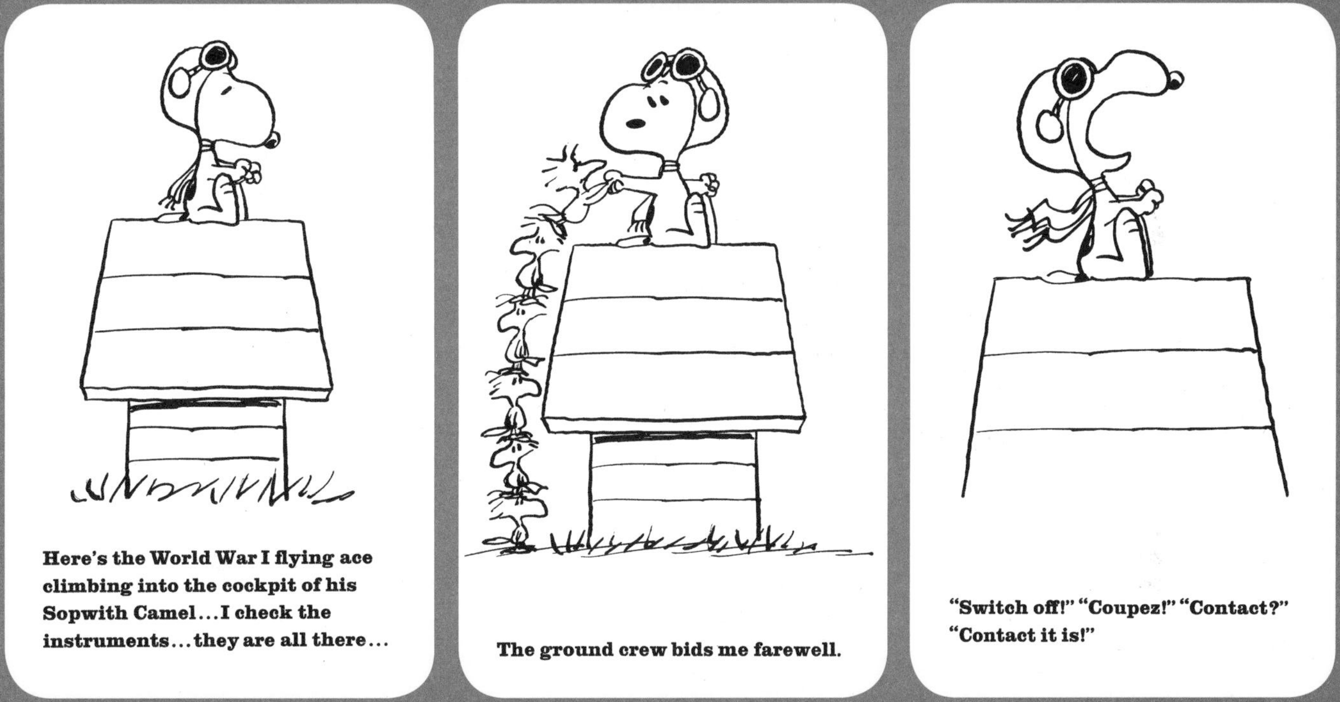
Here's the World War I flying ace climbing into the cockpit of his Sopwith Camel...I check the instruments...they are all there...
The ground crew bids me farewell.
"Switch off!" "Coupez!" "Contact?" "Contact it is!"

My route is along the Somme valley...as the early morning sun begins to warm the sky, I pass Morlancourt Ridge not realizing the dramatic role that this area is someday to play.*

*See my next book.

As I fly over the trenches, I wave to the poor blighters below....

Blighters appreciate your waving to them.

"There it is! There's the ammunition train!"

As I wheel about, puffs of angry
flak appear in the sky.

And then another sound!
Machine-gun bullets tear through
the side of my Sopwith Camel...
it's the Red Baron!

Fighting the controls with every
ounce of my strength, I manage to
bring my stricken craft down
behind enemy lines.

I leap out of the burning cockpit,
and run for cover.

I've got to find that ammunition train, and destroy it.

What's this? I can't believe it! It's the shy country lass...she's talking to the train engineer... that girl is a spy!

To think that I almost lost my heart to her...I would have taken her back to the states with me, if she hadn't been so ugly.

I'll put on my famous disguise, and find out their plans...

"Wo ist der root beer hall?"

Suddenly, I see my chance... I leap for the ammunition train, and destroy it.

A desperate bid for freedom!

Here's the World War I flying ace, back at the aerodrome somewhere in France...he thinks of the war, the simple country lass who deceived him, and the Red Baron... and he is plagued by the eternal question....

"Where's my toasted English muffin?"

The End

SNOOPY and "It Was a Dark and Stormy Night"

BY CHARLES M. SCHULZ

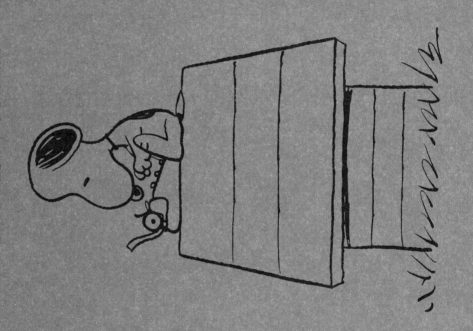

Sometimes, when you are a great writer, the words come so fast you can hardly put them down on paper...

Sometimes.

Part I

It was a dark and stormy
night.

**"Your novel has a very
exciting beginning."**

"Thank you."

**"Good luck with the
second sentence."**

Suddenly, a shot rang out!

My plot is thickening.

"Stop raining on my novel!"

A door slammed.
The maid screamed.

Suddenly, a pirate ship
appeared on the horizon!

**This twist in the plot will
baffle my readers.**

Page 145

"I hear you're working
on a novel..."

"I'm a good artist so if you'll
start thinking about what you'd
like on the cover of your book,
I'll draw it for you."

How about a bunch of pirates
and Foreign Legionnaires
fighting some cowboys with
some lions and tigers and
elephants leaping through the
air at this girl who is tied to
a submarine?

While millions of people
were starving, the king
lived in luxury.
   Meanwhile, on a small
farm in Kansas, a boy was
growing up.

**In Part Two, I'll tie all of this
together.**

Part II

A light snow was fall-
ing, and the little girl
with the tattered shawl
had not sold a violet
all day.

At that very moment, a
young intern at City
Hospital was making an
important discovery.

**I may have written myself
into a corner.**

The mysterious patient in Room 213 had finally awakened. She moaned softly.

Could it be that she was the sister of the boy in Kansas who loved the girl with the tattered shawl who was the daughter of the maid who had escaped from the pirates?

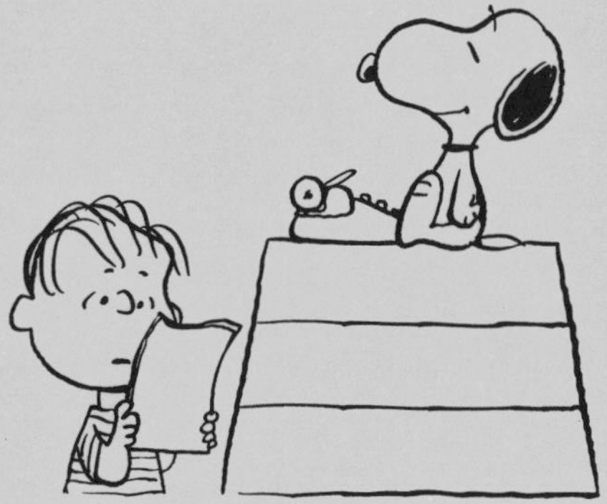

"But what about the king?"

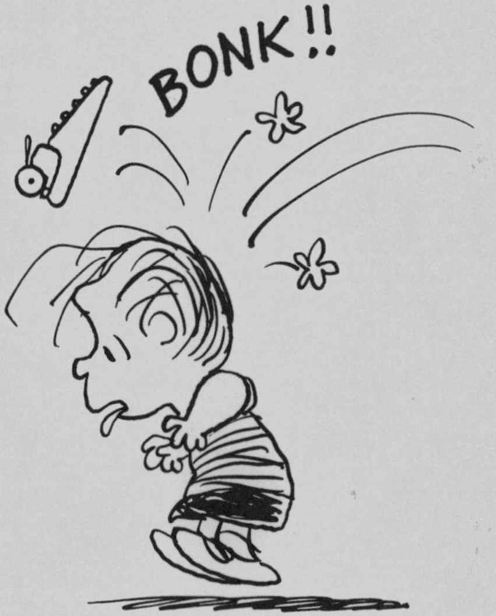
BONK!!

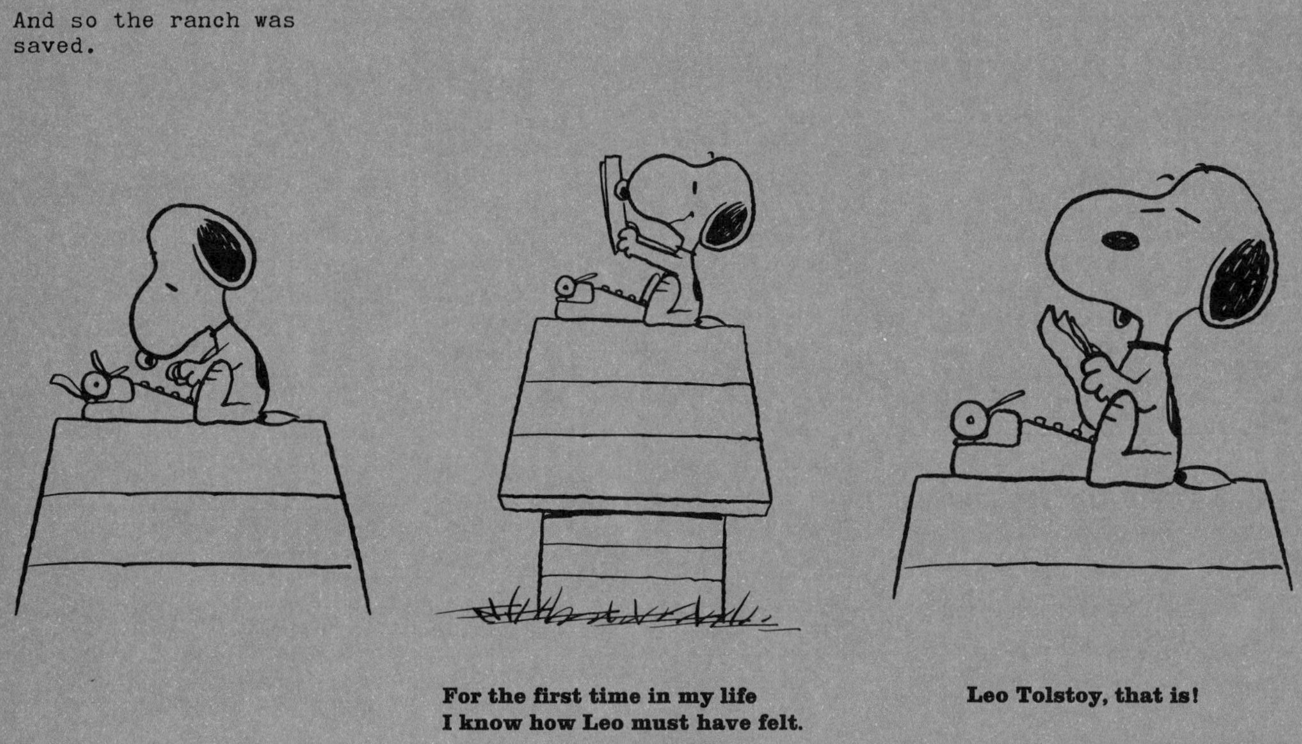
And so the ranch was saved.
For the first time in my life I know how Leo must have felt.
Leo Tolstoy, that is!

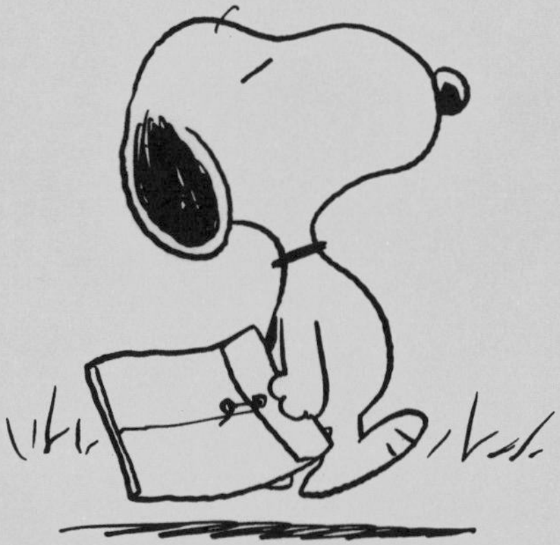

Here's the world-famous novelist walking to the mailbox to send his manuscript away.

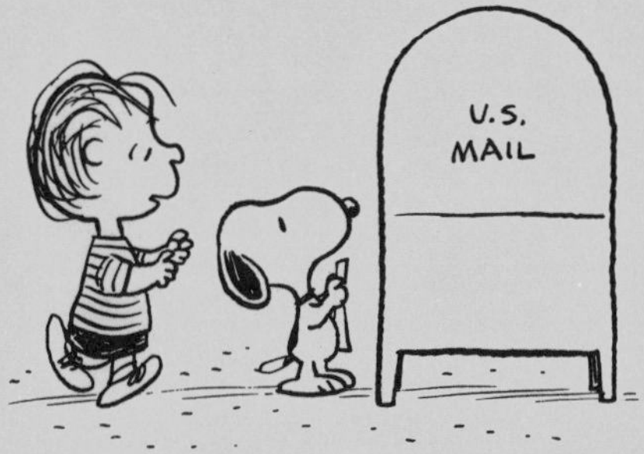
U.S.
MAIL

"Here, let me help you..."

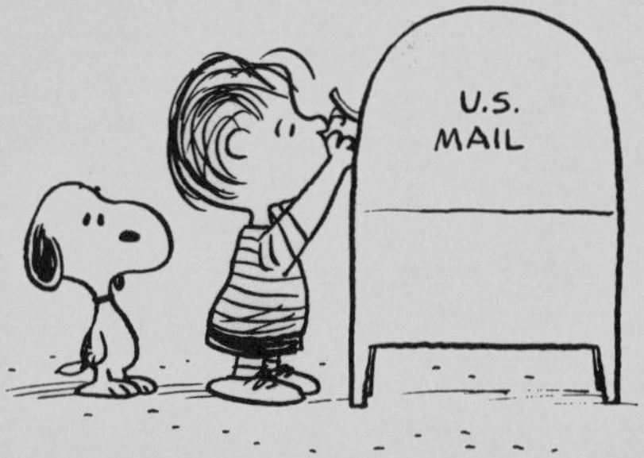
U.S.
MAIL

My career almost came to an end.

"Oh, excuse me."

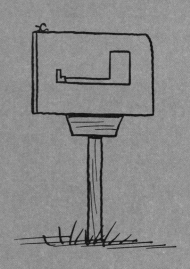

"That's all right...I'm expecting word from my publisher."

Dear Sir:
It gives me great pleasure
to inform you of our
decision to publish your
book....

"I'm an author!"

It Was a Dark and Stormy Night

A NOVEL BY Snoopy

It Was a Dark and Stormy Night

by Snoopy

Holt, Rinehart and Winston

New York   Chicago   San Francisco

For Woodstock,
my friend of friends

PART

II

It was a dark and stormy night. Suddenly, a shot rang out! A door slammed. The maid screamed.

Suddenly, a pirate ship appeared on the horizon! While millions of people were starving, the king lived in luxury. Meanwhile, on a small farm in Kansas, a boy was growing up.

PART III

light snow was falling, and the little girl in the tattered shawl had not sold a violet all day.

At that very moment, a young intern at City Hospital was making an important discovery. The mysterious patient in Room 213 had finally awakened. She moaned softly. Could it be that she was the sister of the boy in Kansas who loved the girl with the tattered shawl who was the daughter of the maid who had escaped from the pirates? The intern frowned.

"Stampede!" the foreman shouted, and forty thousand head of cattle thundered down on the tiny camp. The two men rolled on the ground grappling beneath the murderous hooves. A left and a right. A left. Another left and right. An uppercut to the jaw. The fight was over. And so the ranch was saved.

The young intern sat by himself in one corner of the coffee shop. He had learned about medicine, but more importantly, he had learned something about life.

THE END

"A LIGHT SNOW WAS FALLING..."

A malevolent, self-centered monarch, a midwestern farm boy, a young, street-corner florist in a tattered shawl—these and many more keenly etched characters come together in this deeply moving and strangely compelling novel of growth, change, and recognition. Drawn with sparse clarity and measured cadence, **It Was a Dark and Stormy Night** is reminiscent of many works. Relevant to readers of all ages, here is a remarkable first novel by an inventive young author from whom more will undoubtedly be heard in years to come.

PHOTO BY LOCKHART AND STERNER

Snoopy was born at the Daisy Hill Puppy Farm, one of a litter of eight pups. His hobbies are reading, baseball, flying, and "just sort of lying around." He is currently at work on a book of short stories.

Holt, Rinehart and Winston / 383 Madison Avenue, New York 10017

Here's the world-famous author
reading a review of his book.

I can see the headlines now,
"Author bites book reviewer
on the leg!"

Here I am on the way to my
first autograph party.

I hate it when the line doesn't
extend clear around the block.

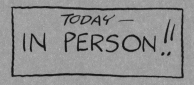

TODAY —
IN PERSON!!
The Author!

Autograph parties are terrible when two million people show up.

Autograph parties are terrible when nobody shows up.

What I need is a unique signature.

"I Never Promised You an Apple Orchard" The Collected Writings of SNOOPY

BY CHARLES M.SCHULZ

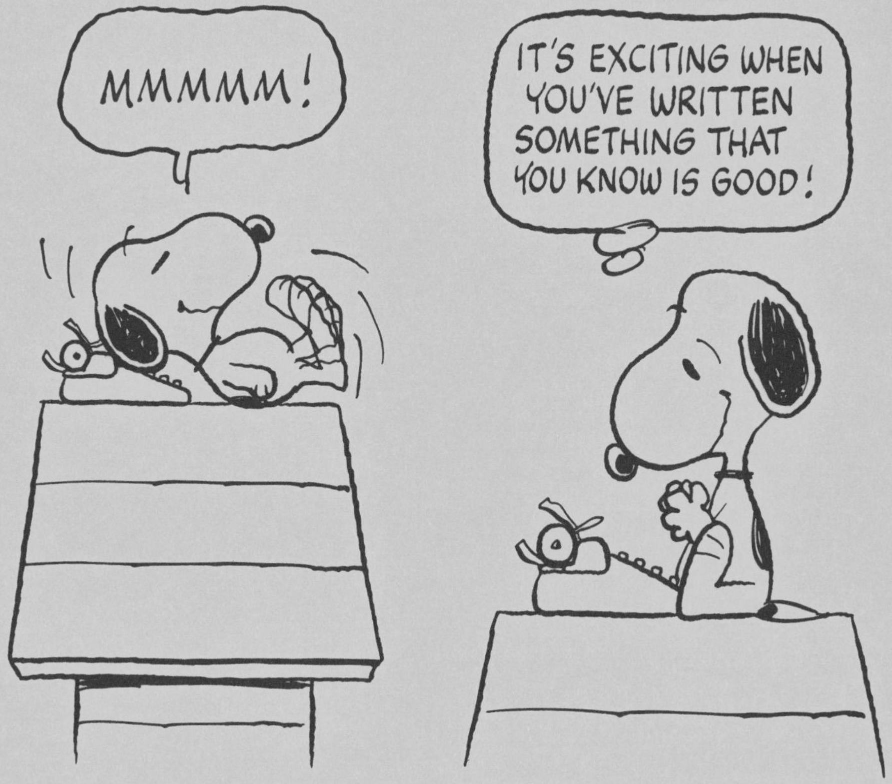
MMMMM!
IT'S EXCITING WHEN YOU'VE WRITTEN SOMETHING THAT YOU KNOW IS GOOD!

Edith had refused to marry him because he was too fat.

"Why don't you go on a diet?" suggested a friend. "You can't have your cake and Edith, too!"

Though her husband often went on business trips, she hated to be left alone.

"I've solved our problem," he said. "I've bought you a Saint Bernard. Its name is Great Reluctance. Now when I go away, you shall know that I am leaving you with Great Reluctance!"

She hit him with a waffle iron.

His wife had always hated his work. "You'll never make any money growing toadstools," she complained.

"On the contrary," he declared. "My toadstool business is mushrooming!"

She creamed him with the electric toaster.

Joe Anthro was an authority on Egyptian and Babylonian cultures. His greatest accomplishment, however, was his famous work on the Throat Culture.

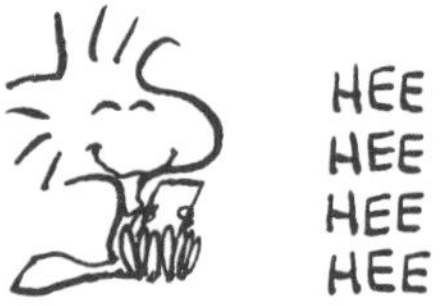
HEE
HEE
HEE
HEE

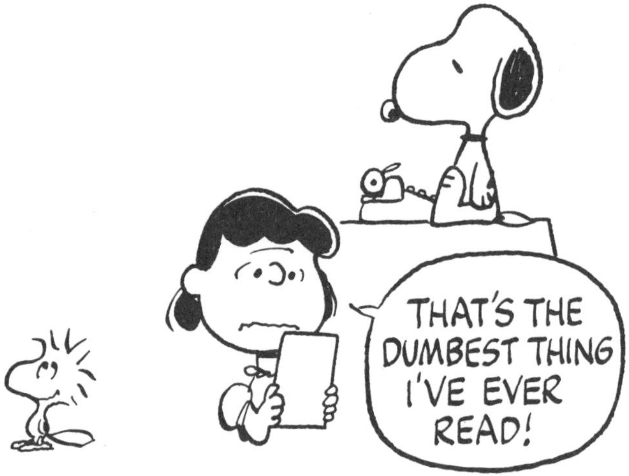
THAT'S THE DUMBEST THING I'VE EVER READ!

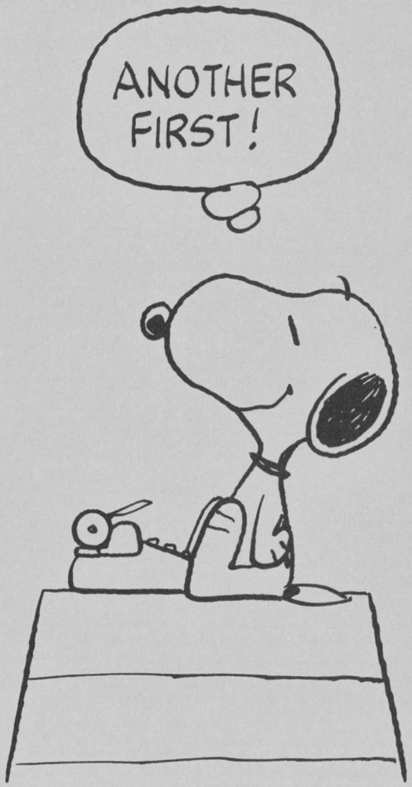
ANOTHER FIRST!

A few thoughts concerning a lost love . . .

Rats!

"You've always ignored me," she said. "And now you say you want to marry me. Every night you play cards. I'm really afraid that you love cards more than you love me. If you could say something nice to me just once, perhaps I'd marry you."

" ♢♣♡♠ "

"You blew it!" she said, and walked out of his life forever.

AH! MY SECRETARY WITH THE MORNING MAIL!

"Dear Contributor,
Thank you for submitting your manuscript. We regret that it does not suit our present needs."

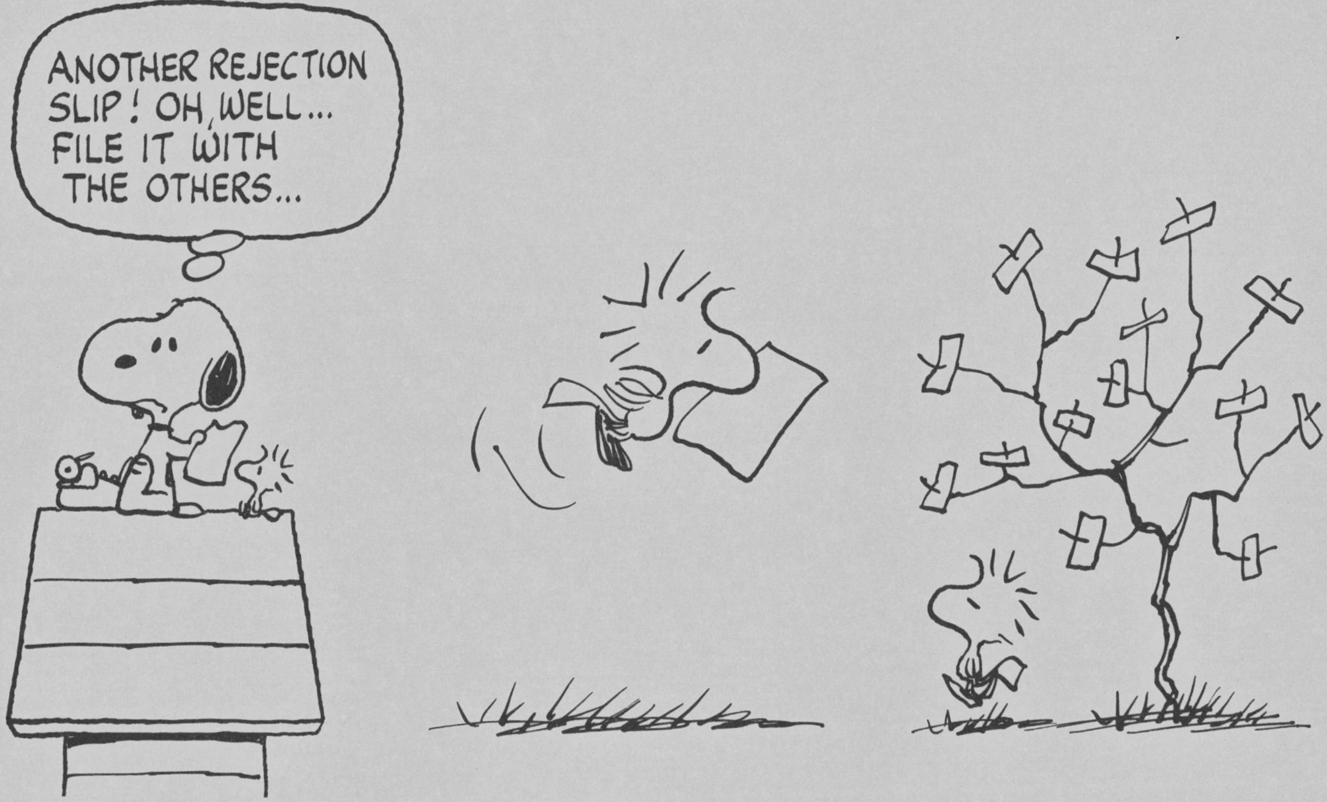
ANOTHER REJECTION SLIP! OH, WELL... FILE IT WITH THE OTHERS...

Her real name was Dorothy Fledermaus, but all her friends called her "Dee." Thus, she was frequently referred to as "Dee Fledermaus."

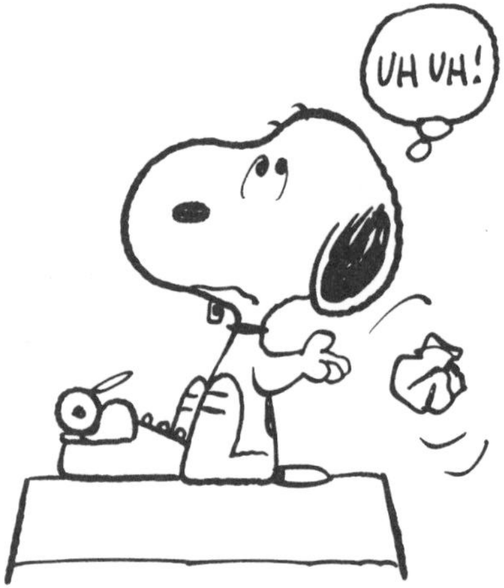
UH UH!

The last car drove away. It began to rain. And so our hero's life ended as it had begun . . . a disaster. "I never got any breaks," he always complained.
He had wanted to be rich. He died poor. He wanted friends. He died friendless. He wanted to be loved. He died unloved. He wanted laughter. He found only tears.

He wanted applause. He received boos. He wanted fame. He found only obscurity. He wanted answers. He found only questions.

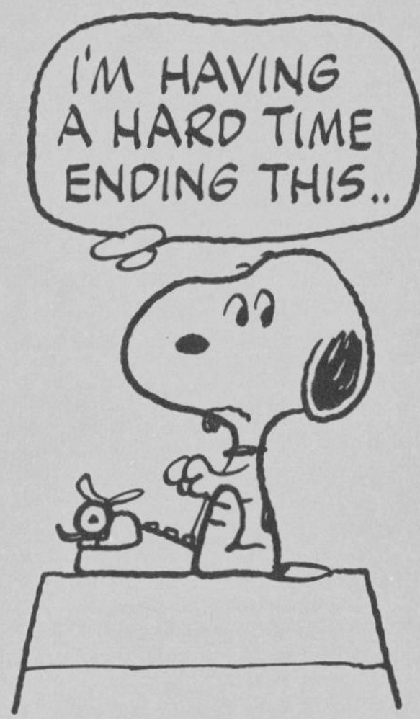
I'M HAVING A HARD TIME ENDING THIS..

They had named their Great Dane "Good Authority."
One day, she asked her husband if he had seen her belt.
"Belt?" he said. "Oh, I'm sorry. I thought it was a dog collar. I have it on Good Authority."
Shortly thereafter, their marriage began to go downhill.

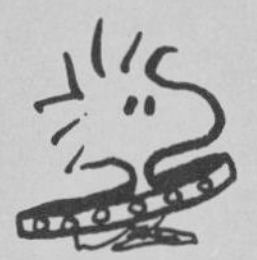

Immediately after he won the golf tournament, he was interviewed on TV.
"This is the most exciting moment of my life!" he said.
"I saw you on TV," said his wife. "I thought the day we got married was the most exciting moment of your life."
In the next tournament, he failed to make the cut.

"I love you," she said, and together they laughed. Then one day she said, "I hate you," and they cried. But not together.
The first time he saw her she was playing tennis.
"Ours was a Love Set," he said, "but we double-faulted."

A Love Story
by
Erich Beagle

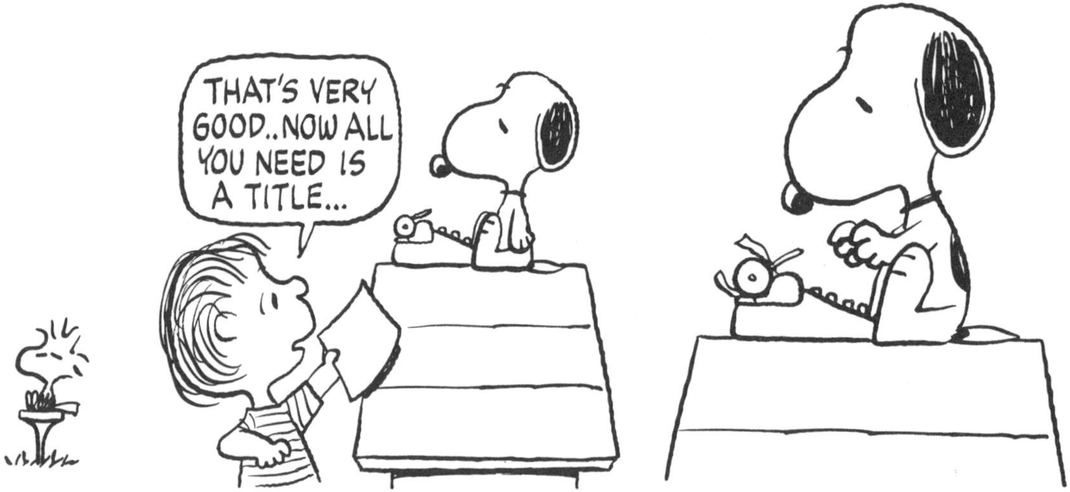
THAT'S VERY GOOD..NOW ALL YOU NEED IS A TITLE...

"Do you love me?" she asked.
"Of course," he said.
"Do you really love me?" she asked.
"Of course," he said.
"Do you really really love me?" she asked.
"No," he said.
"Do you love me?" she asked.
"Of course," he said.
So she asked no more.

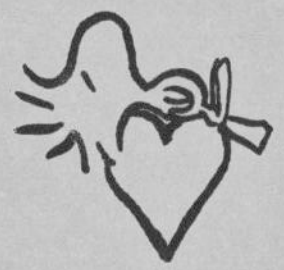

"Our love will last forever," he said.
"Oh, yes! yes! yes!" she cried.
"Forever being a relative term, however," he said.
She hit him with a ski pole.

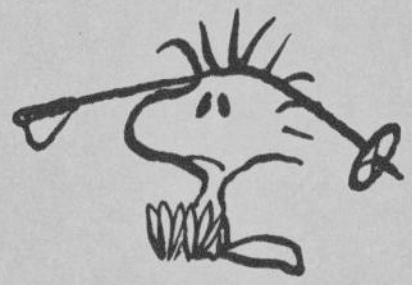

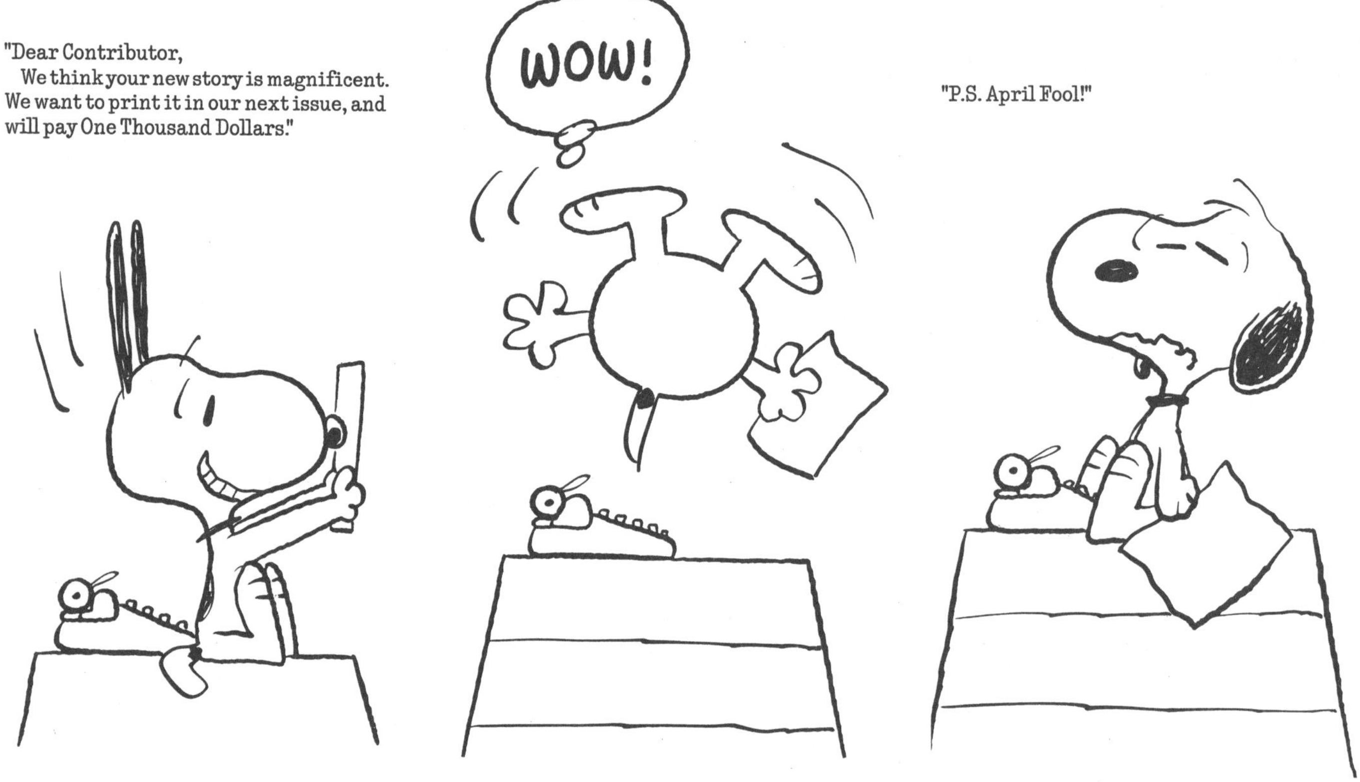
"Dear Contributor,
We think your new story is magnificent. We want to print it in our next issue, and will pay One Thousand Dollars."
WOW!
"P.S. April Fool!"

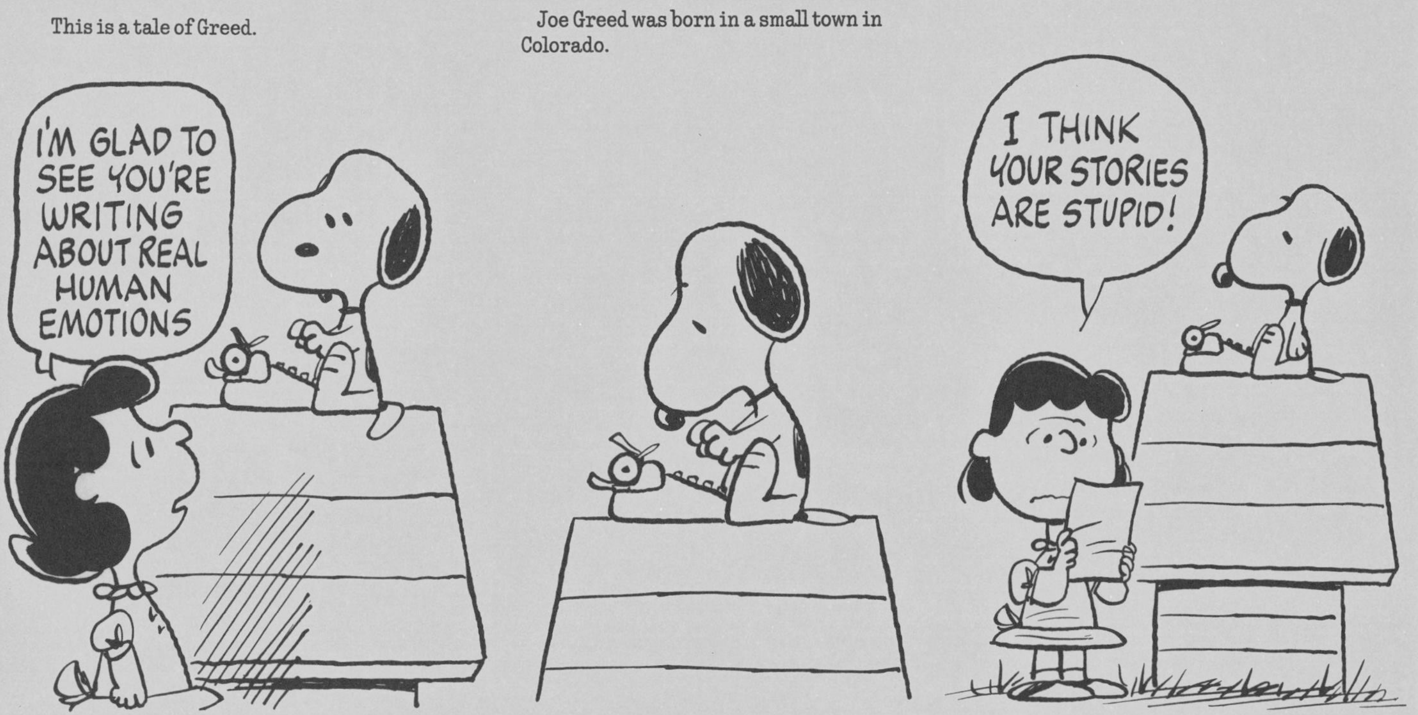

This is a tale of Greed.
I'M GLAD TO SEE YOU'RE WRITING ABOUT REAL HUMAN EMOTIONS
Joe Greed was born in a small town in Colorado.
I THINK YOUR STORIES ARE STUPID!

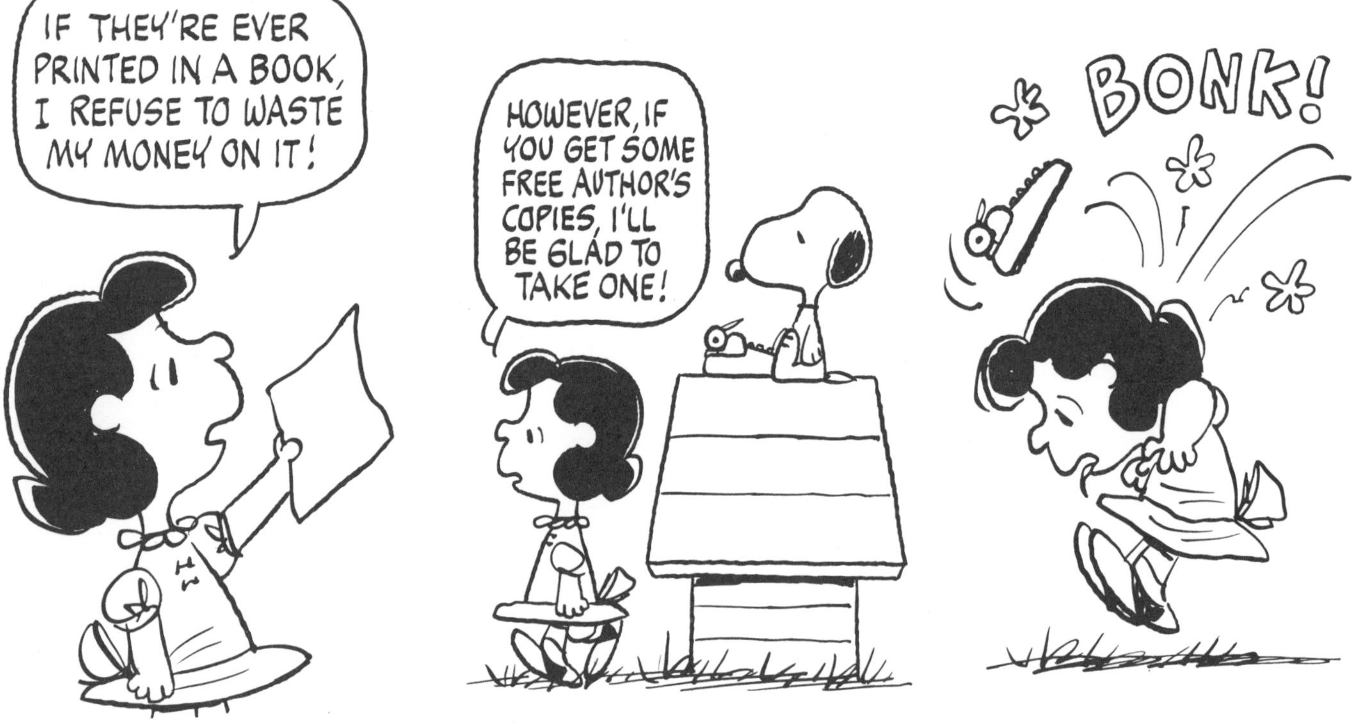
IF THEY'RE EVER PRINTED IN A BOOK, I REFUSE TO WASTE MY MONEY ON IT!
HOWEVER, IF YOU GET SOME FREE AUTHOR'S COPIES, I'LL BE GLAD TO TAKE ONE!
BONK!

To Whom It May Concern

Dear Whom:

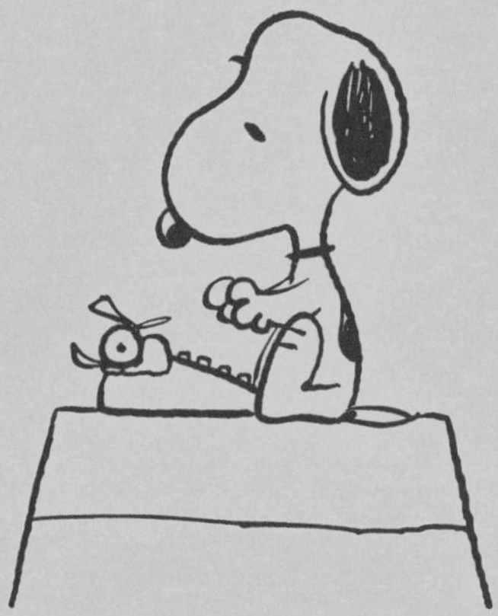

The Bunnies . . . A Tale of Mirth and Woe
"Ha Ha Ha," laughed the bunnies.
"Ha Ha Ha Ha Ha Ha Ha Ha Ha Ha"

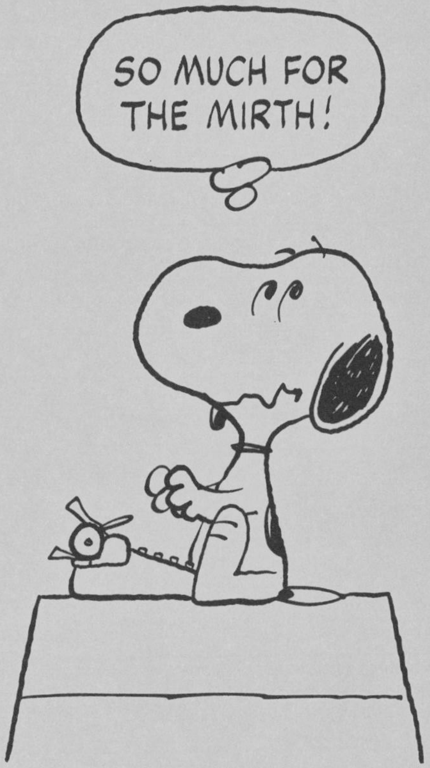
SO MUCH FOR THE MIRTH!

Joe Sportscar spent ten thousand dollars on a new twelve-cylinder Eloquent.

"You think more of that car than you do of me," complained his wife. "All you ever do these days is wax Eloquent!"

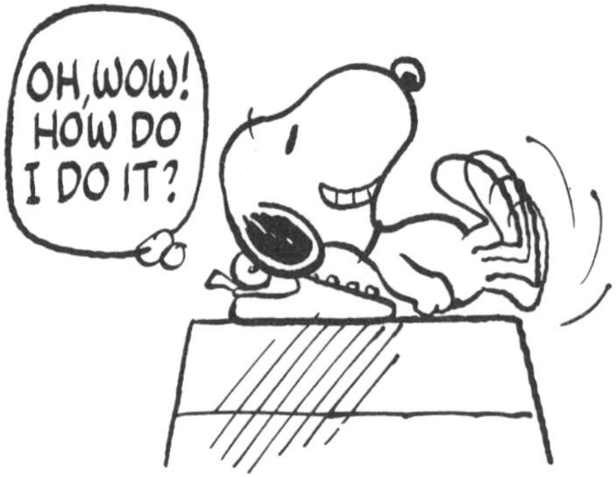
OH, WOW! HOW DO I DO IT?

This is the story of two mice who lived in a museum.

One evening after the museum had closed, the first mouse crawled into a huge suit of armor. Before he knew it, he was lost. "Help!" he shouted to his friend. "Help me make it through the knight!"

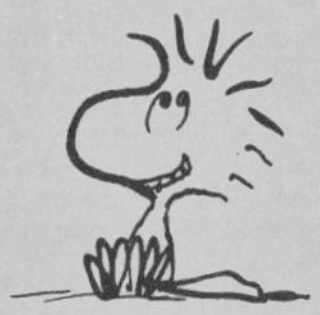

"Dear Contributor,

Thank you for submitting your story to our magazine. To save time, we are enclosing two rejection slips . . ."

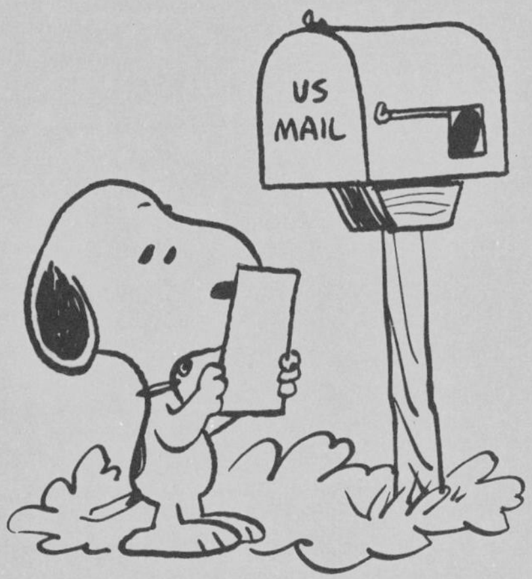
US
MAIL

"One for this story, and one for the next story you send us."

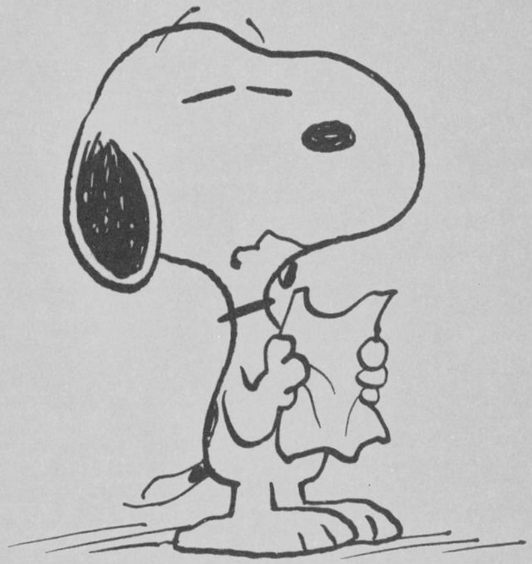

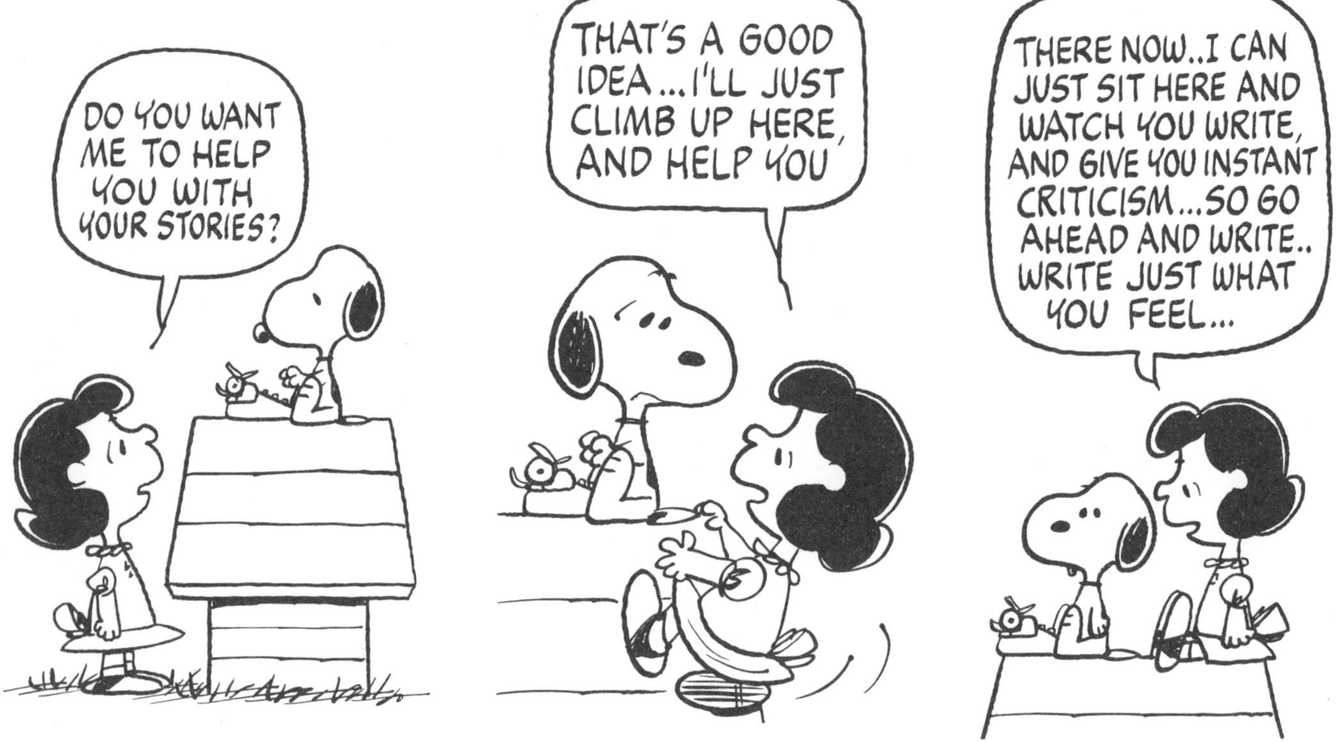
DO YOU WANT ME TO HELP YOU WITH YOUR STORIES?
THAT'S A GOOD IDEA ... I'LL JUST CLIMB UP HERE, AND HELP YOU
THERE NOW..I CAN JUST SIT HERE AND WATCH YOU WRITE, AND GIVE YOU INSTANT CRITICISM ... SO GO AHEAD AND WRITE.. WRITE JUST WHAT YOU FEEL...

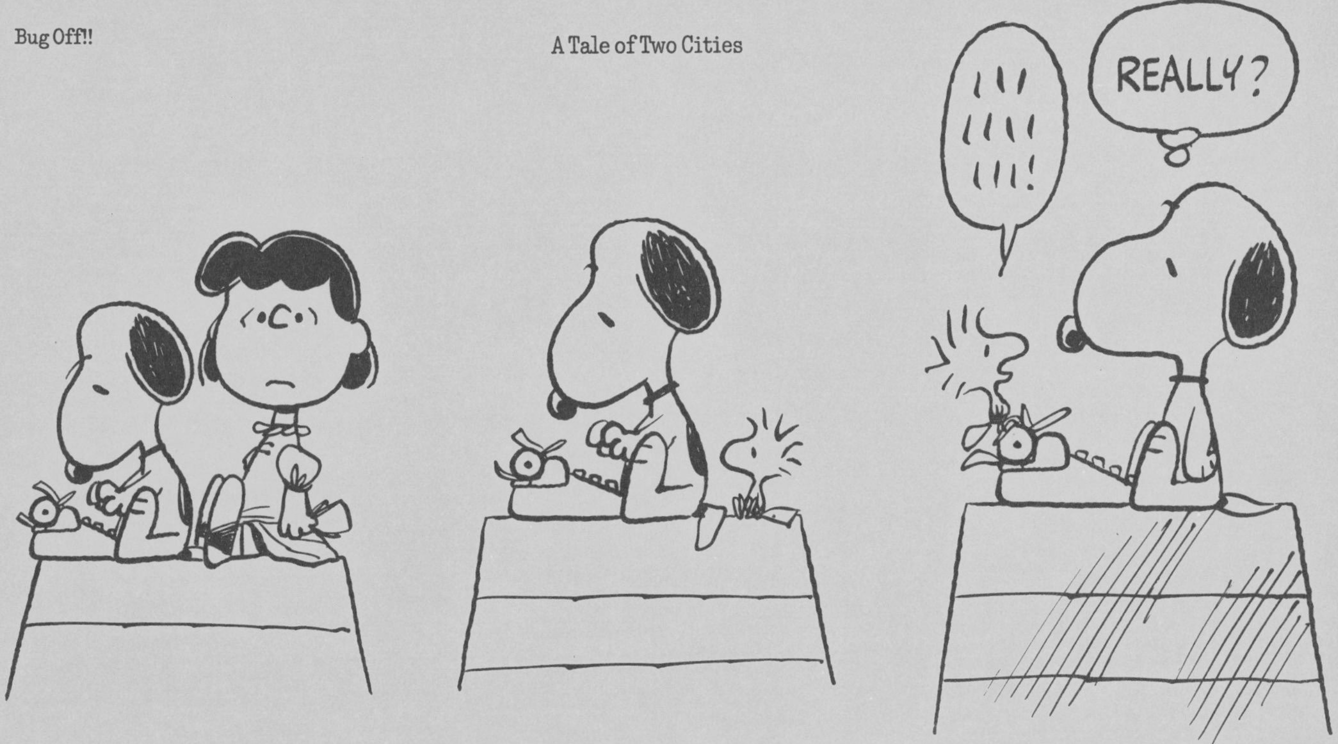
Bug Off!!
A Tale of Two Cities
REALLY?

Of Human Bondage

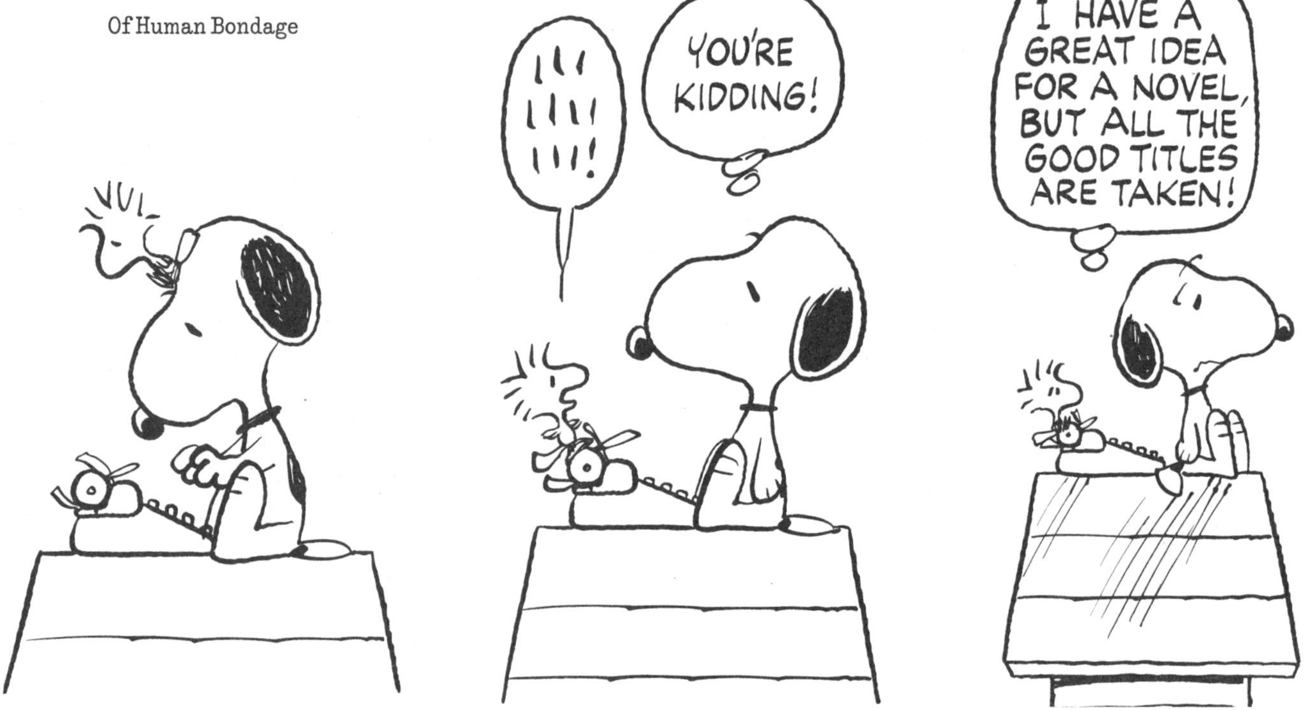

"Toodle-oo, Caribou!"
A Tale of the Frozen North

Other books by the author

It Was a Dark and Stormy Night

One morning Joe Eskimo went out to his barn to milk his polar cow. As he walked through the barn, tiny polar mice scampered across the frozen floor.

The stall was empty!

"Someone has stolen my polar cow!" shouted Joe Eskimo. "This is the work of Joe Jacket, who hates me!"

Joe Eskimo and Joe Jacket were rivals for the heart of Sally Snow who lived south of the iceberg. Joe Eskimo thought back to the night when he first shook her hand. Now, he was about to lose her.

Quickly, he harnessed his dog team and sped into town. He found Joe Jacket and Sally Snow sitting in a small café drinking polar tea.

"You'll never take Sally Snow away from me, you scoundrel!" shouted Joe Eskimo.

"And just what do you think you're going to do about it?" sneered Joe Jacket.

"Stop it, you two!" said Sally Snow. "You're creating a scene. I don't want to marry either of you. I've decided to join the Women's Tennis Tour. That's where the money is!"

"You don't know how to play tennis," said Joe Eskimo.

"I can learn, can't I? There's a pro out at the club who's giving group lessons. I'm going to sign up."

"Do you have a racket?" asked Joe Jacket.

"Of course," said Sally. "I bought one today."

"Wood or metal?"

"Wood, of course. I'm a traditionalist."

"Gut or nylon?"

"Gut, if you must know! And now, if you'll excuse me, I'm going to take my first lesson. Thank you for the polar tea. Toodle-oo, Caribou!"

Thus, Joe Eskimo and Joe Jacket became good friends, having been driven together by the same shattering blow. They worked the polar ranch together, and eventually became very wealthy.

Sally Snow went on to become only a mediocre player, for her volley was weak. After three years on the tour, she married an Australian who struck her from behind one day during a mixed-doubles match.

"When will you learn to stay on your side of the court?" he shouted.

Sally began to cry, and ran off to the locker room. That evening she took a plane to Vancouver. From her hotel room she placed a phone call to Joe Eskimo in Alaska.

"Hello, Joe? Is that you, Joe?" she sobbed.

"Which Joe do you want?"

"Which Joe?"

"Yes, there are two Joes living here. Which Joe do you wish to speak to?"

"Oh, forget it!" said Sally, and she hung up.

The snow began to fall gently past the window of her hotel room, and the lights of the city sparkled below. Sally lay back on the bed, sighed, and closed her eyes.

"Toodle-oo, Caribou!" she said.

Gentlemen,

I have just completed my new novel. It is so good, I am not even going to send it to you.

Why don't you just come and get it?

Gentlemen,

Yesterday, I waited all day for you to come and get my novel and to publish it, and make me rich and famous. You did not show up. Were you not feeling well?

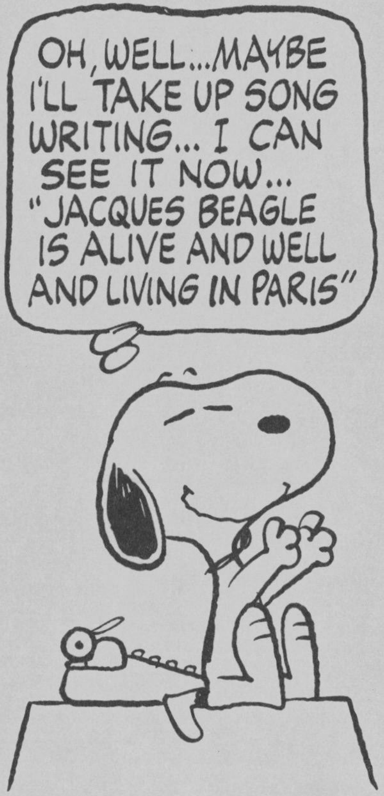
OH, WELL...MAYBE I'LL TAKE UP SONG WRITING... I CAN SEE IT NOW... "JACQUES BEAGLE IS ALIVE AND WELL AND LIVING IN PARIS"

THINGS I LEARNED

In 1981, Holt, Rinehart and Winston published *Things I Learned After It Was Too Late (And Other Minor Truths)*, which they followed up in 1984 with *Things I've Had To Learn Over and Over and Over (Plus a Few Minor Discoveries)*.

Things I've Had To Learn
Over And Over And Over
(Plus a Few Minor Discoveries)

Chatter is not conversation.

Don't waste too much effort on an English theme if there isn't going to be any media coverage.

Never jog on a golf course. You could run into a string of double bogeys.

The early bird need not
pursue the worm when he can
order pizza at midnight.

A hug is better than
all the theology in the world.

Candy bars are like years.
We're paying more,
but they're getting shorter.

How sharper than
a serpent's tooth
is a sister's "See?"

Stocking caps are great . . .
if you don't mind getting
your ears wrinkled.

If you don't got it,
you don't have it.

It's hard to tell everybody
they can go home
if nobody shows up.

Never try to visit the tree where you were born.

Small trophies are for hollow victories.

You can't discuss something with someone whose arguments are too narrow.

No one should be expected to solve a math problem that has a "twelve" in it.

The only time a dog gets complimented is when he doesn't do anything.

If they go on a cruise and don't get kissed, it's always the travel agent's fault.

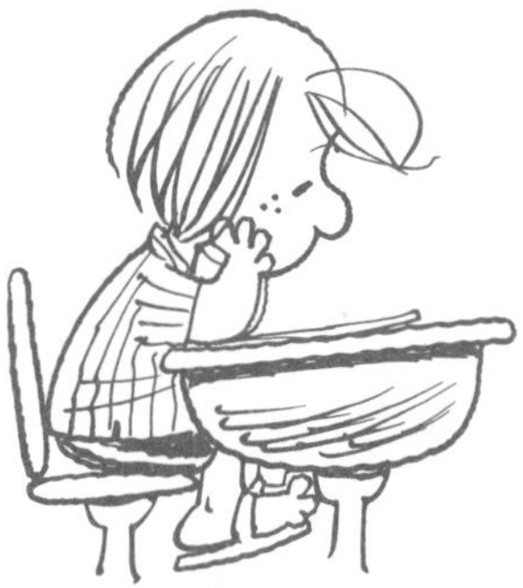

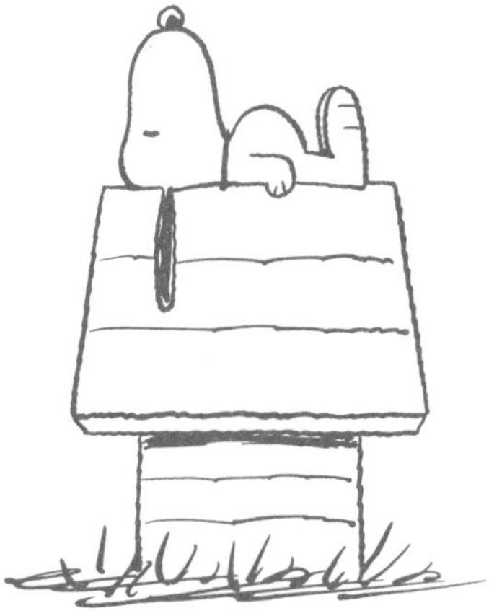

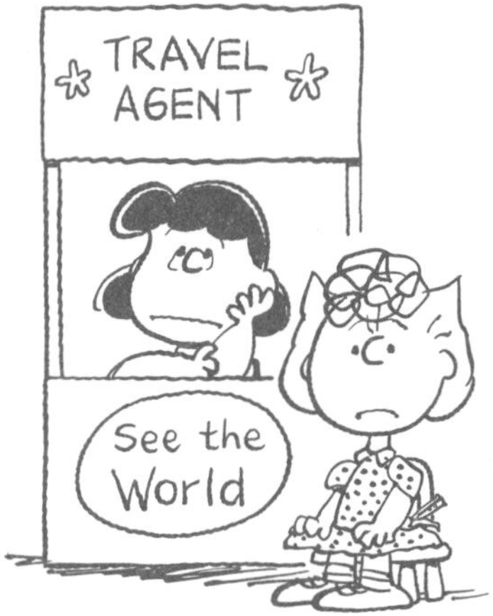
TRAVEL AGENT
See the World

**I'm not good at names,
but I never forget a slight.**

**You can't sulk in
a dining room chair.**

You can't eat compliments.

**Always get off the ice
before the Zamboni starts.**

Always turn out your closet light. Otherwise, you'll get up some morning and find you can't start your closet.

Never complain about the weather. . . . Whimper, but don't complain.

If they ask you to convert Fahrenheit to Celsius, remember that it's easier just to put on a sweater.

Seasick is bad,
carsick is bad . . .
nestsick is the worst.

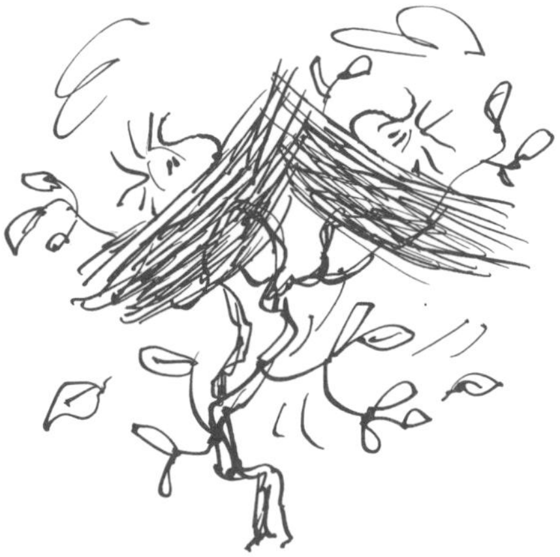

Education can be painful
if you get your finger
caught in your binder.

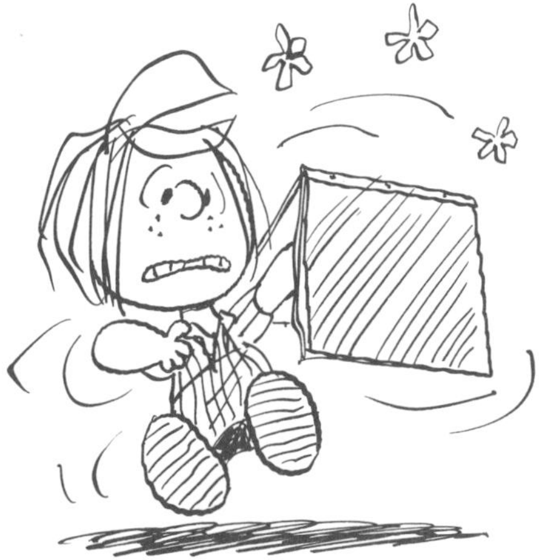

The pen may be mightier
than the sword,
but not a sister's mouth.

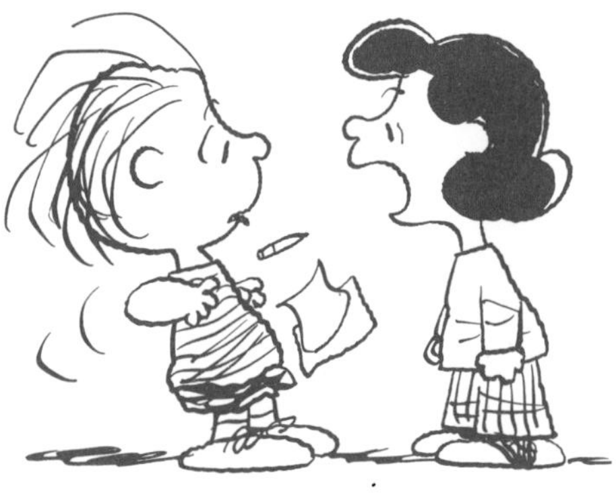

What are friends for if
you can't forget them?

If your life is going by
too fast, maybe someone
pushed the fast-forward button.

If life seems to have
more questions than answers,
try to be the one
who asks the questions.

MADAM FULLCHARGE

It's hard to sleep at night if you're worried that a ten-pound frog from Southern Cameroon may come and jump on your stomach.

Fat is not mature.

When you're waiting for your supper, a watched back door never opens.

Don't worry about the world
coming to an end today.
It's already tomorrow
in Australia.

It's too late to crawl
back into the egg.

When it's hot in the
classroom, and you fall asleep
at your desk, your math paper
sticks to your head.

Life is like a
ten-speed bicycle.
Most of us have
gears we never use.

Eating in the rain tends to cool down your pizza.

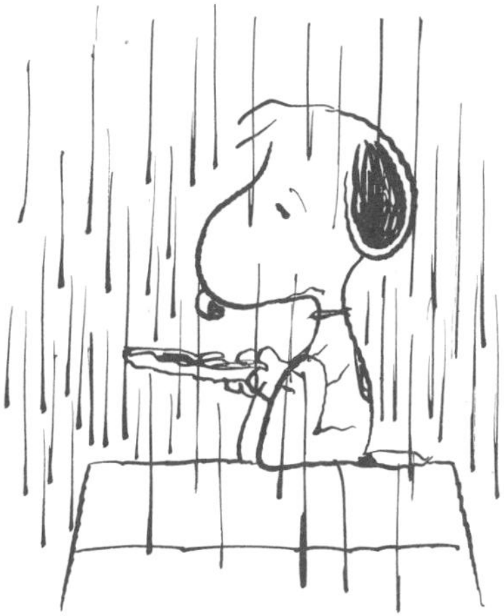

If life is like a baseball game, try to find out how many innings they're playing.

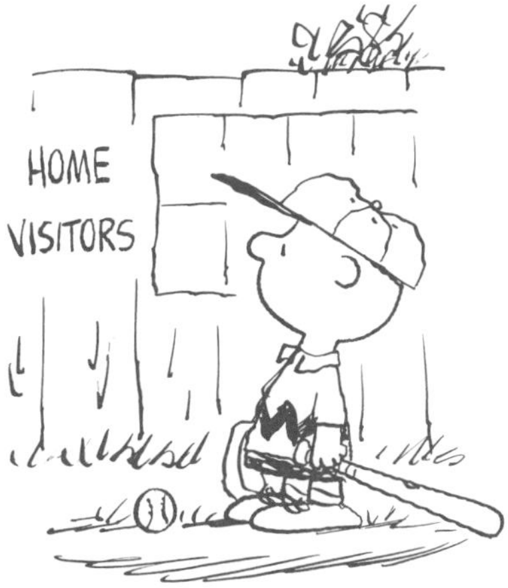
HOME
VISITORS

School can be very helpful, but, like a prescription, should be taken only as directed.

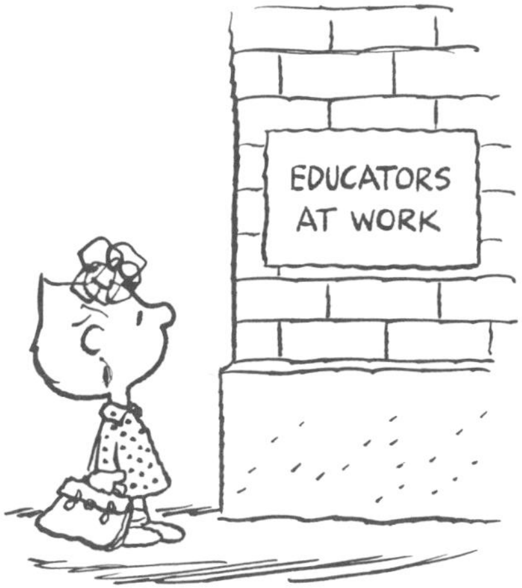
EDUCATORS AT WORK

They say we all have to
deal with the law from
the very day we're born . . .
so sue a baby!

If you're not sure she loves you,
blockhead her out of your mind.

The only real way to look younger
is not to be born so soon.

Most of us have to be
satisfied if we just
look good at a distance.

You know it's cold when you
can hear your feet coughing.

Those who believe in the
"balance of nature" are
those who don't get eaten.

Never neglect writing letters
of appreciation to someone
who has been good to you.

Dear Supper Dish,

You can't survive by sucking
the juice from a wet mitten.

Birthday presents from
Grandma are a problem.
The sweaters are too big
and the money is too small.

When lawyers say, "*sine mora*,"
they mean "without delay,"
but lawyers say a lot of things.

When you leave for the afternoon, be careful how your secretary signs your letters.

Life can be as full as a grocery cart . . . unless you have six items or less.

Decorate your home. It gives the illusion that your life is more interesting than it really is.

S/w
(Dictated, but not worth reading)

To avoid getting sick while
traveling, be careful what
you eat, and stay home.

It's not difficult to find
your way in the wilderness if
you remember that Hollywood is
in the West and the moon
is always over Hollywood.

A Christmas story should
always have a character in it
whom everyone can love.

Tiny Jim

What's good about hiking is there's no "offside."

Yelling at your brother three times is one more than the recommended daily allowance.

If you're busy, you don't have to answer the phone, and sleeping is busy.

Try to avoid
long good-byes.

Be thankful and drink
a toast to the man who
invented the roof.

And when all else fails,
blame it on the media.

Things I Learned After It Was Too Late
(And Other Minor Truths)

He who lives by the dirty rotten little drop shot dies by the dirty rotten little drop shot!

Nothing echoes like an empty mailbox.

Unfortunately, it's very hard to forget someone by drinking root beer!

Every time there's a good suggestion, someone brings up the budget!

All the best coaches are in the stands.

Subtraction is the awful feeling that you know less today than you did yesterday.

$$2,956 \\ -743$$

**My life is going by too fast....
My only hope is that
we go into overtime.**

**There's a lot more to life
than not watching TV!**

**The sins of the stomach
are visited unto the body.**

To stay warm in winter, insulate the ol' attic!

When you have to get up at 7:00, 6:59 is the worst time of day!

Joggers have to be careful— it's easy to run into a barbed comment!

**When no one loves you,
you have to pretend
that everyone loves you.**

Necks hate to exercise.
If necks were feet,
you'd never go anywhere.

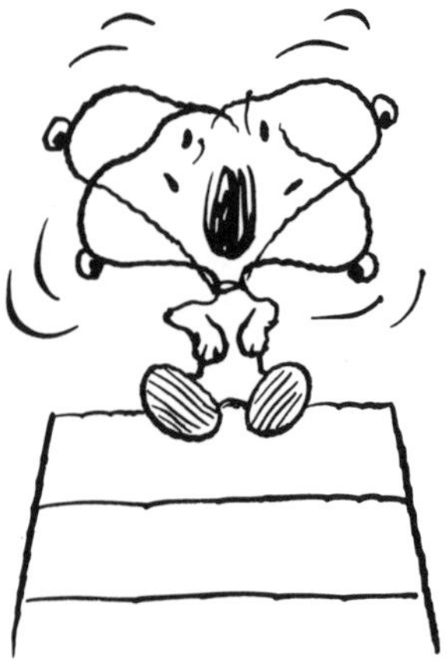

Summers always fly...
winters walk!

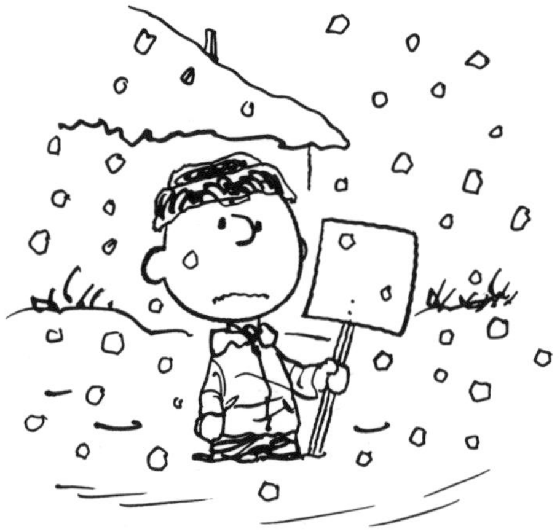

When you're depressed,
it helps to lean your head on
your arm and stare into space—
if you're unusually depressed,
you may have to change arms.

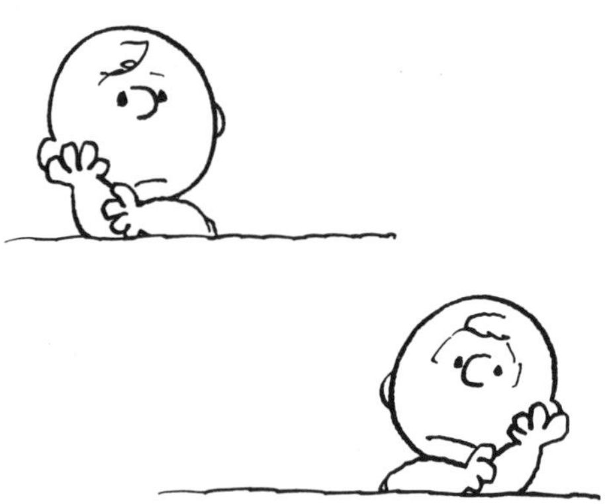

No matter how hard you try, you can't steer a dog dish!

The worst thing about swimming is crossing a hot parking lot!

If light travels so fast, how come the afternoons are so long?

**"How to grill a swordfish":
Ask him a lot of tough questions!**

**A good education is
the next best thing
to a pushy mother!**

**Feet are always mad
about something....**

As soon as I get up in the morning, I feel like I'm in over my head.

If you hold your hands upside down, you get the opposite of what you pray for.

The best trips are the kind where you can be home by noon.

**One of the great joys in life
is scarfing junk food!**

If no one answers the phone, dial louder.

You can't write a term paper before breakfast.

Never drop a box of sequins on a shag rug!

Never lie in bed at night asking yourself questions you can't answer....

There's nothing more embarrassing than barking up the wrong tree!

There's a difference between a philosophy and a bumper sticker!

HAVE A NICE DAY

**Keep an eye on your lunch box
so it doesn't get ripped off.**

**Life is easier if you only
dread one day at a time.**

**Ten minutes before you
go to a party is no time
to be learning to dance!**

Never ask your secretary to read something back.

Vitamin C does not keep you from getting wet!

Feet should stay awake in case you have to go some place in a hurry!

Mention marriage to a musician, and you get drowned out!

No matter how hard you try, you can't build a rainman.

A watched supper dish never fills.

**No book on psychology
can be any good if
you can understand it!**

**Classes can ruin
your grade average!**

**Lovers don't send
form letters.**

**I'm always sure about things
that are a matter of opinion.**

The late bird does not even catch the late worm!

One thing I've learned about algebra: Don't take it too seriously.

It's impossible to be gloomy when you're sitting behind a marshmallow.

$a(b \cdot c) = ab - ac$

**Sidewalks always win...
knees always lose!**

**A thumb tastes best
at room temperature!**

**"Quiet beauty" is nice
to have, but it should
speak up now and then.**

**Never share your pad
with a restless bird!**

**Being crabby all day
makes you hungry.**

**When we lose, I'm miserable....
When we win, I feel guilty!**

**I would have won,
but I got off to a bad finish!**

**Life is like an ice cream cone:
You have to learn to lick it!**

**Don't blame people
who are born with crabby genes.**

It's always difficult to talk
from one generation to another.

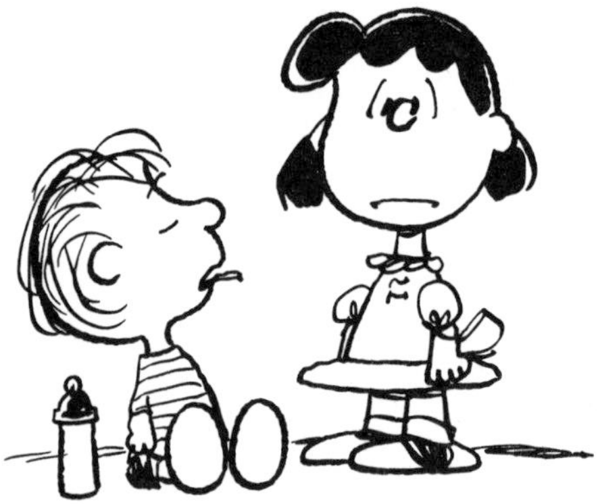

It's all right to look interested,
but looking bored
is easier on the eyes....

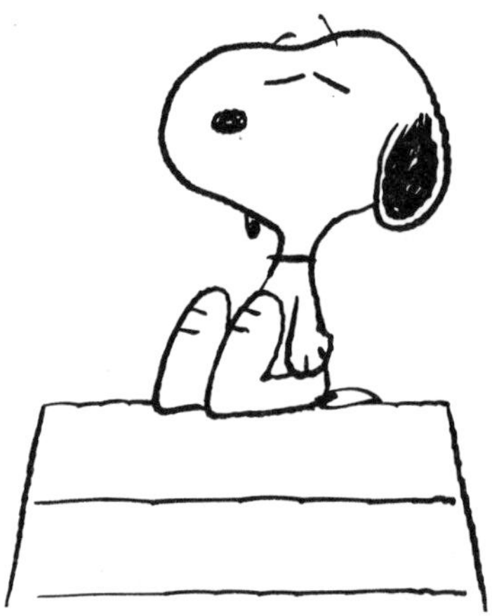

The secret to life is
to be in the right room!

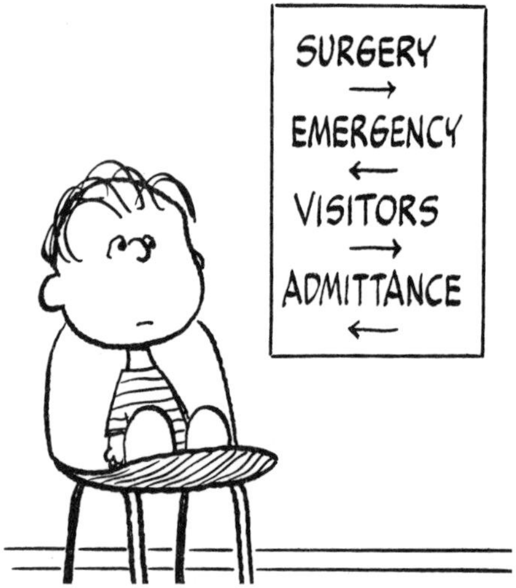
SURGERY →
EMERGENCY ←
VISITORS →
ADMITTANCE ←

**Life is full of choices,
but you never get any!**

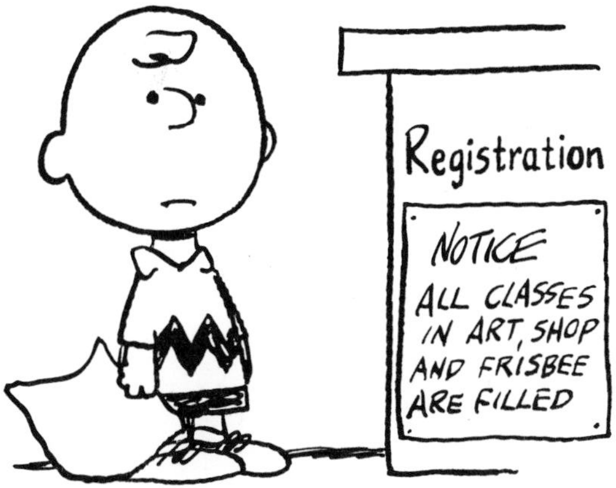

Registration
NOTICE
ALL CLASSES IN ART, SHOP AND FRISBEE ARE FILLED

GOLF

Schulz gave the world of golf a lot of attention. He created a stream of single-panel cartoons and illustrations for the programs for the Bing Crosby Pro-Am golf tournament (in which he also played), for golf associations, and for books.

    Snoopy's Grand Slam, published in 1972, contains the material you see here (some of which originally appeared in golf tournament programs while other parts were new), plus an April 1968 strip sequence about Snoopy playing in the Masters.

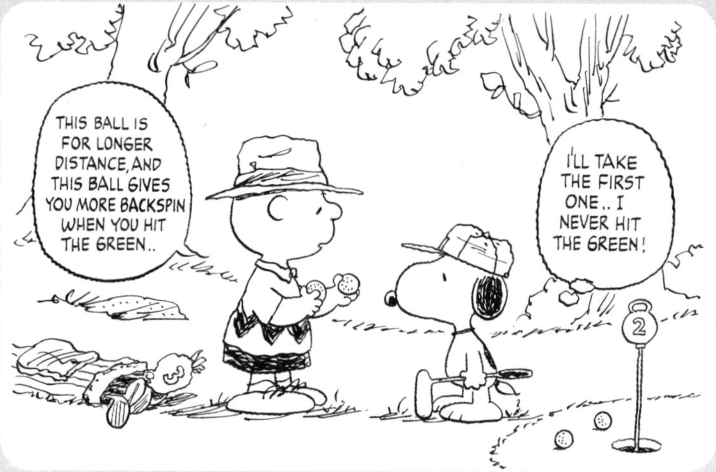

THIS BALL IS FOR LONGER DISTANCE, AND THIS BALL GIVES YOU MORE BACKSPIN WHEN YOU HIT THE GREEN..
I'LL TAKE THE FIRST ONE.. I NEVER HIT THE GREEN!
2

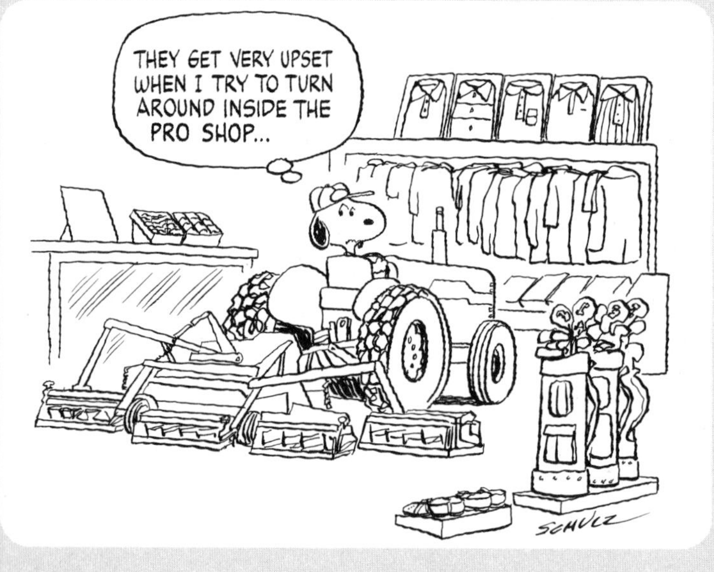

THEY GET VERY UPSET WHEN I TRY TO TURN AROUND INSIDE THE PRO SHOP...
SCHULZ

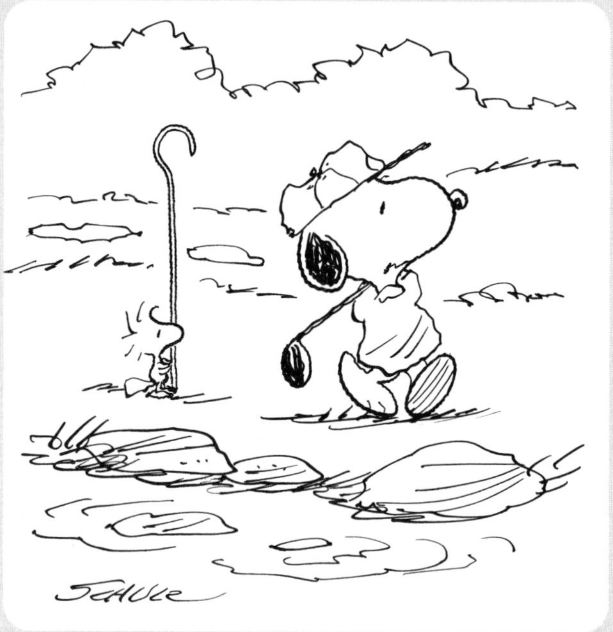

SCHULZ

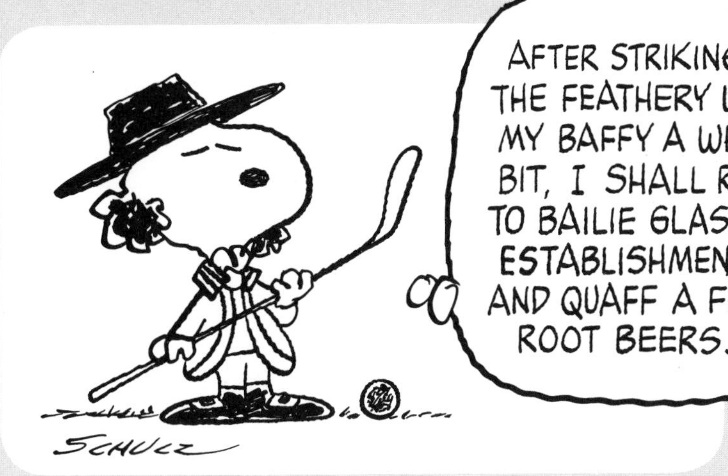
AFTER STRIKING THE FEATHERY WITH MY BAFFY A WEE BIT, I SHALL REPAIR TO BAILIE GLASS'S ESTABLISHMENT, AND QUAFF A FEW ROOT BEERS...
SCHULZ

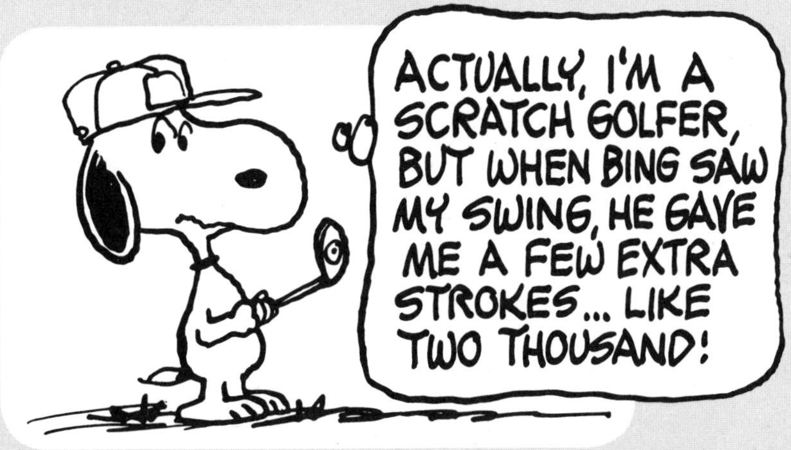
ACTUALLY, I'M A SCRATCH GOLFER, BUT WHEN BING SAW MY SWING, HE GAVE ME A FEW EXTRA STROKES... LIKE TWO THOUSAND!

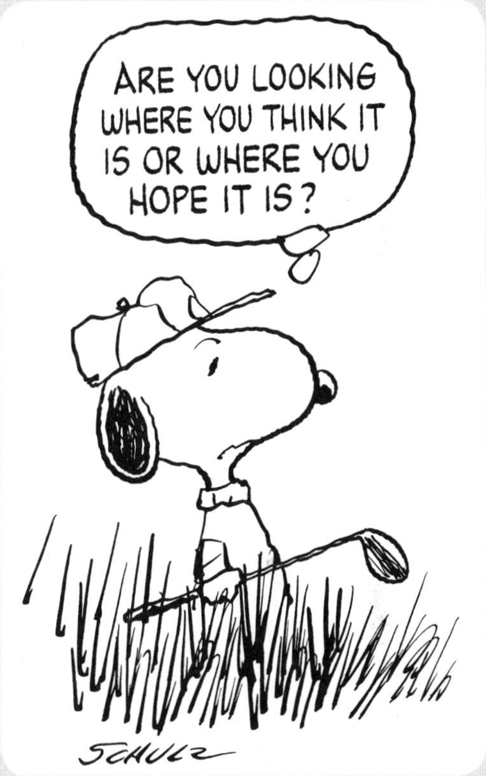
ARE YOU LOOKING WHERE YOU THINK IT IS OR WHERE YOU HOPE IT IS?
SCHULZ

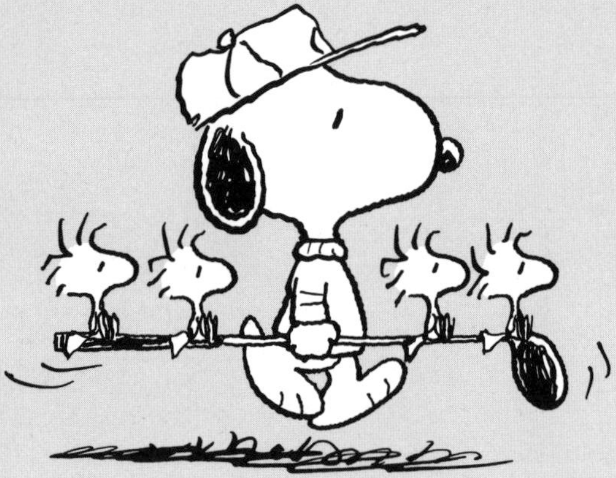

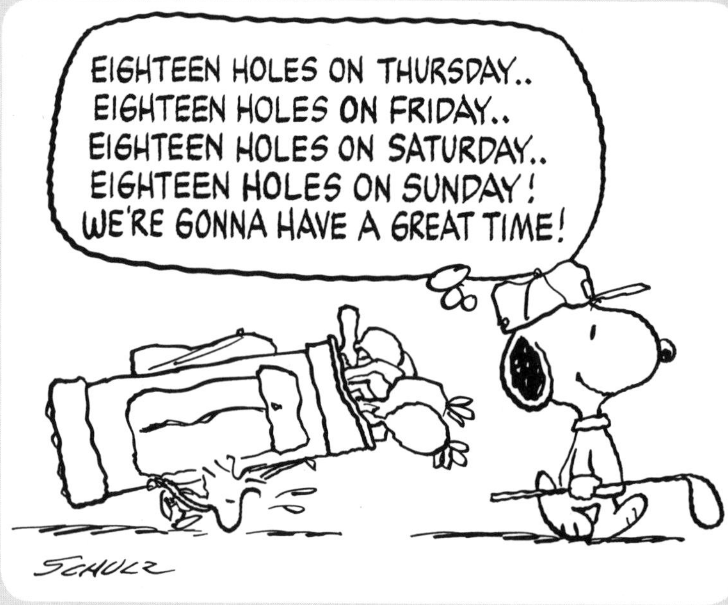
EIGHTEEN HOLES ON THURSDAY..
EIGHTEEN HOLES ON FRIDAY..
EIGHTEEN HOLES ON SATURDAY..
EIGHTEEN HOLES ON SUNDAY!
WE'RE GONNA HAVE A GREAT TIME!
SCHULZ

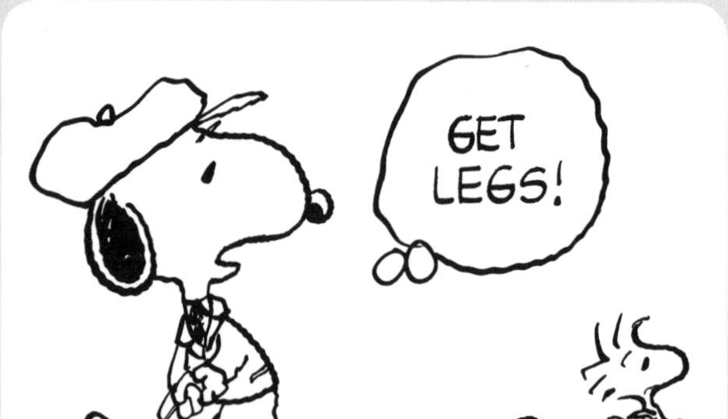
GET LEGS!
SCHULZ

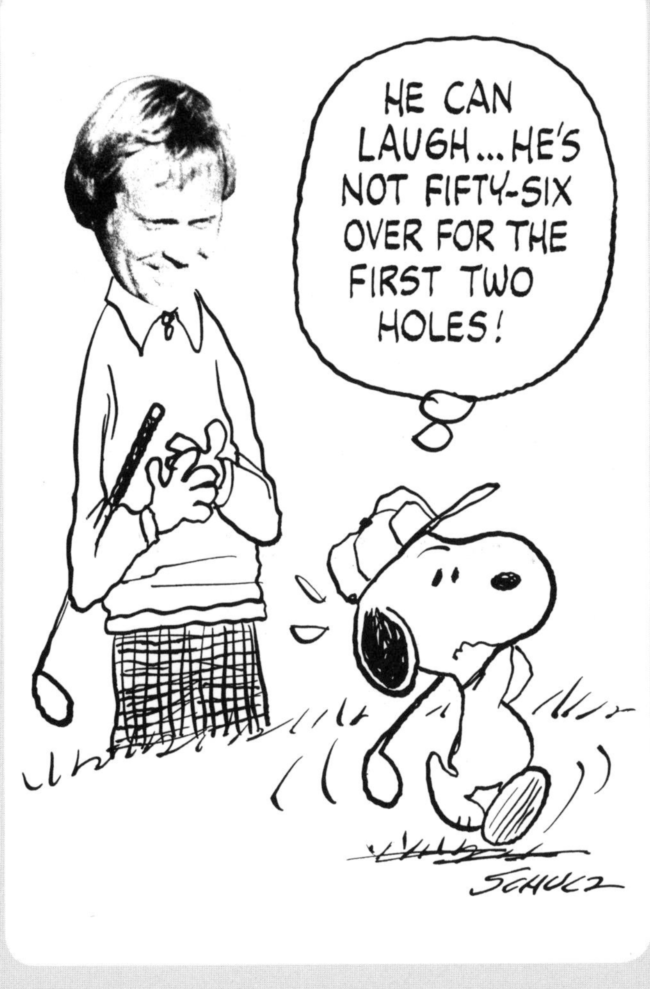
HE CAN LAUGH...HE'S NOT FIFTY-SIX OVER FOR THE FIRST TWO HOLES!
SCHULZ

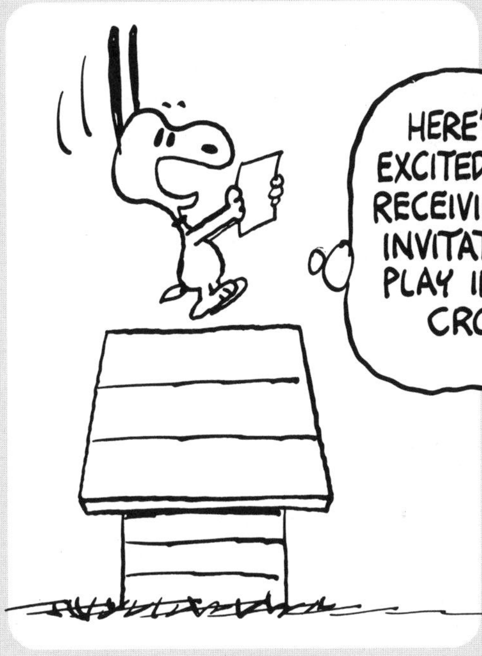
HERE'S THE EXCITED AMATUER RECEIVING HIS INVITATION TO PLAY IN THE CROSBY..

Happiness is not cutting the ball after topping a nine-iron.

Happiness is when your pro says "You sure saved us on that hole, Partner!"

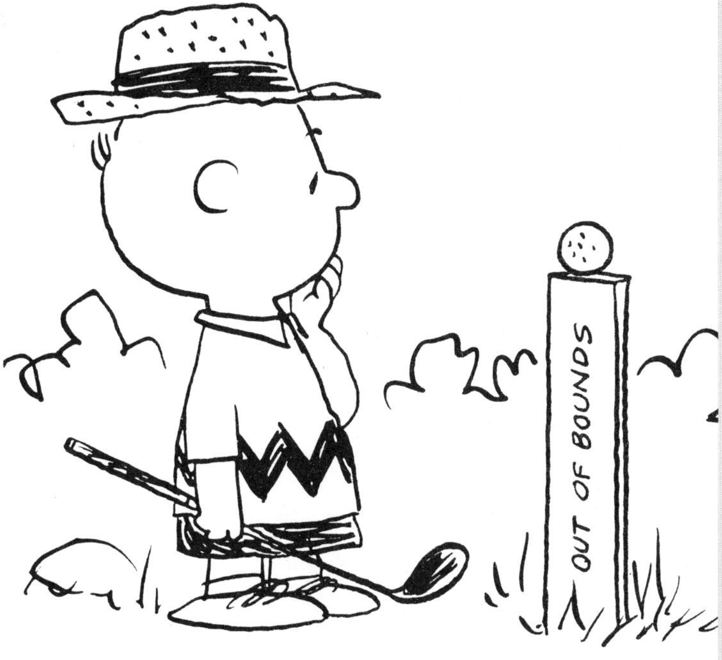
OUT OF BOUNDS

Happiness is discovering you're not "Out of Bounds" after all.

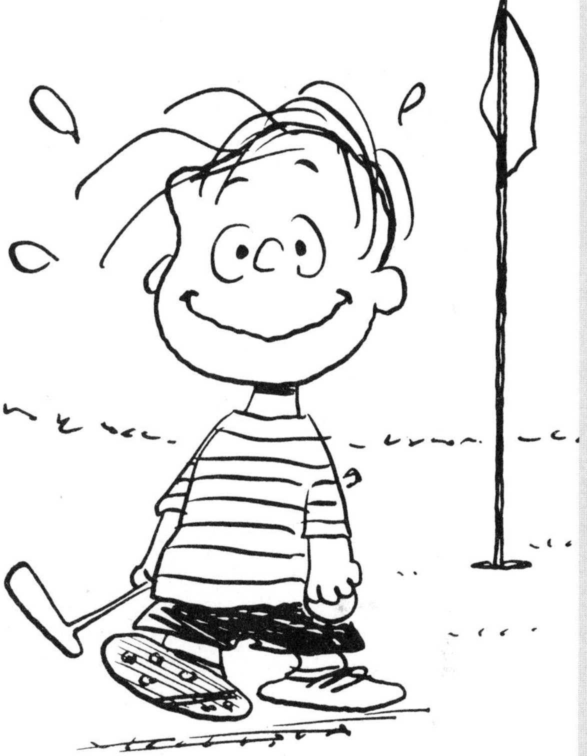

Happiness is getting past the eighth and ninth holes at Pebble Beach without botching the whole round.

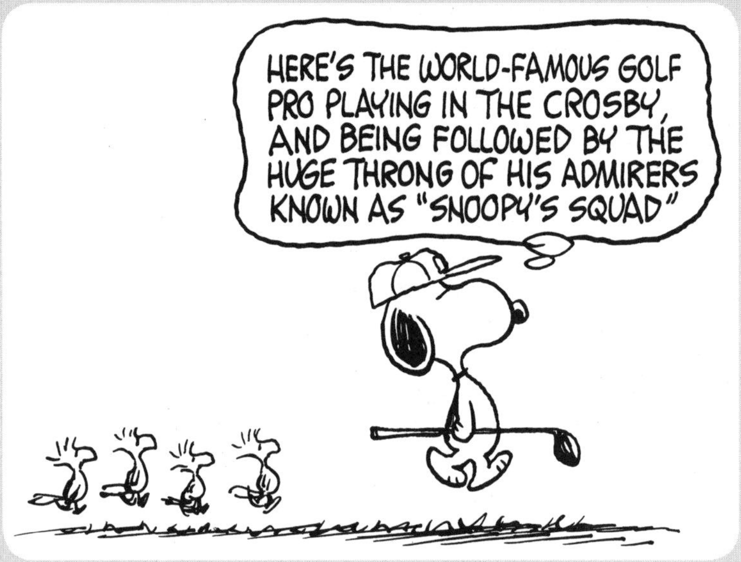
HERE'S THE WORLD-FAMOUS GOLF PRO PLAYING IN THE CROSBY, AND BEING FOLLOWED BY THE HUGE THRONG OF HIS ADMIRERS KNOWN AS "SNOOPY'S SQUAD"

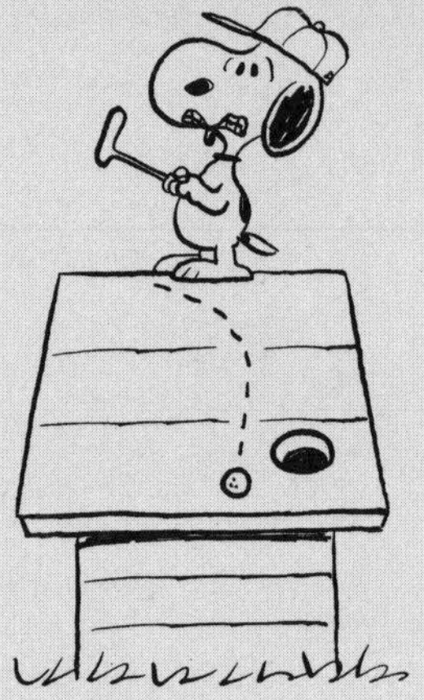

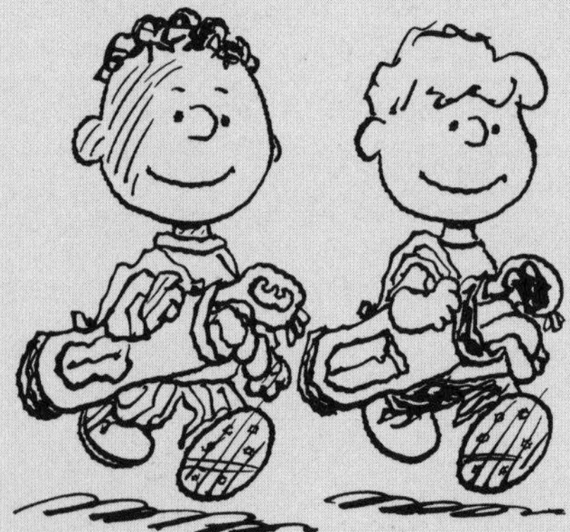

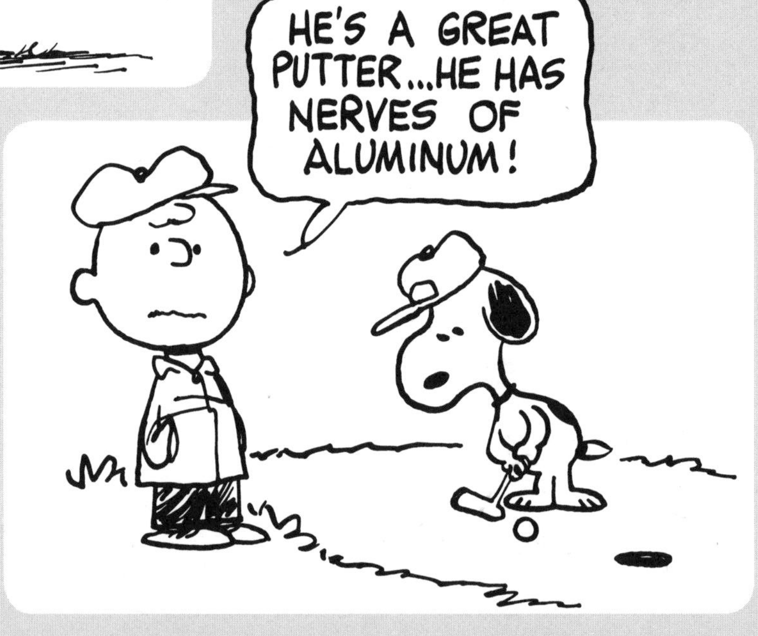
HE'S A GREAT PUTTER...HE HAS NERVES OF ALUMINUM!

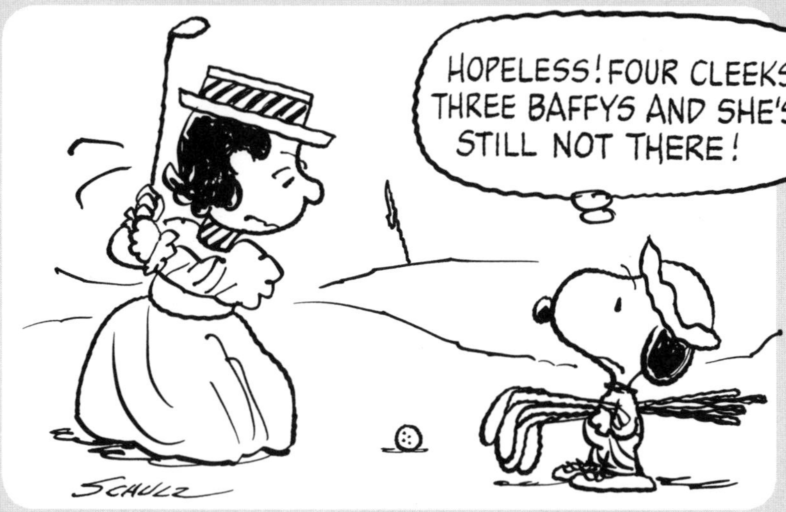
HOPELESS! FOUR CLEEKS, THREE BAFFYS AND SHE'S STILL NOT THERE!
SCHULZ

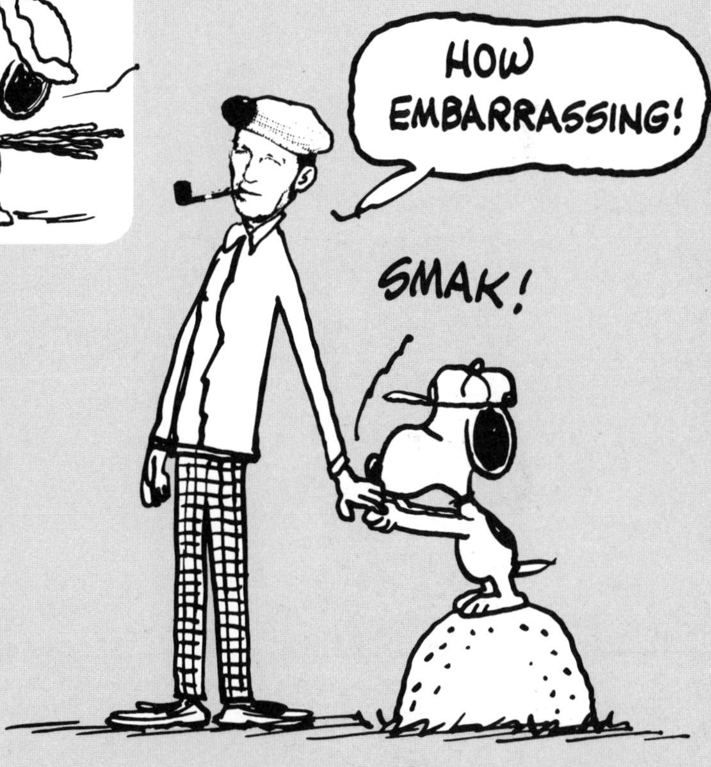
HOW EMBARRASSING!
SMAK!

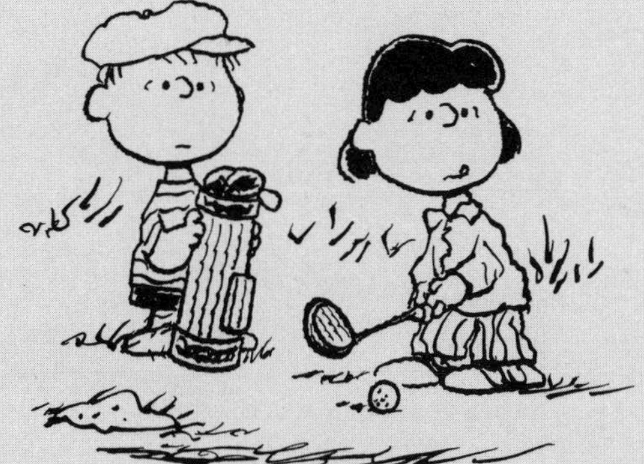

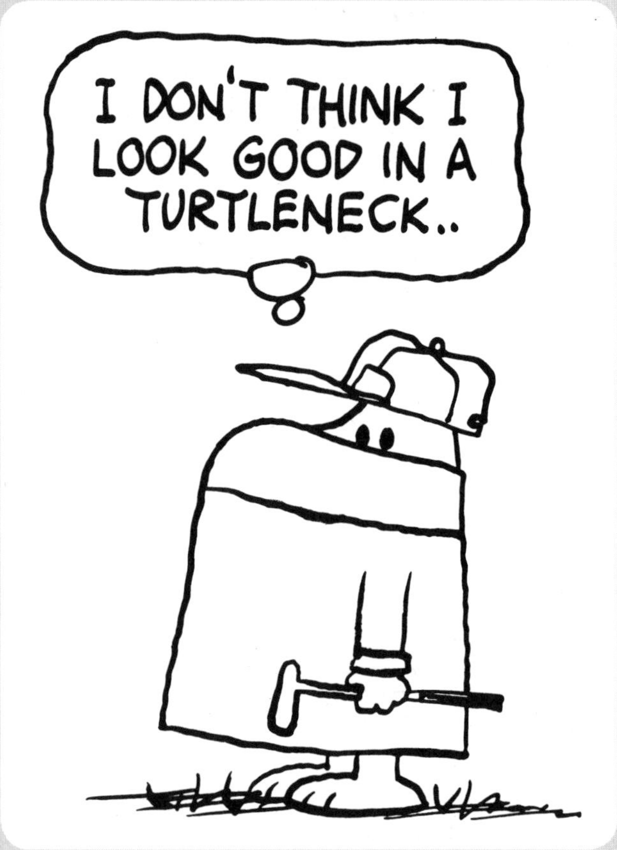
I DON'T THINK I LOOK GOOD IN A TURTLENECK..

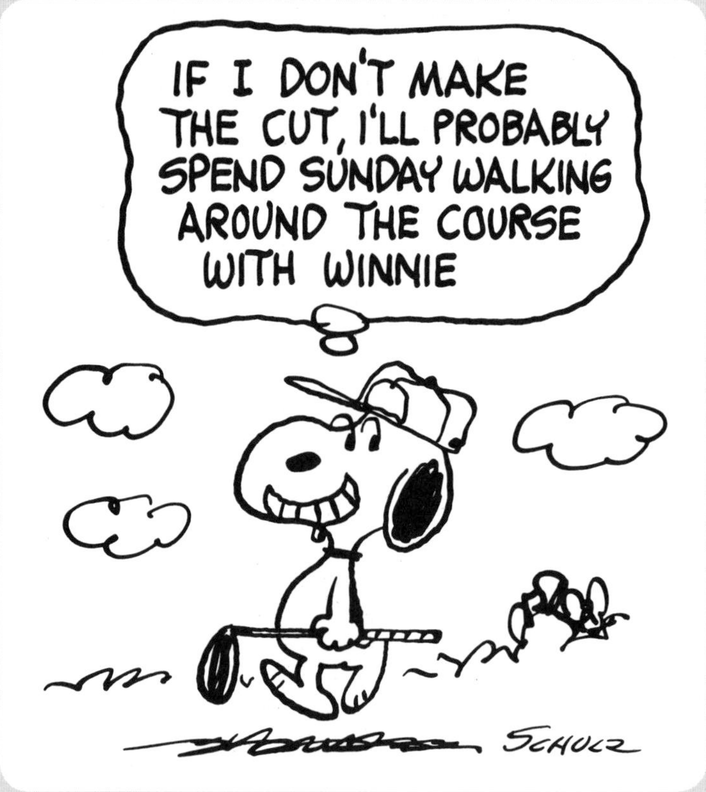
IF I DON'T MAKE THE CUT, I'LL PROBABLY SPEND SUNDAY WALKING AROUND THE COURSE WITH WINNIE
SCHULZ

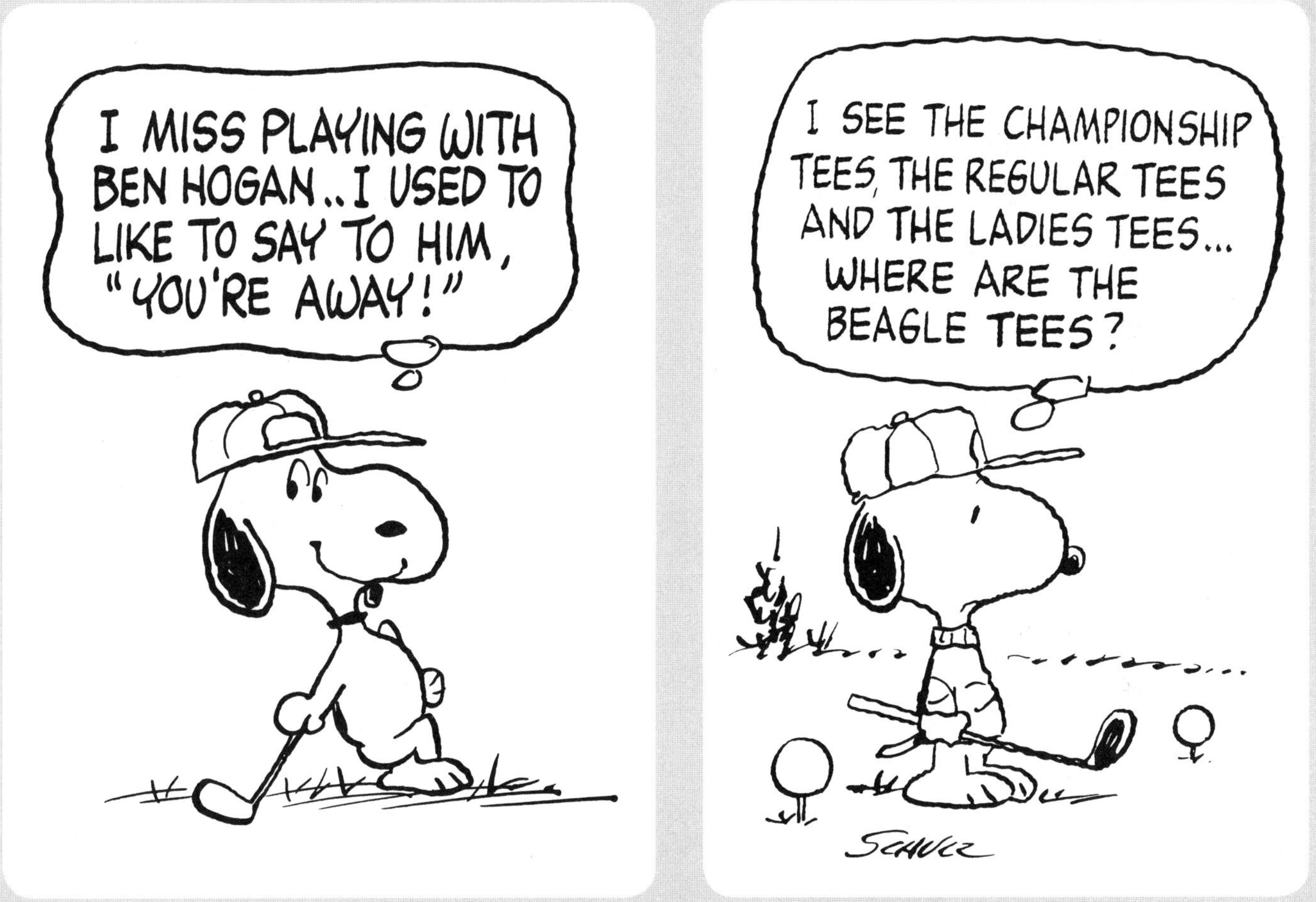
I MISS PLAYING WITH BEN HOGAN..I USED TO LIKE TO SAY TO HIM, "YOU'RE AWAY!"
I SEE THE CHAMPIONSHIP TEES, THE REGULAR TEES AND THE LADIES TEES... WHERE ARE THE BEAGLE TEES?
SCHULZ

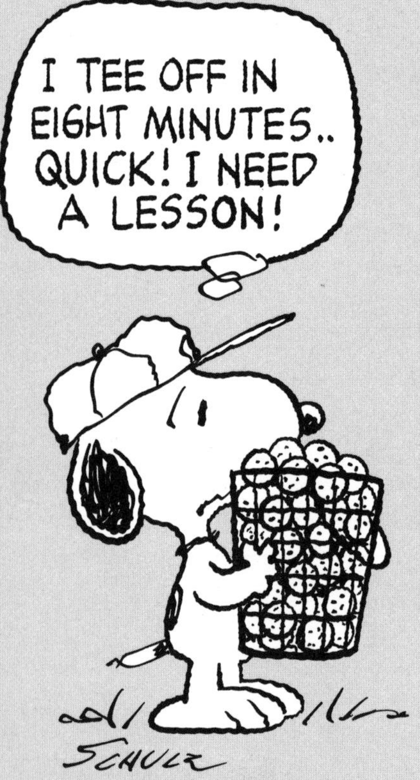
I TEE OFF IN EIGHT MINUTES.. QUICK! I NEED A LESSON!
SCHULZ

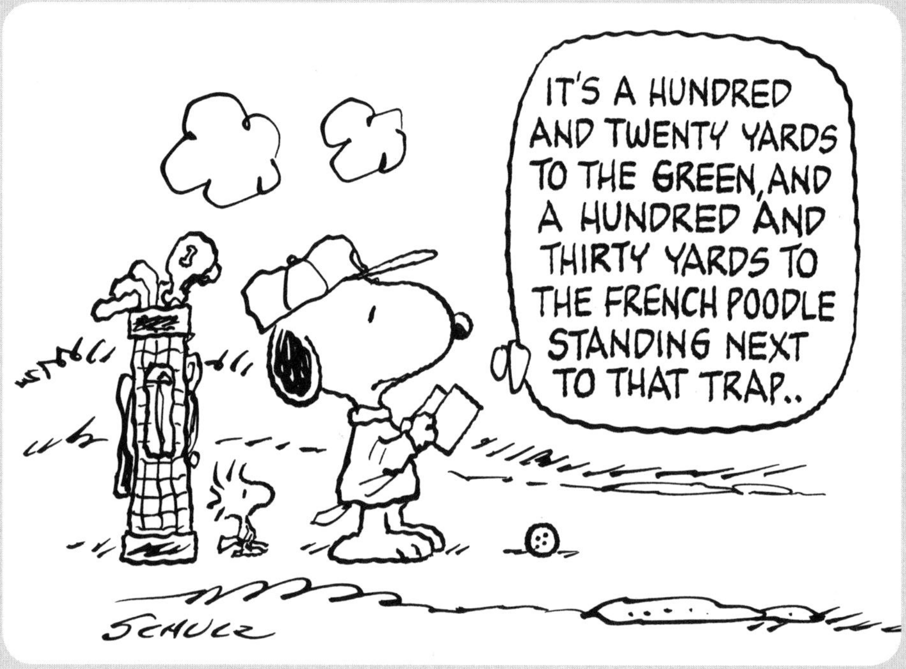
IT'S A HUNDRED AND TWENTY YARDS TO THE GREEN, AND A HUNDRED AND THIRTY YARDS TO THE FRENCH POODLE STANDING NEXT TO THAT TRAP..
SCHULZ

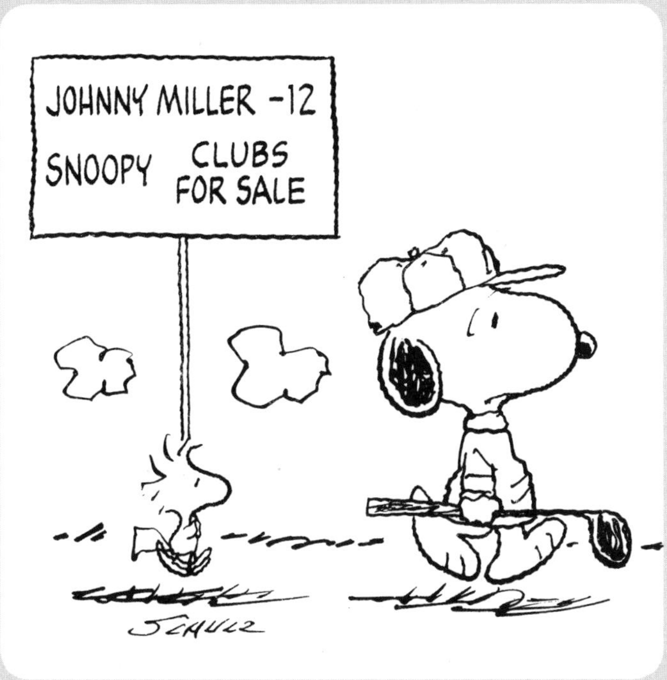
JOHNNY MILLER -12
SNOOPY CLUBS FOR SALE
SCHULZ

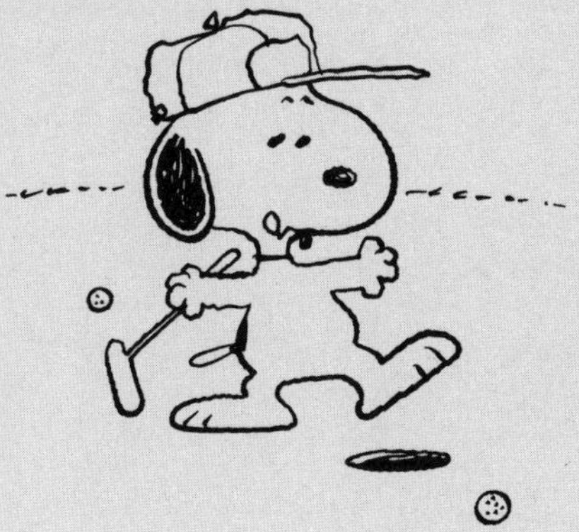

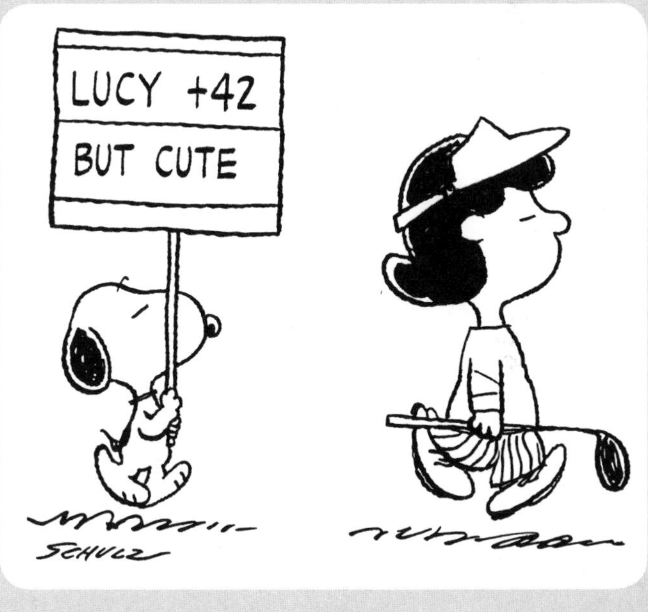
LUCY +42
BUT CUTE
SCHULZ

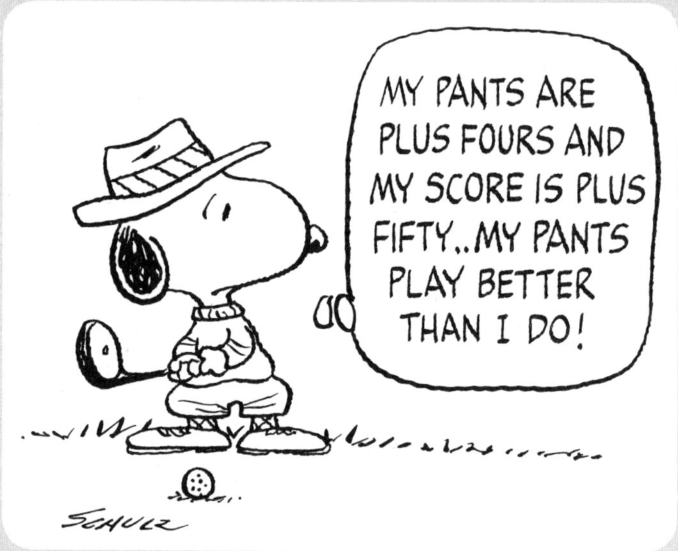
MY PANTS ARE PLUS FOURS AND MY SCORE IS PLUS FIFTY..MY PANTS PLAY BETTER THAN I DO!
SCHULZ

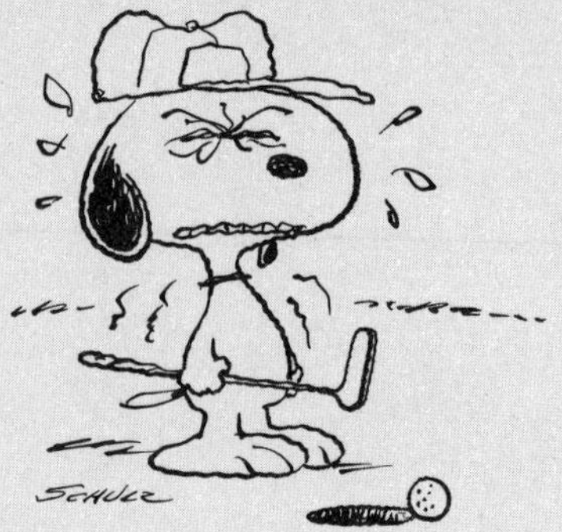
SCHULZ

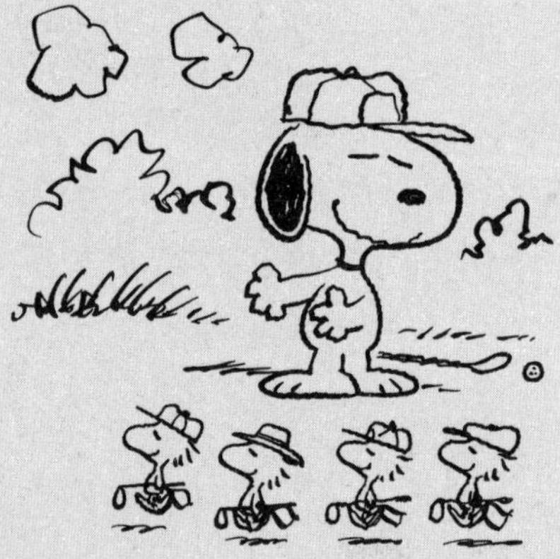

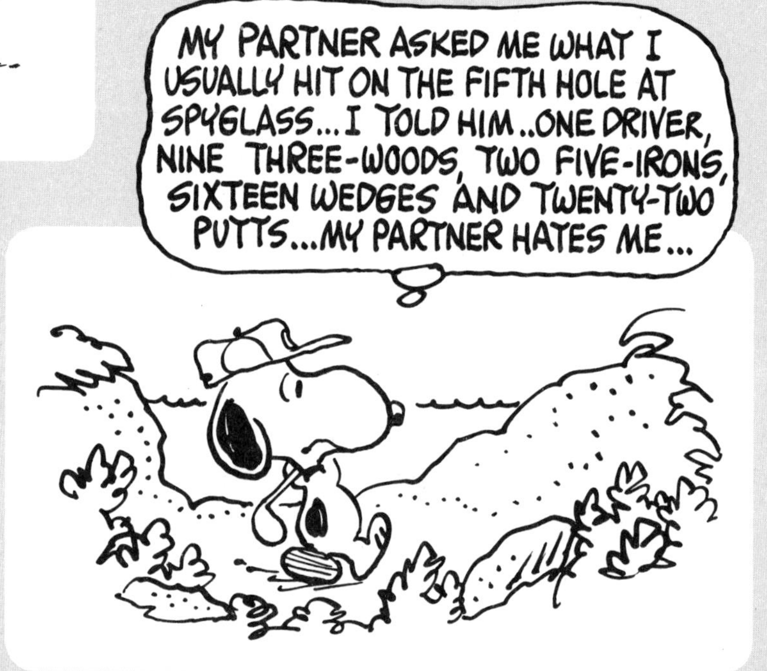
MY PARTNER ASKED ME WHAT I USUALLY HIT ON THE FIFTH HOLE AT SPYGLASS...I TOLD HIM..ONE DRIVER, NINE THREE-WOODS, TWO FIVE-IRONS, SIXTEEN WEDGES AND TWENTY-TWO PUTTS...MY PARTNER HATES ME...

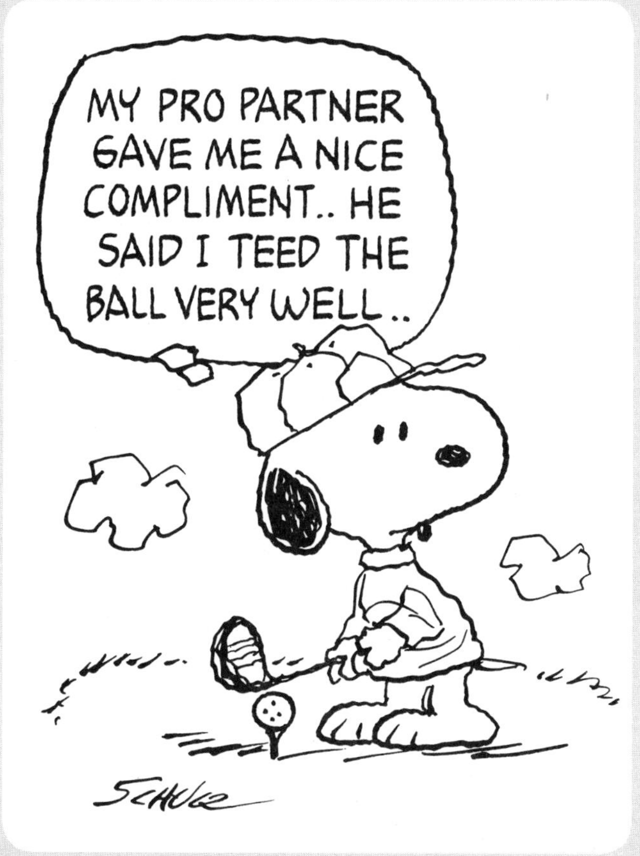
MY PRO PARTNER GAVE ME A NICE COMPLIMENT.. HE SAID I TEED THE BALL VERY WELL..
SCHULZ

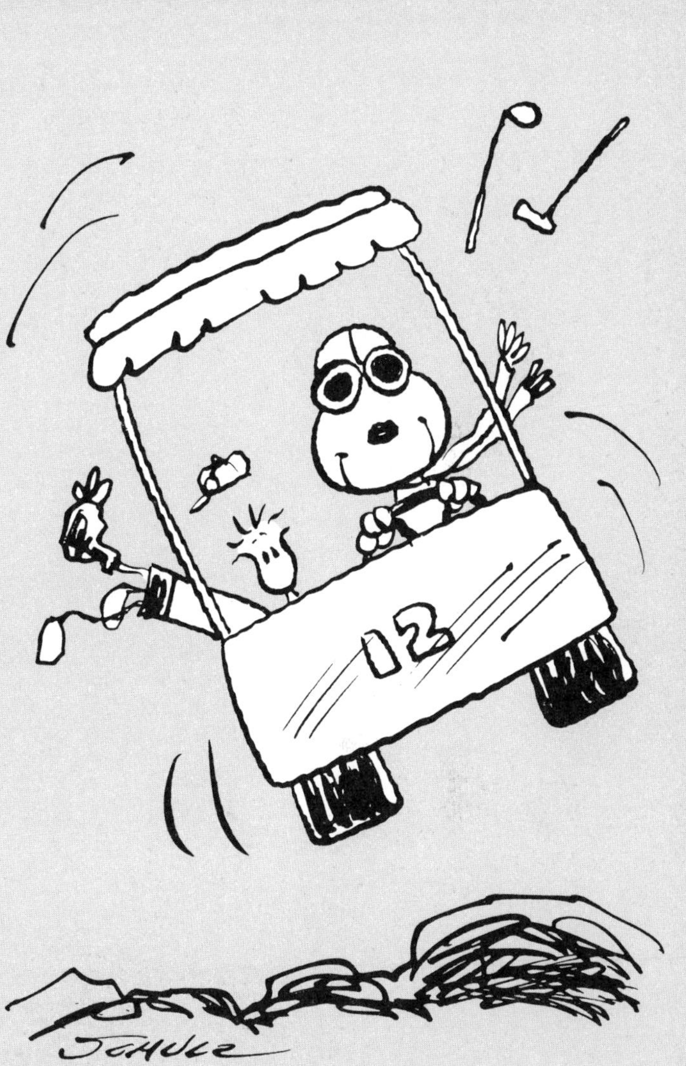
12
SCHULZ

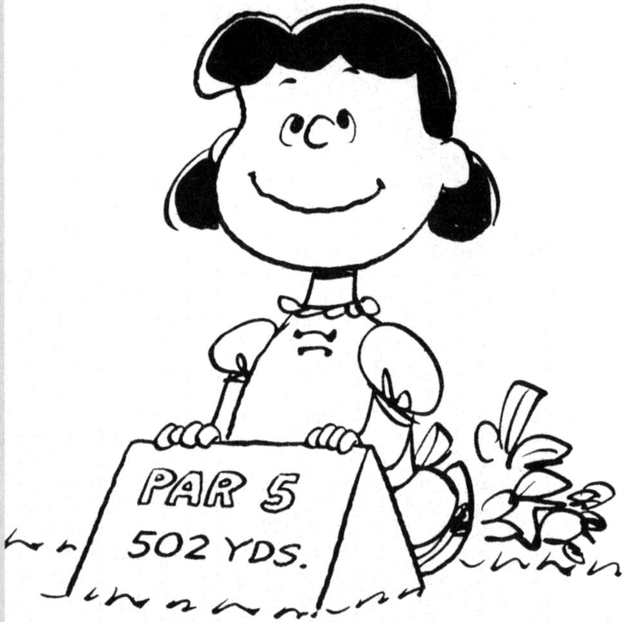
PAR 5
502 YDS.

Security is being the first spectator to the tee when Arnold Palmer drives.

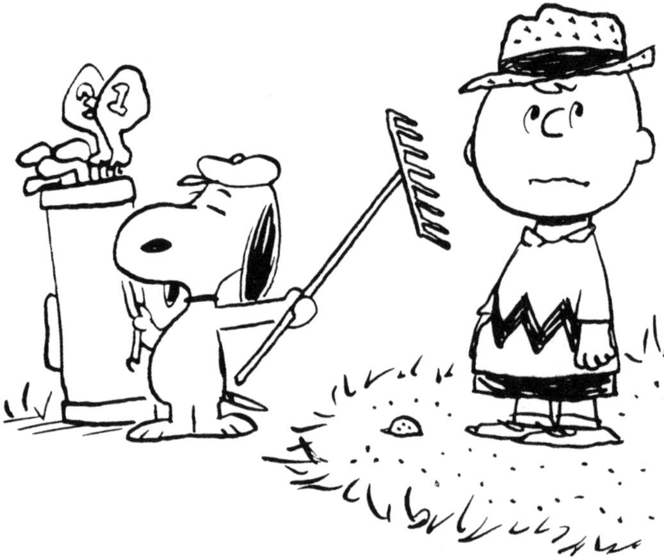

Security is having a caddy who knows just what club you should use.

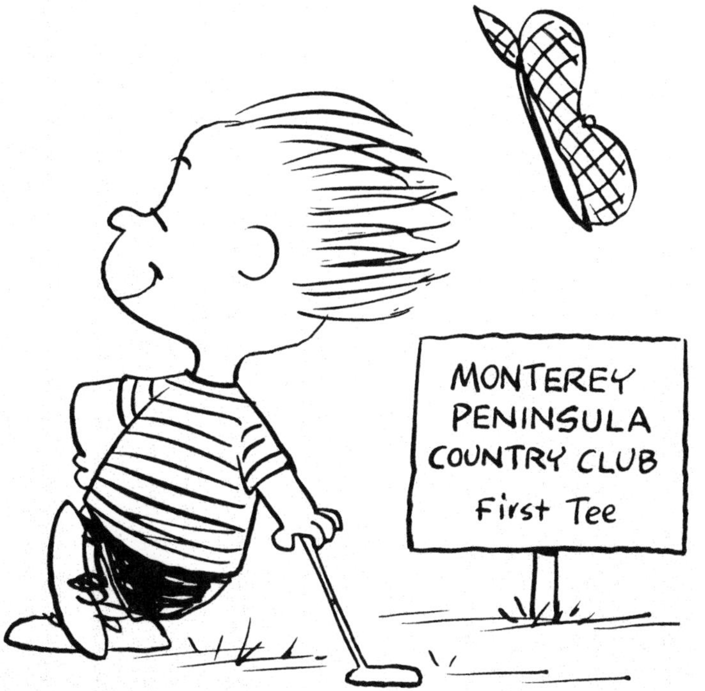
MONTEREY
PENINSULA
COUNTRY CLUB
First Tee

Security is not having to play Pebble Beach on the windiest day of the tournament.

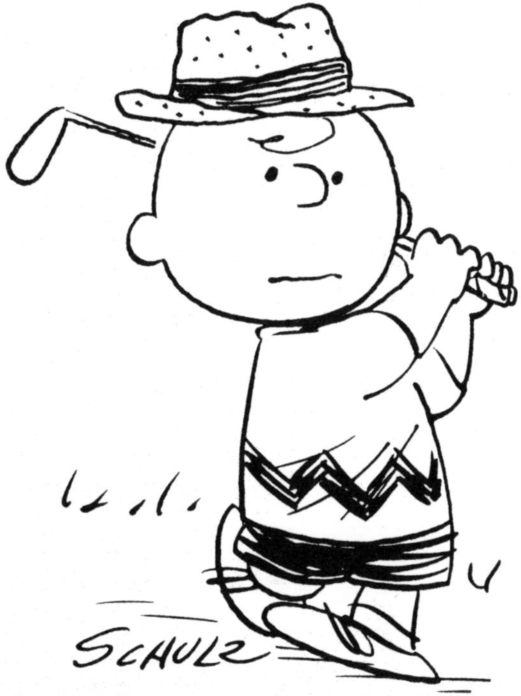
SCHULZ

Security is playing it safe with a four iron on the sixteenth hole at Cypress.

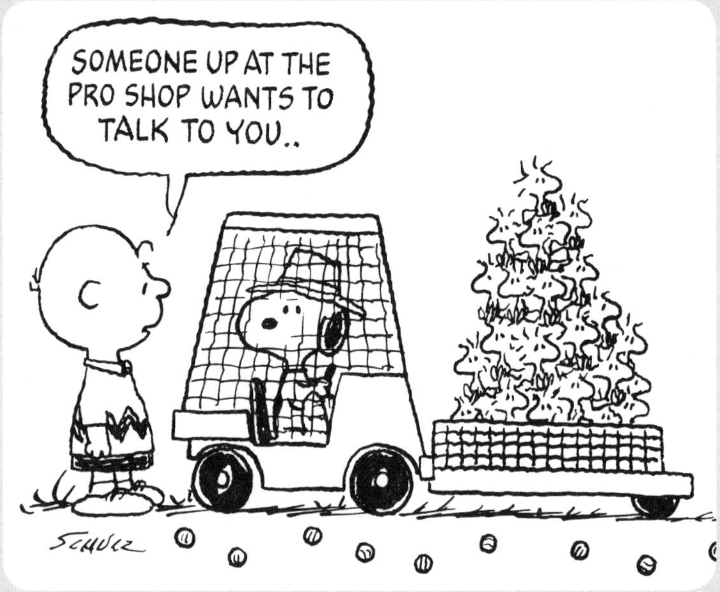
SOMEONE UP AT THE PRO SHOP WANTS TO TALK TO YOU..
SCHULZ

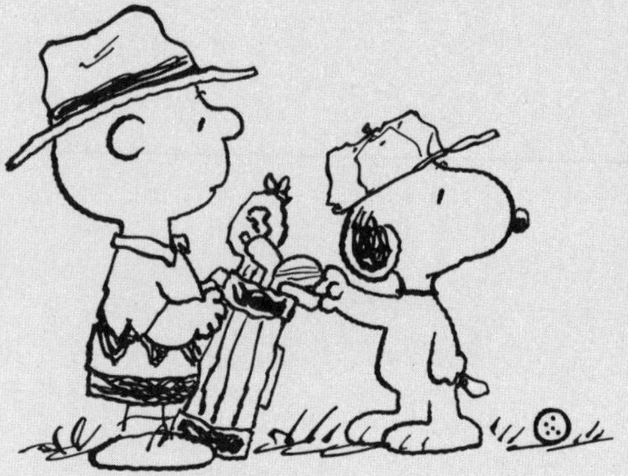

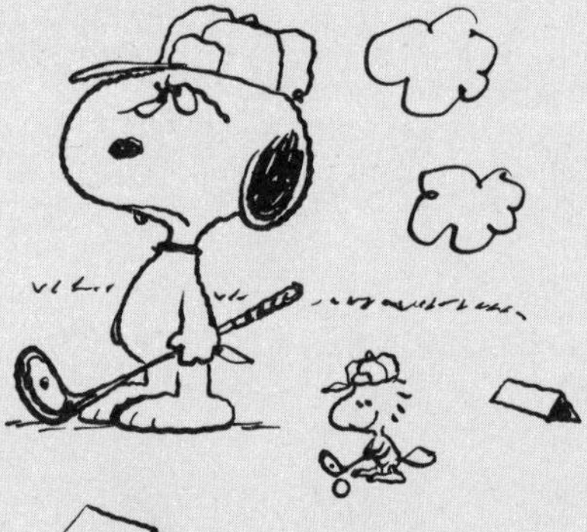

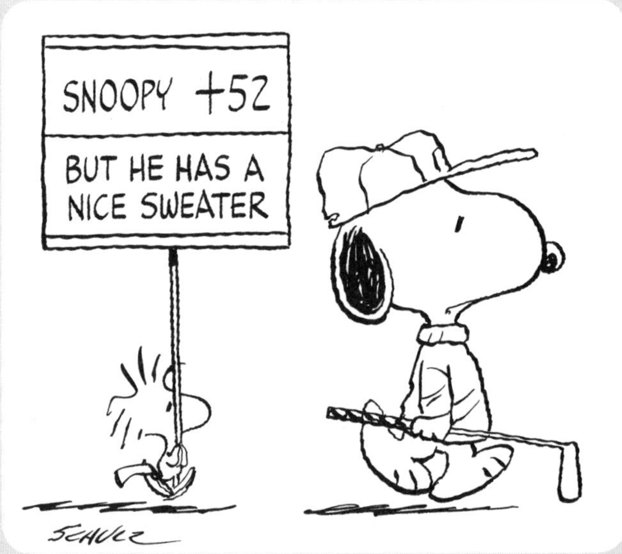
SNOOPY +52
BUT HE HAS A NICE SWEATER
SCHULZ

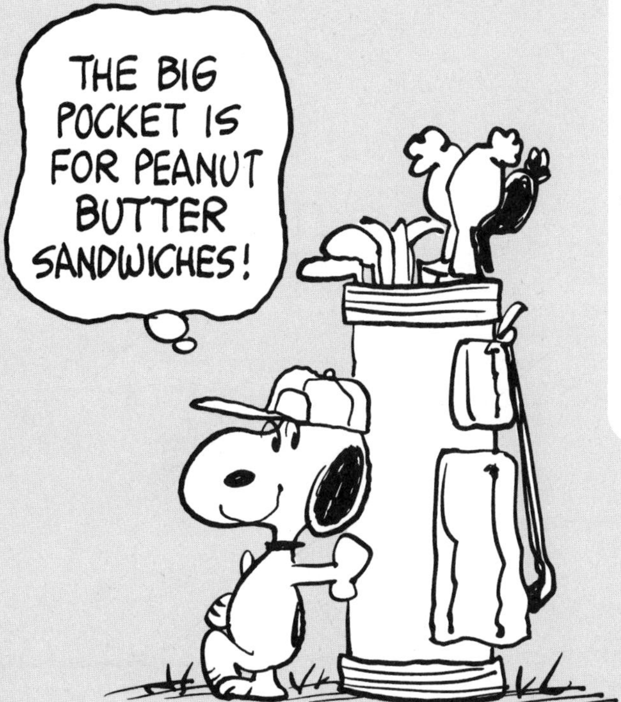
THE BIG POCKET IS FOR PEANUT BUTTER SANDWICHES!

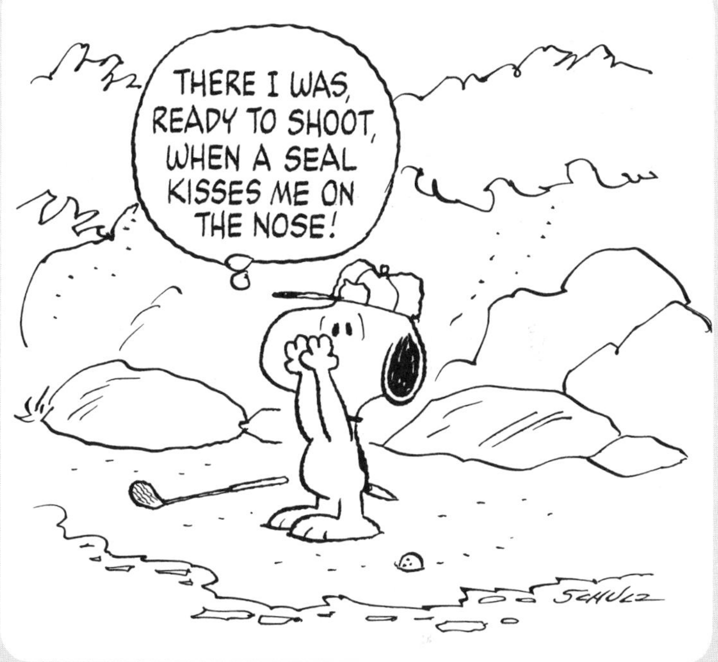
THERE I WAS, READY TO SHOOT, WHEN A SEAL KISSES ME ON THE NOSE!
SCHULZ

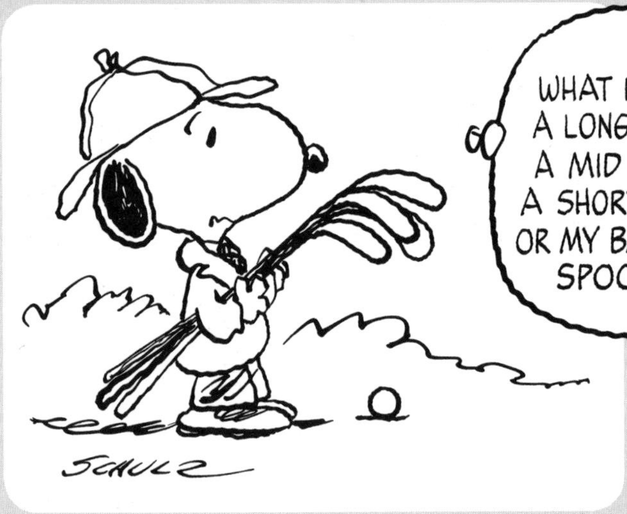
WHAT DO I HIT, A LONG SPOON, A MID SPOON, A SHORT SPOON OR MY BAFFING SPOON?
SCHULZ

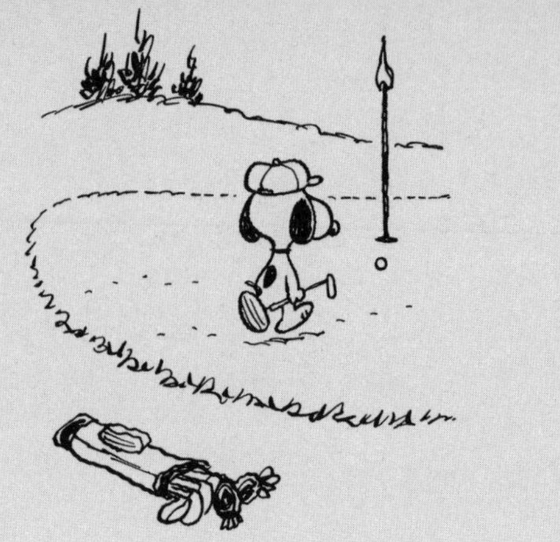

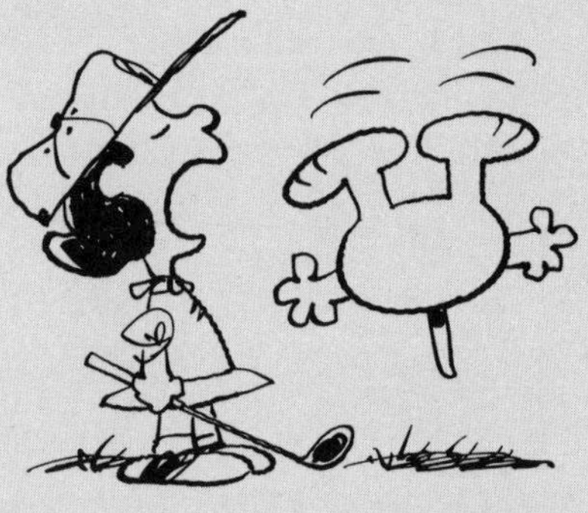

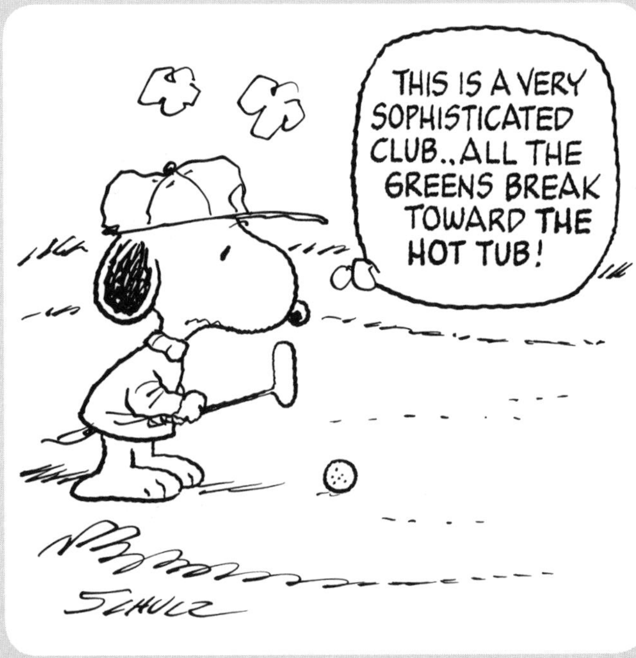
THIS IS A VERY SOPHISTICATED CLUB..ALL THE GREENS BREAK TOWARD THE HOT TUB!
SCHULZ

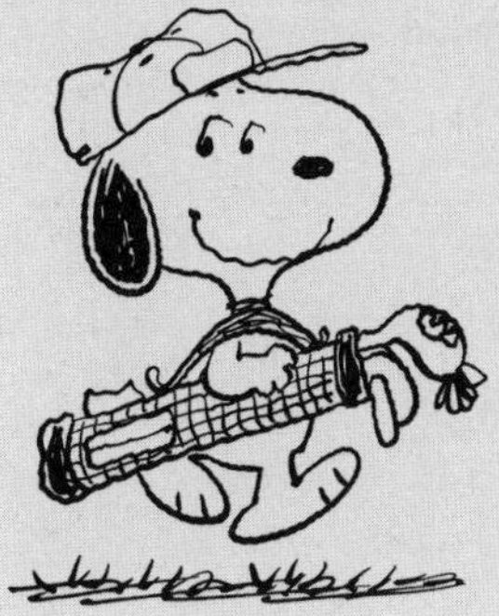

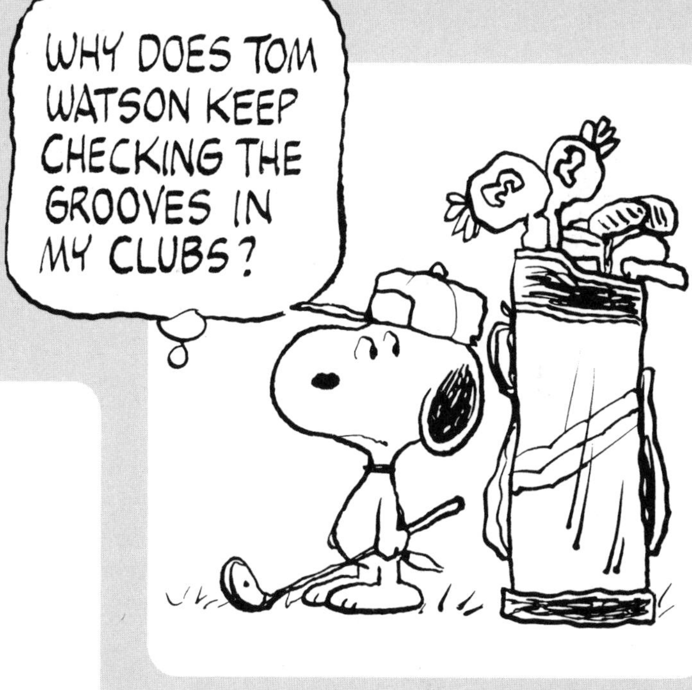
WHY DOES TOM WATSON KEEP CHECKING THE GROOVES IN MY CLUBS?

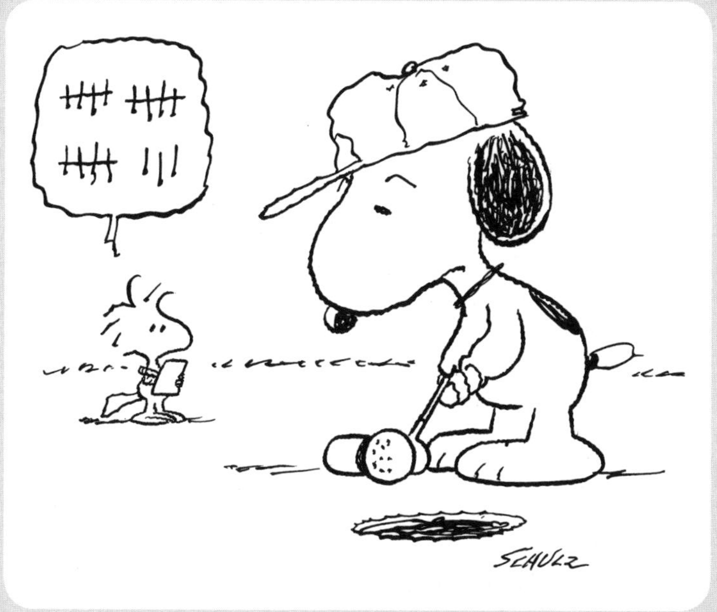
SCHULZ

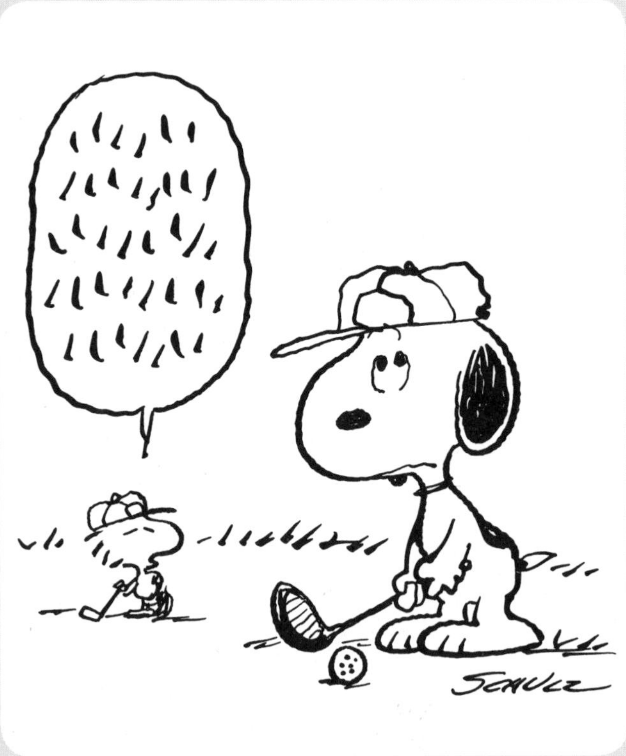

SCHULZ

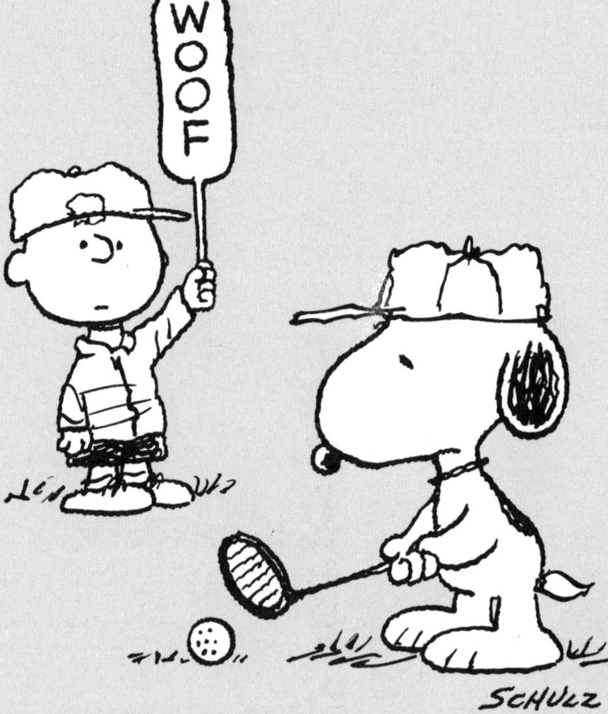

WOOF
SCHULZ

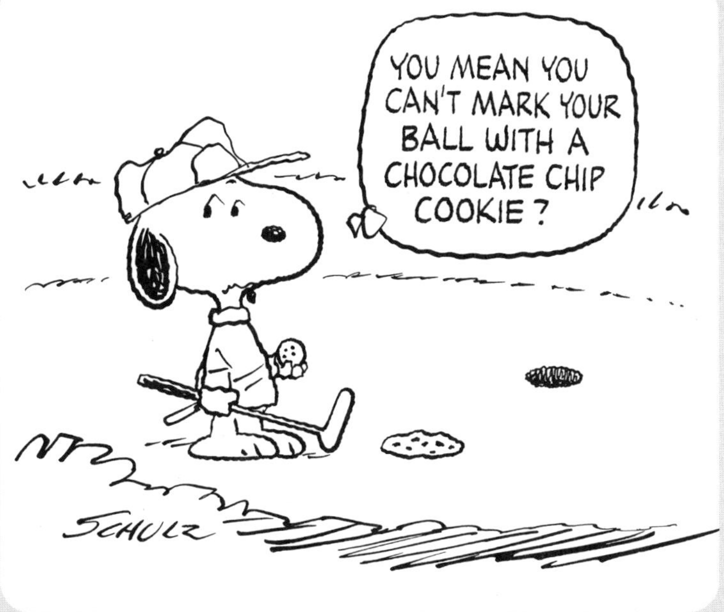
YOU MEAN YOU CAN'T MARK YOUR BALL WITH A CHOCOLATE CHIP COOKIE?
SCHULZ

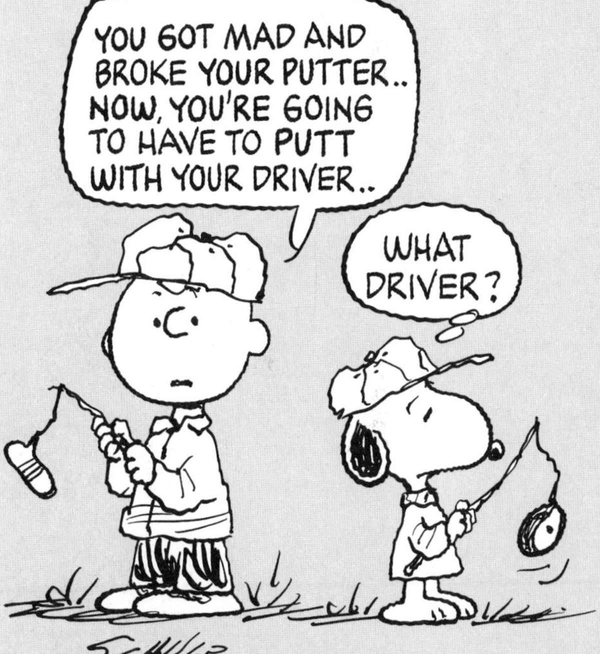
YOU GOT MAD AND BROKE YOUR PUTTER.. NOW, YOU'RE GOING TO HAVE TO PUTT WITH YOUR DRIVER..
WHAT DRIVER?
SCHULZ

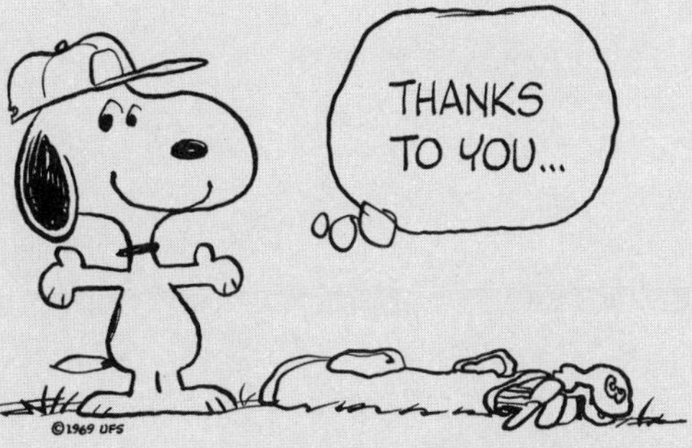
THANKS TO YOU...
©1969 UFS

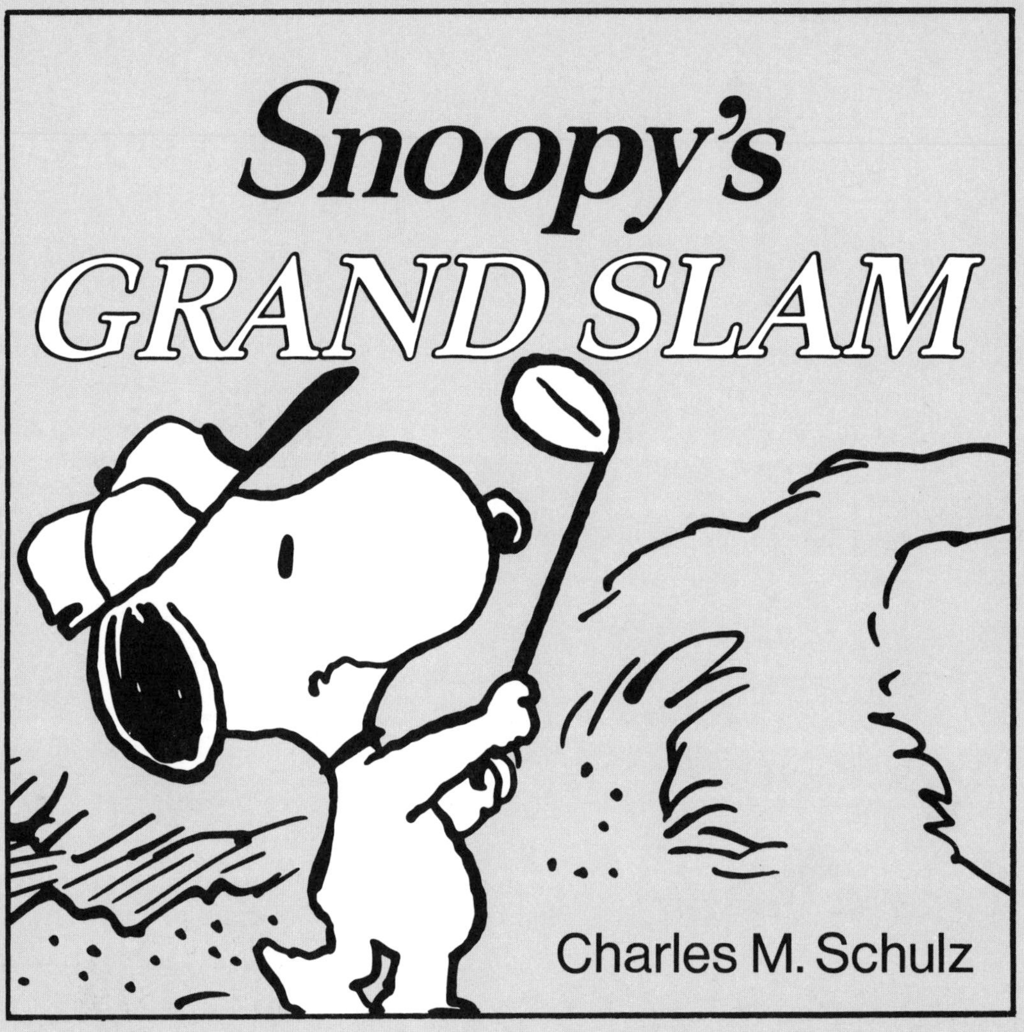
Snoopy's
GRAND SLAM
Charles M. Schulz

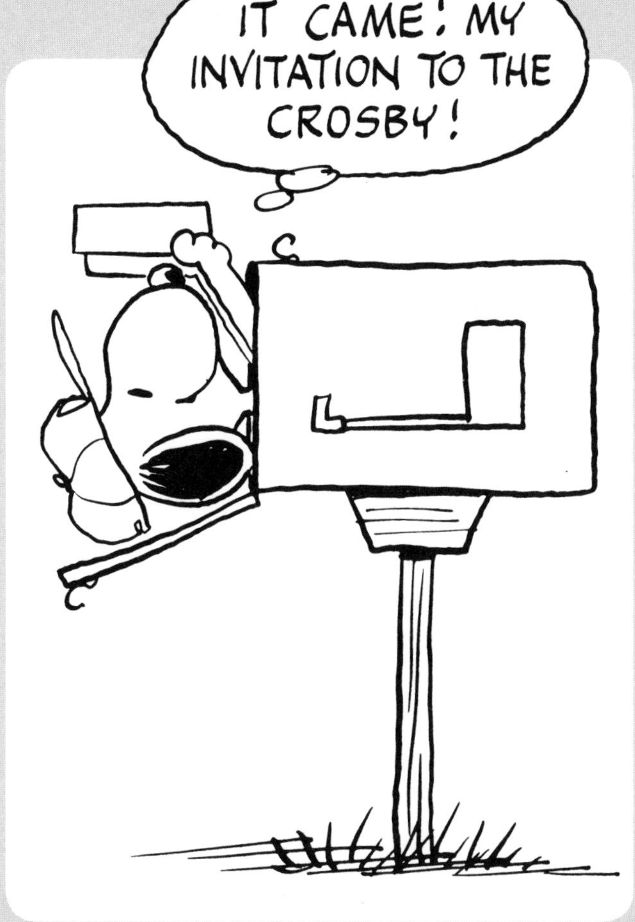
IT CAME! MY INVITATION TO THE CROSBY!

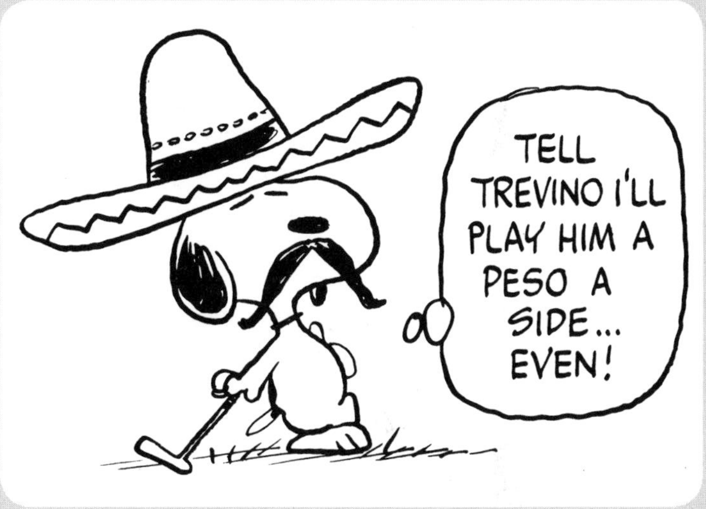
TELL TREVINO I'LL PLAY HIM A PESO A SIDE... EVEN!

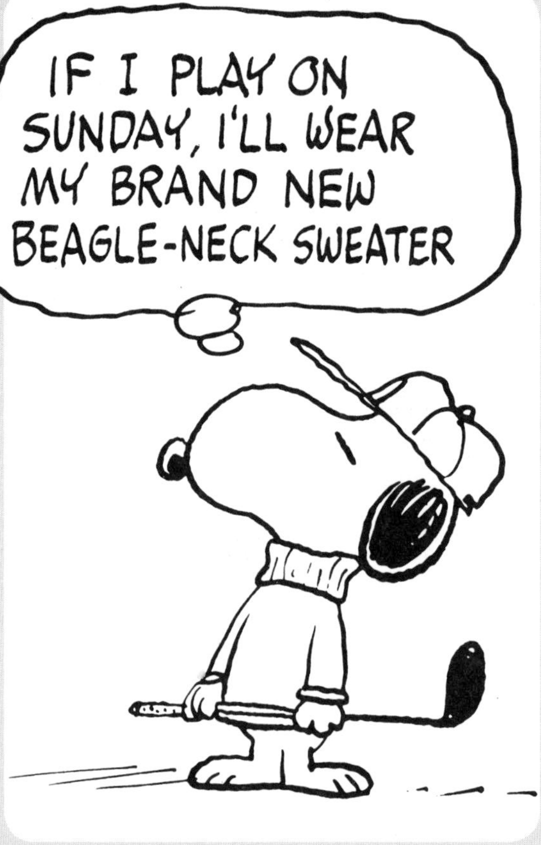
IF I PLAY ON SUNDAY, I'LL WEAR MY BRAND NEW BEAGLE-NECK SWEATER

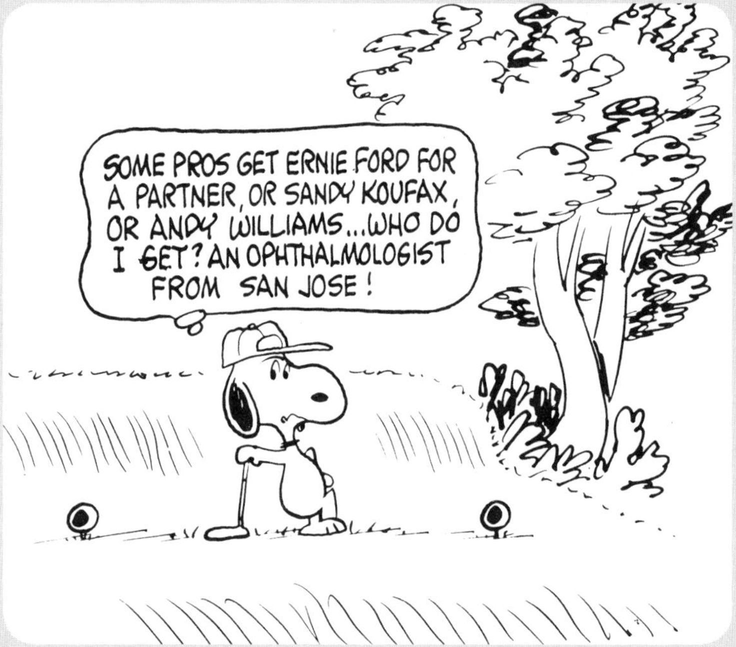
SOME PROS GET ERNIE FORD FOR A PARTNER, OR SANDY KOUFAX, OR ANDY WILLIAMS...WHO DO I GET? AN OPHTHALMOLOGIST FROM SAN JOSE!

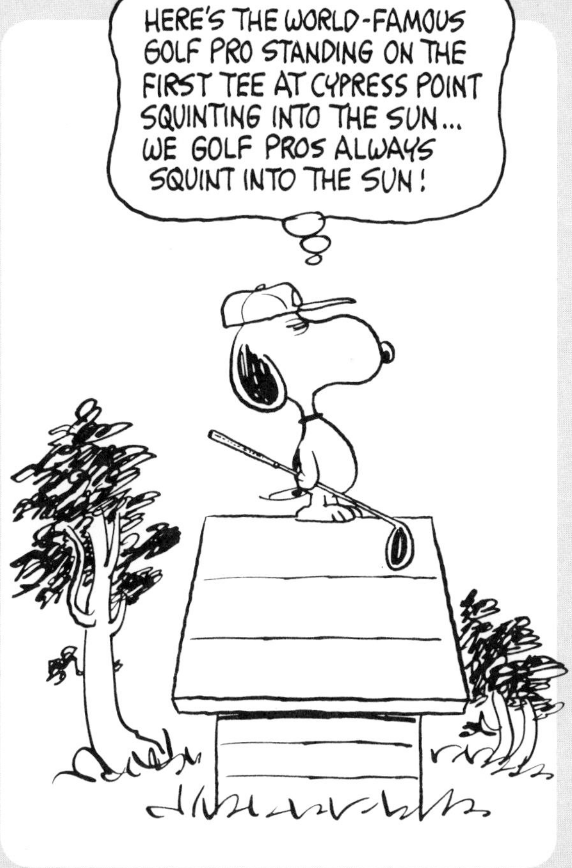
HERE'S THE WORLD-FAMOUS GOLF PRO STANDING ON THE FIRST TEE AT CYPRESS POINT SQUINTING INTO THE SUN... WE GOLF PROS ALWAYS SQUINT INTO THE SUN!

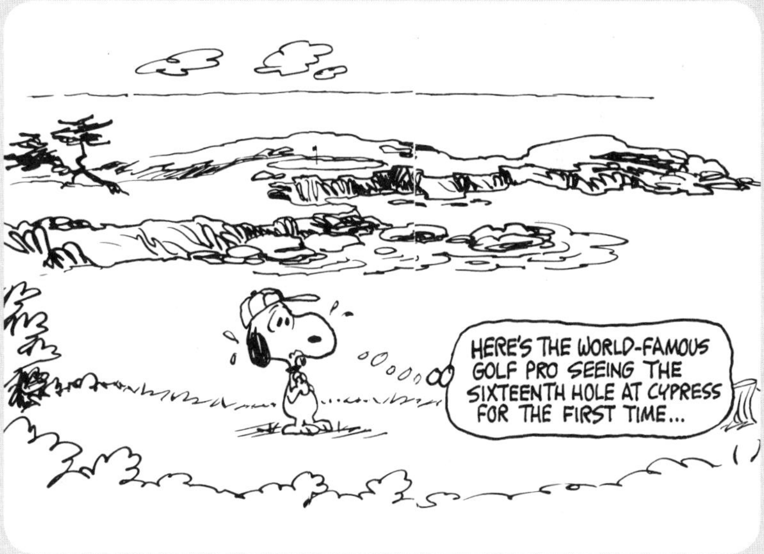
HERE'S THE WORLD-FAMOUS GOLF PRO SEEING THE SIXTEENTH HOLE AT CYPRESS FOR THE FIRST TIME...

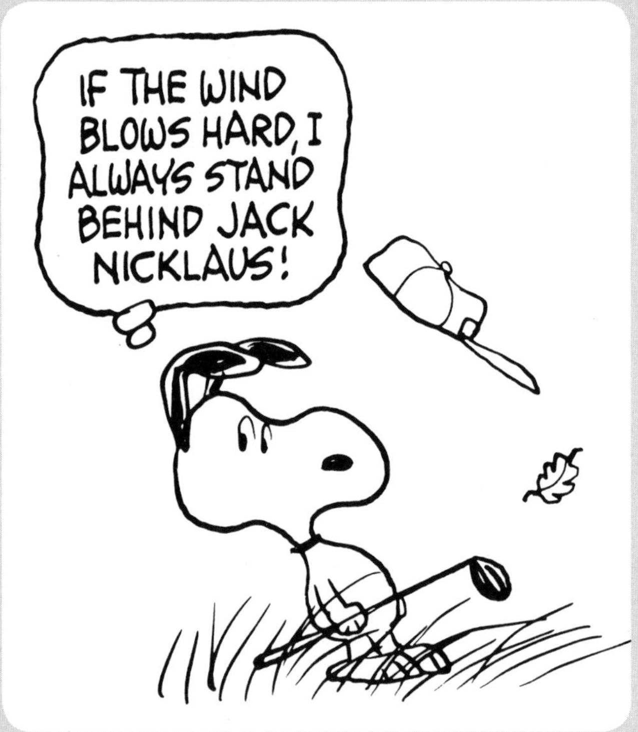
IF THE WIND BLOWS HARD, I ALWAYS STAND BEHIND JACK NICKLAUS!

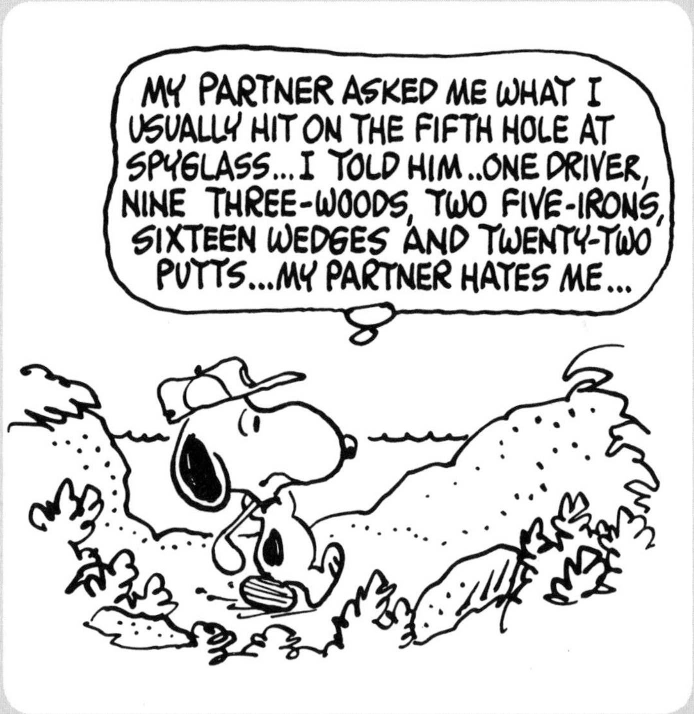
MY PARTNER ASKED ME WHAT I USUALLY HIT ON THE FIFTH HOLE AT SPYGLASS... I TOLD HIM ..ONE DRIVER, NINE THREE-WOODS, TWO FIVE-IRONS, SIXTEEN WEDGES AND TWENTY-TWO PUTTS...MY PARTNER HATES ME...

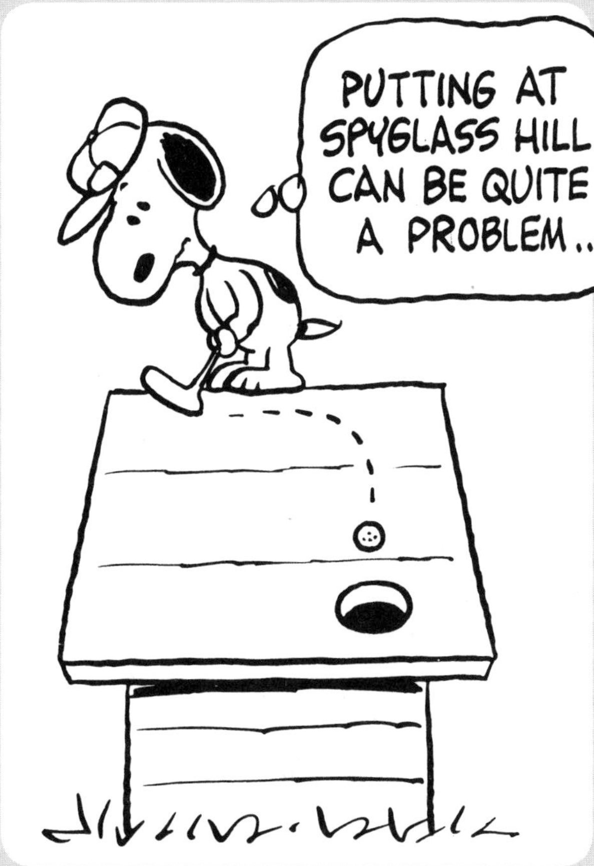
PUTTING AT SPYGLASS HILL CAN BE QUITE A PROBLEM..

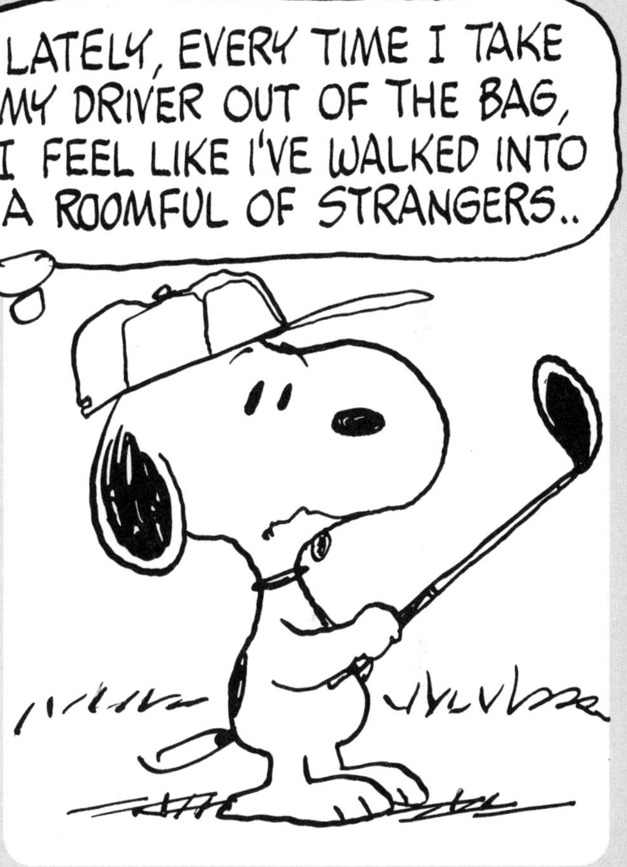
LATELY, EVERY TIME I TAKE MY DRIVER OUT OF THE BAG, I FEEL LIKE I'VE WALKED INTO A ROOMFUL OF STRANGERS..

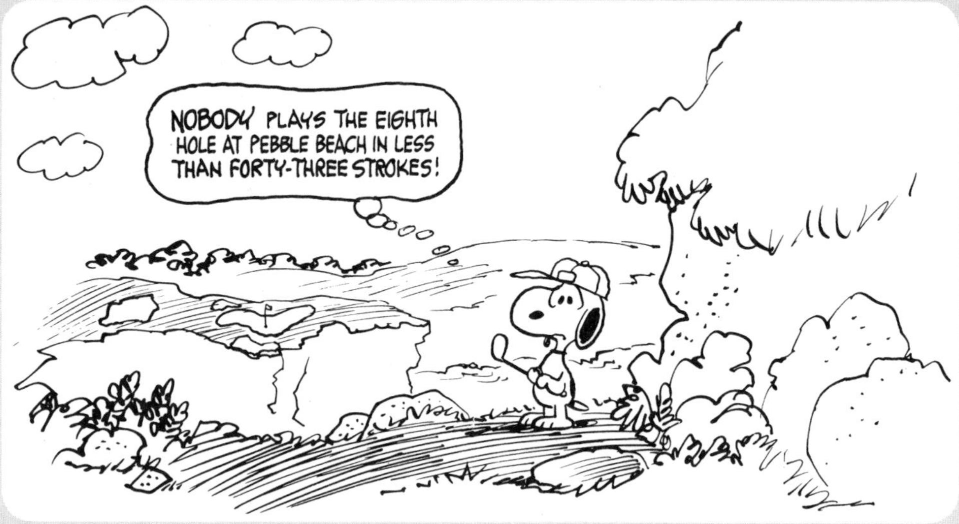
NOBODY PLAYS THE EIGHTH HOLE AT PEBBLE BEACH IN LESS THAN FORTY-THREE STROKES!

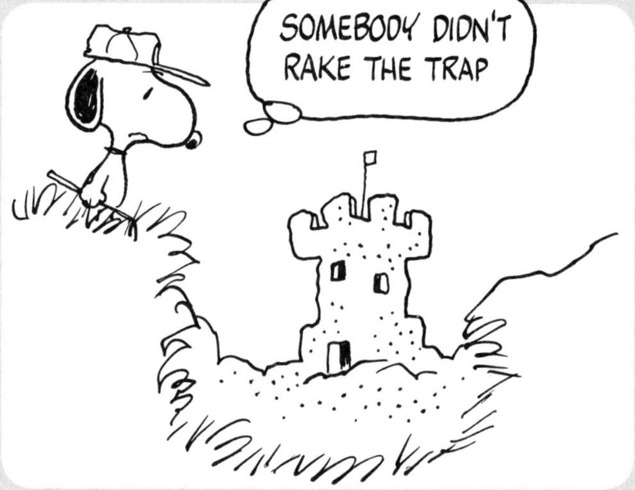
SOMEBODY DIDN'T RAKE THE TRAP

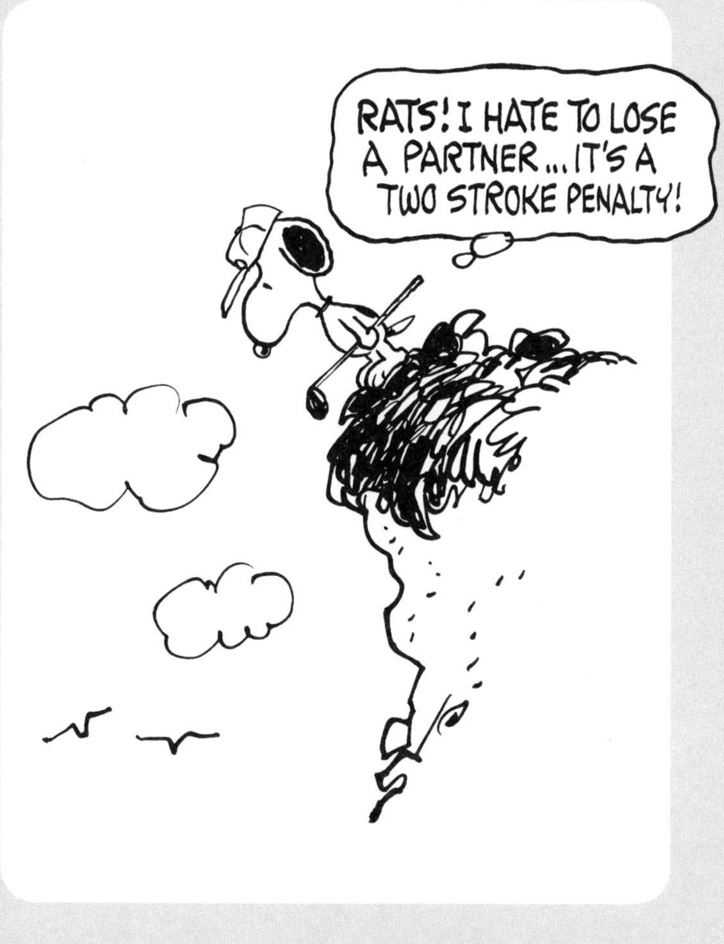
RATS! I HATE TO LOSE A PARTNER...IT'S A TWO STROKE PENALTY!

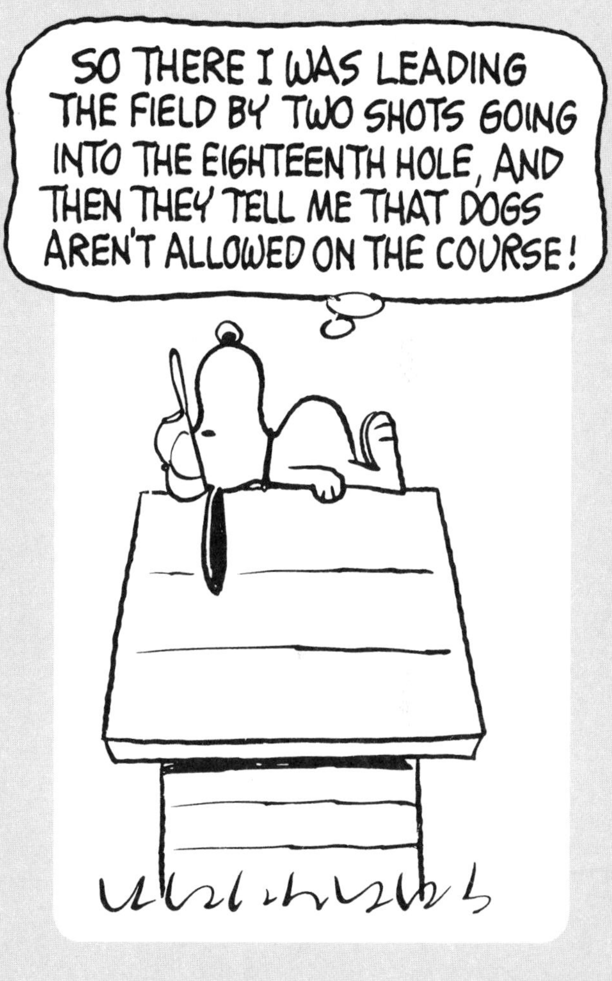
SO THERE I WAS LEADING THE FIELD BY TWO SHOTS GOING INTO THE EIGHTEENTH HOLE, AND THEN THEY TELL ME THAT DOGS AREN'T ALLOWED ON THE COURSE!

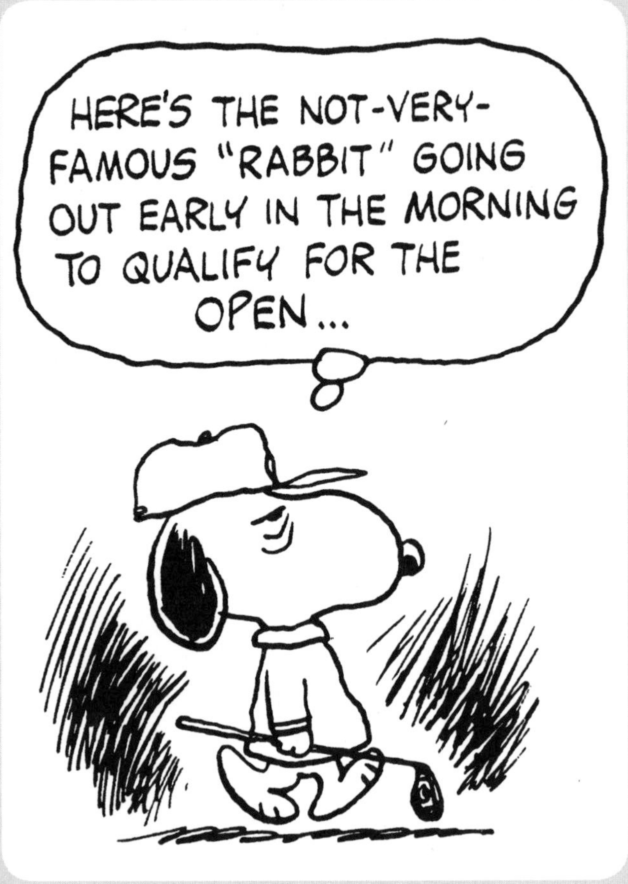
HERE'S THE NOT-VERY-FAMOUS "RABBIT" GOING OUT EARLY IN THE MORNING TO QUALIFY FOR THE OPEN...

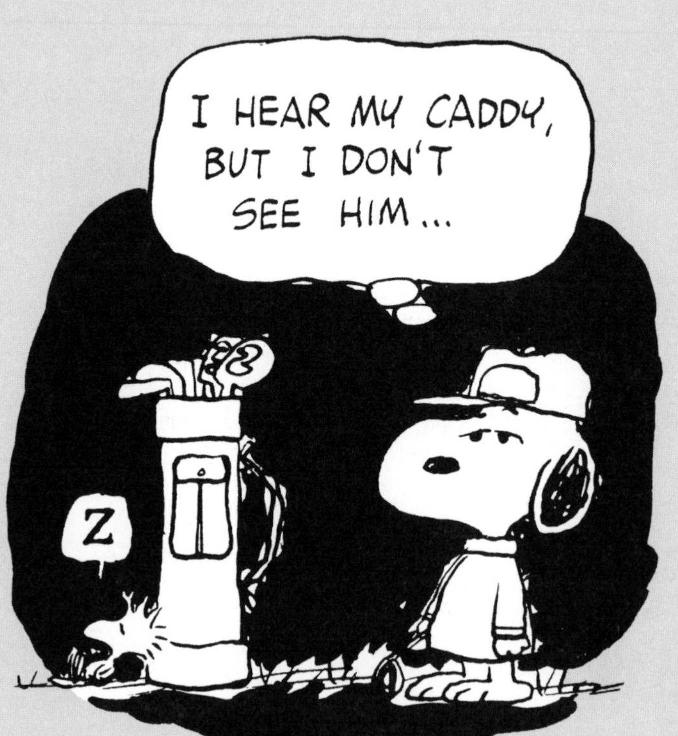
I HEAR MY CADDY, BUT I DON'T SEE HIM...
Z

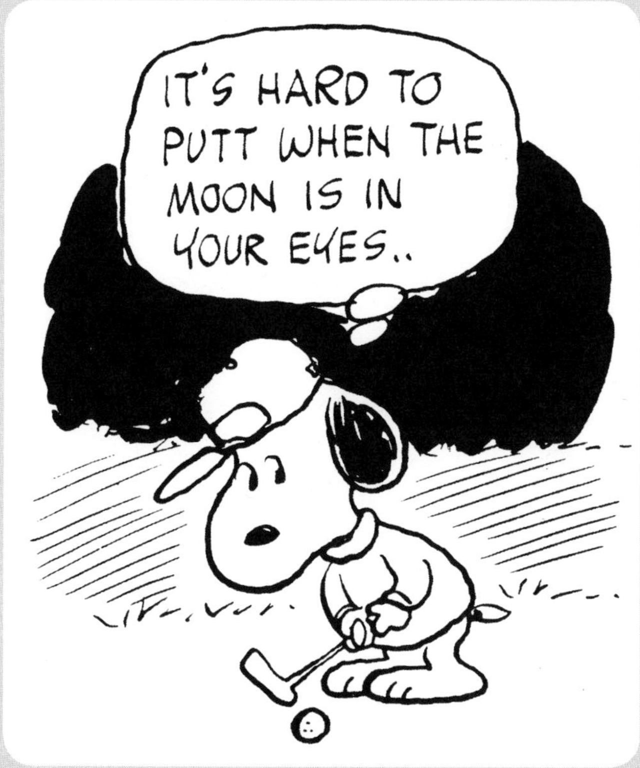
IT'S HARD TO PUTT WHEN THE MOON IS IN YOUR EYES..

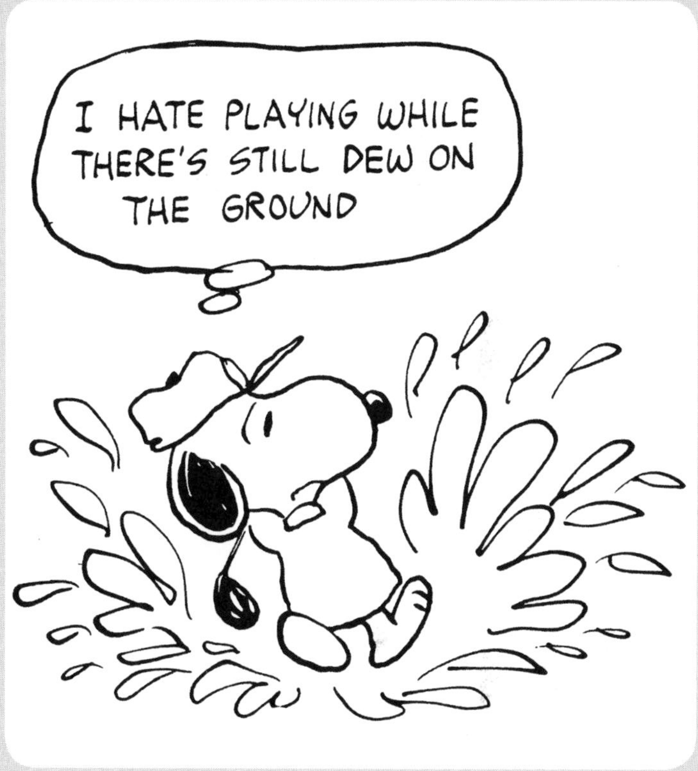
I HATE PLAYING WHILE THERE'S STILL DEW ON THE GROUND

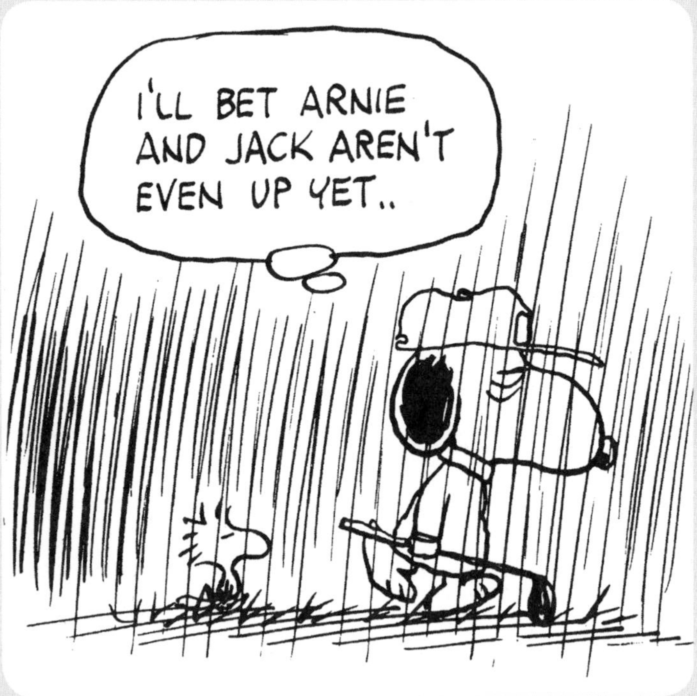
I'LL BET ARNIE AND JACK AREN'T EVEN UP YET..

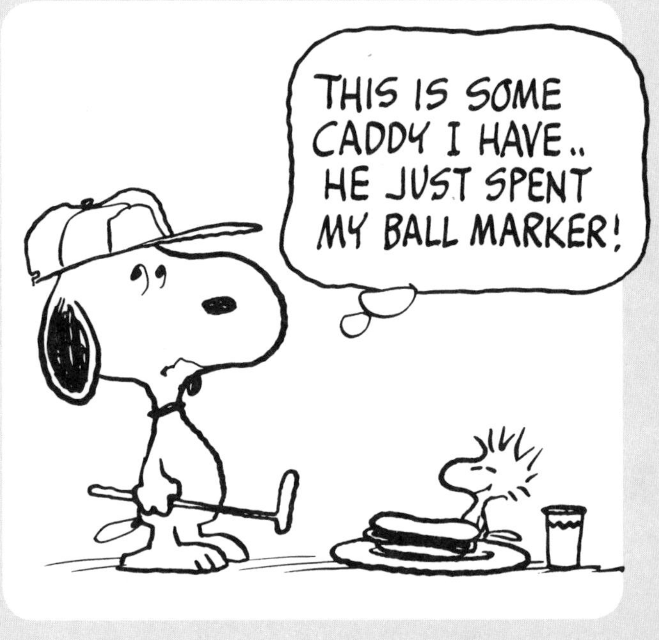
THIS IS SOME CADDY I HAVE.. HE JUST SPENT MY BALL MARKER!

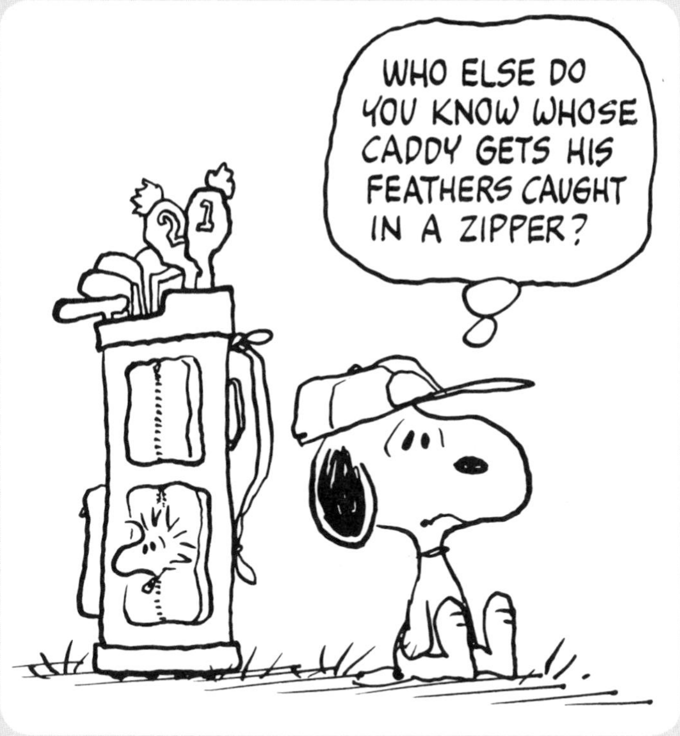
WHO ELSE DO YOU KNOW WHOSE CADDY GETS HIS FEATHERS CAUGHT IN A ZIPPER?

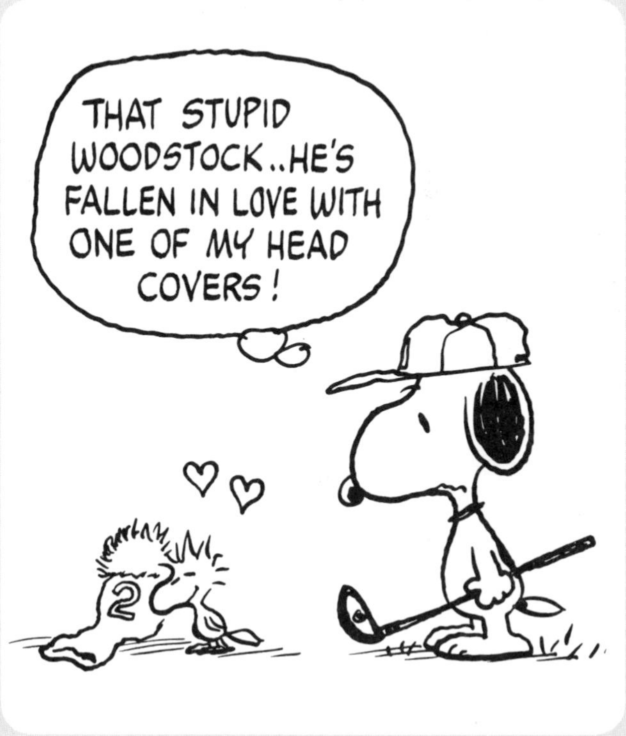
THAT STUPID WOODSTOCK..HE'S FALLEN IN LOVE WITH ONE OF MY HEAD COVERS!

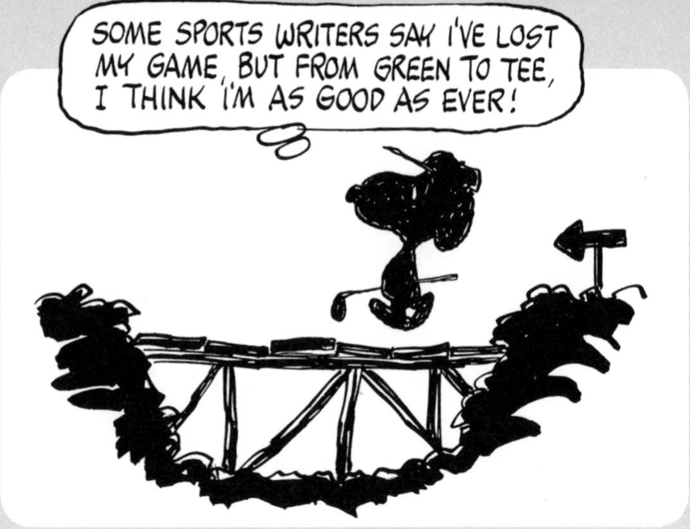
SOME SPORTS WRITERS SAY I'VE LOST MY GAME, BUT FROM GREEN TO TEE, I THINK I'M AS GOOD AS EVER!

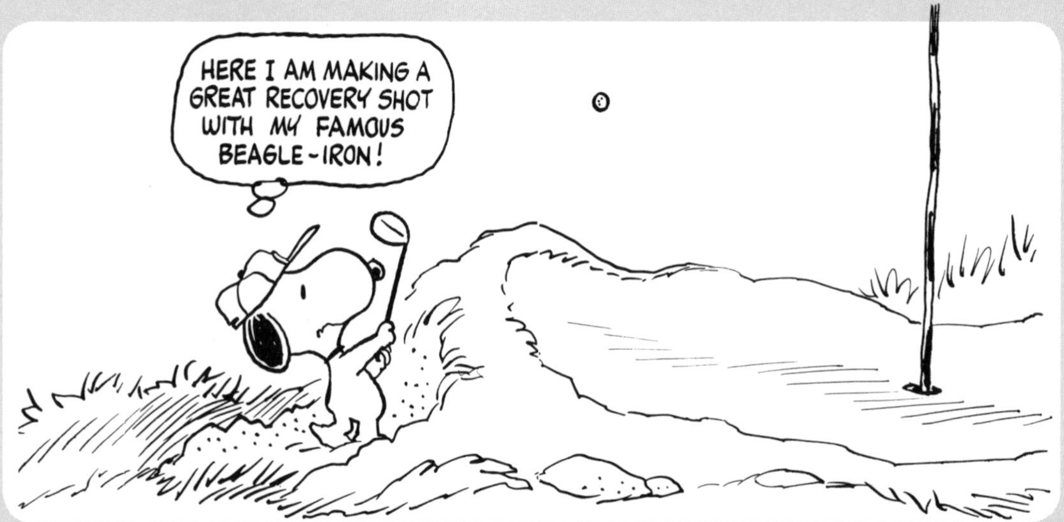
HERE I AM MAKING A GREAT RECOVERY SHOT WITH MY FAMOUS BEAGLE-IRON!

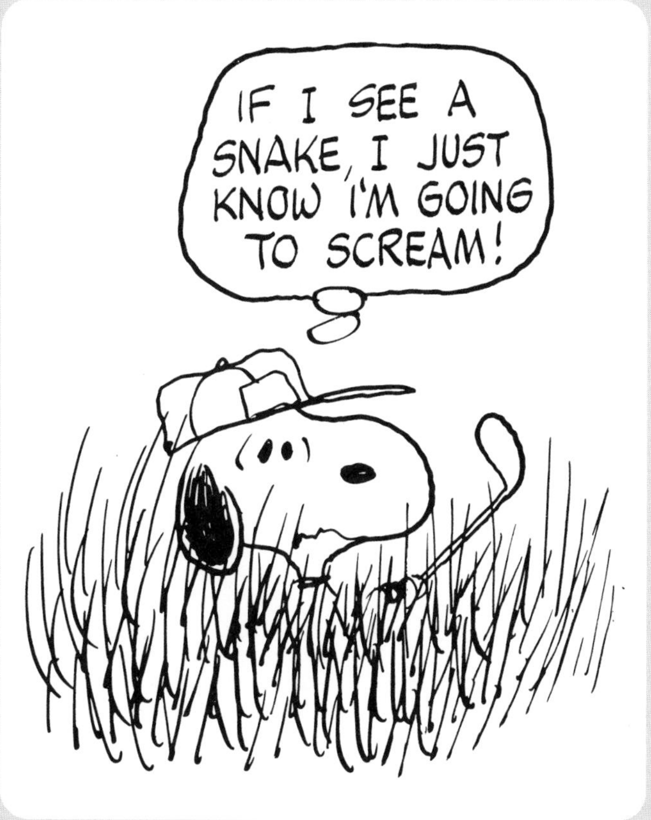
IF I SEE A SNAKE, I JUST KNOW I'M GOING TO SCREAM!

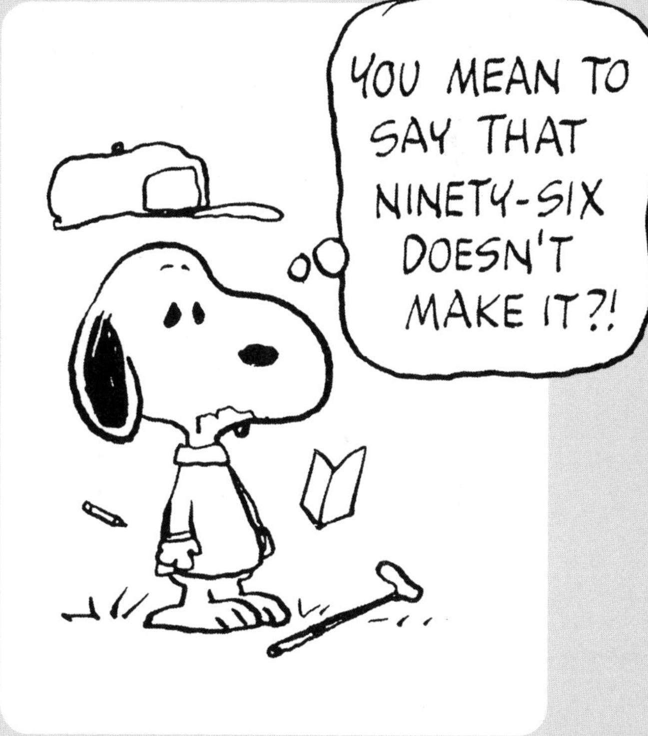
YOU MEAN TO SAY THAT NINETY-SIX DOESN'T MAKE IT?!

WELL, I COMPLETED MY GRAND SLAM ... I PLAYED IN THE CROSBY, THE MASTERS AND THE OPEN, AND I LOST ALL OF THEM!
SIGH

TENNIS

Tennis was another of Schulz's passions and captured a fair share of his attention. The work that follows, published in 1979 under the title *Snoopy's Tennis Book*, mixed tennis-themed strip reprints with two original sequences: *Snoopy at Wimbledon* and *Snoopy's Tournament Tips*.

SNOOPY AT WIMBLEDON

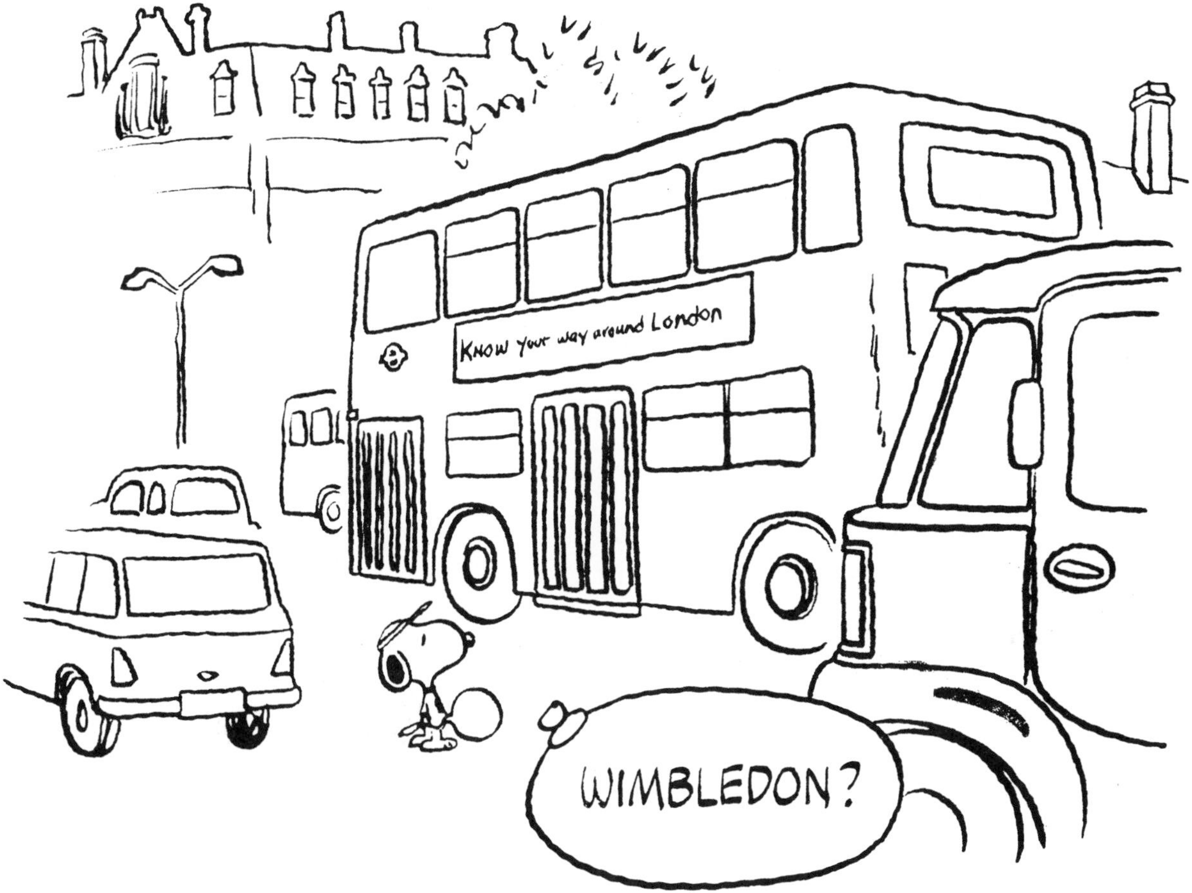
KNOW your way around London
WIMBLEDON?

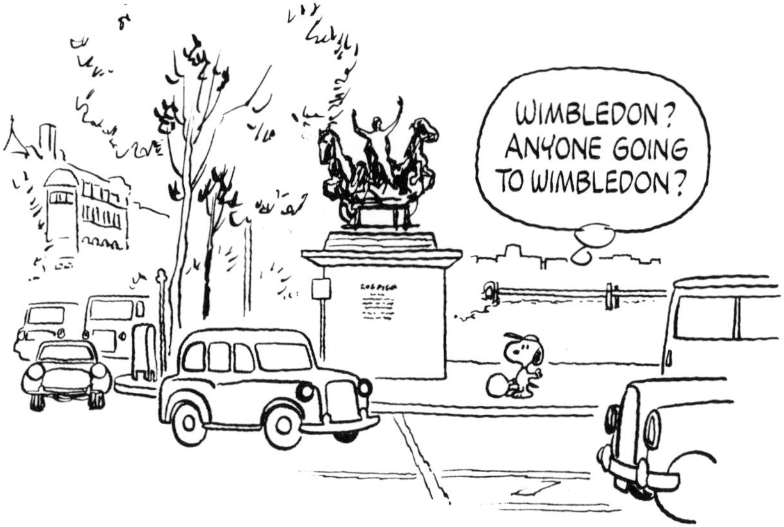
WIMBLEDON? ANYONE GOING TO WIMBLEDON?

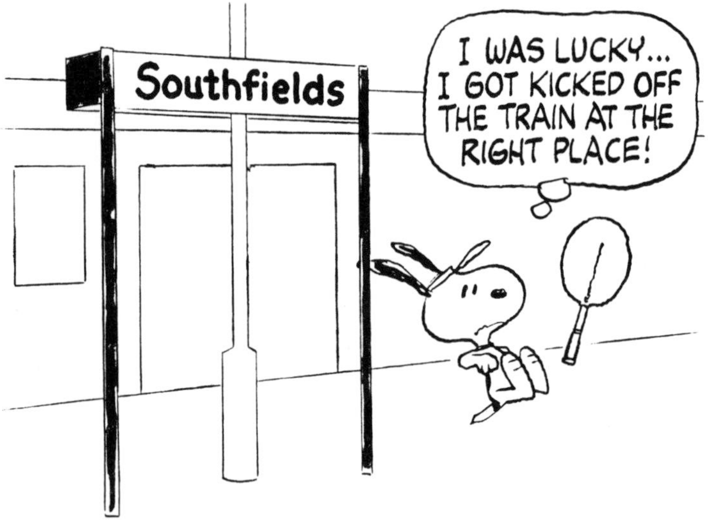
Southfields
I WAS LUCKY... I GOT KICKED OFF THE TRAIN AT THE RIGHT PLACE!

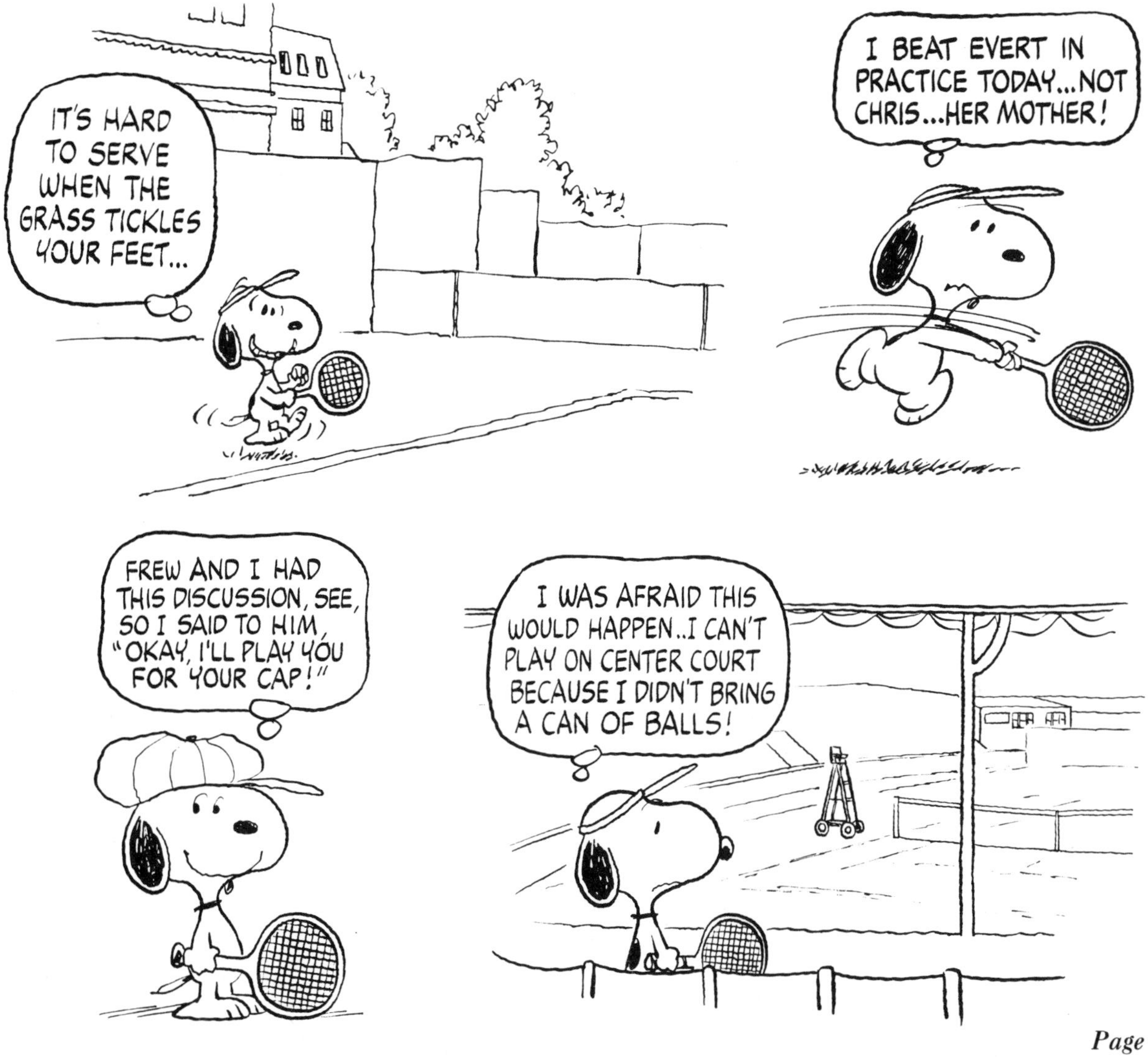
IT'S HARD TO SERVE WHEN THE GRASS TICKLES YOUR FEET...
I BEAT EVERT IN PRACTICE TODAY...NOT CHRIS...HER MOTHER!
FREW AND I HAD THIS DISCUSSION, SEE, SO I SAID TO HIM, "OKAY, I'LL PLAY YOU FOR YOUR CAP!"
I WAS AFRAID THIS WOULD HAPPEN..I CAN'T PLAY ON CENTER COURT BECAUSE I DIDN'T BRING A CAN OF BALLS!

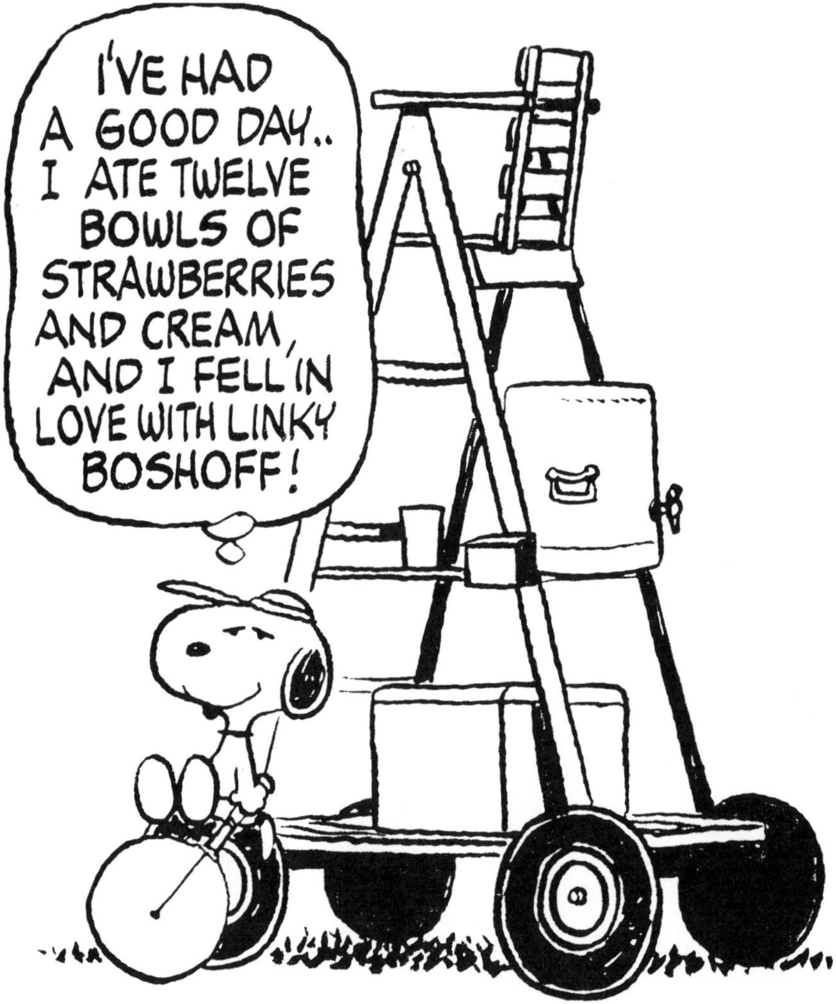
I'VE HAD A GOOD DAY.. I ATE TWELVE BOWLS OF STRAWBERRIES AND CREAM, AND I FELL IN LOVE WITH LINKY BOSHOFF!

Snoopy's Tournament Tip #1

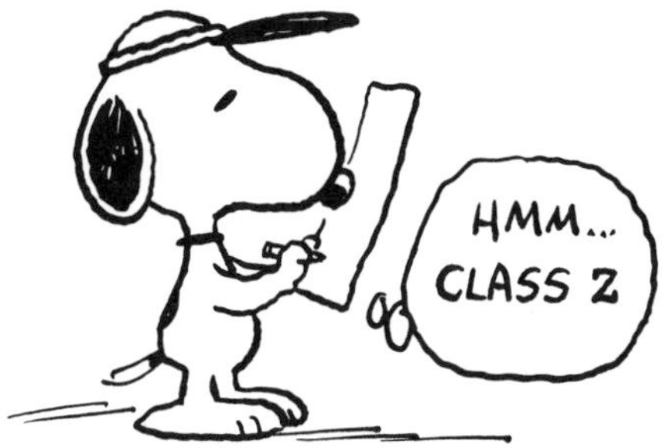
HMM...
CLASS Z

When filling out the entry blank, make certain you place yourself in the proper category.

Snoopy's Tournament Tip #2

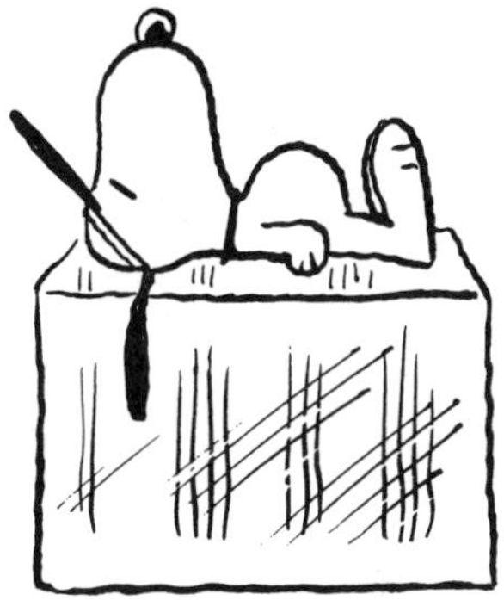

After a strenuous practice session you may want to pack your arm in ice . . . (or, preferably, your whole body).

Snoopy's Tournament Tip #3

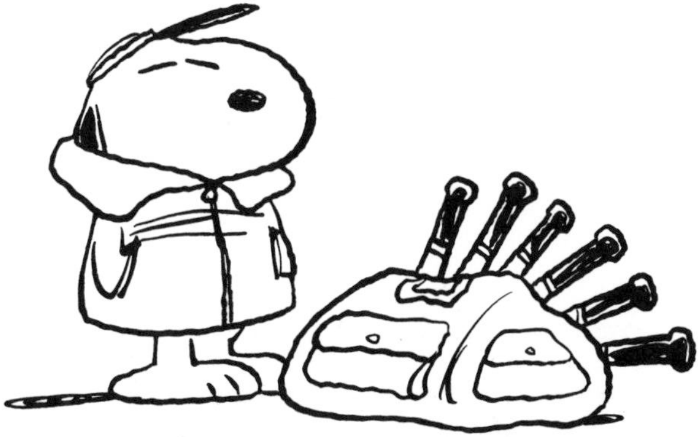

Some people are easily impressed by clothing and equipment . . . therefore, a flashy warm-up jacket and several extra rackets can be important.

Snoopy's Tournament Tip #4

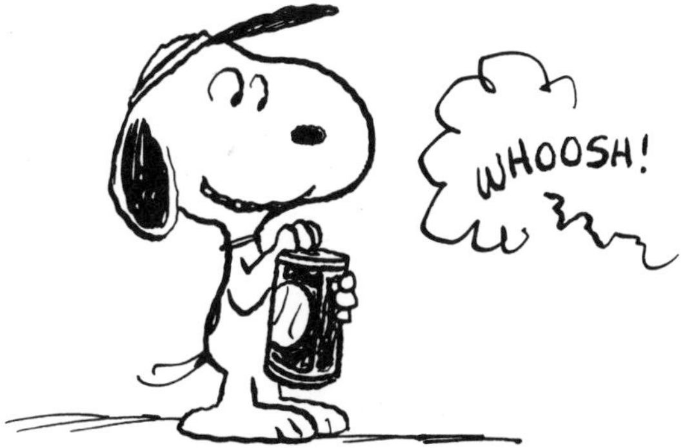
WHOOSH!

Always offer to open a new can of tennis balls, but do it as slowly as reaching for a dinner check. If care is taken, one unopened can should last the entire season.

Snoopy's Tournament Tip #5

During the warm-up, ask your opponent if you may hit a few overheads, but do so knowing that he'll find out you don't really have an overhead.

Snoopy's Tournament Tip #6

It is considered improper to bounce the ball excessively so as to annoy the receiver, but go ahead and try it anyway.

Snoopy's Tournament Tip #7

It is not necessary to argue about a suspected bad call . . . sometimes a slight look of dismay will do the trick.

Snoopy's Tournament Tip #8

If your opponent has a hard first serve, don't let it bother you . . . if he or she has a hard second serve, you can let *that* bother you.

Snoopy's Tournament Tip #9

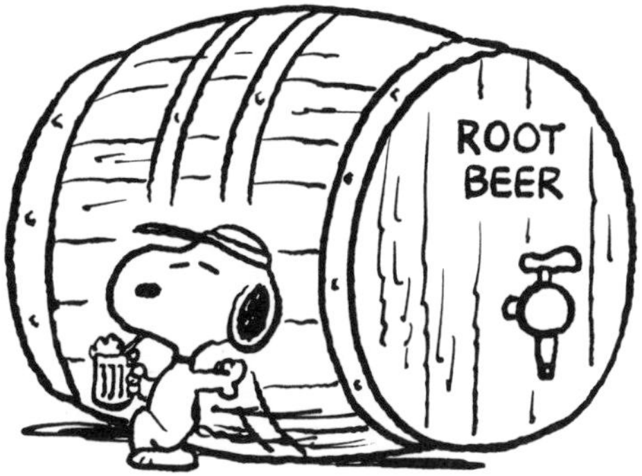
ROOT
BEER

It is always wise to bring along something to drink between sets.

Snoopy's Tournament Tip #10

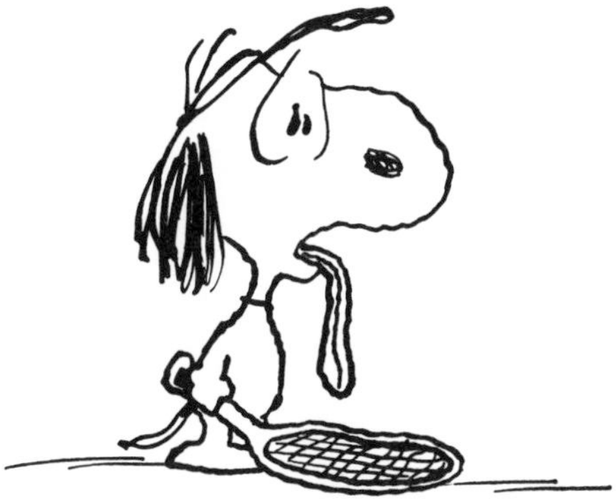

If your opponent runs you from side to side, avoid obvious signs that you are tiring.

Snoopy's Tournament Tip #11

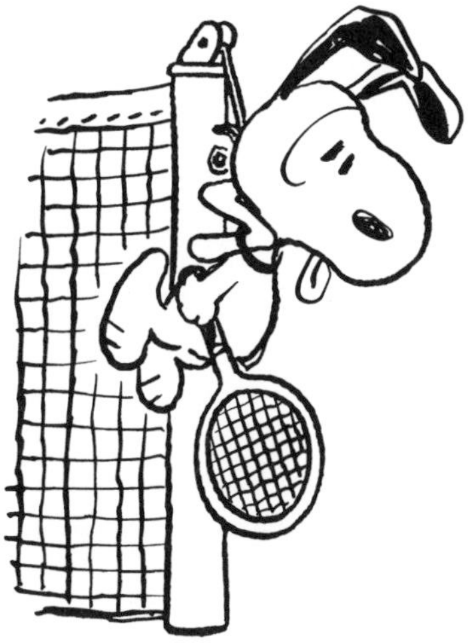

It is admirable to try to run down every shot, but also unwise to attempt grandstand plays that could cause foolish injury.

Snoopy's Tournament Tip #12

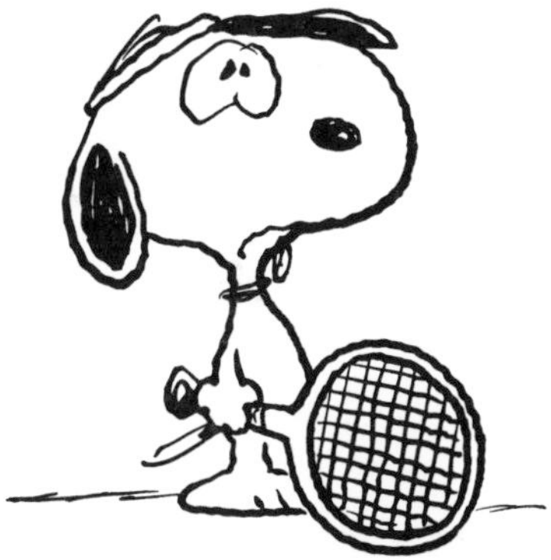

Remember, in playing singles, you actually have no one to blame your losses on but yourself . . . therefore, you may want to take up doubles.

Snoopy's Tournament Tip #13

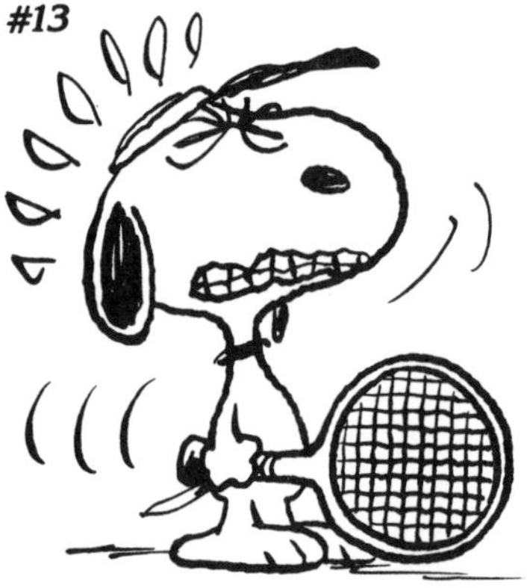

When playing doubles, refrain from saying anything if your partner hits a cold put-away into the net.

Snoopy's Tournament Tip #14

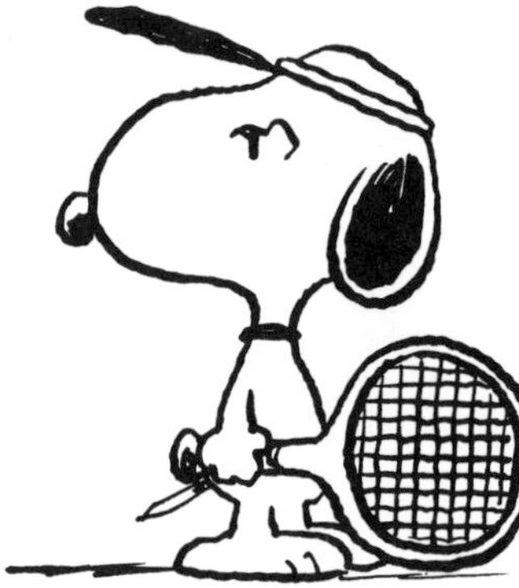

If your partner double faults four times in a row, you may want to suggest that he or she throw the ball higher . . . or take up bowling!

Snoopy's Tournament Tip #15

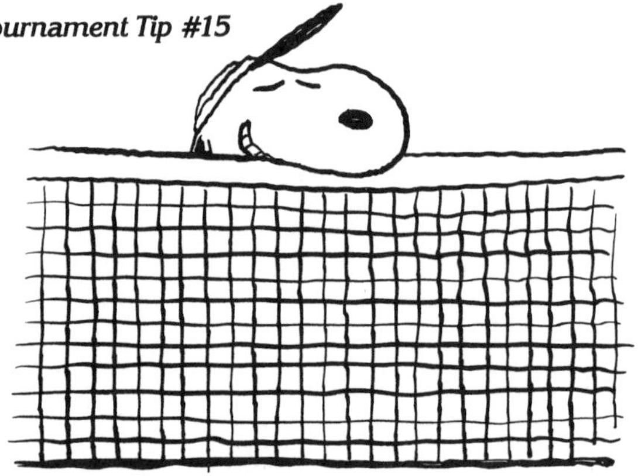

If you have won, always approach the net graciously to congratulate your opponent on a match well played.

Snoopy's Tournament Tip #16

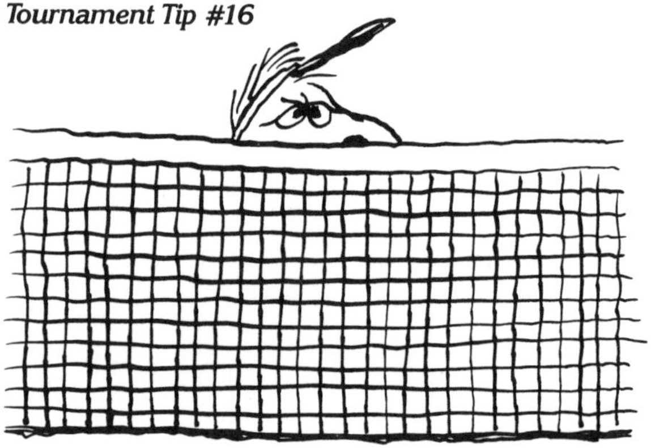

If you have lost, always approach the net graciously to congratulate your opponent on a match well played.

Snoopy's Tournament Tip #17

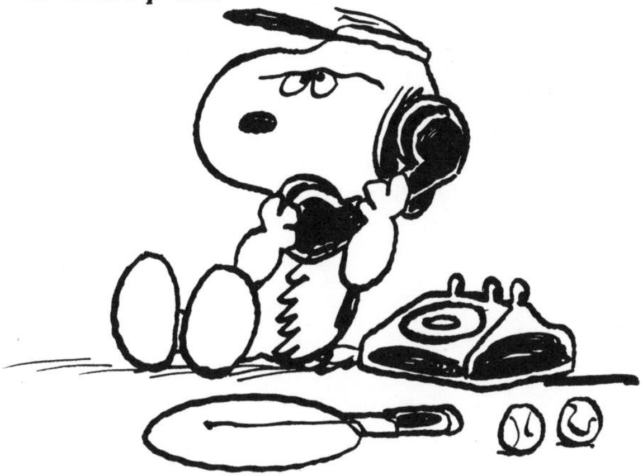

And remember, once a match is over and you have returned home, it is probably too late to call a serve "out."

SPOT DRAWINGS

Charles Schulz drew countless cartoon spot-drawings over his fifty-year career. In the following pages is a sprinkling of some of these lively drawings taken from hither and yon. Each is a small marvel of nuanced design and expression. We have focused on Snoopy here because Schulz clearly showered much of his wit and sweetness and sense of humor on the Beagle. These little drawings reminds one of Schulz's deep understanding that a good cartoonist always knows how to "draw funny."

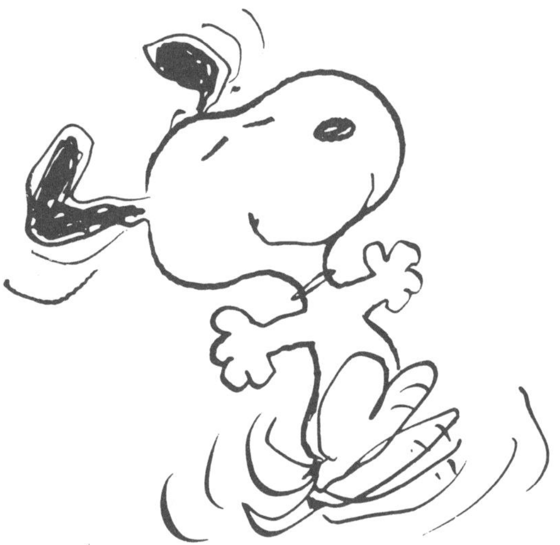

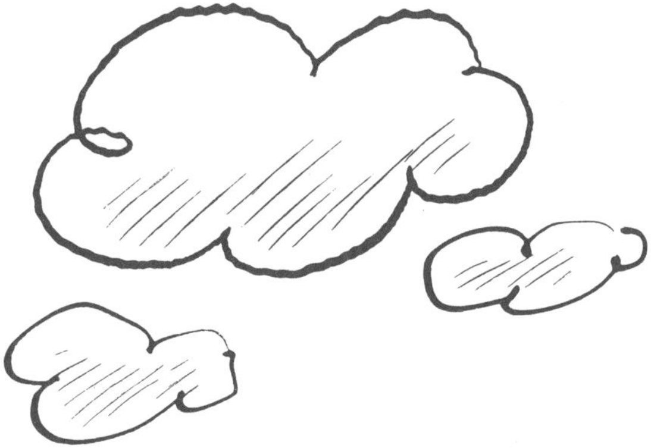

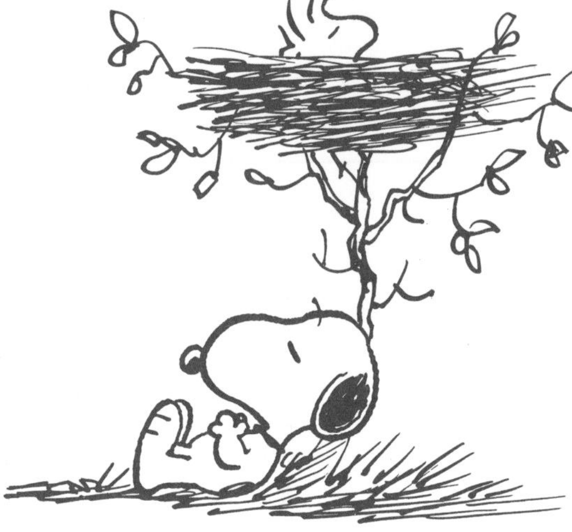

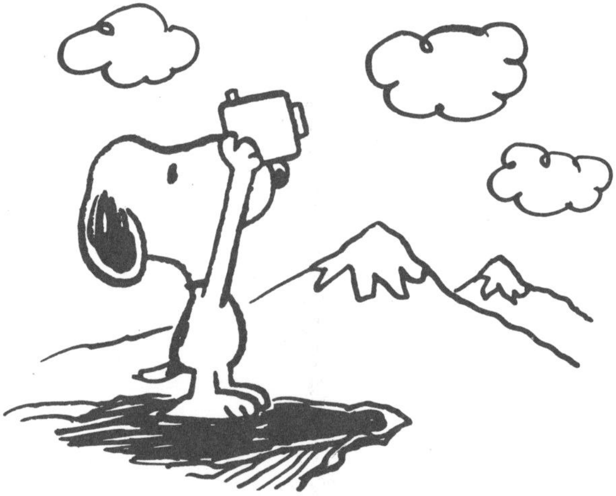

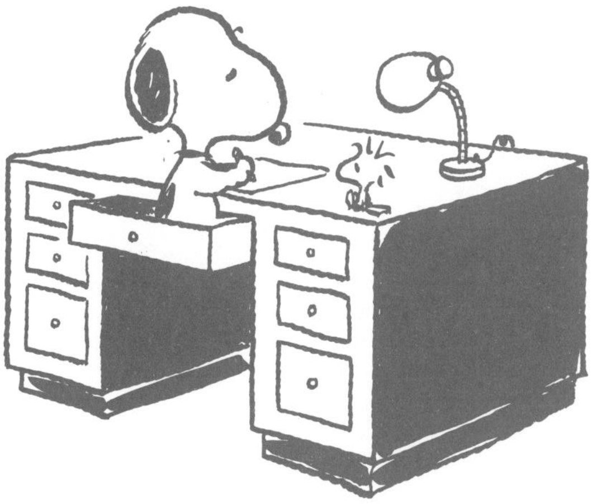

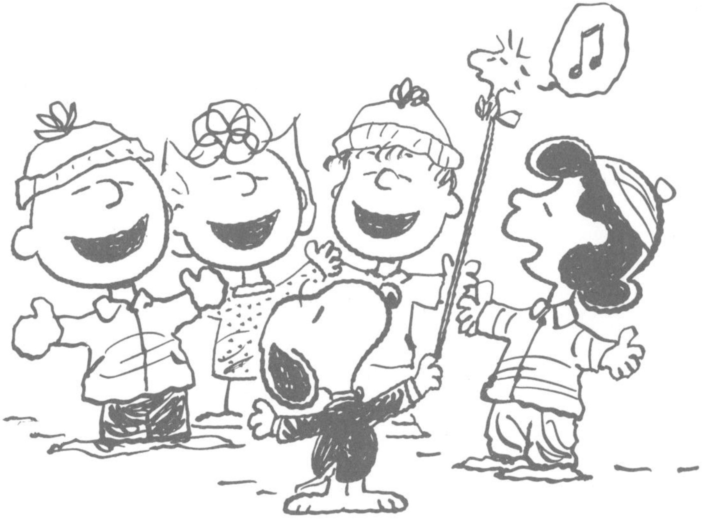

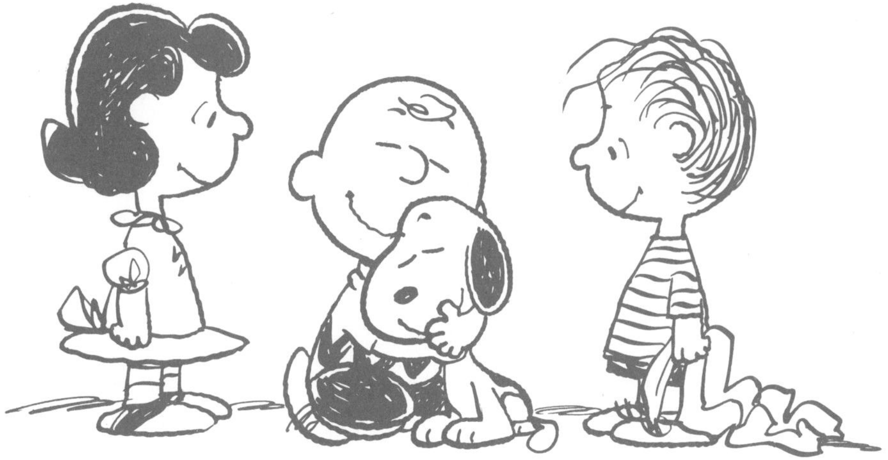

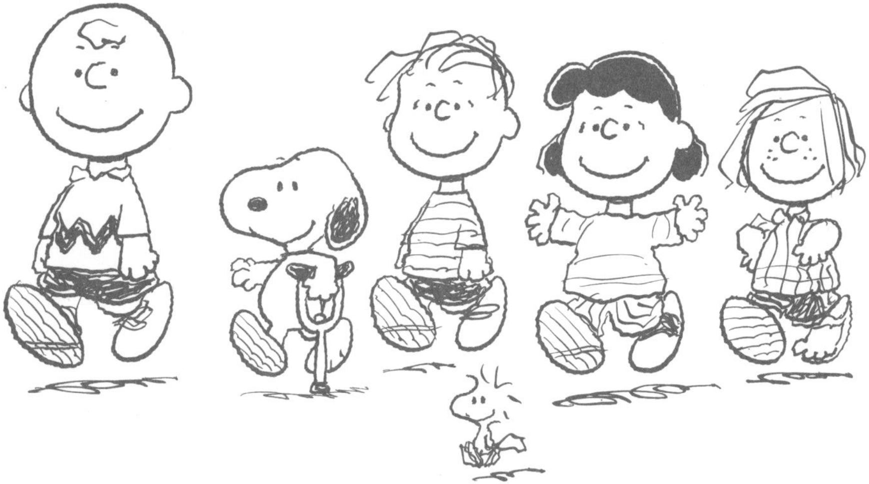

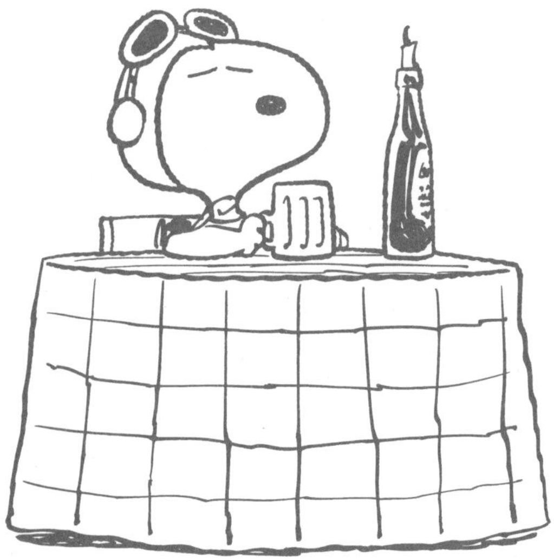

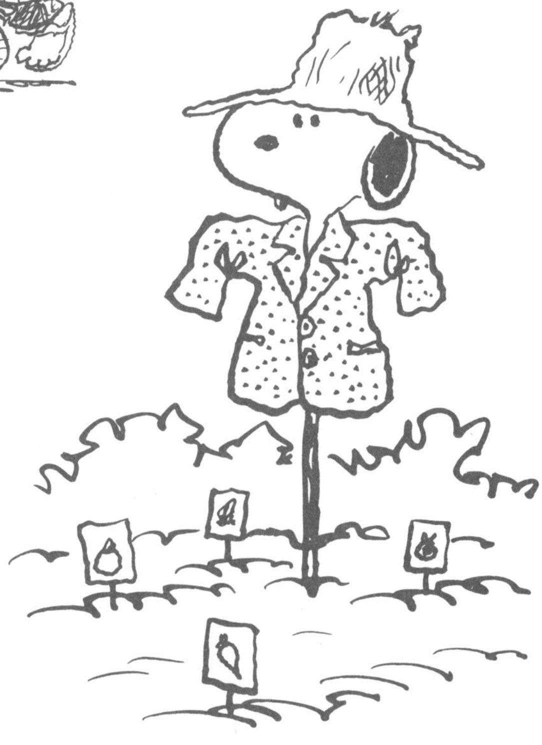

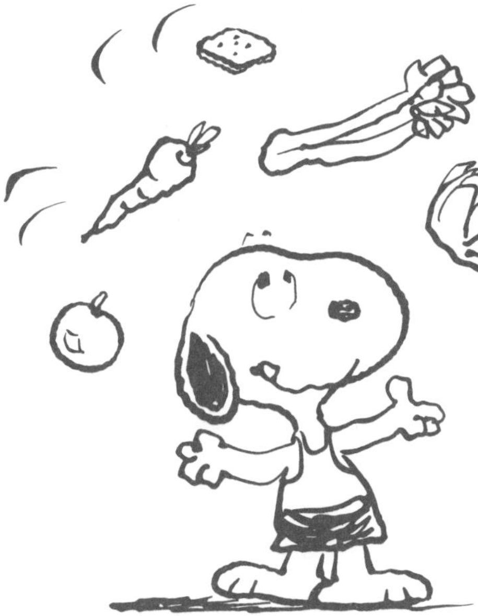

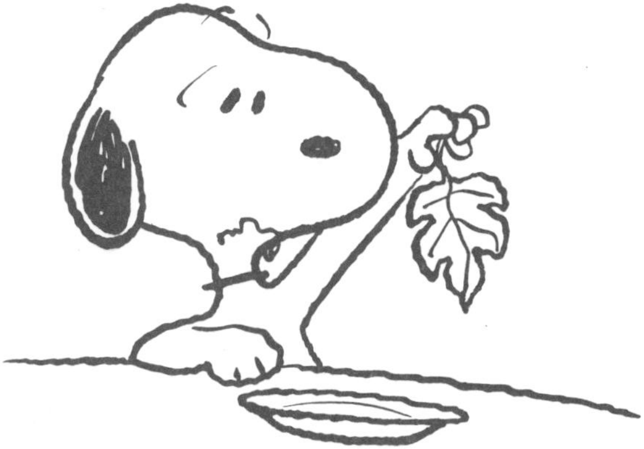

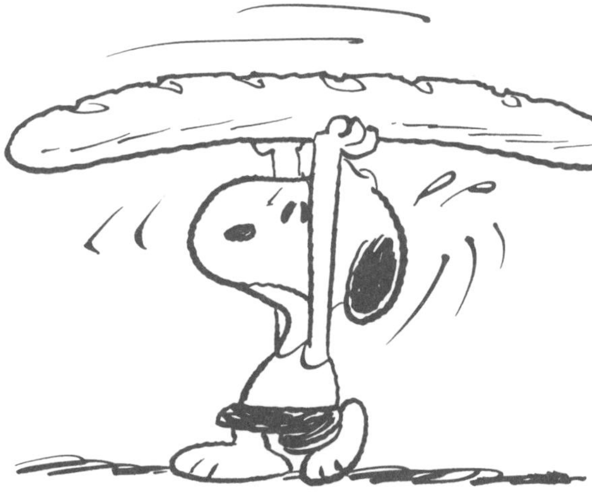

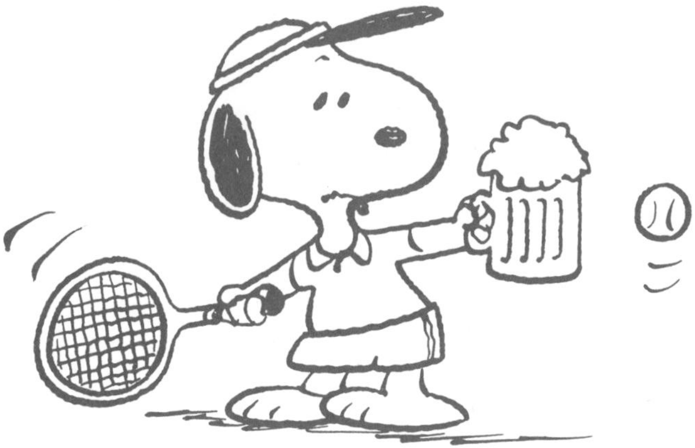

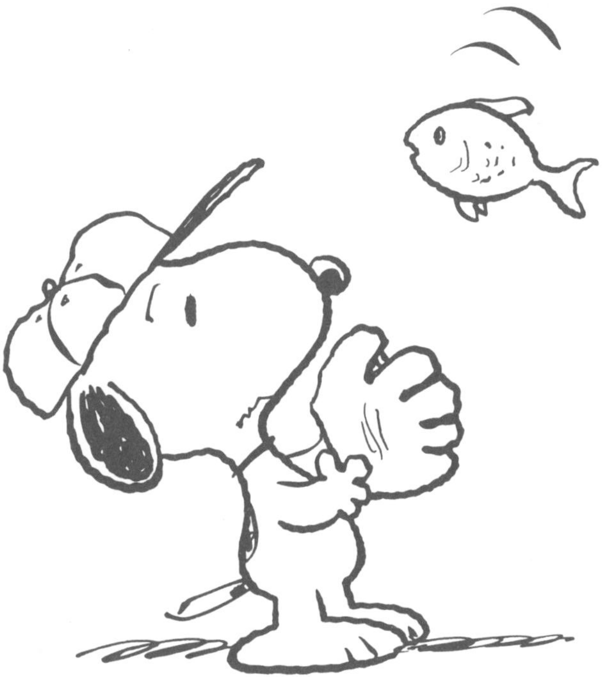

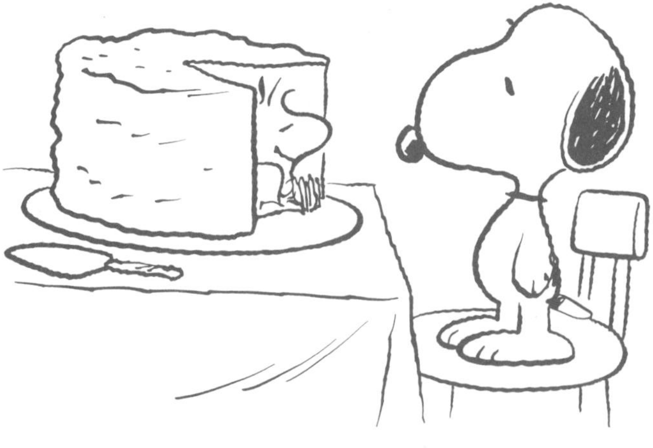

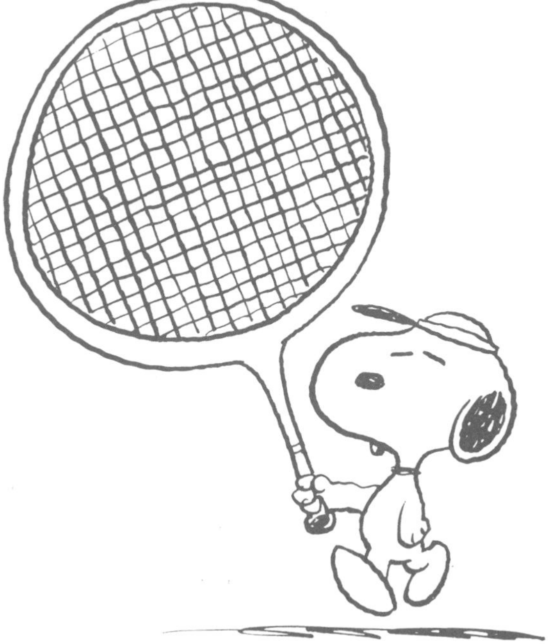

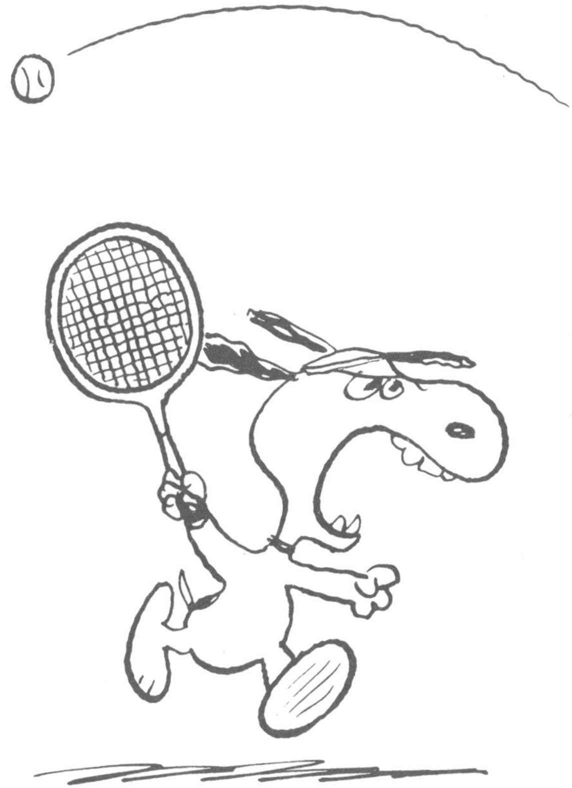

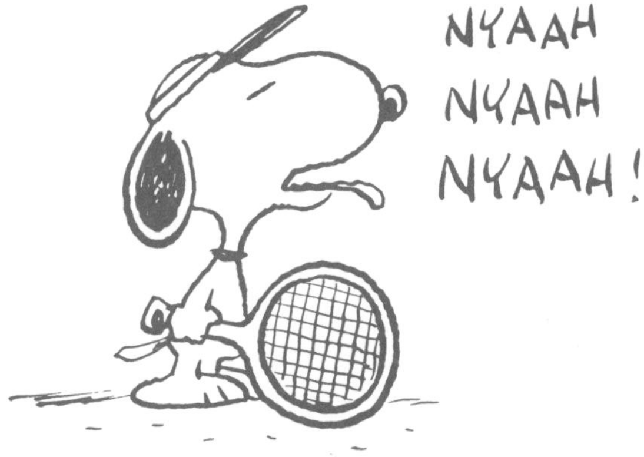
NYAAH
NYAAH
NYAAH!

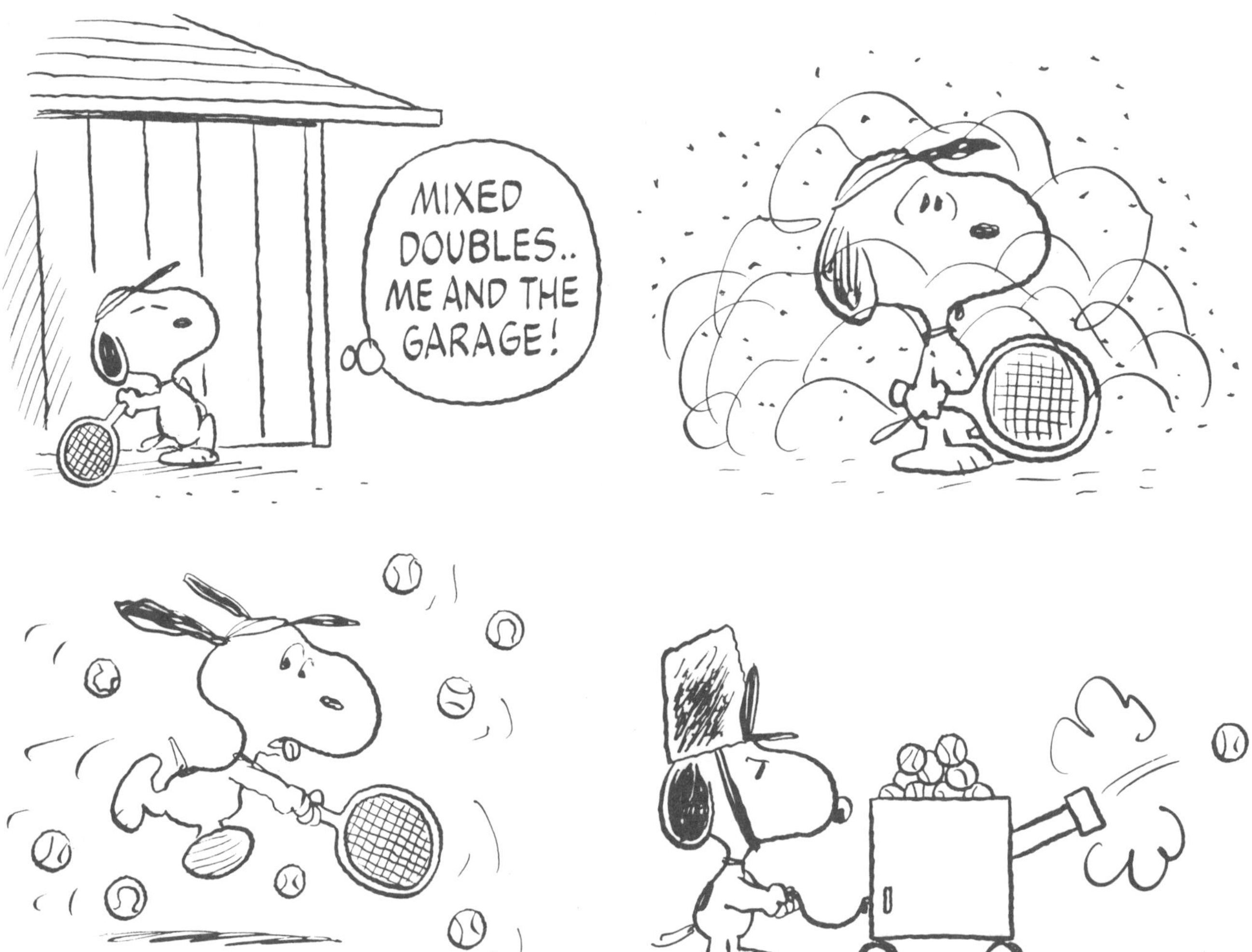
MIXED DOUBLES.. ME AND THE GARAGE!

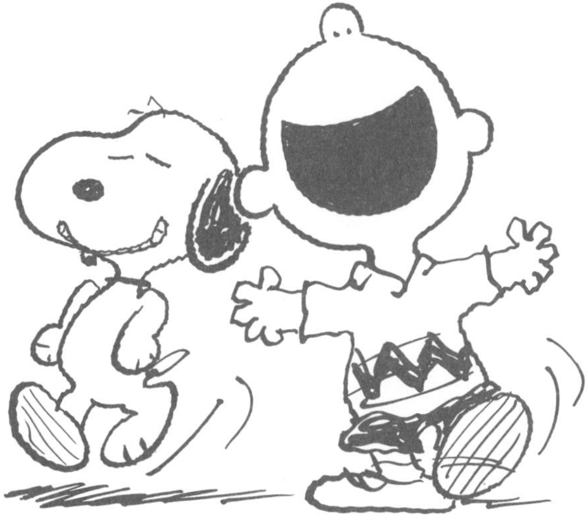

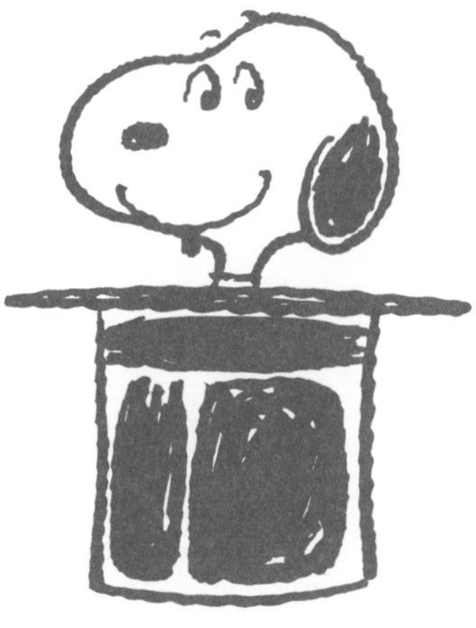

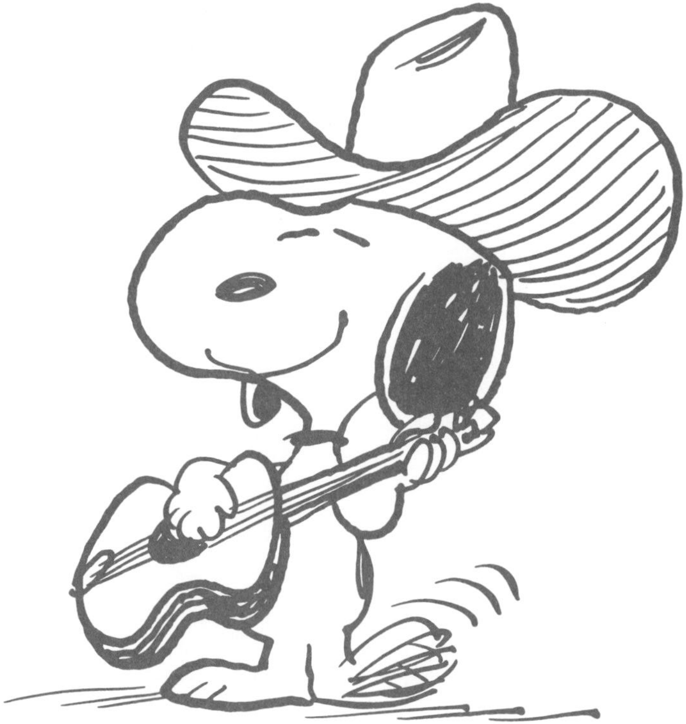

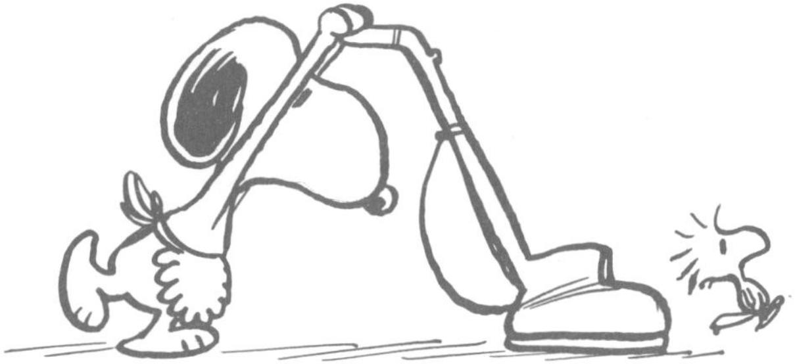

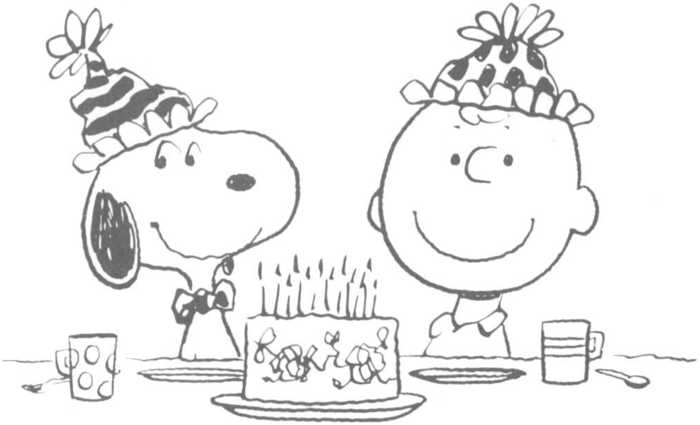

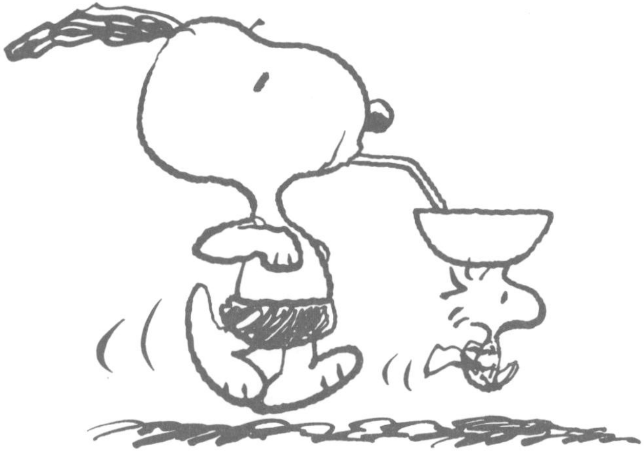

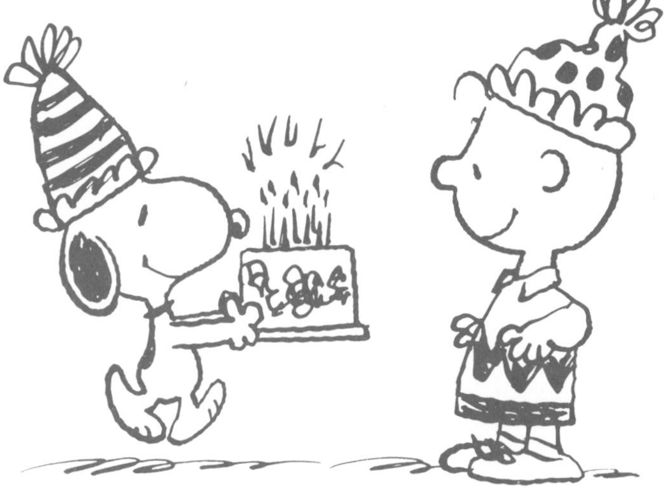

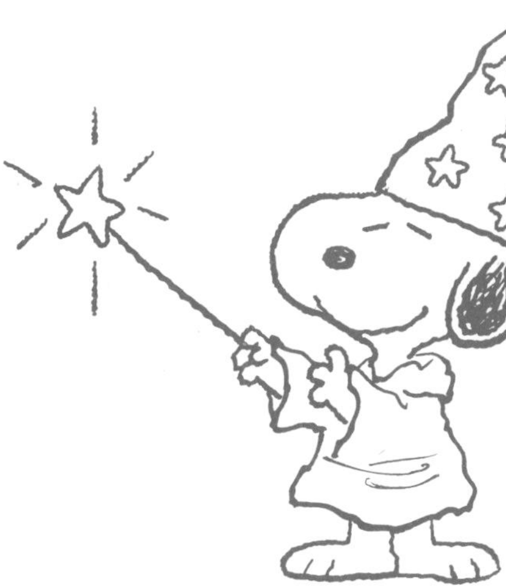

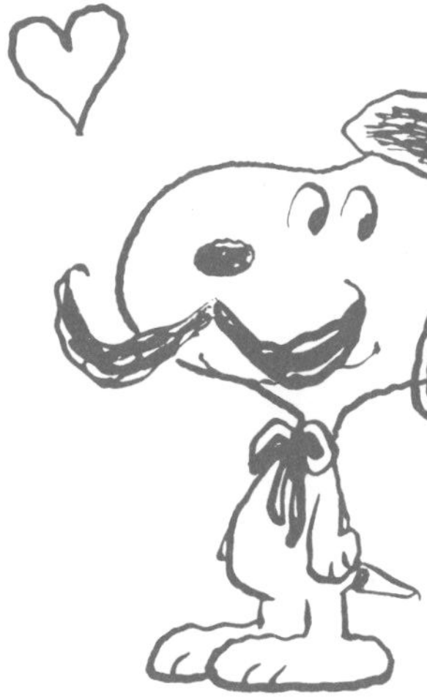

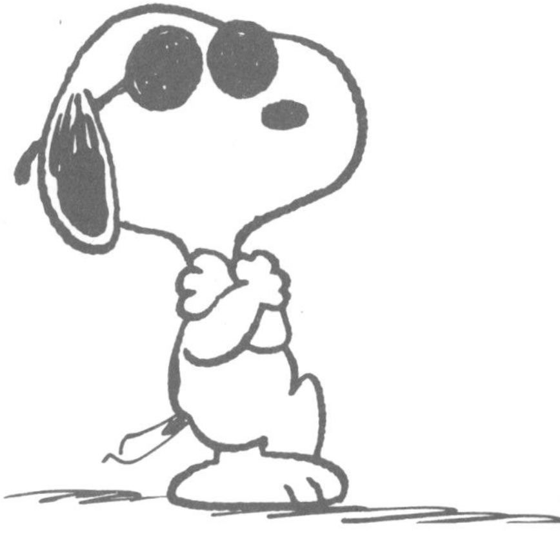

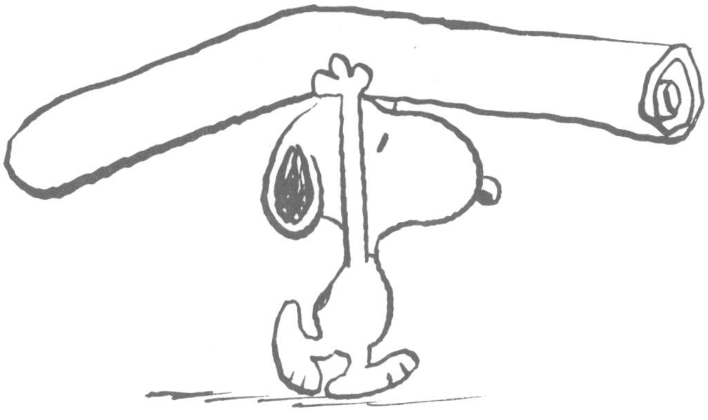

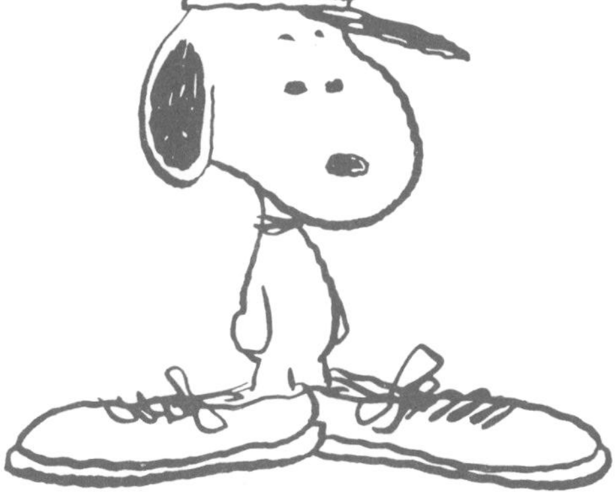

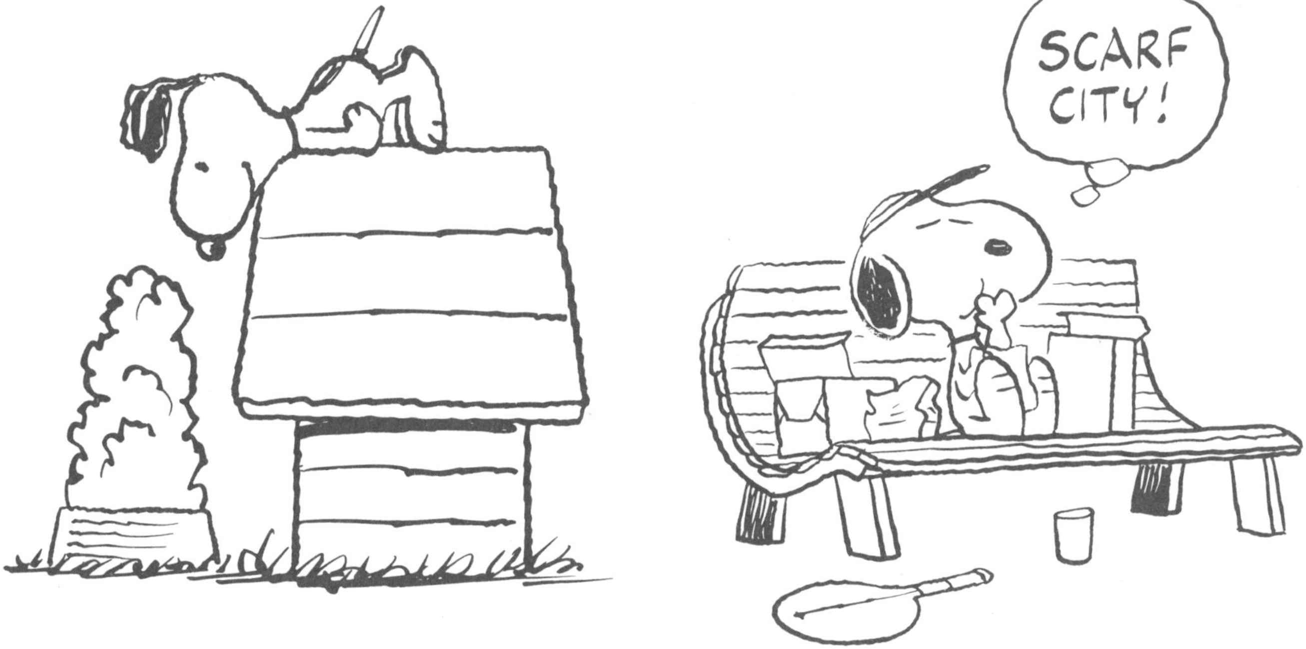
SCARF CITY!

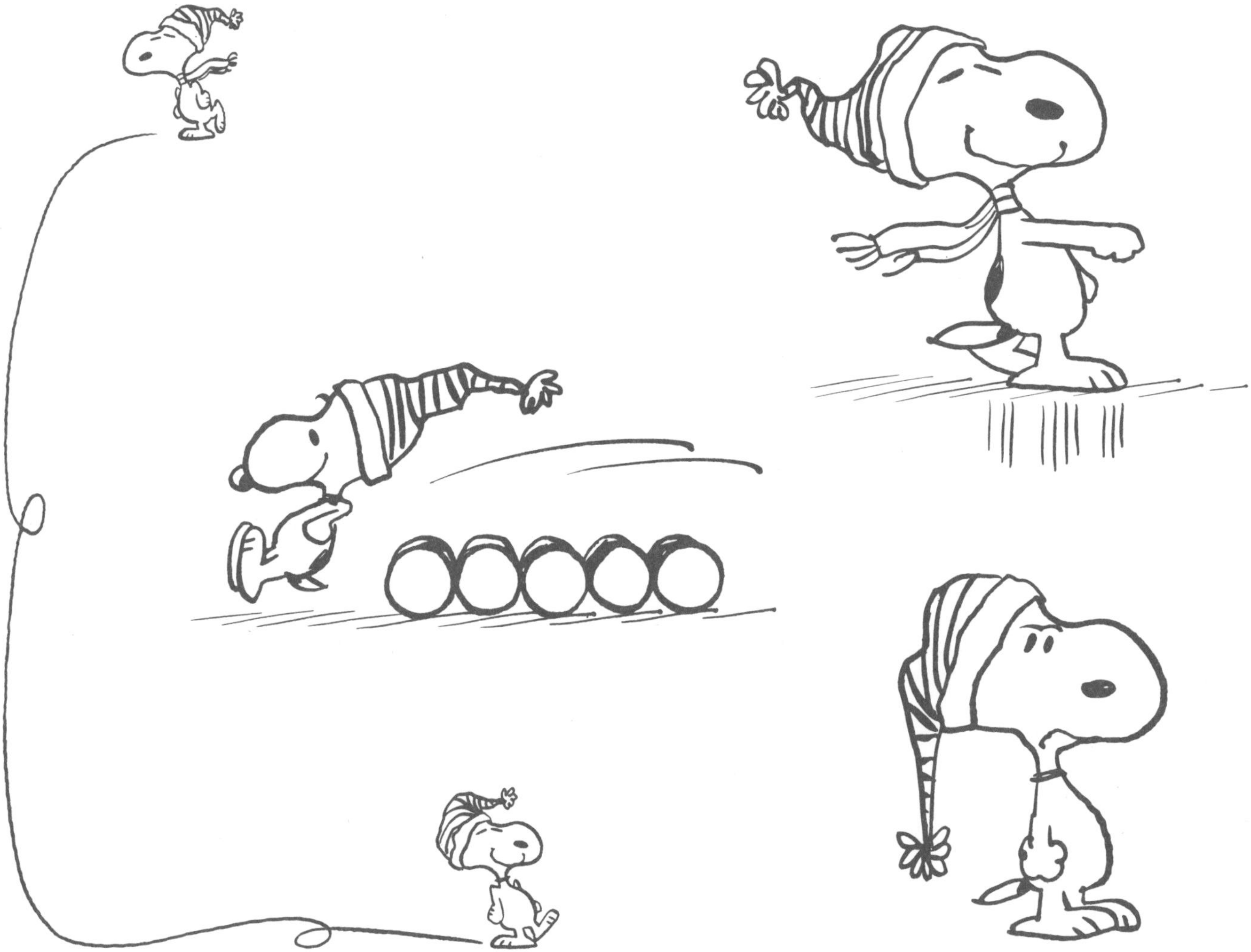

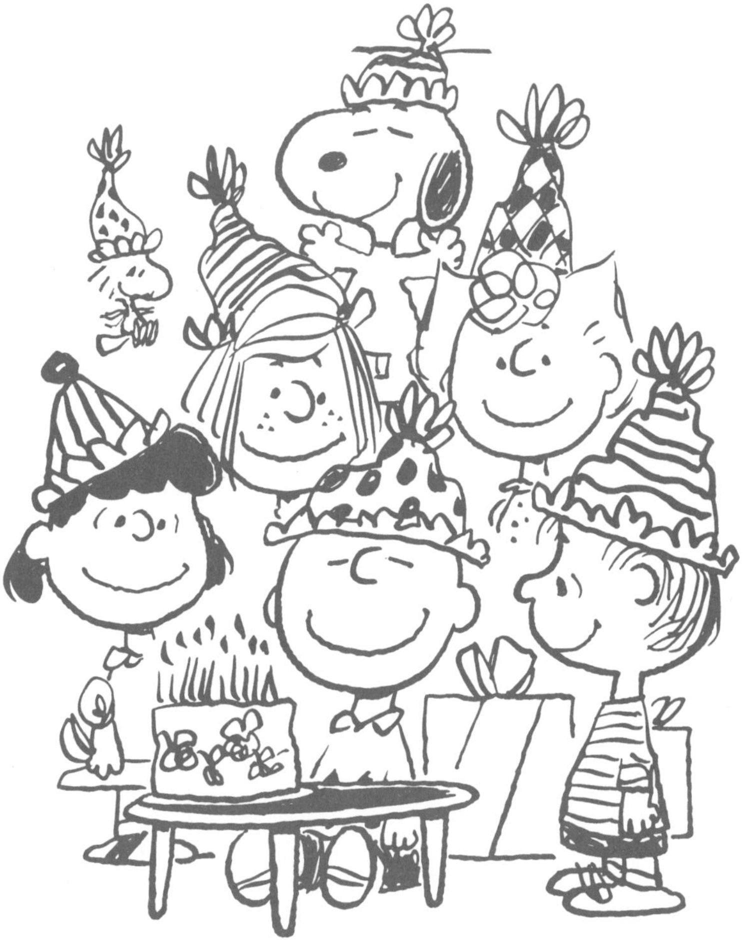

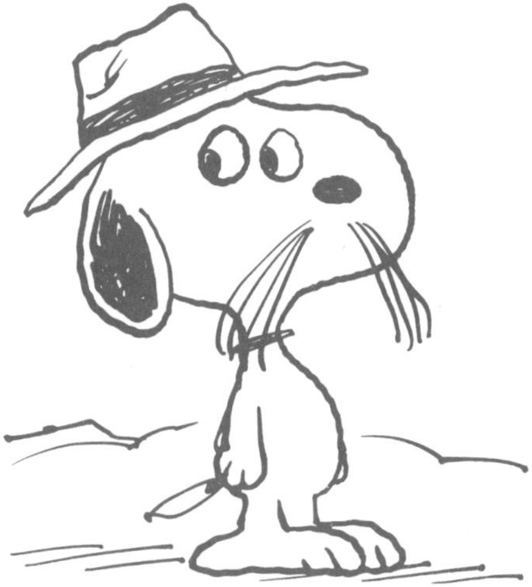

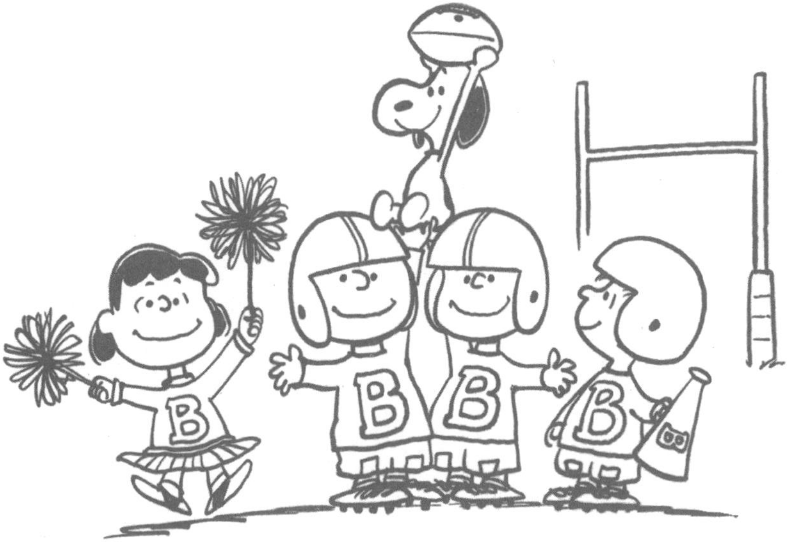

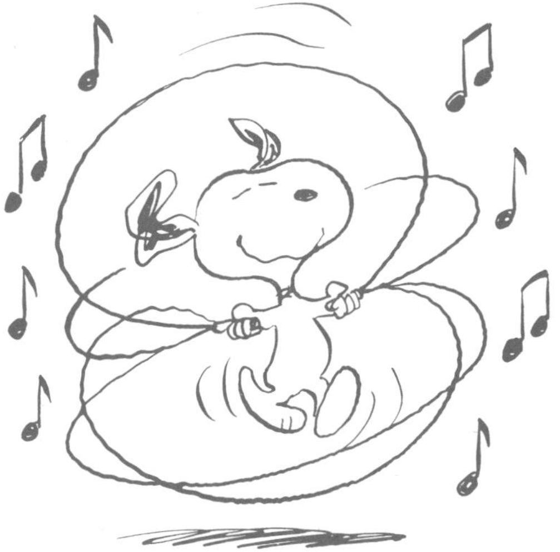

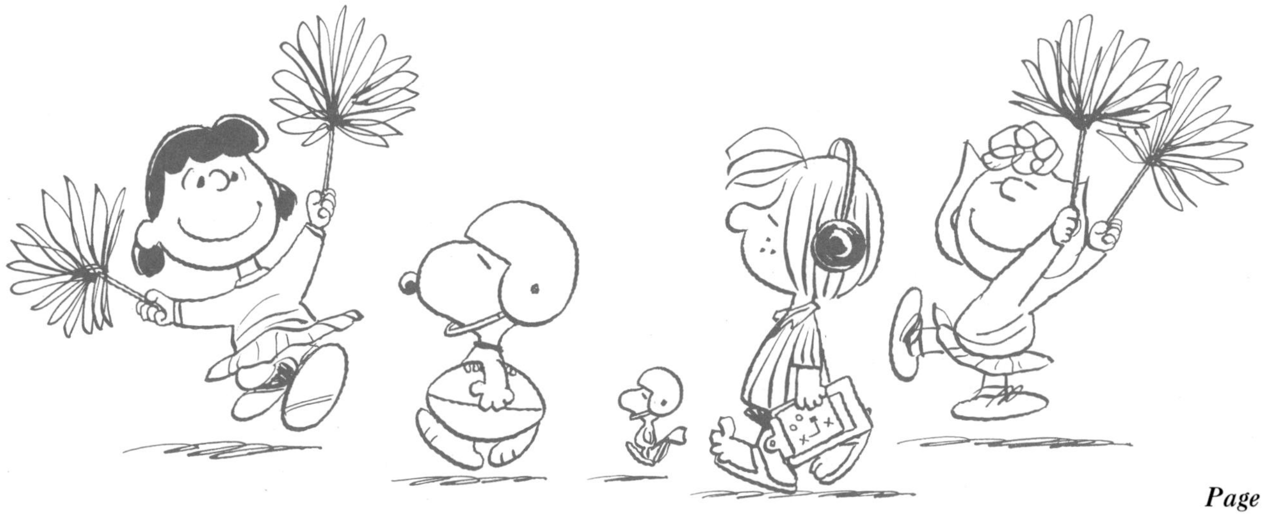

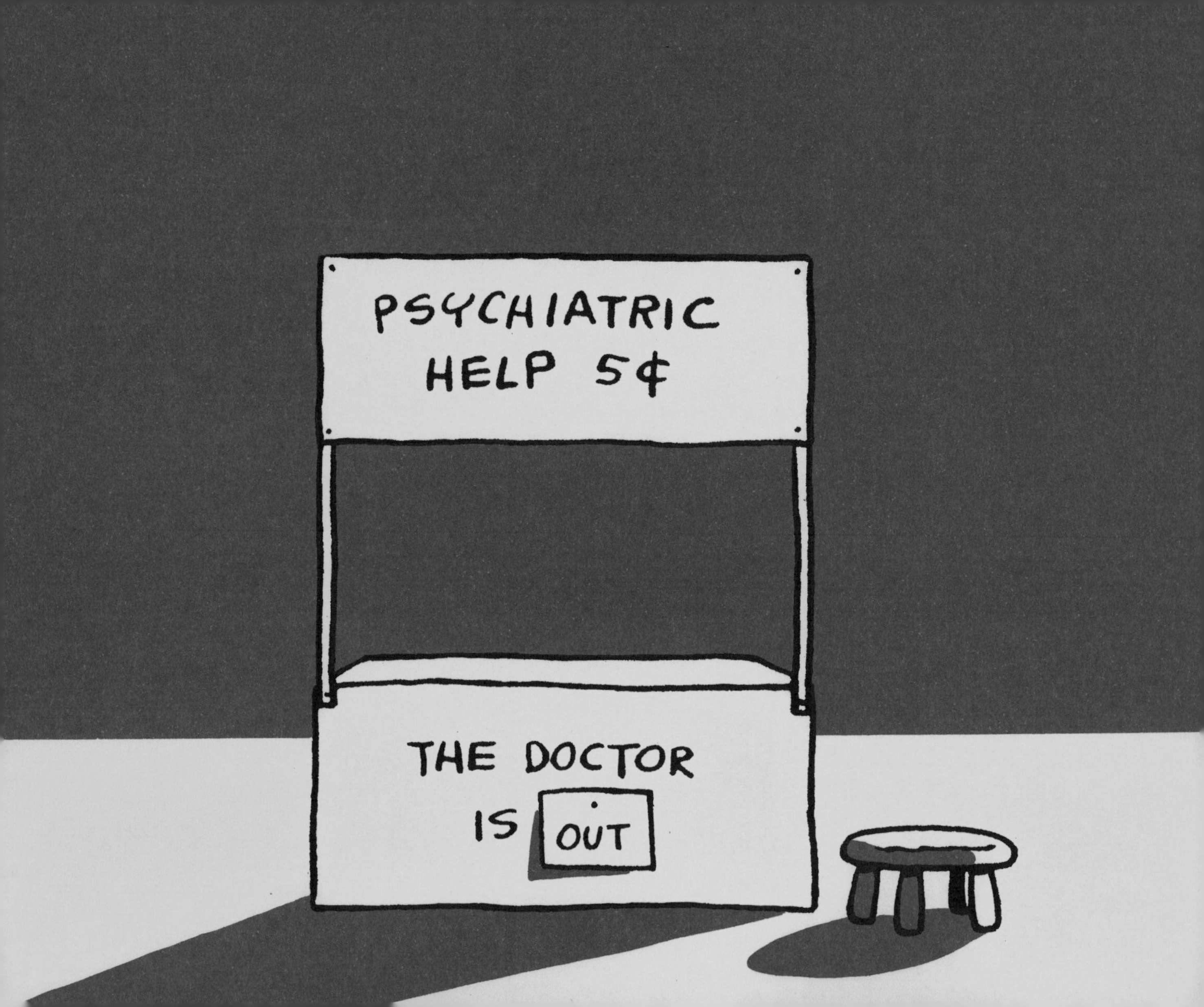
PSYCHIATRIC
HELP 5¢
THE DOCTOR
IS OUT

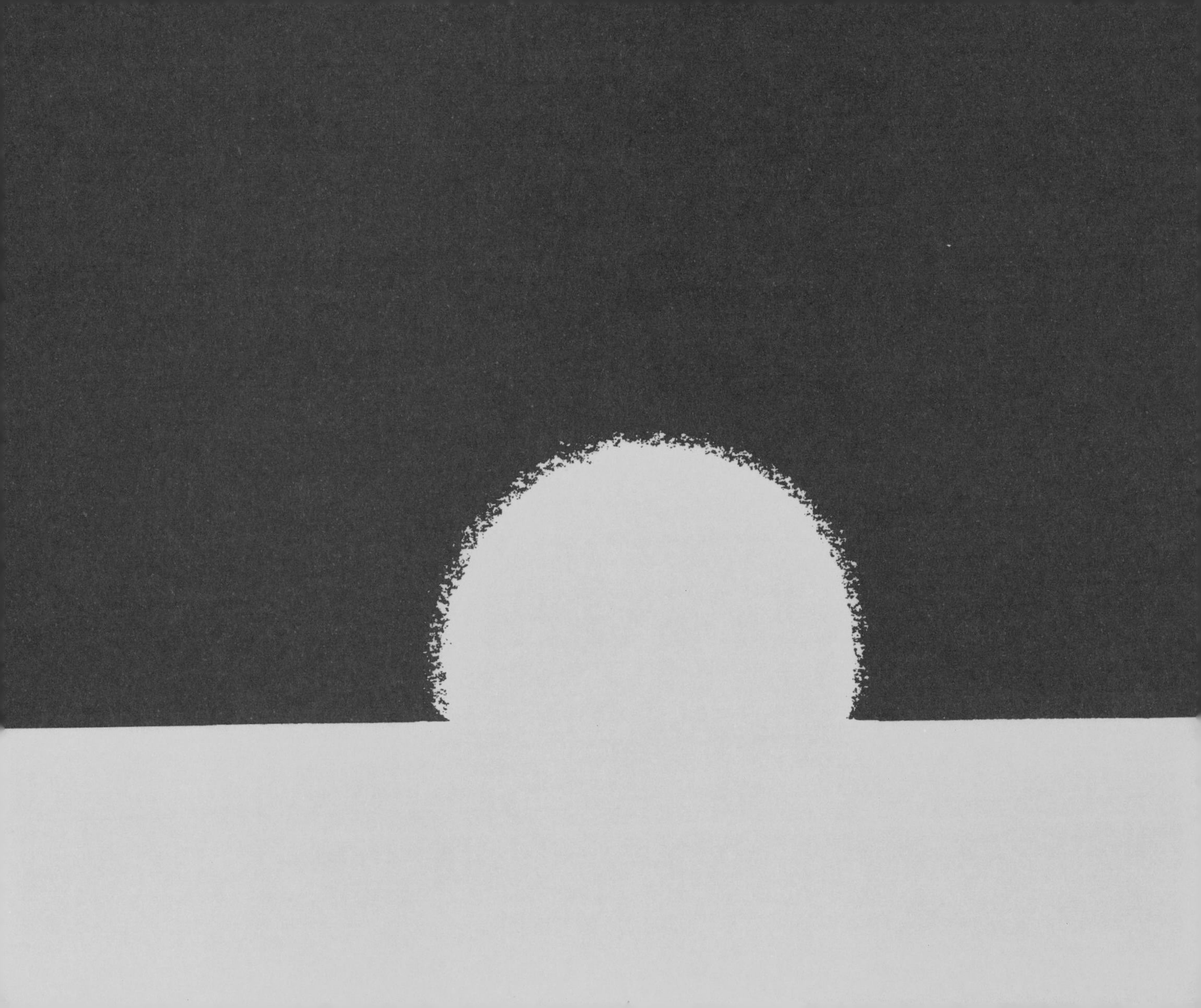

SPARKY by JEAN SCHULZ

I spend a great deal of my time at the Charles M. Schulz Museum, and I am always happy to talk to visitors and answer their questions. One thing I generally explain, upon being introduced as Charles Schulz's wife, is that his nickname was "Sparky."

Recently, I was asked if I helped Sparky with the comic strip. When Sparky and I married in 1973, he had been drawing *Peanuts* for almost twenty-three years. He was thoroughly professional in his work and in his work habits, and he had developed strong opinions about the profession he loved. He said a cartoonist couldn't sustain a comic strip if he didn't draw on the authenticity of his own life — and no, he didn't need any help from me or anyone else. Because he took his keen insights into the people around him and crafted them into his work, all he needed was for me and everyone else to go on being ourselves.

He also believed that to be successful, a comic strip had to have many themes to play upon. He used to say he had a full keyboard — so he did not need to play the same note over and over. He had already drawn more than 8,000 comic strips, written three television shows, two movies, and multiple books, answered mountains of fan mail, taught Sunday school, *and* helped to raise five children, assisting them with schoolwork and coaching them in sports. He was fond of saying his own kids had given him six (in my recollection the number varied, but it was never very many) ideas over the years, and he added with a laugh, "That is not enough to sustain a comic strip."

Sparky's life story has been told in so many interviews that to repeat it seems redundant, but here is the short version. Sparky loved cartoons for as long as he could remember. As a youth, he drew all the time at home. As a teen, he preferred retreating to a corner of the house with his pen and pencil rather than playing outside with his country cousins during family visits to Wisconsin. Although he and his parents lived in several houses and apartments over the years, what Sparky talked about was the card table set up in the kitchen that he used as his drawing desk.

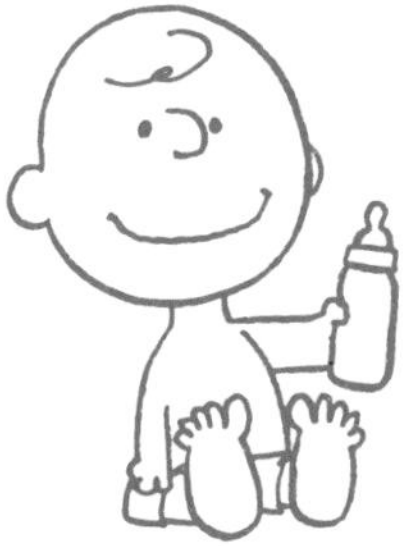

Sparky did not just read the cartoons in the newspapers in the 1920s and 1930s — he studied them. Early on, his parents encouraged his interest by buying him comics and drawing books. Later, he bought his own. Sparky dreamed of creating an adventure strip as beautifully drawn and detailed as *Prince Valiant*. His background in comics was so thorough that when he did begin drawing *Peanuts*, he had a wealth of cartoon traditions and images in his mind to draw from.

It was Frank Wing, a principal instructor at Art Instruction, Inc. in Minneapolis (the correspondence school where Sparky worked after World War II, correcting the lessons mailed in by the students) who told him that his little-kid cartoons were his best work, and he should concentrate on them.

And so, after five years of mailing and hand-carrying his submissions to newspaper syndicates, he was offered a contract, and the first *Peanuts* strip was published October 2, 1950.

Sparky and I met at the ice arena during the time that he was drawing in offices upstairs while he waited for his Studio at #1 Snoopy Place to be completed. My daughter and a friend were skating the early morning sessions, and I was driving them back and forth. Sparky stopped me one day to ask about my comings and goings. I told him I was on my way to play tennis.

"What is your name?" he asked. "My name is Jeannie."

What was it about that brief encounter that got to him? He wrote a poem about it:

You hurried by
        and caught my eye
And love sat near

"My name is Jeannie"
        "I'm so glad that you like me"
And the square at Ghirardelli
        and love moved closer

Can two people kiss
        In the sun among the crowd
While others pay no mind
        and love moves closer?

You hurried by
        and caught my eye
And loved joined us forever.

Sparky told me later that the simplicity of my
answer encouraged him to ask me to sit down with
him and have a cup of coffee.

A little over a year later, we were married.

What I observed in 1973 was a man who
seemed to do his work so easily, so naturally, and
who made it look so simple that it was difficult to
think of it as work. He seemed to naturally fold the
new things that came with a new marriage and a
new household into the pattern of his daily routine

at his drawing board. He was obsessive about his
work, and fortunately for our home life, his obses-
sion ended when he left the studio. But no matter
what he was doing, the *Peanuts* characters were
never far away.

Sparky was not demanding, and in fact was
very appreciative of all my efforts around the house
and in the community. I can't imagine a better husband for me. I don't think I ever walked into his
studio that he didn't say how happy he was to see
me; and it was the same when I phoned him there.
My hope is that I was as good a wife to him as he
was a husband to me. It hadn't occurred to me that
I had been looking for someone to adore me, so it
was a delightful surprise that he did.

Sparky was proud of the simplest things I did,
but he also recognized when I was in over my head,
and he was there to help. A silly example: when
I was invited to throw out the honorary first pitch
at a San Diego Padres baseball game (on behalf of
Canine Companions for Independence — one of
the dogs trotted the ball out to me at the pitcher's
mound), he took me out onto our ball field and
showed me how to get my elbow up and my
shoulder back so I didn't throw "like a girl."
I thought it was very cute of him. At a more serious
time, when a complicated, contentious issue came
before a non-profit board on which I served,

Sparky's calm support and wisdom helped me through a difficult decision.

Another time, in the 1990s, I had to make the two-hour drive from Santa Rosa to Sacramento to give a deposition involving a different non-profit on whose board I also served. Sparky insisted on accompanying me, so he spent his entire working day driving and observing. He sat impassively through the deposition and even remained in the room with the complainant when we took a recess. His equanimity amazed me, and the fact that he remained perfectly calm through it all helped me to keep my own cool. He regularly maintained that calm demeanor during many trying meetings and other situations. I admired it and I learned from it.

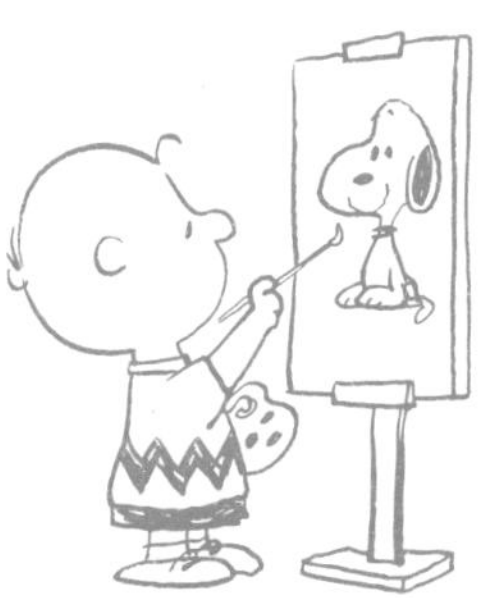

He saw me working for a couple of years on a book about my father's writings, much of which I discussed with him. When it was nearly finished he said, "You should have this published." He reminded me that friends of ours were in the book printing business. They agreed to edit and publish it — and I wound up with a beautiful tribute book to my father, which I have happily shared with family and interested friends.

We quickly became "Sparky and Jeannie" to our friends. We moved in a small circle: Sparky's work, the ice arena, family, and a few social events that revolved around some of my non-profit boards.

Sports were an important part of our lives in the early days of our marriage. Sparky had been playing hockey regularly at the Redwood Empire Ice Arena since its opening in 1969. (He and his first wife, Joyce, had built it for the community, and it became like a second home to him.) Golf was a lifelong sport for him, and he took up tennis again when we married, as it was a sport I enjoyed. Sparky already had a tennis court next to his new studio near the ice arena. We played there with friends and colleagues who worked in his studio. We both took tennis lessons, and for many years our weekends were often busy with tennis tournaments — generally at home, but occasionally out of town in places like Palm Springs and Reno. Five years into our marriage, we built an indoor tennis court. Then, inspired by Billie Jean King's World Team Tennis event, we began an evening mixed-doubles league, which went on for several years. Today the court is used more than ever.

There was a period in the 1980s when Sparky was regularly invited to golf tournaments, including the Dinah Shore. I played in the tennis portion there with professionals invited by the organization. At the end of each day, he was as eager to hear about my matches as he was to talk about his time on the golf course.

At home, we quickly developed a regimen of meeting three times a week after work at the junior college where we could run on the soft track — and sometimes up and down the bleachers. As we jogged around, we would discuss our day. When we got home to dinner and teenage children, we had already had good catch-up time together. It was a simple routine that suited us well.

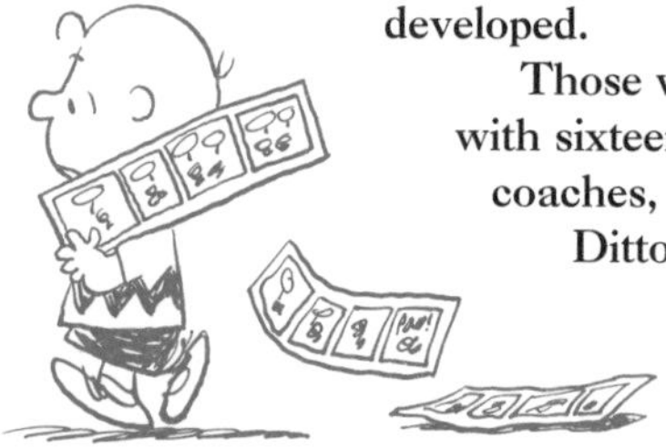

In addition to playing hockey, Sparky also refereed junior hockey games at the ice arena, and his senior hockey team played in some out-of-town tournaments. I began taking adult skating lessons on Monday nights. Sparky would watch the lessons and then we would skate together at the following public session.

Recently, a woman in the parking lot of the ice arena introduced herself and told me that she had skated those sessions, too, in the 1970s. She described Sparky and me skating hand-in-hand and how sweet it looked. Listening to her, I was briefly transported back to those days and the sheer joy of the moment.

My daughter also was skating, taking lessons, and competing at a preliminary level. Sparky's two daughters were more advanced skaters, and their competitions frequently took place out of town. Sparky, or both of us, accompanied them. All three girls skated on the medal-winning drill team that the Redwood Empire Ice Arena's instructors developed.

Those were exciting days. When you go off with sixteen teenage skaters, parents, and coaches, it is always a vibrant experience. Ditto going off with the senior hockey team, wives, and coaches. In 1982, Sparky played the role of our mascot when our ladies' tennis team went to the playoffs in Orange County. He loved "hanging around" in these situations being "one of the gang," and not the center of attention.

Sparky took up golf as a teenager and became obsessed with it. He lettered in golf in high school, and he took great pride in winning the caddie championship at Highland National Golf Course in St. Paul. He had to forego the game while he was overseas in the army during the war, but he took it up again when he returned, even before he was discharged. When he went back to civilian life, he found a group of golf friends, and they played frequently. At one point, he was close to a scratch golfer. One of his favorite memories from that time was being able to follow his hero, Sam Snead, in the gallery at the St. Paul Open. He was later known to say that, back then, he would have loved to play on the professional golf tour, like Snead.

When I expressed interest in learning golf in the 1980s, Sparky enthusiastically encouraged me. He loved to share his passions with others. When we played together he patiently showed me all the touch shots around the green. Now when I play, I can feel him there, and I remember his instructions. The dignity of the game was important to him, and he imparted that feeling to everyone who played with him. Golf, tennis, hockey — all were important in his life and in our life together.

Home with Sparky

The two questions people ask me more than any other are: "What was Sparky like at home?" and "Could you tell when he was thinking about his characters?"

My answer is that I assume the *Peanuts* gang was always lurking in the recesses of his mind.

Whether he was watching a sports program on TV, attending a movie, or just reading, those characters had to have been with him because we see it later in the strip. Sally's gentle absurdity imparts a certain philosophical nonsense that mirrored Sparky's opinions: "The world is coming to an end — Details at 11" (11/19/95). Peppermint Patty seeks reassurance in the routine at the theater: "Have you heard any announcements? I always like the announcements. I love the announcements." To which Marcie replies, "You're very weird, sir." (5/24/99).

Just about everything he observed was translated into a comic strip and, of course, Sparky has conceded that Charlie Brown, Linus, and Lucy all mirror parts of him. He readily accepted that he had a "Lucy" side, and his rebukes had a sting to them. Often the sting came because they were so right-on. His advice and comments came in short sentences — with a self-confidence that often left me with no rejoinder.

And, what *was* Sparky like, at home and elsewhere? Besides being an "easy keeper" (his favorite meals were simple: tuna casserole, bacon and eggs, a tuna sandwich), his entertainment was simple: a movie, a bridge game, an afternoon of golf, and then dinner with friends.

Sparky was a good sport, jumping in to help me with my never-ending projects. After we built a new home in 1980, we both sweated over a steep bank on our property that we covered with rocks we had gathered from the acreage — which was mostly rocks! It is basically hidden, so he couldn't really show it off. However, another wall that we call "Sparky's Wall" is famous on our property. Sparky worked on his wall of small rocks and mortar for several years. Family and visitors made a pile for him of the right-size small rocks and he would work on it each weekend. It looks much like the wall the kids lean on in the comic strip. I don't think he intended this, but that's the way it evolved. Another project I roped him into was spreading turkey manure in the garden. (Our gardener then was elderly, and, I felt, not up to the work.) After three years of the hauling and spreading — and the smell, which lingered for weeks — Sparky declared that he thought we had done enough of this, and maybe we should hire someone to do this job if I wanted it done. But he was a good sport about it for several years.

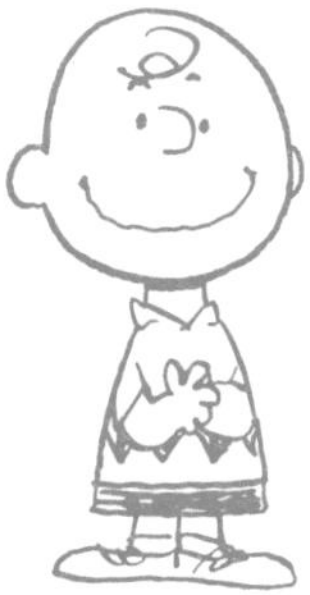

Gala dance parties were popular fundraisers in Santa Rosa in the 1970s and 1980s. Sparky was willing to take up in mid-life what he had missed earlier. So we began dancing lessons upstairs in the ice arena and Sparky talked several friends into joining us. Sparky felt most comfortable at the dances that took place in the arena (with a floor laid over the ice and elaborate decorations, which completely belied the arena's primary purpose). These consisted of a tea dance after "The Woodstock" golf tournament (Sparky's idea) and the volunteer center's "Sweetheart Ball," which included a mini ice show on a quarter of the uncovered ice. Sparky enjoyed hosting these fundraisers. He was proud of what the arena contributed to these community events, and was always generous, underwriting the cost of the arena and donating comic strips for their auctions.

Sparky had a really silly side and loved practical jokes. He loved to relate the antics of his five children and pranks they played on friends at their home in Sebastopol, California. He teased TV producer Lee Mendelson about his telephone calls — after hanging up from a call, Lee would call right back to tell you what he had forgotten.

One day Sparky got back at Lee. He called Lee's answering machine and said, "I bet you have never read *War and Peace*. You should." Sparky then began on page one and read several pages, redialing when the answering machine cut him off.

Sparky laughed about that joke for many years. (I'm sure Lee did, too.)

Sparky also poked fun at Lee in a comic strip: Charlie Brown chases his croquet ball into the street and up against a phone booth. Stepping into the booth Charlie Brown says, "Yes … call me when it's my turn, will you? The number here is …" and there he put Lee's seven-digit telephone number. Telephones across the country rang that Sunday morning, and at Lee's house, the first surprise call was very early in the morning, a small voice saying, "It's your turn, Charlie Brown."

Sparky loved the unexpected when it was presented as good fun. Once I greeted him outside his favorite barbershop, perched on the hood of his car. "I'm your new hood ornament," I announced. Sparky loved that, and he told the story again and again. "You'll never guess what Jeannie surprised me with." Was he at all concerned about possible scratches to his car? Not in the least. Those things didn't bother him.

Another time, at a tennis court at a tournament, I had taken a big gulp of water. I turned toward him and began coughing uncontrollably — and sprayed it all over him. Rather than being upset at the "shower," he found it hilarious and showed off his soaked shirt to everyone. Sparky also loved to show his wintergreen trick. To impress guests at our home, he would cajole them into the pantry, close the door, and crack apart a wintergreen Life Saver to make it sparkle in the pitch darkness. These stories show his slapstick and playful side.

Sparky was also a very quick and strategic thinker. I used to say that if I were in a life-threatening situation there is no one I would rather be with than Sparky. It was uncanny how clearly he could assess a situation and hone in on what needed to be done. This applied both to physically dangerous situations and when his children came home with problems. He went right to the core of the situation. As I think about it, I imagine this was the quality that his commanding officers saw in him and was the reason he was elevated to staff sergeant while at Camp Campbell during the war.

In his 2006 biography, David Michaelis discussed Sparky's depression at length. I prefer to call it "melancholy" because depression feels like a much deeper and more continuous condition that leads to a sort of mental paralysis, which I saw only occasionally in our twenty-seven years. Much of it is probably the same northern melancholy that is mirrored in Garrison Keillor's *Prairie Home Companion* radio program. Sometimes it is a melancholy that comes from thinking too much. In the 6/17/1998 strip, Charlie Brown, reclining against a mound of earth with Snoopy says, "Sometimes I wonder if I even know what it would take to make me happy…" Snoopy stands up and tosses a ball past Charlie Brown, then lies back into the pose from the first panel and thinks, "That usually works with dogs." This strip shows Sparky's honest reflection on his own personality, and the humor that he knows makes a truth easier to accept. But the searching goes back as far as 1958 when, in the 11/14 strip, Charlie Brown says to Lucy, "I wish I could be happy … I think I could be happy if my life had more purpose to it. I also think that if I were happy, I could help others to be happy … does that make sense to you?" A bored Lucy says, "We've had spaghetti at our house three times this month!" To me, this shows Sparky's awareness that "navel gazing" is truly an unproductive activity.

And in the 10/30/69 strip he says: "How come I never wake up thinking I'm going to have a good day, and then really have a good day? Or how come I never wake up thinking I'm going to have a bad day, and then have a good day?" The last panel ends, "My stomach hurts …"

This sort of introspection in the comic strip is awfully hard on Charlie Brown. It is what readers relate to and may have been a sort of catharsis for Sparky.

Sparky once said to me, "You and I are the same; we don't belong anywhere." Without needing to ask exactly what he meant, I took this as a truth. It went straight to my heart, and I have thought about it for all the years since then. I still wonder exactly what it meant to *him*, but to me it meant and still means that, in belonging nowhere, we belong everywhere — and I do think it is a clue to his deeper feelings.

Rheta Grimsley Johnson, author of the first Charles Schulz biography written for adults, delved into Sparky's depression right off the bat, on page 37. Rheta reported that that particular chapter received more commentary and feedback than any other aspect of her book. A psychologist with whom I spoke suggested that a great deal of that reaction represented readers' projections of their own feelings — just as Sparky was somehow comforted by reading biographies and learning of the subject's insecurities and struggles. I often felt that he used the lives of others as a touchstone for his own life, measuring his emotions and feelings against a subject he admired, assuring himself that his own feelings were not an aberration.

Sparky was a great observer of people. He had a good ear for language and idiom, and he made good use of that facility. Whenever he overheard a quirky turn of phrase or a new piece of jargon from the teenagers around us or the kids at the arena, he knew just which *Peanuts* character for whom it would be the perfect fit. As an artist, Sparky was always observing his environment. He said frequently that when sitting in a meeting he was always "drawing with [his] eyes," noticing the fold of a shirt next to the collar and the drape of a curtain. (Many artists speak of having this propensity.)

Sparky was also a curious man whose curiosity led him to delve into things others might let pass unnoticed. I think this came from the fact that his focus was not on the external world, but on his internal world. Everything was fodder for *Peanuts*. Though I observed his creativity for twenty-eight years and can now spot the kinds of ideas that Sparky would have keyed in to, I don't have his creative mind, and I have no idea *how* he would have used them.

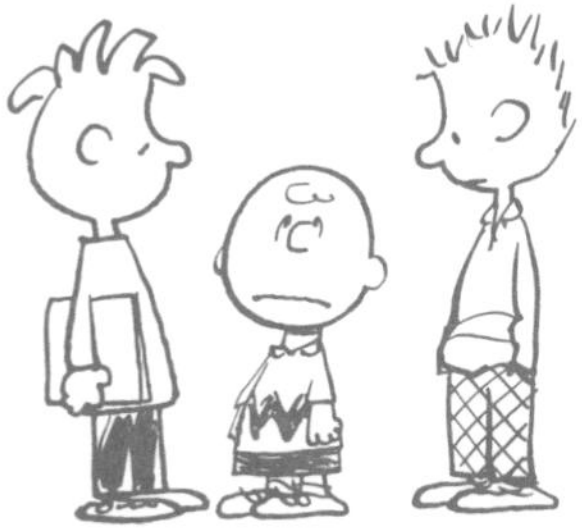

For example, the heavens and the mysteries of the universe intrigued him. He would have surely played with the information in 2010 about the announcement of the number of newly calculated stars in the sky. Can't you just see him loving the number 300 sextillion? And we know he would have found a way to use it. Ditto the unfolding theory of Saturn's rings. And the discovery that microbes that exist on arsenic may inhabit other planets (Sally says, "How gross!"). And the star called HIP 13044 (sounds like a zip code, right?), which began its life in another galaxy that was cannibalized by our galaxy, the Milky Way. All of these things would have been fodder for the strip. I suspect he would have zeroed right in on the argument among astronomers about Pluto's status as a planet (The International Astronomical Union "demoted" Pluto to dwarf planet status in 2006. Sparky might have noticed that the "demoting astronomer" had the last name of Brown).

In addition to these issues in the news, I think Sparky would have noticed the recently discovered Higgs boson and would have found a way to work it into the strip — and in a context with a humorous twist. If you don't believe me about his penchant to collect and use odd facts, see the 1/17/64 strip in which Charlie Brown talks about a Diatryma. "He was a bird who stood seven feet tall and had a head as large as that of a horse! He had a huge sharp bill and powerful legs with which he could run down small animals ... He is now extinct ... in fact, he hasn't been around for sixty billion years ..." Snoopy thinks, "And we won't miss him a bit!" Speaking of current events, can't you see Woodstock as the ultimate tweeter? Joe Cool thinking about his Facebook page? And Sally freaking out when she hears that advertisers "want her eyeballs?"

It was wonderful to be at dinner or a small group with Sparky because he always kept the conversation going — often with questions that I might have thought too probing. But Sparky had a demeanor that resonated as interested rather than prying. A frequent question of Sparky's was, "What did your father do?" This question often took people back to their memories, and created a rapport between them. Another favorite was, "How did your parents meet?" I know Sparky missed having had an opportunity to ask this and similar questions of his own parents. He often said that he simply had been too immature to ask; and then, as we know, the opportunity passes. There was a period of several years when he gave talks to younger audiences and spoke of the importance of asking your parents questions about *their* lives. I would like to think that the advice stuck in the minds of these young people, and that the beginnings of some great conversations ensued, and a different understanding was established between generations.

At gatherings with creative people, Sparky was always able to keep the conversation going with questions that were honest and probing, but never sycophantic or trite. Of course, it was easy for him to discuss cartooning, but he loved to discuss music also. Although Sparky had no formal musical training, he had spent many, many hours listening to classical records beginning when he worked at Art Instruction. He and several of the other instructors would whistle a theme from the great symphonies and concertos and see who could identify it. He loved the patterns in music, and from years of active listening he understood where the music was heading. So at the symphony, he was not simply an observer; he listened with anticipation.

Sparky was comfortable in these discussions, so it made it easy for me. I got to listen to all these great conversations and was spared from exposing my own ignorance. I wished many times that I had Sparky's storytelling ability to remember and share the stories for the pleasure of others.

Sparky was also known for really off-the-wall questions. One neighbor remembered Sparky asking him pretty much out of the blue, "What do you think about The Resurrection?" I'm not sure Pete had thought about the Resurrection since college religion class, and it surprised him so much he says he will never forget the surge of feelings that welled up from racing through his mind to re-examine his thoughts about such a fundamental question.

Sparky once asked a business colleague who was a Mormon, "What do you think of the fellow

Joseph Smith?" My friend said she remembers it now, twenty-five years later, and that it actually made her think about something to which she had paid little attention previously.

Composer Ellen Zwilich said that Sparky asked if she had played a toy piano as a child. Ellen said she figured that Sparky wanted to see if she was in the same league as Schroeder, who could play the Hammerklavier Sonata on *his* piano.

I believe that Sparky asked those questions to make the conversation richer. Tennis-player-turned-philanthropist Andrea Jaeger said Sparky "looked into your heart and always wanted to hear more."

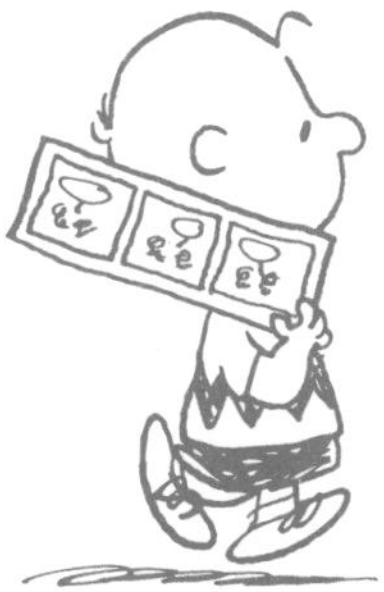

On a few formal occasions, Sparky met with heads of state, cultural ministers, and ambassadors. Again, I was happy to let him take the lead. We met President Jimmy Carter in the Oval Office. The group consisted of Sparky, me, my son Brooke Clyde, Lee Mendelson (producer of the Charlie Brown TV shows), Robert Metz (president of United Media), and two officers of United Media. Sparky pretty much carried the conversation, but at the end, Lee Mendelson said to Mr. Carter, "Thank you, Mr. President, for never giving a speech to preempt one of our Charlie Brown specials." Lee recalls the President answering, "I'll tell you something. I've done a lot of stupid things in my life, but I'm not that stupid."

When meeting President Reagan and Queen Elizabeth II in the reception line during her state visit to San Francisco, it was a simple handshake and a nod ("Mr. President." "Your Majesty."), which the formality of the occasion required. But when he met Jack Lang, the French Minister of Culture, in a less formal ceremony to be invested as a Commandeur de l'Ordre des Arts et des Lettres (Commander of the Order of Arts and Letters), they had many short conversations about art, music, and culture. Two years later in Italy, when he was presented with the Ordine al merito della Repubblica Italiana (Order of Merit of the Italian Republic), there was a formal lunch with Peter Secchia, the American ambassador to Italy, and his wife, Joan.

Sparky's grace, authenticity, and dignity carried him through situations such as these that he could never have imagined when he was starting out in his career.

Sparky worked hard to keep his life simple. Although he was proud of the recognition and honors he received, he never made more of them than they were. He was fortunate that his greatest joy was sitting at the drawing board feeling the pen nib pass over the paper as he executed his comic strip.

Our life together included new friends we had met through sports and old friends from our earlier days, with whom we became re-acquainted as a couple. Many of these friends knew what Sparky did, of course, but they seemed to take him and *Peanuts* for granted. Again, I think it was because he made it seem so easy — and he preferred to ask other people questions about their lives rather than talk about himself.

When plans were made to produce the twenty-fifth *Peanuts* anniversary show in 1975, Phyllis George was selected as the host. Phyllis George was a very popular Miss America and one of the first women to break through as a major sports writer and TV reporter. Sparky was excited about working with her, and he invited some friends to drop by his studio. Meeting Phyllis George and watching the filming seemed to make them look at Sparky differently. But Sparky had not asked them over to impress them; he just wanted to share the fun of meeting Phyllis George. As far as Sparky was concerned, he was a regular person — but Phyllis George was a star.

I'm reminded of Lee Mendelson's story of filming a documentary about Sparky in the 1960s and taking a film crew to the bowling alley in Sebastopol, where Sparky and his first wife Joyce were in a bowling league. As the crew was filming Sparky, one of the bowlers came over and said to the cameraman, "If you want to film a good bowler, you should come see Jack over here — he can really bowl." The people in the bowling league were seemingly oblivious to Sparky's celebrity status and couldn't imagine a film crew following him. (It *was* a more innocent time.)

In the 1960s, Sparky joined with one of his bowling friends, Tony Martin, to coach his sons, Monte and Craig, in the Forestville Little League, and again he was pretty much "one of the dads." He was fortunate that Sebastopol in the 1960s was a place where he could stay off the radar of tabloid celebrity newspapers.

Sparky didn't think of himself as a celebrity. For most of his early career he worked in a solitary environment with only occasional requests from reporters for interviews. *Peanuts* and its characters were beloved by fans, but Sparky felt himself to be more or less anonymous.

In a 1993 interview in Minneapolis, Sparky explained to Pat Miles, "I suppose the turning point might have been about 1958 when Snoopy got up on his hind legs and started to walk and think. Then, not long after that, we got on the cover of *Time* magazine. The *Time* 1965 cover opened up everything and everyone realized we were in the paper." Still, Sparky lived a simple and unpretentious life on a quiet lane outside of the sleepy town of Sebastopol.

There were people who "found" him, though. In 2010, Randy Alfred, writing for *California*, the Cal Alumni magazine, described how he and a friend had set out in 1967 to see if they could find Sparky's home and meet him. They did, and they did. Randy writes in the 2010 article, "We could scarcely believe our luck. The world's most successful cartoonist was holding forth on his art... Schulz asked us about ourselves. He seemed especially interested in my studies in the sociology of religion." It is a charming story, and again speaks to the "simplicity" of an earlier era, and shows that Sparky's curiosity and interest in others was simply part of his personality.

Now, all these years later, I continue to live in Sparky's world and the admonitions he gave me resonate. He would say to me, "You try to do too much," and "You should learn to 'hang out.'" He said my attempts at multi-tasking made me forget important things and made me lose track of what I was doing. Now I tell everyone that Sparky knows I need help and is looking after me! I say that Sparky helps me find things. It has happened so many times in the first few years that now I just

expect it. If I lose my credit card or my driver's license, I know that if I relax Sparky will help me find it or remind me where I left it. Recently, I was going to the lab to get some blood work. I ran back into the kitchen for something else and there was the lab slip I had forgotten. I gave a nod of recognition — "Thank you, Sparky, you saved me the frustration of getting to the lab with no slip and having to drive twenty-five minutes home to get it — or plan another day with no breakfast so I could do the blood test."

By the time we married, Sparky was thoroughly professional. The comic strip seemed to flow smoothly from him like water from a pitcher — only occasionally coming out unevenly in the creative equivalent of getting caught up in ice cubes. I recognized his genius, but on a day-to-day basis, I took it all for granted.

Sparky had strong opinions about the profession, which he expressed in interviews and with certain friends. It is a mistake, however, for interviewers or readers of those interviews to think his life and opinions were static. It is true that he had certain answers "grooved" and they are much the same in the 1960s as in the 1980s and 1990s, but much of that is because interviewers tend to ask the same questions year after year. Also, one learns to avoid controversy. Occasionally, an interviewer's questions would be particularly challenging, and out would come some different thoughts and answers. I particularly enjoyed an interview done at one of the Reuben weekends (the cartoonists' annual award celebration). Sparky's answers here are distinctly different because he knew his interviewer was more informed. And, of course, a TV interview in 1998 by Charlie Rose is superior. We play that interview daily in the theater at the Museum.

Divided into Thirds

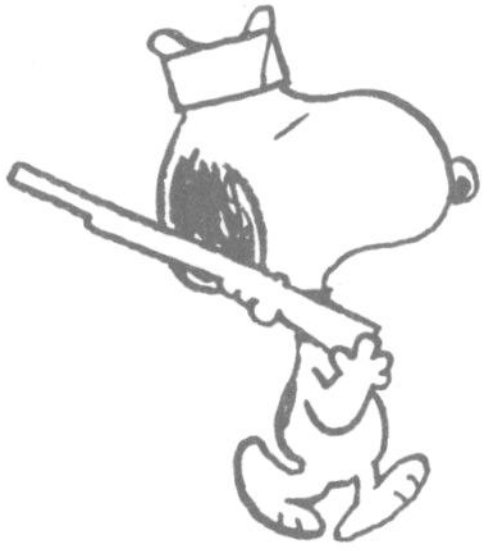

I think of Sparky's life divided into thirds: his youth and the cusp of adulthood when he found himself in the army; his budding career and his first marriage; and the last twenty-five years, when his children were mostly grown and became parents themselves. Each of these periods is reflected in the comic strip: from the "little kid stage" through the explosive 1960s and 1970s into a mature, thoughtful 1980s and 1990s. There is a very important subsegment of that first third of Sparky's life. It is the period of perhaps five years, which encompasses his mother's death, his three years in the military, and the year or two after his discharge before he landed at Art Instruction School.

There is an interesting correlation between Sparky's experiences as an adult and his memories of his childhood. I don't think I clearly realized this before working with David Michaelis when he was writing Sparky's biography.

David, in his deep research, followed many threads to weave a wonderful story of Sparky's parents, his early life, and his rise as a cartoonist. Reading about his early life and seeing the photos of the intense boy and young man, it is difficult not to be drawn into Sparky's dream. Through David, I was able to meet and talk to people from Sparky's past. At one point I quipped to David, "I think *we* now know more about Sparky than he knew about himself."

I had known of his sadness at being drafted just as his mother was dying, but until I met Don Schaust — who, because of their last names, sat next to Sparky on the train from St. Paul to Camp Campbell — I didn't recognize the chasm that Sparky had entered when he left for boot camp.

Don said it was a very awkward train ride sitting next to Sparky because Sparky hardly spoke during the entire journey. Later Don learned that Sparky's mother had just died, and then Don was able to understand a bit more. Hearing this story, sixty years later, from Don's point of view, was much more powerful than hearing something similar from Sparky. Many of these stories wouldn't have come out without David's work.

There is a wonderful parallel story line in the strip that goes for four weeks in 1973 — Charlie Brown discovers that he has a rash on his head with lines that make it look like a baseball. He puts a sack over his head to hide the rash, and goes off to camp. The mysterious nature of "Mr. Sack" intrigues the other campers. They begin to ask him questions and discover that his answers provide solutions to their problems.

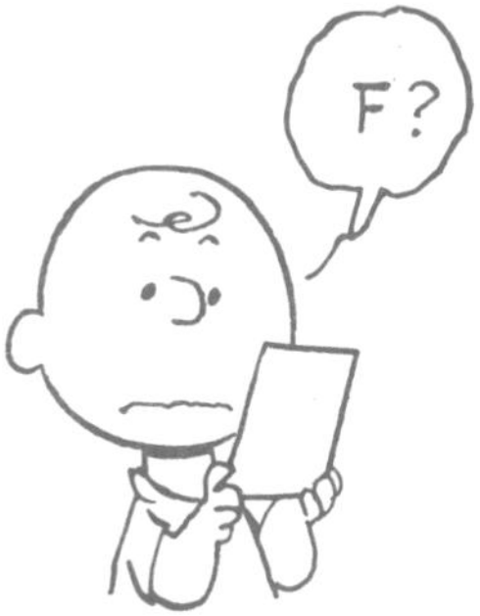
F?

Many of us who discuss the Mr. Sack sequence read this story as a parallel to Sparky's army career. He left St. Paul for Camp Campbell, Kentucky under the cloud of his mother's death, his head in a figurative paper bag. After some lonely weeks he made friends with Elmer Hagemeyer, ten years his senior and a St. Louis policeman before he was drafted. This friendship helped Sparky through his eighteen months at Camp Campbell, and the two remained close friends until Sparky's death.

During his time at Camp Campbell, Sparky flourished as a soldier, earning an expert marksman badge and the respect of the twelve-man squad that he was appointed to lead. The good feelings of his accomplishments continued through his six months in Europe in 1945 and the time that followed when he was stationed stateside. But, Sparky said later, when he returned to civilian life, like the rest of the de-mobilized soldiers looking for nonexistent jobs, he fell right back into being his old insecure self. He felt just like poor Charlie Brown returning home from significant success at camp — only to be quickly deflated by Lucy.

Now, I feel sure Sparky didn't write the Mr. Sack sequence as an allegory. He began simply enough with the stitch-like marks on Charlie Brown's head. Then his imagination kicked in and he thought that Charlie Brown could wear a grocery bag to hide them — and the story took on its own life.

Sparky was proud of what he had accomplished in the army. As he said, "I went in a know-nothing kid and I learned to be a leader, a staff sergeant in charge of a twelve-man squad." Just as Charlie Brown went to camp and discovered a new person inside himself.

Still, the timing of it all was devastating, as Rheta Grimsley Johnson says in her book. It was devastating not to be able to mourn with those who knew and loved his mother. No wonder the loss was seared into his memory, to come out in Charlie Brown's camp adventure thirty-some years later.

Sparky was not the only one who was proud of his army record. Others noticed it, too. One of his relatives later commented to me that what impressed him most was that Sparky "went in a buck private and came out a staff sergeant." He seemed to be saying that that was an uncommon occurrence in his experience and he expressed admiration for Sparky's accomplishment.

After Sparky was discharged from the military and still looking for a job, Carl Schulz, Sparky's father, realizing his son was having a difficult time, introduced him to a pastor from the Church of God. This pastor had ministered to Sparky's mother in her dying days and had preached at her funeral. The minister invited Sparky to church and Sparky, fortunately, followed up. This was probably the first real church community experience Sparky had, and it helped to fill the void of his mother's passing.

Sparky found a group of young people in the church and he soon began participating in services and Bible study. He told me that he had read through the entire Bible three times — and of course it comes out in the first TV special and in the more than 150 strips he drew which have a Biblical reference.

When he and Joyce moved to Sebastopol in 1958, Sparky taught adult Sunday school at the Sebastopol Methodist Church for several years until, he realized, "I didn't have anything else to say." His students have told me that he never "preached," he just asked their opinions of Biblical passages. That was the basis of their discussions.

Ultimately, Sparky's conclusion was simple. He frequently said, "Jesus's message is love, but there is no money in that." Interestingly, while the Biblical references in *Peanuts* are spread throughout its fifty years, more than half are in the final two decades. Perhaps Sparky became more philosophical in his own 60s and 70s.

But he was never dogmatic, so it's disturbing when someone tries to use *Peanuts* as a tool to push an agenda. The first example of that was *The Gospel According to Peanuts*. The plain fact is that Sparky never advocated a particular view, religious or otherwise. Every day, he called upon everything he knew "simply" to create a funny comic strip.

Fifty Years of *Peanuts*

Just as the seventy years of Charles Schulz's life can be divided into thirds, so, similarly, can the fifty years of *Peanuts*. Although his peers in the National Cartoonists Society honored Sparky in

1955 with a Reuben, their most prestigious award, and the number of newspapers subscribing to the strip grew steadily, the strip seemed to appeal mostly to a niche audience of college students, other artists, and cartoon aficionados.

Those first years were somewhat standard comics fare: the birds are birds, flying and hopping; the kids are kids, building forts and making mud pies; and Snoopy follows them around on all fours. The main themes were established: the triangle of Schroeder, Beethoven, and Lucy; Charlie Brown and his baseball team and disastrous kite adventures; Linus and his blanket; crabby, know-it-all Lucy; Pig-Pen with his trailing cloud of dust. But in 1959, Snoopy stands upright to slide into third base (4/21/59) and walks upright with Lucy while dressed as a baby (6/24/59). Soon he is on his hind legs doing his happy dance, and by November he is enjoying the view from the top of his doghouse.

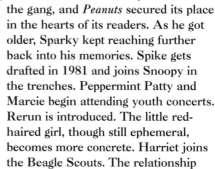

After a decade, the strip exploded in the 1960s — and to many that decade was the apotheosis. Certainly the 1960s and the 1970s saw these earlier themes continue and two of the most popular *Peanuts* themes appear: the Great Pumpkin and Snoopy as the World War I flying ace. Actually, the Great Pumpkin is first mentioned in a series of six strips in October 1959. The Great Pumpkin reappears each year and is joined by the World War I flying ace in the 1966 television show, *It's the Great Pumpkin, Charlie Brown*.

In the strip's final two decades, the gang continued to have adventures, storylines continued to be developed that broadened the experience of the gang, and *Peanuts* secured its place in the hearts of its readers. As he got older, Sparky kept reaching further back into his memories. Spike gets drafted in 1981 and joins Snoopy in the trenches. Peppermint Patty and Marcie begin attending youth concerts. Rerun is introduced. The little red-haired girl, though still ephemeral, becomes more concrete. Harriet joins the Beagle Scouts. The relationship between Woodstock and Snoopy becomes richer. (Sparky says, "The two of them have a really neat friendship, and, of course, as in any friendships, there are fights.")

Like any artist in any medium, Sparky was working to push the boundaries of his art, developing new themes — Sparky played with a Sunday page with over a hundred of Snoopy's friends and relatives in the gallery as he prepares to tee off in the last tournament of the year (8/9/92). This is reminiscent of the strips with Linus talking to the audience of snowmen, which he did multiple times in the 1990s (12/5/93, 12/3/95, 11/10/96, 11/5/98, 11/10/98). In this period, the strips became more philosophical, while, at the same time, Sparky employed many sight gags, as he'd done in the early years of the strip. One of my favorites is 9/3/83 — Snoopy can't sleep and steals Woodstock's "Z" — and the wonderful three-day series in March of 1991 when Charlie Brown is on the mound in the rain while everything imaginable goes floating by.

Sparky felt his drawing technique continued to develop, becoming looser and more expressive. Because he was continually pushing himself, he was critical of the work he had done previously. He didn't want to see ten-year-old art on the licensed products, which made it difficult for United Media to keep up with new art for the licensees.

The discussion about the "best era/best decade" in *Peanuts* remains a subject of debate among readers, journalists, and the public. My theory is that just as Sparky discovered a theme that pleased him and made him want to go back to it again and again with infinite variations so, too, an individual reader discovers a *Peanuts* moment that hits his or her heart (or head) and becomes a fan. But a person's

first connection with *Peanuts* also has a lot to do with where he or she is in his or her own life, much like the effect music has when a certain theme can take us back to a time we remember with great yearning. By the time readers have followed *Peanuts* for a few years, they have constructed their own reality of the *Peanuts* world — and that may be one reason people have such a strong reaction to things that don't fit into their construction.

Sparky spoke about the developments in the strip in its last two decades. He pointed out that they weren't sudden changes — that the kids' personalities and situations had been changing from the start. In the beginning, nobody loves Charlie Brown — or, as he says to Lucy, "Nobody important loves me." (5/15/52). But in the later years, there are *two* girls trying to claim his attention: Peppermint Patty and Marcie. "Now he is in real trouble," says Sparky, because he has to think ahead about what he says to whom, and no matter what, he is in trouble with someone.

There is also the development of Rerun, whose original "gig" was riding on the back of his mom's bicycle. This particular theme developed from me describing the mishaps I had when my children rode on the back of my bike. But Sparky took it beyond a single theme and developed Rerun into his own character. When one looks back at the last decade one can see that Rerun develops as the only "normal" kid. He tags along in the other kids' shadows and the only thing he wants is a dog, a bike, and to be able to get the ball into the basket — very normal childhood desires. Rerun isn't plagued with the neuroticism of the rest of the *Peanuts* gang. One wonders where he came from.

Sparky bridled against the "He should quit, he's past his best work" comments. In response, he would refer to the 10/8/96 strip with Snoopy and Linus: "Everyone brings something to the party." He was very proud of that strip and felt it was as good as anything he had ever done. But there are many more strips Sparky was proud of and which we at the Museum feel are classics in the *Peanuts* oeuvre. Because of the breadth of the characters in *Peanuts*, Sparky could introduce themes that simply would not work in other strips.

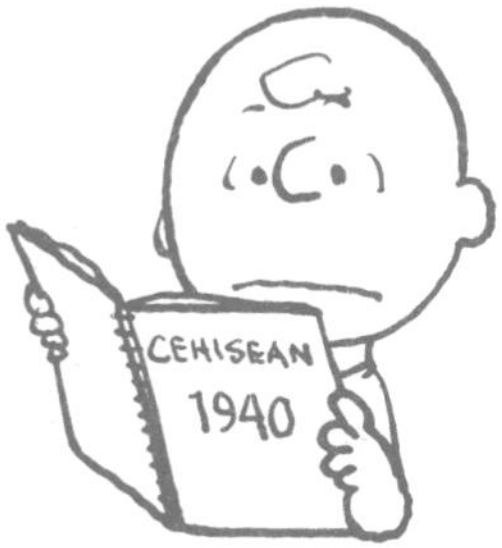
CEHISEAN
1940

For example, in early November 1970, the storyline has Snoopy accompanying Woodstock south for the winter. On November 11, Snoopy suddenly realizes that it's Veterans' Day, the day he always quaffs a root beer with Bill Mauldin, so he stops at a telephone booth to phone Bill. Sparky enjoyed recognizing his hero, and he drew a total of nineteen strips honoring the famed World War II cartoonist, including one in the pumpkin patch. *Peanuts* often moved between the real world and the fantasy world, but not many strips can do that.

In 1997 Sparky asked two young women attending the Santa Barbara Writers' Conference if they had ever read the works of Ernie Pyle, the legendary World War II correspondent who was killed in the Pacific Theatre. They had not, and Sparky immediately went looking for a book by Pyle, but the bookstore did not have any. At home, he found one of his own books by Pyle and mailed it to them. From this encounter came that year's Veterans' Day strip (11/11/97). Snoopy makes his annual visit to Bill Mauldin and tells him about going into a bookstore to get something by Ernie Pyle. They'd never heard of him. Snoopy leans his head onto his paw, and sighs, "I don't know, Bill ... I just don't know." So art follows life.

Snoopy

Snoopy has proved to be one of the most popular characters in *Peanuts* — at times, he is even more popular than Charlie Brown himself.

Of course, dogs have been central figures in comic strips from the beginning. Little Nemo has a dog. Little Orphan Annie has Sandy, Blondie has Daisy, Buster Brown has Tige. Artists and authors in other genres have recognized the importance of dogs to humans and have included them in their storytelling. Just the other day I noticed in Puccini's *The Girl of the Golden West* that the lonely gold miners wonder if their dogs will remember them when they return to their homes. In *Mr. Hulot's Holiday*, one of the first scenes in the French seaside village has a funny episode of a car coming across the local dog lazing in the middle of the street. Dogs have been artistic fodder because of their deep human connection and for their ability to provide comic relief.

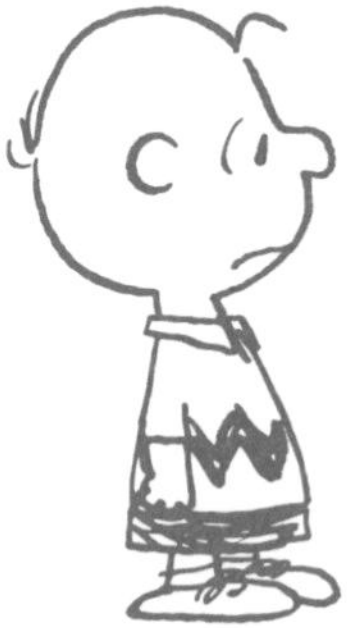

Sparky had a deep affinity for dogs. He found them amusing and "honest." In the 3/26/91 installment, Charlie Brown says, "and I feel having a dog for a friend can make an ordinary life a beautiful life." On 8/17/94, he says "...dogs protect you, give you comfort, love, joy and companionship ... that's their job..." "Talk about stress," thinks Snoopy.

Sparky spoke frequently about the unique personalities of many of the dogs he had owned. Anyone who has read very much about Sparky or *Peanuts* will know about Sparky's dog, Spike, who reportedly understood fifty words, and, when given a chance, terrorized the neighborhood kids but, of course, was a model of good behavior in the family.

He often spoke about their St. Bernard, Lucy, a family dog in the 1960s, who loved to say "goodbye" when the family was all dressed up to go out. As Lucy approached, wagging her head and drooling, everyone would run from her yelling, "No, Lucy, no!"

Shortly after Sparky and I married, his daughter Jill brought her dog Rufie to live with us. Rufie was a mixed breed that seemed to be mostly Sheltie. He would sit on a picture windowsill so he could see the world outside and thus never have anyone sneak up on him. Sparky loved this aspect of Rufie's personality and always spoke affectionately about Rufie years after he was gone from our lives.

Readers of some of his books will remember a short essay Sparky wrote about carrying a "dog cookie" in his pocket when he drove to the arena for breakfast. There was a dog who lived in a small fenced yard across from the ice arena where Sparky parked. Sparky delighted in being greeted every morning and giving him one small Milk-Bone dog biscuit and a cheery, "How are you today?"

Researchers have now looked at scans of dogs' brains and have discovered that making eye contact with a human releases oxytocin, the pleasure hormone, in a dog's brain. It seems to me that Sparky felt this connection on a very basic level.

Karen Kresge, the choreographer of our Christmas ice show during the 1990s, engaged an act by skater Kirk Wyse and his dog Scrapette. Kirk skated a Charlie Chaplin Little Tramp sketch, and he and Scrapette had some wonderful warm, funny, and slapstick bits. Sparky fell in love with Scrapette, and every night he would watch the show at least until that act was finished; then he would be satisfied and could come home. During rehearsals and between shows, Sparky enjoyed sitting with Kirk and Scrapette. He insisted Karen ask Kirk to come back the following year and he was just as charmed by the act even though it was exactly the same. Several years later, we heard that Scrapette had died. Sparky was very sad.

Then there was Andy, the foundling we "rescued" in 1985, and who stole Sparky's heart. Many later strips speak of Charlie Brown "going home to take care of my dog." Nothing pleased Sparky more than to sit in his leather chair and fall asleep with Andy on his lap. The 10/8/96 strip Sparky was so proud of embodies the feeling of perfect contentment he felt with Andy sleeping on his lap.

I love what a friend wrote to me: "Just to hear the name 'Snoopy' makes one feel warm and fuzzy all over. To me, Snoopy is the Spirit of the U.S. in mind and spirit — all mixed together and portrayed as man's best friend — the lovable dog."

From the very beginning, Snoopy, even while still on all fours, supplied plenty of visual humor, such as 4/9/55 and 6/22/54 when his ears become the joke. Snoopy even used his ears to support his "head stand." Sparky's fascination with the personalities of dogs provided him with plenty of humor.

It is easy for readers to focus on the story and the engaging characters and not recognize how the deceptively simple drawing is a critical part of their enjoyment. Sparky spoke of that frequently, saying that good design within each panel and characters who are pleasant to look at contribute greatly to a reader's appreciation of a comic strip.

In an interview with Don Tracewell (another Northern California cartoonist and member of the Northern California Cartoonist and Humorist Association) during the Phoenix Reuben Awards weekend in 1992, Sparky was talking about how important good drawing is. "You don't have to be a Wyeth or a Picasso," he said, "but you need to know how to draw something before you can cartoon it." He added that he was a strong proponent of "mild drawing," adding, "it is a mistake to get involved in extreme caricature in a comic strip if you are going to draw characters that have to show some emotion such as great joy or sadness. People should know where the eyes are and the mouth are …"

Sparky felt his drawing got more fluid and more expressive each year. Nick Meglin, the former editor of *Mad* magazine, recalled that, during a talk at a subsequent Reuben Awards weekend, "when asked if he ever thought about giving up drawing the *Peanuts* feature, Sparky responded, 'I would only do that if the feeling and the sound of the pen gliding over the page no longer excites me. It still does as much today as it did when I first started the strip.'"

Sparky told me he heard murmurs of agreement from the audience of his fellow cartoonists when he said that. They all shared a profound connection with their art, which extended even to the physical act of creating it.

It is my pleasure to guide many visitors through the Museum, and I have been astounded by what I learn from each of them. One visitor, a symphony conductor from France, was looking through the strip gallery and he came over to me excitedly. He said something like, "Charles Schulz understood silence." He pulled me over to a thee-panel strip that starts with Rerun in bed (12/3/98). Lucy announces that it is snowing outside and all the

schools are closed. The expression on Rerun's face in the second panel expresses complete contentment. The last panel says simply, "poetry." The conductor compared the second panel to the important, deliberate softening and silence in a piece of music that prepares the audience for the dramatic notes to follow.

Another visitor, an art historian who teaches and writes about painting, talked to me about the integrity of Sparky's line and how no line crosses another unless there is a reason. "Every line serves a purpose," she emphasized. All these people have opened my eyes to the enormous complexity in the strip which I, and I am sure others, have taken for granted all these years.

I have talked about Sparky's life as a fairy tale: a boy had a dream; through pluck and a little luck, he made it come true; he got to live a long and happy life in his castle; and then his life ended. It is very difficult to be sad about a life lived well.

But we can be sad about the end of an era.

Sparky saw an era ending when he spoke to the National Cartoonists Society at their Reuben Awards weekend in San Antonio, Texas, in 1999, his final appearance before that group.

Corporate boardroom decisions are based on numbers, Sparky said, adding that he had no reason to believe that most of the executives at

Scripps Howard (then the owner of the *Peanuts* copyright) even read comic strips.

In 2009, Scripps Howard made a business decision to sell United Media, the licensing arm of the company. They did not approach us, the family of the artist who had created millions of dollars in revenue for them for more than fifty years, to make any sort of collaborative arrangement or even have the courtesy to notify us of their plans. They held a blind auction in which we were treated like any other bidder. That is the way "business" happens in the twenty-first century.

It was truly the end of an era, and I am glad Sparky was not here to see it.

The good news is that the Charles M. Schulz Museum, which opened in 2002, was already welcoming visitors from around the world and continuing to bring the happiness embodied in the saga of the *Peanuts* gang.

Sparky once said that he would be satisfied if his tombstone read: "He made people happy!"

He did. And he still does.

The End

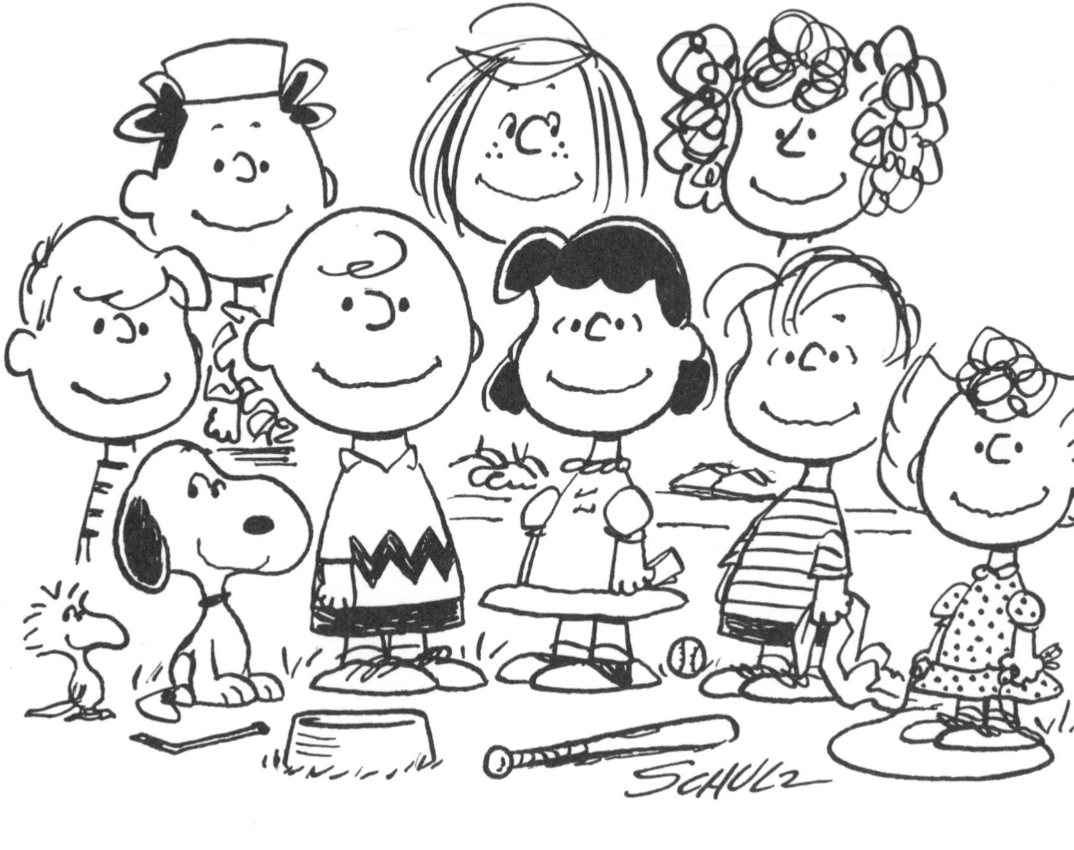
SCHULZ

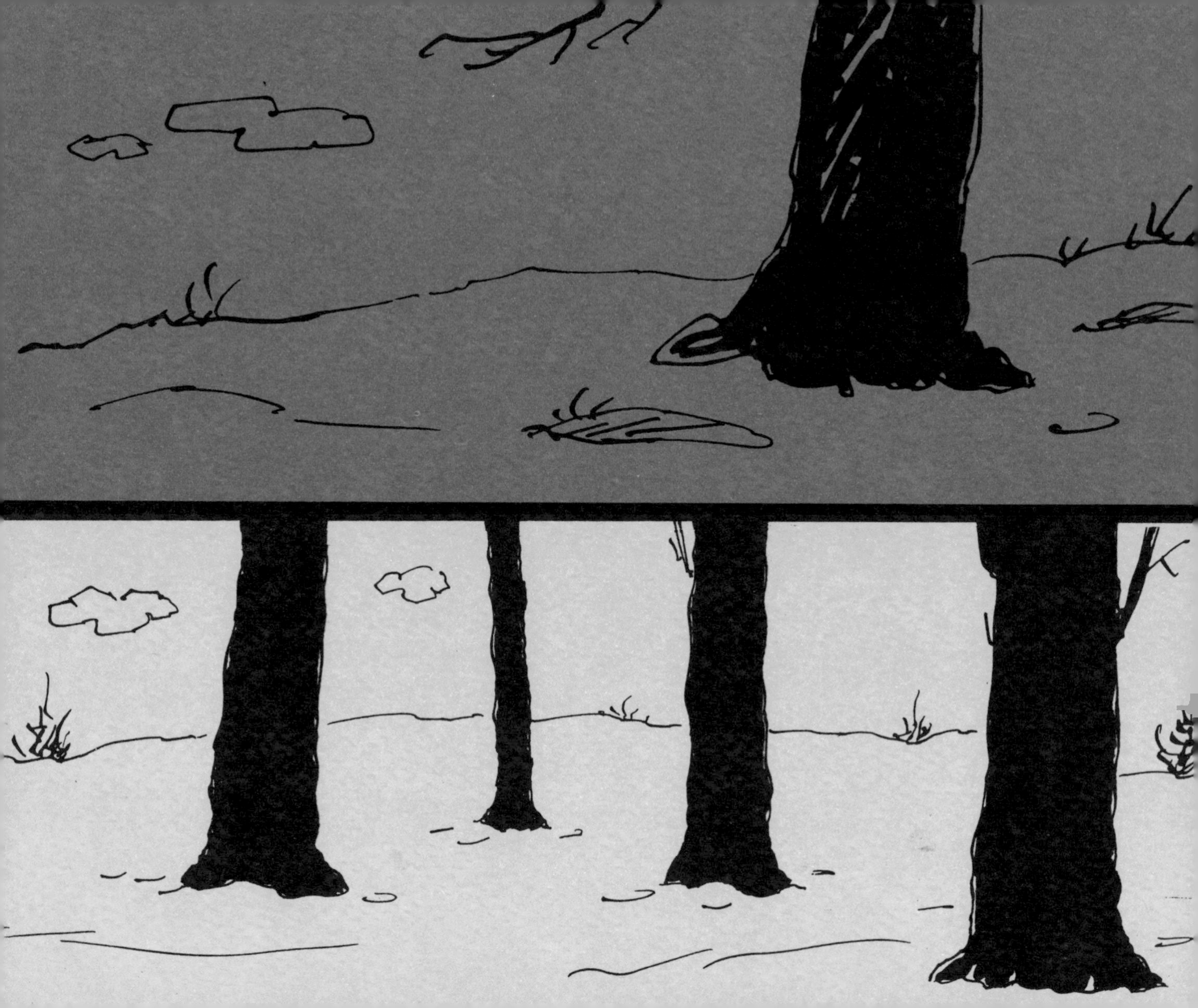